SOCIALISM ACROSS THE IRON CURTAIN

This innovative pan-European history of post-war socialism challenges the East-West paradigm that still dominates accounts of post-war Europe. Jan De Graaf offers a comparative study of the ways in which the French, Italian and Polish socialist parties and the Czechoslovakian Social Democratic Party dealt with the problems of socio-economic and political reconstruction. Drawing on archival documents in seven languages, De Graaf reveals the profound divide which existed in all four countries between socialist elites and their grassroots as workers reacted hostilely to calls for industrial discipline and for further sacrifices towards the reconstruction effort. He also provides a fresh interpretation of the political weaknesses of socialist parties in post-war continental Europe by stressing the importance of political history and social structure. By placing the attitudes of the continental socialist parties in their proper socio-historical context he highlights the many similarities across and divergences within the two putative blocs.

JAN DE GRAAF is a postdoctoral researcher at KU Leuven, Belgium. He graduated with the highest distinction from Utrecht University in 2009 and obtained his PhD from the University of Portsmouth in 2015. Since 2015, he has been working on a four-year postdoctoral project on wildcat strikes as a pan-European phenomenon, funded by the Research Foundation – Flanders (FWO).

NEW STUDIES IN EUROPEAN HISTORY

Edited by
PETER BALDWIN, *University of California, Los Angeles*
CHRISTOPHER CLARK, *University of Cambridge*
JAMES B. COLLINS, *Georgetown University*
MIA RODRIGUEZ-SALGADO, *London School of Economics
and Political Science*
LYNDAL ROPER, *University of Oxford*
TIMOTHY SNYDER, *Yale University*

The aim of this series in early modern and modern European history is to publish outstanding works of research, addressed to important themes across a wide geographical range, from southern and central Europe, to Scandinavia and Russia, from the time of the Renaissance to the present. As it develops the series will comprise focused works of wide contextual range and intellectual ambition.

A full list of titles published in the series can be found at:
www.cambridge.org/newstudiesineuropeanhistory

SOCIALISM ACROSS THE IRON CURTAIN

*Socialist Parties in East and West and the
Reconstruction of Europe after 1945*

JAN DE GRAAF

KU Leuven, Belgium

CAMBRIDGE
UNIVERSITY PRESS

CAMBRIDGE
UNIVERSITY PRESS

University Printing House, Cambridge CB2 8BS, United Kingdom

One Liberty Plaza, 20th Floor, New York, NY 10006, USA

477 Williamstown Road, Port Melbourne, VIC 3207, Australia

314–321, 3rd Floor, Plot 3, Splendor Forum, Jasola District Centre, New Delhi – 110025, India

79 Anson Road, #06-04/06, Singapore 079906

Cambridge University Press is part of the University of Cambridge.

It furthers the University's mission by disseminating knowledge in the pursuit of education, learning, and research at the highest international levels of excellence.

www.cambridge.org
Information on this title: www.cambridge.org/9781108425087
DOI: 10.1017/9781108639781

© Jan De Graaf 2019

First published 2019

Printed and bound in Great Britain by Clays Ltd, Elcograf S.p.A.

A catalogue record for this publication is available from the British Library.

Library of Congress Cataloging-in-Publication Data
Names: Graaf, Jan de, author.
Title: Socialism across the iron curtain : socialist parties in East and West and the reconstruction of Europe after 1945 / Jan De Graaf, Katholieke Universiteit Leuven, Belgium.
Description: New York: Cambridge University Press, 2018. |
Series: New studies in European history
Identifiers: LCCN 2018038869 | ISBN 9781108425087 (hardback) |
ISBN 9781108441179 (paperback)
Subjects: LCSH: Socialism – Europe – History – 20th century. |
Socialist parties – Europe – History – 20th century. |
Europe, Eastern – Politics and government – 20th century. |
Europe, Western – Politics and government – 20th century. |
BISAC: HISTORY / Europe / General.
Classification: LCC HX238.5.G724 2018 | DDC 335.094/0904–dc23
LC record available at https://lccn.loc.gov/2018038869

ISBN 978-1-108-42508-7 Hardback

Contents

Acknowledgements

This book could not have been written without the generous support of various research institutes and funding organisations. First and foremost, I want to thank the Centre for European and International Studies Research at the University of Portsmouth for providing me with a three-year PhD fellowship in 2011. I am also grateful to the German Historical Institute in Warsaw, the Society for the Study of French History, and the British Association for Slavonic and East European Studies for making possible archival sojourns in Poland, France, and the Czech Republic, respectively. On a more general level, I would like to express my gratitude to all the staff in the various archives that I visited during my doctoral studies, and especially to Frédéric Cépède at the Office Universitaire de Recherche Socialiste in Paris for his assistance in providing the cover image for this book. Last but not least, I am indebted to all those who were involved in the realisation of the book: Elizabeth Friend-Smith, Michael Watson, Abigail Walkington, and Natasha Whelan at Cambridge University Press, Dawn Preston, who managed the production process, and Luke Finley for the copy-editing.

Sections of Chapters 2 and 3 appeared in 'More than Canteen Control: Italian and Polish Socialists Confronting Their Workers, 1944–1947', *International Review of Social History*, 59/1 (2014), pp. 71–98. Chapters 6 and 8 are derived in part from 'European Socialism between Militant and Parliamentary Democracy: A Pan-European Debate, 1945–8', *European Review of History/Revue européenne d'histoire*, 26 (forthcoming; www.tandfonline.com/doi/full/10.1080/13507486.2018.1491530). I want to thank both journals for allowing me to reprint the sections in question.

The book is much better for the discussions I had with and the feedback I received from various colleagues along the way, including two anonymous referees and Stefan Berger, Christiane Brenner, Robert Brier, Simona Colarizi, Martin Conway, Geoff Eley, Paul Flenley, Lex Heerma van Voss, Duco Hellema, Peter Heumos, Padraic Kenney, Gareth Pritchard,

Jakub Šlouf, and Marcin Zaremba. My special thanks goes out to Wolfram Kaiser, who supervised my PhD project at the University of Portsmouth. His expert feedback, delivered at astonishing speed, much improved the very first drafts of the chapters that appear in this book. His impressive network of academic contacts opened doors for me that would otherwise have remained closed. Most importantly, he taught me a lot about what it meant to be a professional historian. I have now been my own man (that is, no longer a PhD student) for two-and-a-half years, but I still find myself thinking 'What would Wolfram advise here?' every now and again. That, more still than publications, should count as academic impact.

Above all, however, I want to thank my wife Myrte for her love and support. I am extremely grateful for her decision to move with me from the Netherlands to Portsmouth and for the can-do spirit that landed her a PhD fellowship within six months of getting there. I will always remember the trips we made together to various European cities as I was working on this project. More than that still, I will cherish the time we spent in beautiful Portsmouth, making our daily cycle trips along the seafront, playing board games on Wednesday and Saturday evenings, and finally making it up the Spinnaker Tower during the last weeks of our four-year stay in the city. As we have moved on to yet another country, our son Max and daughter Tessa, who were born as I was completing this book, have brought fresh joy to our lives. It is to them that I want to dedicate this book.

Abbreviations

AAN	Archiwum Akt Nowych (Poland)
ACS	Archivio Centrale dello Stato (Italy)
AdL	Archivio del Lavoro (Italy)
ADN	Archives Departmentales du Nord (France)
AMP	Archiv Města Plzně (Czech Republic)
ANM	Archiv Národního Muzea (Czech Republic)
APŁ	Archiwum Państwowe w Łodzi (Poland)
CDL	Departmental Liberation Committees/Comités Départementaux de Libération (France)
CGT	General Confederation of Labour/Confédération Générale du Travail (France)
CHS	Centre d'Histoire Social (France)
CHSP	Centre d'Histoire des Sciences Po (France)
CKW	Centralny Komitet Wykonawczy (Poland)
CLN	National Liberation Committee(s)/Comitato/i di Liberazione Nazionale (Italy)
CLNA	Company National Liberation Committee(s)/Comitato/i di Liberazione Nazionale Aziendale (Italy)
CNR	National Council of the Resistance/Conseil National de la Résistance (France)
Cominform	Communist Information Bureau
Comintern	Communist International
COMISCO	Commission of International Socialist Conferences
CRR	Commissariat Régional de la République (France)
CUP	Central Planning Office/Centralny Urząd Planowania (Poland)
ČSDSD	Czechoslovakian Social Democratic Workers' Party/Československá Sociálně Demokratická Strana Dělnická (Czechoslovakia)

ČSL	Czechoslovakian People's Party/Československá Strana Lidová (Czechoslovakia)
ČSM	Czechoslovakian Youth Union/Československý Svaz Mládeže (Czechoslovakia)
ČSNS	Czech National Socialist Party/Česká Strana Národně Sociální (Czechoslovakia)
ČSSD	Czechoslovakian Social Democratic Party/Československá Sociální Demokracie (Czechoslovakia)
DC	Christian Democratic Party/Democrazia Cristiana (Italy)
DNA	Norwegian Labour Party/Det Norske Arbeiderpartiet (Norway)
DS	Slovakian Democratic Party/Demokratická Strana (Czechoslovakia)
FDP	Popular Democratic Front/Fronte Democratico Popolare (Italy)
FFT	Fondazione di Studi Storici Filippo Turati (Italy)
FJJ	Fondation Jean Jaurès (France)
FLB	Fondazione Lelio e Lisli Basso Isocco (Italy)
FN	Fondazione Nenni (Italy)
GSE	Socialist Enterprise Groups/Groupes Socialistes d'Entreprise (France)
IISH	International Institute of Social History (the Netherlands)
INSMLI	Istituto Nazionale per la Storia del Movimento di Liberazione in Italia (Italy)
ISRT	Istituto Storico della Resistenza in Toscana (Italy)
JS	Young Socialists/Jeunesses Socialistes (France)
KOR	Provincial Trade Union Council/Krajská Odborová Rada (Czechoslovakia)
KPP	Polish Communist Party/Komunistyczna Partia Polski (Poland)
KSČ	Czechoslovakian Communist Party/Komunistická Strana Československá (Czechoslovakia)
LHASC	Labour History Archive and Study Centre (United Kingdom)
MRP	Popular Republican Movement/Mouvement Républicain Populaire (France)
MSzDP	Hungarian Social Democratic Party/Magyarországi Szociáldemokrata Párt (Hungary)

MUP	Movement of Proletarian Unity/Movimento di Unità Proletaria (Italy)
NA	Narodní Archiv (Czech Republic)
NSZ	National Armed Forces/Narodowe Siły Zbrojne (Poland)
NV	National Committee(s)/Narodní Výbor(y) (Czechoslovakia)
OURS	Office Universitaire de Recherche Socialiste (France)
PCF	French Communist Party/Parti Communiste Français (France)
PCI	Italian Communist Party/Partito Comunista Italiano (Italy)
PdA	Action Party/Partito d'Azione (Italy)
PDL	Democratic Labour Party/Partito Democratico del Lavoro (Italy)
PKWN	Polish National Liberation Committee/Polski Komitet Wyzwolenia Narodowego (Poland)
PLI	Italian Liberal Party/Partito Liberale Italiano (Italy)
PNF	National Fascist Party/Partito Nazionale Fascista (Italy)
PPR	Polish Workers' Party/Polska Partia Robotnicza (Poland)
PPS	Polish Socialist Party/Polska Partia Socjalistyczna (Poland)
PRI	Italian Republican Party/Partito Repubblicano Italiano (Italy)
PRS	Radical Party/Parti Républicain, Radical et Radical-Socialiste (France)
PSDR	Romanian Social Democratic Party/Partidul Social Democrat Român (Romania)
PSI	Italian Socialist Party/Partito Socialista Italiano (Italy)
PSIUP	Italian Socialist Party of Proletarian Unity/Partito Socialista Italiano di Unità Proletaria (Italy)
PSL	Polish Peasant Party/Polskie Stronnictwo Ludowe (Poland)
PSLI	Italian Socialist Workers' Party/Partito Socialista dei Lavoratori Italiani (Italy)
PSU	Unitary Socialist Party/Partito Socialista Unitario (Italy)
PvdA	Dutch Labour Party/Partij van de Arbeid (the Netherlands)
PZPR	Polish United Workers' Party/Polska Zjednoczona Partia Robotnicza (Poland)

RGR	Rally of Republican Lefts/Rassemblement des Gauches Républicaines (France)
RPF	Rally of the French People/Rassemblement du Peuple Français (France)
SD	Democratic Party/Stronnictwo Demokratyczne (Poland)
SDKPiL	Social Democratic Party of the Polish and Lithuanian Kingdom/Socjaldemokracja Królestwa Polskiego i Litwy (Poland)
SdP	Sudeten German Party/Sudetendeutsche Partei (Czechoslovakia)
SFIO	French Socialist Party/Section Française de l'International Ouvrière (France)
SIA	Socialist International Archives
SILO	Socialist Information and Liaison Office
SL	People's Party/Stronnictwo Ludowe (Poland)
SNB	National Security Corps/Sbor Národní Bezpečnosti (Czechoslovakia)
SOA	Státní Oblastní Archiv (Czechoslovakia)
SP	Labour Party/Stronnictwo Pracy (Poland)
SPD	German Social Democratic Party/Sozialdemokratische Partei Deutschlands (Germany)
SPÖ	Austrian Socialist Party/Sozialistische Partei Österreichs (Austria)
UJRF	Union of the Republican Youth of France/Union de la Jeunesse Républicaine de France (France)
UNRRA	United Nations Relief and Rehabilitation Administration
ÚRO	Central Council of Trade Unions/Ústřední Rada Odborů (Czechoslovakia)
VA	Všeodborový Archiv (Czech Republic)
WiN	Freedom and Independence/Wolność i Niezawisłość (Poland)
WRN	Freedom, Equality, Independence/Wolność, Równość, Niepodległość (Poland)

Introduction

On the eve of the liberation of France, André Philip, the socialist minister of interior affairs in the French government in exile, urged his colleagues to waste no time in implementing the necessary socio-economic and political reforms once the Second World War had come to an end. 'Everything can be done in the first year following the liberation', he explained in an often-quoted statement. 'What is not done in the first year will never be done, because by then all the old habits will have been resumed.'[1]

Historians of post-war Europe are so fond of this quote for more than one reason. First and foremost, they use it to represent the great aspirations that accompanied the liberation of the continent. In this narrative, the first months and years that followed the Second World War were witness to a 'radical openness' during which a different Europe, based on various forms of industrial and participatory democracy, seemed in the making. This radical moment was ephemeral, running from the liberation in 1944–45 to the onset of the Cold War in 1947–48 at the latest, and quickly made way for fossilisation around the American and Soviet models.[2] If the quote already neatly captures the fleeting nature of this putative opportunity to transform Europe, it gets all the more powerful as it was delivered by a socialist. For where the communists and Christian democrats, the other major power brokers in post-war (continental) Europe, had clearly and

---

[1] Quoted in Andrew Shennan, *Rethinking France: Plans for Renewal 1940–1946* (Oxford: Oxford University Press, 1989), p. 292.
[2] On the 'radical openness' of the situation in post-liberation Europe see Geoff Eley, *Forging Democracy: The History of the Left in Europe, 1850–2000* (Oxford: Oxford University Press, 2002), pp. 287–98 and especially his 'Legacies of Antifascism: Constructing Democracy in Postwar Europe', *New German Critique*, 67 (1996), pp. 73–100. He quotes Philip's words in both of these accounts. More generally on the moment of liberation as a missed opportunity to remake Europe from below: Tom Behan, *The Long Awaited Moment: The Working Class and the Italian Communist Party in Milan, 1943–1948* (New York: P. Lang, 1997); Rebecca Boehling, *A Question of Priorities: Democratic Reforms and Economic Recovery in Postwar Germany: Frankfurt, Munich, and Stuttgart under U.S. Occupation, 1945–1949* (Providence, RI: Berghahn Books, 1996).

early on chosen sides in the emerging Cold War, historians have often
associated the post-war socialist parties[3] with the search for a 'third way'
between American capitalism and Soviet communism.[4] In their efforts
to bring together democracy and socialism, and to keep open channels
between East and West in doing so, the socialists were then the main
exponents of the more radical Europe that never was.

Such claims about the post-war European socialist parties, as we will see
at various points in this book, are often based on anecdotal observations.
In fact, the historiography of post-war European socialism rarely moves
beyond a narrow political perspective or addresses how the socialist parties
were rooted in their respective societies. This stands in stark contrast to
the profusion of social and socio-political histories of post-war communism[5] and Christian democracy[6] that have appeared in recent decades.
What many of these studies have in common is that they only accord the
Cold War a minor role in their explanatory frameworks. Instead, these
works tend to trace back the post-war fortunes of their subject matter to a

[3] The Socialist International has historically always consisted of both parties describing themselves as
'socialist' and parties describing themselves as 'social democratic'. For the sake of clarity, the adjective
'socialist' will be used throughout to describe the broader party family to which both socialist and
social democratic parties belonged. The adjective 'social democratic' will only be used where we are
dealing with an individual party or a group of parties describing itself or themselves in that manner
(e.g. the German Social Democratic Party or the Scandinavian social democratic parties).
[4] Peter Heumos (ed.), *Europäischer Sozialismus im Kalten Krieg: Briefe und Berichte, 1944–1948*
(Frankfurt am Main: Campus Verlag, 2004), p. 45. Many individual socialist parties in post-war
Europe, or at least left-leaning elements within these parties, espoused visions of a 'third way' or a
'third force', which was often conceived as 'a bridge' between East and West. See Christian Bailey,
'The European Discourse in Germany, 1939–1950: Three Case Studies', *German History*, 28/4 (2010),
pp. 453–78, 457–64; Klaus Misgeld, 'As the Iron Curtain Descended: The Co-ordinating Committee
of the Nordic Labour Movement and the Socialist International between Potsdam and Geneva
(1945–1955)', *Scandinavian Journal of Social History*, 13/1 (1988), pp. 51–7; Fritz Weber, *Der kalte
Krieg in der SPÖ: Koalitionswachter, Pragmatiker und revolutionäre Sozialisten* (Vienna: Verlag für
Gesellschaftskritik, 1986), pp. 126–8; Jonathan Schneer, 'Hopes Deferred or Shattered: The British
Labour Left and the Third Force Movement, 1945–49', *The Journal of Modern History*, 56/2 (1984),
pp. 197–226.
[5] To name just three of the most prominent examples: Mark Pittaway, *The Workers' State: Industrial
Labor and the Making of Socialist Hungary, 1944–1958* (Pittsburgh, PA: University of Pittsburgh
Press, 2012); Gareth Pritchard, *The Making of the GDR, 1945–1953: From Antifascism to Stalinism*
(Manchester: Manchester University Press, 2000); Padraic Kenney, *Rebuilding Poland: Workers and
Communists, 1945–1950* (Ithaca, NY: Cornell University Press, 1997).
[6] See e.g. Rosario Forlenza, 'A Party for the Mezzogiorno: The Christian Democratic Party, Agrarian
Reform, and the Government of Italy', *Contemporary European History*, 19/4 (2010), pp. 331–49;
Frank Bösch, *Die Adenauer-CDU: Gründung, Aufstieg und Krise einer Erfolgspartei 1945–1969*
(Stuttgart: Deutsche Verlags-Anstalt, 2001); Gerd-Rainer Horn and Emmanuel Gerard (eds.),
Left Catholicism, 1943–1955: Catholics and Society in Western Europe at the Point of Liberation
(Louvain: Leuven University Press, 2001).

series of longer-term socio-economic and political developments that were strengthened and accelerated by the Second World War.

In his seminal work on the impact that the Second World War had on Eastern Europe, for example, Jan Gross has suggested that the 'social consequences' of the war paved the way for a communist take-over well before the Red Army set foot in the region. In the first place, the elimination of the Jewish and German urban bourgeoisie, through racial extermination and population transfers, respectively, had significantly reduced the ranks of the one social class most likely to oppose the communists. Secondly, with the introduction of economic planning and the mass expropriation of private property, the state had already taken on a much increased role in economic life during the war years. Thirdly, the sheer levels of violence to which the region had been exposed did great damage to the moral fabric of its societies, making them more vulnerable to authoritarian impulses.[7] Building upon Gross's thesis, other historians have gone back further in time to add to the equation[8] such dimensions as the skewed age pyramid produced by the First World War and the manifest failure of the interwar bourgeois-conservative state – all leading to the conclusion that 'no conservative reconstruction was actually possible' in post-war Eastern Europe.[9]

Where all of these historians stop short of explicitly suggesting that Eastern Europe would also have gone communist without Soviet interference, Martin Conway's scholarship on post-war Western Europe has been credited with demonstrating 'very powerfully' how the political hegemony of Christian democratic parties in the region 'can be explained without significant reference to the Cold War'.[10] In his work on post-war Belgium, and on (continental) Western Europe more generally, Conway points out that the occupation and liberation had 'changed the social balance of

---

[7] Gross developed his thesis in a series of well-known chapters and articles: 'Themes for a Social History of War Experience and Collaboration', in István Deák, Jan T. Gross, and Tony Judt (eds.), *The Politics of Retribution in Europe: World War II and Its Aftermath* (Princeton, NJ: Princeton University Press, 2000), pp. 15–36; 'War as Revolution', in Norman Naimark and Leonid Gibianskii (eds.), *The Establishment of Communist Regimes in Eastern Europe, 1944–1949* (Boulder, CO: Westview Press, 1997), pp. 17–40; 'Social Consequences of War: Preliminaries to the Study of Imposition of Communist Regimes in East Central Europe', *East European Politics and Societies*, 3/2 (1989), pp. 198–214.

[8] Bradley F. Abrams, 'The Second World War and the East European Revolution', *East European Politics and Societies*, 16/3 (2002), pp. 623–64.

[9] This was the conclusion that Mark Mazower drew after hearing a joint workshop paper by Martin Conway and Timothy Snyder on the 'Problems of Reconstruction in Eastern and Western Europe'. See Jessica Reinisch, 'Comparing Europe's Post-War Reconstructions: First Balzan Workshop, Birkbeck College, London, 28 October 2005', *History Workshop Journal*, 61/1 (2006), pp. 299–304.

[10] Holger Nehring, 'What was the Cold War?' *The English Historical Review*, 127 (2012), pp. 920–49, 931–2.

power'.[11] Contrary to the conventional historiographical wisdom that the industrial working class had emerged 'strengthened and radicalised' from the war,[12] however, he argues that the rural and middle classes were in fact the 'principal beneficiaries of the social changes of the 1940s'.[13] As economic power in post-liberation Europe lay primarily with those producing food or having the means to buy it, these groups were able to improve their position vis-à-vis the working class in the informal economy that existed alongside the official state rationing system. This new alliance between rural and middle-class interests found its 'political expression' first and foremost in the Christian democratic parties, whose decades-long domination of so many governments across post-war Western Europe reflected the transformed 'social realities' on the ground.[14]

If we can attribute the post-war strength of the communists in Eastern Europe and of the Christian democrats in Western Europe to the social changes wrought during the interwar and war years, can we account for the post-war weakness of the European socialist parties in a similar way? That is what this book sets out to achieve. In doing so, it will draw on some of the general observations that Conway made on the precarious situation in which the working class found itself at the moment of liberation. The effects of military conscription, forced labour in the Reich, and the aerial bombing of industrial centres had hit urban working-class communities 'disproportionally hard', he explains, while the wartime demobilisation of the labour movement put the working class on the back foot politically in the aftermath of the liberation.[15] To these general points, the book will add a set of social, economic, and political consequences of the interwar and war years that specifically confounded the work of the socialist parties in post-war (continental) Europe. With this socio-political approach to the history of post-war European socialism, the book offers an alternative to the narrative of victimisation so prevalent in accounts placing the Cold War front and centre in their analysis.

---

[11] Martin Conway, *The Sorrows of Belgium: Liberation and Political Reconstruction, 1944–1947* (Oxford/New York: Oxford University Press, 2012), p. 7.

[12] Conway, 'The Rise and Fall of Western Europe's Democratic Age, 1945–1973', *Contemporary European History*, 13/1 (2004), pp. 67–88, 73.

[13] Conway, *The Sorrows*, p. 8.

[14] Conway, 'The Rise and Fall', p. 81. See also Conway, 'The Age of Christian Democracy. The Frontiers of Success and Failure', in Thomas Kselman and Joseph Buttigieg (eds.), *European Christian Democracy: Historical Legacies and Comparative Perspectives* (Notre Dame, IN: University of Notre Dame Press, 2003), pp. 43–67.

[15] Conway, 'The Rise and Fall', p. 74.

To this end, the book focuses on four socialist parties that repeatedly refused to dance to the tune of the Cold War: the Czechoslovakian Social Democratic Party (ČSSD) and the Polish Socialist Party (PPS) in Eastern Europe, as well as the French Socialist Party (SFIO) and the Italian Socialist Party (PSIUP)[16] in Western Europe. Upon the liberation of their countries, each of these four parties took office in the broad-based centre-left coalition governments, comprising communist, socialist, and anti-fascist centrist or centre-right parties (often Catholic or Christian democratic parties, but also peasant or liberal parties) that were so typical for post-war continental Europe. As these coalitions began to disintegrate in 1946–47, however, the four socialist parties resolved on widely divergent strategies. On the one side, the Italian and Polish socialists, sharing the conviction that the Left should close ranks to prevent fascists from ever taking power again, stood by the communist-socialist united front. On the other, the Czechoslovakian social democrats and French socialists, increasingly viewing communism as the greater threat to democracy, began veering towards their centrist and centre-right coalition partners. If clearly not the result of some premature geo-political division of the continent, how can we explain these similarities across and differences within the two putative 'blocs'?

To answer this question, the book challenges the Cold War paradigm that is still so dominant in the historiography of post-war European socialism. Rather than teleologically projecting back the Iron Curtain that separated the parties after 1947–48, therefore, the book focuses on the set of problems that really dominated the agendas of post-war socialists in East and West: the problems of socio-economic and political reconstruction. The 'problems of post-war reconstruction', even if we confine these to their socio-economic and political dimensions, of course represent a vast interpretative category that could not possibly be covered in the space of one book. For that reason, the book will deal specifically with those two aspects of post-war reconstruction that were particularly controversial within or among the European socialist parties. In the first place, it explores

---

[16] From its creation in 1892 to 1943, the Italian Socialist Party went by the name Partito Socialista Italiano (Italian Socialist Party – PSI). In August 1943, after a merger with the Resistance group Movimento di Unità Proletaria (Movement of Proletarian Unity – MUP), the party changed its name to Partito Socialista Italiano di Unità Proletaria (Italian Socialist Party of Proletarian Unity – PSIUP). Amid fears that the party's anti-communist wing, which had broken away at the January 1947 PSIUP congress, would start using the old name, the PSIUP changed its name back to PSI in 1947. For the sake of clarity, the abbreviation PSIUP will be used throughout in this book to describe the post-war Italian Socialist Party. The abbreviation PSI will only be used where we are dealing with the pre-war Italian Socialist Party.

the tensions that the mammoth material demands of the reconstruction effort generated between socialist elites and grassroots. To that end, it analyses how the austerity-driven reconstruction programmes were received by rank-and-file socialists in four socialist strongholds with long traditions of industrial activism: Lille for France, Łódź for Poland, Milano for Italy, and Plzeň for Czechoslovakia. Secondly, it examines what was certainly the most contentious debate between the post-war European socialist parties: the debate over the shape that newfound democracy should take. By placing this debate in its proper social and historical contexts, it arrives at a fresh understanding of the divergences within and the eventual split of the post-war international socialist movement.

In revisiting the histories of the post-war European socialist parties through the prism of post-war reconstruction, the book finds itself in fertile research ground. Having long studied the reconstruction effort only in function of the Cold War or the European integration process,[17] historians have increasingly come to address the theme in its own right. In fact, their work has often shown how the realities on the ground shaped (geo-)political developments rather than the other way around.[18] Much of this revolved around the Balzan Research Project 'Reconstruction in the Immediate Aftermath of War: A Comparative Study of Europe, 1945–1950', which ran from 2003 to 2008. Commissioned by Balzan Prize Winner Eric Hobsbawm and directed by David Feldman and Mark Mazower, this project brought together close to one hundred historians working on different aspects of the reconstruction effort in both Eastern and Western Europe. Summarising its results, Mazower noted that their discussions had raised questions about 'how far "East" and "West" Europe actually existed before the Cold War helped reify them and fill them with meaning'. For during 'those critical years from the end of the war until 1948 it was not at all clear that Bulgaria or Romania shared more with Czechoslovakia or the German Democratic Republic than they did with, say, Greece or that anything useful was to be gained by placing Dresden and Prague in some putative "Eastern Europe"'. By taking 'the common set of problems' that post-war reconstruction presented as its point of departure, the Balzan Project had

---

[17] See, respectively, David Ellwood, *Rebuilding Europe: Western Europe, America and Postwar Reconstruction* (London/New York: Longman, 1992); Alan Milward, *The Reconstruction of Western Europe* (London: Routledge, 1992).
[18] See e.g. Paul Steege, *Black Market, Cold War: Everyday Life in Berlin, 1946–1949* (Cambridge: Cambridge University Press, 2009); Jill Lewis, *Workers and Politics in Occupied Austria 1945–1955* (Manchester/New York: Manchester University Press, 2007).

served as a reminder 'of the contingency of these Cold War categories and the lability of the idea of Europe'.[19]

Few if any of these insights, however, have found their way into the historiography of post-war European socialism.[20] For this is one field of study where the paper walls between East and West have stayed very much in place. Scholarship on post-war Eastern European socialism remains especially beholden to Cold War commonplaces. As a result, the post-war history of the Eastern European socialist parties has often been reduced to a classic story of deceit and betrayal, in which fellow-travelling socialists or downright crypto-communists sold out their parties in the run-up to the enforced communist–socialist mergers of 1947–48.[21] Small wonder, then, that comparative and transnational histories of post-war (Western) European socialism have frequently neglected or dismissed the Eastern European parties. These were supposedly 'nothing but front organisations of the communists'[22] led by 'Molotov socialists'[23] in hock to the Soviet Union, whose sole purpose was to disrupt the dealings of their Western counterparts. Even if other accounts have taken the arguments put forward by the Eastern European socialists more seriously, these still tend to portray post-war Eastern socialism as a homogeneous bloc whose conflicts with Western socialism could ultimately not be resolved.[24] With its focus on the unlikely bedfellows that socialist debates over socio-economic and political reconstruction brought forth, the book demonstrates that the fault lines within the post-war international socialist movement did not run along clear-cut East–West lines.

In doing so, the book not only adds a further pan-European chapter to recent scholarship on the reconstruction effort, but also sheds fresh light on the post-war histories of the four parties that are at the heart

---

[19] Mark Mazower, 'Reconstruction: The Historiographical Issues', *Past and Present*, 210, Supplement 6 (2011), pp. 17–28, 20.

[20] I have discussed the recent historiography of post-war Eastern and Western European socialism in greater detail in Jan de Graaf, 'Outgrowing the Cold War: Cross-Continental Perspectives on Early Post-War European Social Democracy', *Contemporary European History*, 22/2 (2013), pp. 331–42.

[21] This is certainly the approach in the only book-length comparative history of post-war Eastern European socialist and social democratic parties to have appeared to date: László Révész, *Die Liquidierung der Sozialdemokratie in Osteuropa* (Berne: Schweizerisches Ost-Institut, 1971).

[22] Dietrich Orlow, *Common Destiny: A Comparative History of the Dutch, French, and German Social Democratic Parties, 1945–1969* (New York/Oxford: Berghahn Books, 2000), p. 141.

[23] Rolf Steininger, *Deutschland und die Sozialistische Internationale nach dem Zweiten Weltkrieg* (Bonn: Neue Gesellschaft, 1979), pp. 92–3.

[24] Heumos, *Europäischer Sozialismus im Kalten Krieg*, pp. 13–46; Vibeke Sørensen, *Denmark's Social Democratic Government and the Marshall Plan 1947–1950* (Copenhagen: Museum Tusculanum Press, 2001), pp. 55–9.

of its analysis. Insofar as historians have dealt with the post-war Eastern European socialist parties at all, it has frequently been to cast them in a negative light. This is certainly true for the Czechoslovakian ČSSD. The only book-length account of its post-war trials and tribulations is more than thirty years old.[25] Most of the work that has appeared since the end of the Cold War has focused on the three centrist and centre-right parties that made up the 'democratic opposition' to the communists, often treating the social democrats as no more than an appendage to communism.[26] The Polish PPS, by contrast, does have something of a revisionist historiography. Already during the Cold War, some Western historians noted that the Polish socialists had in fact opposed the communists in the factory councils and within the trade union movement.[27] More recently, a series of Polish historians have credited the (leaders of the) post-war PPS with standing up for parliament, attempts to inject some much-needed humanism into communist policies, and taking an overall pragmatic outlook.[28] Yet, for all of these virtues, many misgivings about post-war Polish socialism remain, as there was a fine line between 'pragmatism and betrayal'.[29]

The much more extensive bodies of literature on post-war French and Italian socialism have shown a similar tendency to question or dismiss the line taken by its subject matter. In fact, the historiography of post-war Western European socialism often takes an explicitly social democratic perspective, measuring the continental socialist parties almost exclusively by the extent to which they succeeded in becoming 'modern' catch-all

---

[25] Karel Kaplan, *Das verhängnisvolle Bündnis: Unterwanderung, Gleichschaltung und Vernichtung der tschechoslowakischen Sozialdemokratie 1944–1954* (Wuppertal: Pol-Verlag, 1984).

[26] In his well-known cultural history of the communist take-over in Czechoslovakia, Bradley Abrams lumps significant parts of the ČSSD together with communism, and primarily reserves the term 'democratic socialists' for the centrist-nationalist Czech National Socialists. Bradley Abrams, *The Struggle for the Soul of the Nation: Czech Culture and the Rise of Communism* (Lanham, MD: Rowman & Littlefield, 2004). The post-war ČSSD is likewise largely dismissed as a non-entity led by 'a servile henchman of the communists' in various chapters on the 'political system of the restored republic' in Zdeňka Kokošková, Jiří Kocian, and Stanislav Kokoška (eds.), *Československo na rozhraní dvou epoch nesvobody* (Prague: Ústav pro soudobé dějiny, 2005).

[27] Christoph Kleßmann, 'Betriebsräte, Gewerkschaften und Arbeiterselbstverwaltung in Polen (1944–1958)', *Jahrbücher für Geschichte Osteuropas*, 29 (1981), pp. 185–214; Jaime Reynolds, 'Communists, Socialists and Workers: Poland, 1944–1948', *Soviet Studies*, 30/4 (1978), pp. 516–39.

[28] See, respectively, Anna Pięta-Szawara, 'Socialíści w Sejmie Ustawodawczym wobec zmian ustrojowych w Polsce w 1947 roku', *Polityka i Społeczeństwo*, 6 (2009), pp. 94–102; Michał Śliwa, *Demokracja polska: idee, ludzie, dzieje* (Warsaw: Wydawnictwo Sejmowe, 2010); Eleonora Syzdek and Bronisław Syzdek, *Zanim zostanie zapomniany* (Warsaw: Wydawnictwo Projekt, 1996).

[29] Robert Spałek, 'Między pragmatyzmem a zdradą. Zawłaszczenie PPS w Kraju (1944–1948)', in Robert Spałek (ed.), *Polska Partia Socjalistyczna. Dlaczego się nie udało? Szkice. Wspomnienia. Polemiki* (Warsaw: Instytut Pamięci Narodowej, 2010), pp. 145–242.

parties. Many studies place the experiences of the British Labour Party and/or the Scandinavian social democratic parties – the most successful European socialist parties in electoral terms – at the heart of their analysis. At ease with themselves in practising a reformist politics, these parties had managed to transform themselves into true 'people's parties' and win overall majorities at the polls. Yet the socialist parties on the European continent, unable to muster the resolve to make the same psychological leap, could not emulate these successes. For even if they had de facto embraced reformism too, their continued adherence to a Marxist rhetoric and revolutionary symbolism repelled many voters in the political centre. It was only after the continental socialists belatedly took up the teachings of the British or Scandinavian roads to socialism that they could start dominating (coalition) governments in the 1960s, 1970s, or 1980s.[30]

According to historians of Western European socialism, the French and Italian socialists found themselves furthest behind the curve in this regard. For where the Dutch Labour Party started the process of renewal immediately after the liberation and the German social democrats followed with their Bad Godesberg programme of 1959, it took the self-destruction of the SFIO in the latter part of the 1960s for French socialism to finally come to terms with the electorate.[31] The Italian PSIUP, for its part, literally found itself in a league of its own in the broader context of (Western) European socialism. Stubbornly refusing to renounce their unity pact with the communists as the Cold War took off, the Italian socialists were ostracised from both national government and the international socialist movement. It took the PSIUP decades to recover from the blows it received during its 'two horrible years' of 1947 and 1948, and Italy would only have its first socialist prime minister in the 1980s. Thus by and large failing to partake in the 'golden age' of Western European social democracy, the post-war PSIUP has often been described as an 'anomaly' in the otherwise more harmonious history of anti-communist, governmental, and reformist European socialism.[32]

Placing the post-war histories of Czechoslovakian, Polish, French, and Italian socialism in a broader pan-European context, the book offers a revaluation of the politics pursued by the four parties. For those choices

---

[30] Sheri Berman, *The Primacy of Politics: Social Democracy and the Making of Europe's Twentieth Century* (Cambridge/New York: Cambridge University Press, 1995), pp. 177–99.

[31] Orlow, *Common Destiny*. More specifically on the French socialists: Alain Bergounioux, 'Socialisme français et social-démocratie européenne', *Vingtième siècle, revue d'histoire*, 65 (2000), pp. 97–108.

[32] Luciano Cafagna, *Una strana disfatta: La parabola dell'autonomismo socialista* (Venice: Marsilio, 1996); Giovanni Sabbatucci, *Il riformismo impossibile: Storia del socialismo italiano* (Rome: Laterza, 1991).

that seem so idiosyncratic from an exclusively Eastern or Western perspective begin to make much more sense if we widen our horizons. In terms of the experiences that informed their views on socio-economic and political reconstruction, after all, the continental socialists often had far more in common with their comrades on the other side of the Iron Curtain than with their British or Scandinavian sister parties. The challenges facing the post-war Italian socialists, for example, closely mirrored those of the Polish socialists and Hungarian social democrats – also working in rural and Catholic societies that were emerging from two decades of dictatorship.[33] At the same time, the Czechoslovakian social democrats, in line with the social structure and political history of their country, frequently very much took a 'Western' perspective on the questions of the day. By shifting the spotlight from Europe's divided future to its entangled pasts and presents, therefore, the book brings together for the first time the parallel histories of parties thus far considered worlds apart.

The book is organised around the two broad themes of socio-economic and political reconstruction. After Chapter 1 provides a brief general outline of the pre-war and post-war histories of socialism in Czechoslovakia, France, Italy, and Poland, Chapters 2–4 deal with socio-economic reconstruction. Chapter 2 starts from the bottom up, recounting the sentiments among rank-and-file socialist workers in Lille, Łódź, Milano, and Plzeň on the basis of a wide variety of archival and library sources (including the minutes of socialist factory meetings, local socialist bulletins and newspapers, and police reports of socialist branch gatherings). In doing so, it identifies three worker grievances that were shared right across the four cities: a deep-seated discontent over the insufficient supply of everyday essentials, a stark outrage over the abuses of the black market, and a widespread bewilderment over the remaining socio-economic inequalities under governments in which their leaders participated. Chapter 3 introduces the views taken by socialist leaders, both national and provincial. It explores the arguments that motivated their calls for workers to show industrial discipline, to make sacrifices towards the reconstruction effort, and to participate in the 'battle for production'. Analysing the hostile reception these calls got among hungry and exhausted workers in the four cities, it lays bare a profound divide between socialist elites and their grassroots over

---

[33] I have made the case for a broader, pan-European perspective on the post-war PSIUP in Jan De Graaf, 'Old and New Democracy: Placing the Italian Anomaly in a European Context', in Jens Späth (ed.), *Does Generation Matter? Progressive Democratic Cultures in Western Europe, 1945–1960* (Cham: Palgrave Macmillan, 2018), pp. 151–170.

the nature of socialism. Chapter 4 moves from the material to the moral aspects of post-war reconstruction. It sets out how, for socialist leaders, worker unruliness was part of a broader 'moral crisis' afflicting post-war society in general and such 'disoriented' groups as women and youngsters in particular. But if socialist leaders in each of the four countries agreed that this crisis had its origins in the experience of dictatorship, occupation, and war, it was in their distinct appraisals of the depth and political meaning of societal 'demoralisation' that the four parties began to diverge.

Chapters 5–7 delve deeper into the process of political reconstruction. Chapter 5 outlines the experiences and perceptions that informed socialist attitudes towards the rebuilding of democracy. It explains how very different sets of historical vicissitudes shaped the four parties' views about social and political alliances. These views lay at the root of their widely divergent conceptions of democracy, with the Czechoslovakian social democrats and the French socialists embracing 'bourgeois' democracy and the Italian and Polish socialists advocating a new 'popular' democracy. Chapter 6 examines socialist perspectives on the three principal institutions of 'bourgeois' democracy: elections, parliaments, and constitutions. In doing so, it exposes a deep rift between the two sets of parties. For where the Czechoslovakian social democrats and the French socialists viewed elections, parliaments, and constitutions as sacred principles of democratic politics, for the Italian and Polish socialists the constitutional rulebook was designed to perpetuate bourgeois domination. Chapter 7 elaborates on what was, in theory at least, the defining characteristic of 'popular democracy': direct popular participation in economic and political decision-making. Even though each of the four parties was rhetorically committed to widening grassroots participation in public life, their attitudes towards the participatory bodies that sprang up at the moment of liberation were very different. If the Italian and Polish socialists considered popular participation in such bodies a crucial stepping stone towards democratising society, the revolutionary factory councils and liberation committees represented nothing more than the law of the jungle for the Czechoslovakian social democrats and French socialists.

Chapter 8 assesses the extent to which the divergences and parallels between the four parties were exemplary for post-war European socialism as a whole. To that end, it widens its scope to the debates on socio-economic and political reconstruction within the broader European socialist movement. By revisiting the controversies that ultimately saw the PSIUP expelled from international socialism along with the browbeaten Eastern European parties, it challenges the teleological notion that post-war European socialism had definitively turned the corner towards the acceptance of reformism and parliamentary democracy. The Conclusion will draw on the findings from the seven analytical chapters to arrive at a fresh understanding, rooted in social and political history, of the weakness of socialist parties in post-war (continental) Europe.

CHAPTER I

The National Road to Socialism

In early post-war Europe, talk of 'national roads to socialism' was rife. The conception that the trajectory towards socialism, far from being the same always and everywhere, had to respect national traditions and histories was communist in origins. In their efforts to disassociate themselves and their parties from the feared Soviet model, communist leaders across Europe professed their willingness to work within national political systems and with non-communist national actors. For all of the academic debate as to whether this outreach was genuine,[1] we must not lose sight of the fact that the notion of a 'national road to socialism' was not limited to communism. Indeed, a wide variety of left-leaning individuals took up the premise of a road to socialism that would not repeat the bloody excesses of the Soviet experience.[2] This was certainly true for many socialists, who eagerly embraced the idea of a socialism taking its inspiration from national experiences, traditions, and circumstances rather than universal schemes.[3]

---

[1] The sincerity of the communist outreach has often been measured by national communist leaders' willingness to uphold the concept of 'the national road to socialism' after it fell out of favour with Stalin. In this respect, if we confine ourselves to the four countries under review in this book, scholarship tends to portray Italian and Polish communist leaders as rather more sincere and Czechoslovakian and French communist leaders as rather less sincere in their advocacy of a national road to socialism: e.g. Aldo Agosti, *Palmiro Togliatti: A Biography* (Oxford/New York: I.B. Tauris, 2008); Inessa Iazhborovskaia, 'The Gomułka Alternative: The Untravelled Road', in Norman Naimark and Leonid Gibianskii (eds.), *The Establishment of Communist Regimes in Eastern Europe, 1944–1949* (Boulder, CO: Westview Press, 1997), pp. 123–38; Jiří Pernes, *Takoví nám vládli: komunističtí prezidenti Československa a doba, v níž žili* (Prague: Brana, 2003); Jean-Paul Scot, 'Contradictions d'une tentative de "voie française"', *Nouvelles FondationS*, 3/3–4 (2006), pp. 104–9.

[2] Bradley Abrams, for example, points out how many 'democratic socialist intellectuals ... applauded the "Czechoslovak road" and largely accepted the patriotism and democratic instincts of the Communist Party': 'Who Lost Czechoslovakia? Reconsidering the Communist Takeover 50 Years Later', *Intermarium Online Journal*, 3/3 (1999), pp. 1–13, 9. www.columbia.edu/cu/ece/research/intermarium/vol3no3/abrams.pdf (last consulted: 27 June 2018).

[3] At a December 1946 international conference of socialist and social democratic parties from Central and Eastern Europe, the Polish delegate insisted that 'the road to be followed should be Polish for

This chapter provides the necessary context for the seven analytical chapters by exploring the various national circumstances in which socialists and social democrats in post-war Czechoslovakia, France, Italy, and Poland operated. In the first place, it addresses post-war political developments within the four countries and the four parties. Starting from the formation of the post-war coalition governments, it identifies the key issues, debates, and turning points for each of the four countries and elaborates on the socialist attitudes towards these. Subsequently, the chapter places these attitudes in a broader context by briefly delving into the pre-war histories of the four countries and parties. From the nineteenth-century political and socio-economic climate in which the four parties came into being right to the moment of their countries' liberation, it reconstructs the experiences and traditions that shaped the socialists' responses to their post-war challenges. For it is only from the perspective of their pre-war vicissitudes that we can begin to make sense of what drove the four parties in opposite directions after the Second World War.

The Rise and Fall of the Post-War Coalition

The mainstay of the national road to socialism was a broad-church governmental coalition, consisting of all anti-fascist parties. The shared experience of wartime resistance as well as the national unity required for the reconstruction effort, the rhetoric of the day went, warranted the broadest possible political cooperation. The coalitions that rose to power upon liberation in each of the four countries and by and large remained in place until 1947, accordingly, brought together communists and socialists with a wide variety of (usually three or four) centrist, liberal, peasant, and Catholic and Christian democratic parties. Finding compromise among such a diverse group of parties was always going to be a challenge, however, and so it proved. In the face of ever-increasing tensions between the communists on the one side and the centre-right on the other, the socialists often found themselves right in the middle holding the balance of power.

Poland, Czechoslovak for Czechoslovakia etc.' See 'Bericht über die Konferenz der sozialistischen Parteien Zentral- und Osteuropas in Prag vom 7.–9. Dezember 1946', in Peter Heumos (ed.), *Die Konferenzen der sozialistischen Parteien Zentral- und Osteuropas in Prag und Budapest 1946 und 1947* (Stuttgart: Franz Steiner, 1985), p. 71. Similar sentiments were expressed by leading Western European socialists. See e.g. Lelio Basso, 'La via italiana del socialismo', *Avanti!*, 26 November 1947. www.leliobasso.it/documento.aspx?id=fc1fe3ea2c5115d51c21338b2360bb67 (last consulted: 27 June 2018).

The Provisional Governments

With the communists still moderate in their political behaviour in the immediate aftermath of the liberation, though, the fault lines were initially rather different. In fact, it was frequently the socialist parties which were on the extreme left of the provisional governments that were installed in the wake of liberation. Especially in the two Western European cases, the socialists consistently found themselves outvoted and (near-)isolated in their demands for a more radical economic and/or political settlement.

This was very much the case in post-liberation Italy. After the September 1943 armistice between the Anglo-American Allies and the Italian Kingdom, a military government was formed under Mussolini's former Chief of Staff Pietro Badoglio. The new government, consisting exclusively of erstwhile fascists and accountable to a monarch who had supported fascism all along, quickly ran into conflict with the political-military umbrella organisation of the Italian Resistance – the National Liberation Committee (CLN). The six parties represented in the CLN – the Italian Communist Party (PCI), the Italian Socialist Party (PSIUP), the Action Party (PdA), the Christian Democratic Party (DC), the Democratic Labour Party (PDL), and the Italian Liberal Party (PLI) – initially rejected any cooperation with Badoglio and the king.[4]

All of this changed, however, when communist leader Palmiro Togliatti, upon his return to Italy in April 1944, announced that the PCI would be setting aside its objections to the monarchy for the duration of the war and would seek to join the Badoglio government. This announcement came as a 'cold shower' to the socialists, who, in spite of a Unity of Action Pact with the communists, had not been informed of the pending volte-face beforehand.[5] Yet the PSIUP grudgingly followed the PCI into government and, for a brief period, it appeared that things were moving in the Resistance's direction.

Upon the liberation of Rome in June 1944, Badoglio was replaced by Ivanoe Bonomi (PDL), the president of the CLN, as a new government including all of the six CLN parties took office. As it turned out, though, the liberal Bonomi was opposed to any socio-economic radicalism and set about restoring the unreformed and unpurged fascist bureaucratic

[4] Silvio Pons, 'Stalin and the Italian Communists', in Melvyn P. Leffler and David S. Painter (eds.), *Origins of the Cold War: An International History* (New York/London: Routledge, 2005), pp. 205–20, 207.
[5] Paolo Mattera, *Storia del PSI: 1892–1994* (Rome: Carocci, 2010), pp. 126–7.

apparatus.[6] Exasperated by the near-complete lack of administrative purges and the police's heavy-handed crackdown on peasant land occupations in the southern Italian countryside, the PSIUP provoked a governmental crisis. In late November 1944, the CLN passed a socialist motion of no confidence in the prime minister. But Bonomi refused to even meet with the CLN and instead tendered his resignation to the king. Outraged by this snubbing of the Resistance, the PSIUP refused to join any government that would not explicitly recognise the institutional role of the CLN.[7] Once again, however, the communists left their official partners in the cold and joined the second Bonomi government alongside the three moderate parties (the DC, the PDL, and the PLI).

The liberation of northern Italy in the spring of 1945 offered the PSIUP fresh hopes. In the aftermath of the partisan insurrections in several of the north's large cities, demands for far-reaching socio-economic reforms and a thorough purge returned with a vengeance. This more radical 'wind from the north'[8] made Bonomi's position untenable and, in June, a six-party 'government of the resistance' under former partisan commander Ferrucio Parri (PdA) came into being. Yet the programme that Parri drew up – which included 'a serious purge' and such 'socialist-influenced economic proposals' as wealth redistribution and currency reform – found little favour with the Allies and the Italian liberals.[9] By November, the PLI withdrew from the government. The socialists still tried to save Parri by suggesting that the liberal ministers would be replaced in a new five-party government. But as the DC and the PDL rejected this outright and the PCI remained non-committal, Parri resigned.[10]

The demise of Parri spelt the end of the more radical aspirations of the liberation. Under the new six-party government led by Alcide De Gasperi (DC), in which the liberals 'obtained a stranglehold over economic policy'[11]

[6] Paul Ginsborg, *A History of Contemporary Italy: Society and Politics 1943–1988* (London/ New York: Penguin Books, 1990), p. 53.

[7] For a more detailed account of the socialist demeanour during the crisis of the first Bonomi government, see Simone Neri Serneri, *Resistenza e democrazia dei partiti: I socialisti nell'Italia del 1943–1945* (Manduria/Bari/Rome: Piero Lacaita, 1995), pp. 440–7.

[8] It was with reference to this *vento del Nord* that PSIUP leader Pietro Nenni initially demanded the position of prime minister for the socialists: Francesco Malgeri, *La stagione del centrismo: politica e società nell'Italia del secondo dopoguerra (1945–1960)* (Soveria Manelli: Rubbettino, 2002), p. 14.

[9] Spencer Di Scala, *Renewing Italian Socialism: Nenni to Craxi* (Oxford: Oxford University Press: 1988), p. 29.

[10] A succinct summary of the collapse of the Parri government can be found in Gabriella Fanello Marcucci, *Il primo governo De Gasperi (Dicembre 1945 – Giugno 1946): Sei mesi decisivi per la democrazia in Italia* (Soveria Mannelli: Rubbettino, 2004), pp. 24–32.

[11] Di Scala, *Renewing Italian Socialism*, p. 29.

and which saw the anti-fascist purge result in 'a disastrous failure',[12] the PSIUP adopted a strictly defensive stance. Placing all its hopes on the elections to the Constituent Assembly, which, after painstaking governmental negotiations, had finally been scheduled for June 1946, the party primarily sought to avoid further political crises.

If the interlude between the liberation and the first post-war elections was much shorter in France, it was a similarly frustrating period for the French socialists. In the wake of the August 1944 liberation of Paris, General Charles De Gaulle formed a government of 'national unanimity'. It brought together anti-fascist politicians and parties from right across the political spectrum – with the French Communist Party (PCF) and the French Socialist Party (SFIO) on the left, the newly founded (Catholic) Popular Republican Movement (MRP) and the Radical Party (PRS) in the centre, and a series of mostly non-party liberals and moderates on the right.

Much like their Italian counterparts, the French socialists were frequently ill at ease with the countless compromises that 'national unanimity' entailed. As early as January 1945, the SFIO leadership observed 'a malaise within the country and the government', reflected in an insufficient purge, the absence of a governmental programme, sluggish nationalisations, disagreements over the financial politics, the continuation of state subsidies for faith schools, and the 'anti-constitutional' practices of De Gaulle.[13] During the first months of 1945, though, the socialists lacked both the authority and the Allies to press their views on these questions.

This was especially true for socio-economic questions. A commitment towards nationalisations was part of the 'action programme' of the umbrella organisation of the French Resistance – the National Council of the Resistance (CNR) – which had been underwritten by all the main parties and by De Gaulle in March 1944.[14] Yet the socialists quickly found the nationalisation drive – after the initial wave of 'punitive' expropriations of collaborationist owners in the immediate aftermath of liberation – wanting. The chief culprit, in the SFIO's view, was De Gaulle, who wanted to postpone any further nationalisations until after elections had

---

[12] Ginsborg, *A History of Contemporary Italy*, p. 92.

[13] Martine Pradoux and Gilles Morin, 'Daniel Mayer et la SFIO, 1944–1958', *Matériaux pour l'histoire de notre temps*, 51/52 (1998), pp. 24–32, 26.

[14] The programme has been published in Claire Andrieu, *Le programme commun de la Résistance: Des idées dans la guerre* (Paris: Éditions de l'Érudit, 1984), pp. 168–75.

been held. But in reality, as Augustin Laurent pointed out, the socialists were 'isolated', as both the PCF and the MRP supported the general.[15] The SFIO was likewise on the losing side of the debate on economic planning. The socialists supported Pierre Mendès France – the Radical minister of the national economy – in his proposals for a state-directed economy with strong wage and price control.[16] It was the laissez-faire policies advocated by liberal finance minister René Pleven, however, that won the 'all-important backing' of both De Gaulle and the communists[17] – effectively putting on hold socialist aspirations of indicative planning at least until the October 1945 elections.

If the essential dynamics were very much the same in the two Eastern European cases, the major issues facing their socialists were of a different nature. The post-liberation socialists in Czechoslovakia and Poland, like their counterparts in France and Italy, were frequently on the far left of the post-war coalition governments – their demands for nationalisations and land reform going much further than those of the communists.[18] With large-scale industrial and rural expropriations swiftly implemented in their countries, such socio-economic issues were far less contentious for the Czechoslovakian social democrats and the Polish socialists. Their struggle, in the immediate aftermath of liberation, was above all one for legitimacy.

The Czechoslovakian Social Democratic Party (ČSSD) suffered heavy losses during the war years.[19] The party that took office in the provisional Czechoslovakian government – alongside the Czechoslovakian Communist Party (KSČ), the Czech National Socialist Party (ČSNS), the (Catholic) Czech People's Party (ČSL), and the Slovakian Democratic Party (DS) – was

[15] Office Universitaire de Recherche Socialiste, Paris (hereafter OURS), Archives du Parti Socialiste SFIO, Compte rendu des débats du Comité Directeur, 1944–1969 (hereafter: CD SFIO), 26 February 1945.

[16] On Mendès France's plans: Philip Nord, *France's New Deal: From the Thirties to the Post-War Era* (Princeton, NJ: Princeton University Press, 2010), p. 103.

[17] Jean-Pierre Rioux, *The Fourth Republic 1944–1958* (Cambridge: Cambridge University Press, 1987), pp. 64–6.

[18] Anita Prazmowska, 'The Polish Socialist Party, 1945–1948', *East European Quarterly*, 34/3 (2000), pp. 337–59, 340; Karel Kaplan, 'Tschechoslowakische Sozialdemokratie und tschechoslowakische Kommunisten 1944–1948', in Dieter Staritz and Herman Weber (eds.), *Einheitsfront Einheitspartei. Kommunisten und Sozialdemokraten in Ost- und Westeuropa 1944–1948* (Cologne: Verlag Wissenschaft und Politik, 1989), pp. 280–304, 283.

[19] Whereas Bradley Abrams argues that much of the ČSSD's pre-war leadership was 'too old to continue', Jiří Pernes notes how 'the German occupiers took the life of many of its functionaries'. Abrams, *The Struggle for the Soul*, p. 59; Jiří Pernes, 'Vztahy ČSSD a KSČ v době třetí republiky', in Hynek Fajmon, Stanislav Balík, and Kateřina Hloušková (eds.), *Dusivé objetí: historické a politologické pohledy na spolupráci sociálních demokratů a komunistů* (Brno: Centrum pro Studium Demokracie a Kultury, 2006), pp. 25–33, 26.

in many ways unrecognisable compared with the interwar ČSSD. Its incoming chairman and the provisional government's prime minister, Zdeněk Fierlinger, had never even held a position within the party. As the former Czechoslovakian ambassador to the Soviet Union, however, he did command the trust both of the communists and of President Edvard Beneš (ČSNS).[20]

In fact, the communists had shown a strong preference for representatives of the ČSSD's pre-war left wing during crucial wartime talks in Moscow, propelling such relatively unknown social democrats as Bohumil Laušman and Evžen Erban – the new minister of industry and the secretary general of the united trade union movement, respectively – to positions of real power.[21] If the new ČSSD leadership was initially very close to the communists, though, it was not necessarily out of touch with the party grassroots. The October 1945 ČSSD congress confirmed several pro-communists in leading positions and the principle of cooperation with the communists was shared right across the party.[22]

The post-liberation leadership of the Polish Socialist Party (PPS) experienced far greater difficulties in establishing its legitimacy. These difficulties had their origins in the dispute over the rightful Polish government. In February 1943, the Kremlin had severed diplomatic relations with the Polish government in London exile over the controversy surrounding the Soviet massacre of Polish officers in the Katyń forests.[23] Moscow then proceeded quickly to set up what was effectively a rival government in exile – the heavily communist-dominated Polish National Liberation Committee (PKWN). The PKWN formed the provisional Polish government that took office in Soviet-liberated Lublin in August 1944. The Lublin government was notionally a coalition – of the newly founded (communist) Polish Workers' Party (PPR) as well as three left-wing and centre-left parties with roots in interwar Poland: the Polish Socialist Party (PPS), the Democratic Party (SD), and the People's Party (SL). In

---

[20] There is much debate as to whether Fierlinger, who was instrumental in bringing about the June 1948 merger of the ČSSD and the KSČ, was a communist double agent all along. The who's who of twentieth-century Czechoslovakian history even claims that he had been collaborating with the NKVD – the Soviet Union's secret service – since the mid-1930s: Milan Churaň, *Kdo byl kdo v našich dějinách ve 20. století* (Prague: Libri, 1994), p. 111.

[21] Kaplan, *Das verhängnisvolle Bündnis*, pp. 36–43.

[22] Ibid., pp. 61–2.

[23] The Soviet Union was particularly outraged by the exiled government's efforts to carry out an investigation into the matter on German-occupied territory. See Krystyna Kersten, *The Establishment of Communist Rule in Poland, 1943–1948* (Berkeley/Los Angeles/Oxford: University of California Press, 1991), pp. 14–15.

reality, though, the leaders of the three non-communist parties had often been hand-picked by the PPR and were completely subservient to the communists and the Soviet Union.

This was certainly true for the Lublin PPS. Its leader – Edward Osóbka-Morawski – had been part of a left-wing splinter group of the mainstream PPS underground organisation Freedom, Equality, Independence (WRN). He was among the very few Polish resisters who were willing to work with the communists in the first place. In May 1944, as part of a communist-socialist delegation, he made his way to the territories liberated by the Red Army. Visiting Moscow that same month, he joined forces with pro-communist Polish socialists who had spent the war in the Soviet Union and was promptly appointed as prime minister of the PKWN by Stalin.[24] Dominated by fellow-travellers who had been on the radical left of interwar socialism, then, the Lublin PPS initially bore little resemblance to the pre-war PPS. Small wonder that its legitimacy was fiercely contested by both the London PPS and the WRN, which denounced the Lublin PPS leadership as usurpers of the Polish socialist tradition and branded the party the 'false' or 'concessionary' PPS.[25]

Towards the end of 1944, though, things began looking up both for the Lublin PPS and for the Lublin government. In November, Stanisław Mikołajczyk – the prime minister of the London government – resigned his post in frustration over his fellow ministers' reluctance to compromise with the Lublin government and the Soviet Union. Several London socialists followed in his footsteps and together they entered into negotiations with the Lublin parties. In June 1945, these negotiations led to the creation of a new government – the Provisional Government of National Unity – in which Mikołajczyk became deputy prime minister, leading London socialist Jan Stańczyk became minister of labour, and two further interwar political heavyweights took up ministerial roles. Even if the communists and their partners very much remained in control, the new government was sufficiently representative for the Western Allies to recognise it as the legitimate government of Poland – effectively ending any hopes the London government might still have enjoyed of returning to Poland.

The legitimacy of the Lublin PPS, meanwhile, was strengthened considerably by the inclusion of former Londoners. What is more, the WRN dissolved itself in February 1945.[26] Much of the WRN's rank and file

---

[24] Robert Spałek, 'Między pragmatyzmem a zdradą', pp. 145–242, 145–7.
[25] Prazmowska, 'The Polish Socialist Party', p. 340.
[26] Ibid., p. 341.

seems to have subsequently decided to join the Lublin PPS, which saw its membership rise spectacularly in the first half of 1945. Whatever the origins of the membership surge, it was certainly accompanied by a more independence-minded mood within the Lublin PPS.[27] This became very clear at the party's July–August 1945 congress, where the party leadership failed in its attempt to push through a new party programme and former WRN member Józef Cyrankiewicz replaced former Muscovite Stefan Matuszewski as the party's secretary general.[28] Unlike the two other non-communist parties that had been part of the PKWN, then, the Lublin PPS managed to wrest itself from complete dependency upon the communists. Together with the PPR and Mikołajczyk's new Polish Peasant Party (PSL), it was to become one of the three key forces in post-war Polish politics.

First Electoral Tests

The provisional period came to an end with the first post-war parliamentary elections. Compared with the last pre-war elections, these elections witnessed a strong left-wing surge in each of the four countries. For socialist parties, though, the results were mixed. To be sure, with right-wing parties, liberal parties especially, suffering heavy losses, the socialists were now able to govern without those liberals who had often been their strongest adversaries in the provisional governments. At the same time, however, it was the communists rather than the socialists who turned out to be the main beneficiaries of the post-war swing to the left. Gradually abandoning their post-liberation moderation, moreover, the communist parties began urging socialists to unite with them against the Right – forcing the four parties to show their hands for the first time.

Almost three years after Allied troops first set feet on Italian soil, national elections were finally organised. In certain respects, these elections, which took place on 2 June 1946, were a success story for the Italian socialists. The PSIUP became the largest force on the left in the freshly elected Constituent Assembly, winning 20.7 per cent of the popular vote and 115 seats to the PCI's 18.9 per cent and 104 seats. The socialists were likewise on the victorious side of the institutional referendum, held on the same day as the parliamentary elections, in which more than 54 per cent of the electorate voted to replace the monarchy with a republic. At the same

---

[27] Spałek, 'Między pragmatyzmem a zdradą', pp. 152–3.
[28] Ibid., p. 154; Kersten, *The Establishment of Communist Rule*, p. 179.

time, however, the elections were a major defeat for the Italian Left. The combined Left – even if we include such centre-left parties as the Action Party and the Italian Republican Party (PRI) – fell well short of a parliamentary majority. Both the PSIUP and the PCI, moreover, were dwarfed by the Christian democrats – the DC winning 35.2 per cent of the vote and 207 seats.

In the new De Gasperi government that was formed in the aftermath of the elections – a four-party coalition of the PCI, the PSIUP, the DC, and the PRI – the Christian democrats thus remained very much in charge. The PSIUP's new minister of industry – Rodolfo Morandi – experienced this first-hand. By contemporary European standards, his proposals were far from radical. Widespread nationalisation programmes, by that time well underway in a string of countries in East and West, were not on the table in post-war Italy to begin with. Yet even Morandi's moderate agenda – which included the legal recognition of factory councils and a modicum of state intervention in industrial financing and planning – was consistently voted down by the centre-right parliamentary majority. The 'fourteen points' – a series of planning measures and economic controls to combat rampant inflation and speculation, which Morandi presented to the Council of Ministers in March 1947 – did not even make it that far.[29] '[W]ithin fifteen days', Morandi lamented to the PSIUP Directorate, De Gasperi had created a situation in which the fourteen points 'no longer have value'.[30]

In these circumstances, just as many other Western European socialist parties were moving away from the communists, the PSIUP decided to renew its Unity of Action Pact with the PCI in October 1946.[31] According to the PSIUP's foremost post-war leader, Pietro Nenni, the pact was to reaffirm left unity in the face of the DC.[32] But for the right wing of the party, led by Giuseppe Saragat, the alliance with the 'totalitarian' PCI would necessarily result in the PSIUP's progressive subjugation to and eventual liquidation by the communists. Matters came to a head after the PCI made substantial gains at the PSIUP's expense in November 1946 local elections. In a newspaper interview that had the effect of an 'atomic bomb', Saragat

---

[29] Aldo Agosti, *Rodolfo Morandi: Il pensiero e l'azione politica* (Bari: Laterza, 1971), pp. 421–3.
[30] 'Riunione Direzione' (8 May 1947), Istituto Storico della Resistenza in Toscana, Florence (hereafter ISRT), Fondo Foscolo Lombardi, Partito Socialista Italiano, Direzione Nazionale, Busta 4, Fasc. 20.
[31] The pact has been published in *Orientamenti: Bollettino di Commento e di Indirizzo Politico*, 2/1–2 (1948), pp. 35–7.
[32] Francesca Taddei, *Il socialismo italiano nel dopoguerra: Correnti ideologiche e scelte politiche, 1943–1947* (Milano: Franco Agneli, 1984), p. 305.

denounced the party leadership for harbouring secret desires to merge with the PCI.[33] To settle the debate once and for all, an extraordinary PSIUP congress was called at Rome's Città Universitaria in January 1947. When, at that congress, the motion put forward by Nenni and Lelio Basso, the latter of whom was Saragat's main adversary in the PSIUP leadership, won the backing of 65 per cent of the delegates, Saragat and his supporters left for the nearby Palazzo Barberini. There, they founded the Italian Socialist Workers' Party (PSLI), which, over the next couple of months, was to wean from the PSIUP fifty-two of its parliamentarians.[34]

The first parliamentary elections in post-war France also saw the three large currents of communism, socialism, and Christian democracy take approximately three-quarters of the popular vote. Unlike in Italy, however, there was almost nothing between the three parties in the October 1945 elections to the Constituent Assembly: the PCF emerged as the largest party with 26.1 per cent of the vote, the MRP followed in second place with 25.6 per cent, and the SFIO came third with 24.6 per cent. If the elections returned communists and socialists with an overall majority, nothing much seemed to change initially as the Assembly re-elected General De Gaulle as prime minister. Yet De Gaulle quickly became embroiled in a bitter struggle with the parties dominating the Assembly. At stake was the nature of the new constitution. De Gaulle, viewing strong parliaments as arenas of crippling indecision and petty party squabbles, favoured a presidential system with large powers for the Executive. The three main parties, conversely, by and large wanted to retain the parliamentary system of the pre-war Third French Republic.[35] After the parliamentary groups of the PCF and the SFIO had united to demand a 20 per cent reduction of the military budget, De Gaulle, complaining that 'the exclusive regime of the parties' had reappeared, resigned in January 1946.[36]

A new tripartite government of the PCF, the SFIO, and the MRP was then formed by the socialist Felix Gouin. During its six-month tenure, the new government implemented many of the socialist-supported socio-economic policies that the provisional government had rejected: the gas

---

[33] Di Scala, *Renewing Italian Socialism*, p. 58.

[34] On the schism: Paola Caridi and Ennio Di Nolfo, *La scissione di palazzo Barberini: la crisi del socialismo italiano, 1946–1947* (Napoli: Edizioni Scientifiche Italiani, 1990).

[35] Even if the three parties got their way in the end, the Fourth Republic was of course not an exact replica of the Third. For the new elements, see Emmanuel Cartier, 'The Liberation and the Institutional Question in France', in Andrew Knapp (ed.), *The Uncertain Foundation: France at the Liberation, 1944–1947* (Basingstoke/New York: Palgrave Macmillan, 2007), pp. 23–40.

[36] Quoted in Georgette Elgey, *Histoire de la IVe République: La République des illusions 1945–1951* (Paris: Fayard, 1965), p. 89.

and electricity sectors, and most of the insurance sector, were nationalised, while the SFIO's André Philip set about to realise a state-directed economy as the new minister of the national economy and finance. The three parties could not agree on the new constitution, however. The PCF and the SFIO, mindful of how the upper house had obstructed left-wing governments before the war, were proponents of a unicameral system in which all power lay with the directly elected Assembly and the president would take a largely ceremonial role. The MRP, on the other hand, called for the powers of the Assembly to be counterbalanced by an indirectly elected upper house and for the president to be given real powers. By virtue of their parliamentary majority, communists and socialists managed to put their version of the constitution before the country in the May 1946 constitutional referendum. But the MRP fought a successful anti-communist campaign for a no-vote, leading the constitutional project to be defeated by 10.5 million to 9.4 million votes.[37]

In the elections to a fresh Constituent Assembly that followed in June, the MRP (28.2 per cent) gained, whereas the PCF (25.9 per cent) and the SFIO (21.1 per cent) lost ground. A new tripartite government – led this time by Georges Bidault (MRP) – was to arrive at a compromise over the constitution. This revised constitutional project, which provided for a weak upper house and a president with some powers, was adopted by 9.0 million to 7.8 million votes (on a turnout of just 68 per cent) in October 1946.[38] On the basis of the new constitution, elections to the National Assembly were held in November. In these elections, the last parliamentary elections for five years, the PCF (28.3 per cent) obtained its best ever result, overtaking the MRP (26.0 per cent) and leaving the SFIO (17.9 per cent) well behind.

By that time, the SFIO's steady electoral slide had already resulted in the demise of its post-liberation secretary general, Daniel Mayer. A close ally of the SFIO's pre-war leader Léon Blum, Mayer had sought to broaden the party's appeal by reaching out to Christians and the lower middle classes.[39] But in a party strongly attached to its proletarian character and fiercely anti-clerical in its outlook such designs met with much suspicion. The lack of electoral success sealed Mayer's fate. At the August 1946 SFIO congress,

---

[37] Rioux, *The Fourth Republic*, p. 101.
[38] Ibid., p. 106.
[39] Alain Bergounioux and Gérard Grunberg, *L'ambition et les remords: Les socialistes français et le pouvoir (1905–2005)* (Paris: Fayard, 2005), pp. 168–9; Bruce Desmond Graham, *Choice and Democratic Order: The French Socialist Party, 1937–1950* (Cambridge: Cambridge University Press, 1994), pp. 271–6.

Guy Mollet, whose successful pitch for the party leadership revolved around a reaffirmation of the party's traditional revolutionary rhetoric and a renunciation of anything suggesting that the SFIO had become 'a party of the system', replaced him as secretary general. If Mayer had warned that a victory for Mollet would amount to a major success for the communists,[40] the reality was that his election did not essentially change the party's course.[41] Much like Mayer, Mollet was quick to turn down communist overtures for PCF-SFIO unity of action. And when the new party leadership tried to whip its parliamentary group into supporting the PCF candidate for the prime ministry after the November 1946 elections, 'the fierceness of the reactions' was such that the leadership decided to retreat and give its parliamentarians a free vote.[42]

In Czechoslovakia, the electoral divide between communists and social democrats was even more pronounced. In the May 1946 parliamentary elections, the KSČ came out as the largest party by far with 38.0 per cent of the popular vote, while the ČSSD finished last out of the five parties that had been part of the provisional government with a mere 12.3 per cent. Abysmal as the ČSSD's result may have been, however, the parliamentary elections did see the social democrats emerge as kingmakers in Czechoslovakian politics. With its thirty-seven parliamentary deputies, after all, the ČSSD was in a position to provide both the communists and the three centre-right parties with a majority. In the new government under KSČ leader Klement Gottwald, which was made up of the same five parties that had formed the provisional government, the ČSSD leadership set about to make the most of its role as 'balance-tipper'.[43]

The party, accordingly, abandoned its post-liberation politics of extremely close, almost unquestioned, cooperation with the communists.

---

[40] In a segment of his address that was not without hyperbole, Mayer warned of the Europe-wide repercussions of his defeat. According to Mayer, a majority for Mollet would result in 'the failure of the current politics of the Italian Socialist Party and the victory ... of the [Italian] Communist Party over the Italian Socialist Party. There will be the same type of problems in Belgium. [And] there will be municipal elections in Germany in two weeks. You know of the struggles between the independent Schumacher and the communist Grotter Vohl [sic]. The French Socialist Party has an enormous influence. People are watching what it does, what its leaders think and want.' 'Parti Socialiste SFIO: 38ème Congrès national, 29, 30 31 août et 1er septembre 1946', Fondation Jean Jaurès, Paris (hereafter FJJ), p. 83. http://flipbook.archives-socialistes.fr/index.html?docid=51052&language=fra&userid=0 (last consulted: 27 June 2018).

[41] Bruce Desmond Graham, *The French Socialists and Tripartisme 1944–1947* (London: George Weidenfeld and Nicholson, 1965), p. 214.

[42] André Philip is reported to have said that he would 'rather cut through his wrist' than vote for PCF leader Maurice Thorez. Elgey, *Histoire de la IVe République*, p. 231.

[43] Kaplan, *Das verhängnisvolle Bündnis*, p. 79.

After the elections, this more autonomous line vis-à-vis the KSČ won the support of a clear majority in the ČSSD leadership. In fact, only the 'left-wing group' of the now deputy prime minister Fierlinger still favoured the old formula of 'no struggle on the Left'.[44] But both the 'centrists' around returning minister of industry Laušman and the 'right wing' led by minister of food Václav Majer called for the ČSSD to more emphatically underline its independent character.[45] That did not mean, however, that the party turned its back on the communists altogether: the stronger demarcation between communism and social democracy on the left was to be matched by a commensurate demarcation between the ČSSD and the three parties to its right and, especially for the centrists, the communists very much remained the preferred partners.[46] Yet, with the possibility of conflicts with the KSČ no longer ruled out, the social democrats quickly found themselves at loggerheads with the communists.

For the ČSSD responded to the increasingly authoritarian conduct of communist leaders at the head of key governmental departments and the trade union movement. The social democrats' complaints about the communists chiefly revolved around three issues. In the first place, they protested against the state of affairs at the ministry of the interior, where KSČ minister Václav Nosek was steadily expanding the communist hold over the security forces by centralising command structures and making overtly political appointments. Secondly, they expressed serious misgivings about the methods used by the communist minister of agriculture Július Ďuriš, who repeatedly reverted to street and village campaigns to force the KSČ's ever more radical proposals on land reform through parliament. Thirdly, they sharply condemned 'the communist terror against social democrats' in factories, which sometimes went as far as attempts to liquidate entire ČSSD factory organisations.[47] This more and more heavy-handed demeanour on the part of the communists had two effects upon the ČSSD: it increasingly drove the party into the arms of the three centre-right parties, with which the social democrats voted to amend or defeat significant parts of the legislation put forward by Nosek and Ďuriš, and it decisively pitted the social democratic grassroots against the communists. These twin developments strongly affected ČSSD attitudes when socio-political polarisation reached new heights in the second half of 1947.

---

[44] Kaplan, 'Tschechoslowakische Sozialdemokratie', p. 286.
[45] Pernes, 'Vztahy ČSSD a KSČ', p. 29.
[46] Kaplan, Das verhängnisvolle Bündnis, pp. 78–80.
[47] Ibid., pp. 87–101.

If political relations in Czechoslovakia only truly came under strain after the elections, Poland had effectively been divided into two camps before parliamentary elections were finally held in January 1947. When the Provisional Government of National Unity came into being in mid-1945, the communists had still indicated that elections would be held as soon as possible – with early 1946 mentioned as likely at the time. Yet, over 1945 and 1946, the PPR and the PPS kept pushing the date for elections forward. For both communists and socialists were acutely aware of their weakness vis-à-vis the Polish Peasant Party. The November 1945 elections in Hungary, a country with a social structure similar to that of Poland, had seen a peasant party that was in many ways the mirror image of the PSL win an absolute majority. In Poland, where elections were likely to turn into 'a plebiscite' on the Soviet Union,[48] prospects for the parties most closely associated with the new order were, if anything, even bleaker.

To neutralise the electoral threat from the PSL, communists and socialists first suggested that all (legal) parties, rather than presenting separate lists, would run the elections as a common bloc. In February 1946, the PPR and PPS leaderships published a joint proposal for the creation of a 'bloc of six' – consisting of the four Lublin parties as well as the PSL and the small (Christian democratic) Labour Party (SP). It soon became apparent, however, that the parties could not agree on how parliamentary seats would be distributed after the elections. The original communist-socialist proposal stipulated that the four 'larger' parties (the PPR, the PPS, the SL, and the PSL) would each receive an equal number of seats and the two 'smaller' parties (the SD and the SP) a lower number. Well aware that this would guarantee the PPR and its vassals in the SL and the SD a parliamentary block vote, the PSL demanded instead that, in line with the social make-up of Poland, three-quarters of the seats would be awarded to 'representatives of the countryside'.[49] This was an unacceptable condition for the communists as well as the socialists, though, and the negotiations broke down in mutual recriminations.

In March 1946, the communists decided to postpone the elections again. In their place, a 'popular referendum' was called for June 1946, in

---

[48] This was at least what communist leader Wladyslaw Gomułka expected. See: Kersten, *The Establishment of Communist Rule*, p. 234.

[49] The vagueness of this formulation – the communist-dominated SL, after all, also claimed to represent the countryside – leaves some room for interpretation. Yet, both Anita Prazmowska and Jan Tomicki understand it to mean that the PSL demanded 75 per cent of parliamentary seats for itself: Prazmowska, 'The Polish Socialist Party', p. 349; Jan Tomicki, *Polska Partia Socjalistyczna, 1892–1948* (Warsaw: Książka i Wiedza, 1983), p. 474.

which the Polish people were asked whether they approved the abolition of the upper house (question 1), whether they approved nationalisations and land reform (question 2), and whether they approved the new Polish–German border along the Oder–Neiße line (question 3). Both communists and socialists campaigned for a yes vote on each of these three questions. Yet the PSL urged its supporters to vote no on the first question, effectively turning the referendum into a showdown between the two opposing camps. The communists certainly did everything in their power to obtain the 'three-times-yes' they so desired: the referendum campaign saw a massive propaganda effort for a yes vote and those calling for a (partial) no vote met with administrative obstruction and police intimidation.

Despite all this, as many as 80 per cent of voters may have voted no on the first question, with the second question possibly also defeated.[50] Although the communists, assisted by falsification 'experts' from the Soviet Union, made sure that the official results gave the yes camp a clear victory on each of the three questions (68 per cent on question 1; 77 per cent on question 2; and 91 per cent on question 3), the real outcome spoke volumes about the prospects of the Lublin parties in parliamentary elections. Chiefly on the initiative of the PPS, therefore, socialists and communists renewed their offer of an electoral 'bloc of six' in the aftermath of the referendum.[51] But the PSL remained unwilling to join the bloc on the terms set by the PPR and the PPS and, by late September, the four Lublin parties announced that they would run the January 1947 elections on a common list – as the 'Democratic Bloc'.

The months that followed witnessed the increasing polarisation of Polish society. In November, the PPR and the PPS entered into a united front agreement, the text of which committed the two parties to an eventual merger.[52] The PSL, meanwhile, became the subject of 'mass repression',[53] which included the arrest of countless, frequently local and provincial,

---

[50] The report that the PSL drew up on the abuses surrounding the referendum estimated that 83.3 per cent of voters voted no on the first question. As no full vote count actually took place and the communists simply replaced no with yes ballots, burning or flushing down the toilet the discarded no ballots, it is impossible to verify this claim. We do know some local results, however, and these seem to confirm the PSL report. For even in such industrial towns as Rzeszów and Stalowa Wola, where the communists had expected to perform far better than in the countryside, 79 per cent and 80 per cent of the voters, respectively, voted no on question 1. What was more, these towns also voted no on question 2 by 73 per cent and 69 per cent, respectively. See Kersten, *The Establishment of Communist Rule*, pp. 280–2; John Coutouvidis and Jaime Reynolds, *Poland 1939–1947* (New York: Holmes & Meier, 1986), pp. 253–4.

[51] Kersten, *The Establishment of Communist Rule*, p. 297.

[52] Spałek, 'Między pragmatyzmem a zdradą', pp. 203–4.

[53] Kersten, *The Establishment of Communist Rule*, p. 316.

party leaders, a search of the party headquarters by the security services, and the repeated police interrogation of party activists. The election itself, finally, took place in an atmosphere of intimidation – with Democratic Bloc agitators forcing their way into millions of homes during the campaign, and factory workers and local communities being led to the polling station collectively to cast their vote before the eyes of such agitators on polling day.[54] In these circumstances, the parliamentary elections in Poland, which, after due falsification, returned the Democratic Bloc with 80.1 per cent of the popular vote, were no more than a farce.

The Endgame

The kind of left–right polarisation that came early to Poland gradually took hold across continental Europe. During 1947 and 1948, the post-war grand coalitions were reconstituted on a narrower basis in each of the four countries. At least three (interconnected) factors were at play in the demise of the post-war coalition. In the first place, the coalitions were already crumbling under their own weight. As conventional politics steadily gained the upper hand over the immediate needs of the reconstruction effort, it became increasingly difficult to find common ground among the unlikely bedfellows that made up the post-war coalitions. Secondly, the coalitions were rattled by various forms of social unrest as 1947 progressed. Strikes, street campaigns, and large demonstrations, often instigated by those same actors that had preached moderation and national unity in the aftermath of the liberation, all contributed to putting relations between the parties under strain. Thirdly, the coming of the Cold War was accompanied by fresh pressures upon governments in East and West. As the Americans began to push for the communists to be removed from government in Western Europe and the Soviets instructed the communists to consolidate their hold on power in Eastern Europe, the four parties had to decide where their allegiance lay.

In Italy, the impetus for the denouement of the grand coalition definitely came from the Christian democrats. In the same November 1946 local elections that had seen the PCI overtake the PSIUP for the first time, the DC suffered bad losses. Support for the party had more than halved compared with the June parliamentary elections, while the neo-fascist and populist Front of the Common Man made spectacular gains. The Vatican and the business community then started to press De Gasperi to remove

---

[54] On the many abuses surrounding the elections, see ibid., pp. 316–41.

the Left from his government.[55] But the prime minister, who still needed communists and socialists to back (and share the blame for) the unfavourable peace treaty that the Italian government would have to sign at the Paris Peace Conference in February 1947, did not consider the time ripe just yet.[56] In the absence of any governmental agreement on economic policy, however, inflation remained rampant and, as a consequence, the Christian democrats kept losing support. After another disastrous round of local elections for the DC in April, and buoyed by the removal of the PCF from the French government in early May, De Gasperi finally resigned on 13 May 1947.

Following a brief interlude during which the liberal Francesco Saverio Nitti failed to obtain a majority for a new government, De Gasperi then set about to form a coalition without the PCI and the PSIUP. Yet his preferred partners on the centre-left, the republican PRI and Saragat's PSLI, refused to join. This forced De Gasperi to form a minority DC-only government, which needed the support of the combined Right (including the Front of the Common Man) to get its programme through parliament.[57] The new government's policies reflected this transformed support base. Luigi Einaudi, the liberal minister of the budget charged with bringing inflation under control, swiftly implemented an austerity programme that, in its reliance on the free market, was in many ways the polar opposite of Morandi's fourteen-point agenda. Although the 'Einaudi line' succeeded in bringing down inflation to much lower levels, its severe credit restrictions quickly saw business investment drying up.[58]

The resulting rise in unemployment further aggravated already tense social relations. Mass lay-offs unleashed a wave of mostly spontaneous worker protests and strikes during the autumn of 1947, which were met with an increasingly heavy-handed response by the minister of the interior Mario Scelba (DC). Ever since taking office in February 1947, he had been purging all levels of the police of former partisans. The officers who

[55] Mattera, *Storia del PSI*, p. 145.
[56] During a September 1946 conversation with Henry Tasca, the economic counsellor at the American Embassy, De Gasperi had already indicated that he only foresaw a rupture with the communists after the signing of the Peace Treaty: Marialuisa-Lucia Sergio, *De Gasperi e la 'questione socialista': l'anticomunismo democratico e l'alternativa riformista* (Rome: Istituto Luigi Sturzo, 2004), p. 105.
[57] While officially a single-party DC government, the new government did include some non-DC ministers – most notably Carlo Sforza (PRI) as foreign minister and Luigi Einaudi (PLI) as minister of the budget: Malgeri, *La stagione del centrismo*, p. 50.
[58] La linea Einaudi, therefore, was by no means uncontroversial with Italian employers. In fact, the 'great majority' of protests against the government's credit politics came not from trade unions but from employers' organisations: Agostino Giovagnoli, *L'Italia nel nuovo ordine mondiale: politica ed economia dal 1945 al 1947* (Milano: Vita e Pensiero, 2000), pp. 173–7.

took their place were told to clamp down forcefully on every manifest-ation of left-wing radicalism.[59] And so they did. In the context of Scelba's endeavours to 'conquer the streets', which saw the notorious riot police repeatedly opening fire upon industrial or rural agitations, Basso even spoke of 'a veritable fascist danger'.[60]

In this climate of mounting socio-political polarisation, the PSIUP drew ever closer to the PCI. It was the socialists, who, in November 1947, proposed that the two parties would run the April 1948 parliamentary elections on a common list.[61] After successful experiences with common lists in several local elections, both communists and socialists were con-fident that they would be able to defeat the DC by presenting a united front – and, in December 1947, the Popular Democratic Front (FDP) was formed. The first months of 1948, however, witnessed a sharp upswing in Christian democratic fortunes. As the first Marshall Plan aid began to arrive, the material situation improved. During the election campaign, moreover, the DC benefited greatly from the backing of both the Vatican and the United States.[62] The PCI and the PSIUP, meanwhile, were forced on the defensive by the February 1948 communist coup in Czechoslovakia. After the PSIUP leadership had justified the events in Prague as a 'popular revolution' and sent a congratulatory telegram to Fierlinger, the inter-national socialist movement formally endorsed Saragat's Socialist Unity list against that of the FDP.[63]

All of these factors combined to turn the April 1948 parliamentary elections into a particularly traumatic experience for the PSIUP. Whereas the DC won 48.5 per cent of the vote and an absolute parliamentary majority, the FDP lost almost a quarter of those who had voted communist or socialist in June 1946 and only obtained 31.0 per cent. Worse still for the socialists, the overwhelming majority of votes cast for the FDP had gone

[59] Paul Ginsborg, for example, argues that the police 'were encouraged to intervene incisively and bru-tally against all working-class or peasant protests that transcended narrow boundaries': Ginsborg, *A History of Contemporary Italy*, p. 112.

[60] Quoted in Maurizio Degl'Innocenti, *Storia del PSI. III, Dal dopoguerra ad oggi* (Rome/Bari: Laterza, 1993), p. 90.

[61] As Aldo Agosti points out, the PSIUP offer was motivated in part 'by a desire to camouflage in a single result the expected electoral losses of the socialists, weakened by the split': Agosti, *Palmiro Togliatti*, p. 191.

[62] On the role of the Vatican: Robert Ventresca, *From Fascism to Democracy: Culture and Politics in the Italian Election of 1948* (Toronto/Buffalo: University of Toronto Press, 2004), pp. 177–96. On the role of the United States: Kaeten Mistry, 'The Case for Political Warfare: Strategy, Organization and US Involvement in the 1948 Italian Election', *Cold War History*, 6/3 (2006), pp. 301–29.

[63] Simona Colarizi, 'I socialisti italiani e l'Internazionale Socialista: 1947–1958', *Mondo Contemporaeno*, 1/2 (2005), pp. 1–62.

to communist candidates, leaving the PSIUP with just 41 parliamentarians against 140 for the PCI. The rupture with mainstream Western European socialism that had already been very much on display during the election campaign, moreover, quickly proved beyond repair. When even the new, more autonomist party leadership that was briefly in charge after the election defeat refused to renounce the Unity of Action Pact, the PSIUP was first suspended and then expelled from the international socialist movement, with the PSLI taking its place. It was not until the PSIUP abandoned its alliance with the PCI after the Hungarian Revolution of 1956 that the party would manage to escape from its domestic and international ostracism.

In France, by contrast, the events of 1947 and 1948 made sure that the socialists would remain at the heart of government for most of the next decade. In just how pivotal a position the SFIO found itself already became very obvious during the protracted negotiations following the November 1946 parliamentary elections. After both Maurice Thorez (PCF) and Georges Bidault (MRP) failed to obtain a parliamentary majority to form a new government, eyes turned towards the socialists. To break the deadlock, the SFIO leadership convinced Léon Blum, in old age and poor health, to put himself forward as prime ministerial candidate of a transition government. While the Assembly almost unanimously invested Blum with the power to form a government, he was unable to put together a coalition. As the largest party, the PCF demanded one of the three 'grand ministries' (Interior Affairs, Foreign Affairs, or Defence), but the MRP refused to join the government if Blum were to give any of these posts to the communists. The only option that commanded majority parliamentary support, then, was a temporary single-party SFIO government to address pressing economic issues while seeing the newly founded Fourth Republic through the elections to the presidency and the speaker of the National Assembly.

As soon as these offices were filled, Blum resigned. In the new government subsequently formed by the socialist Paul Ramadier – a four-party coalition of the PCF, the SFIO, the MRP, and the Radical Party (by that time rebranded as the RGR) – the communists did obtain one of their prized ministries: with François Billoux becoming minister of defence (though he was immediately stripped of any command over the armed forces by the creation of three separate ministries for war, for the Air Force, and for the Marine). And it was on military questions that the first cracks in the coalition quickly appeared. By March 1947, the PCF made it clear that it could no longer support the colonial war France was waging in Indo-China. Ramadier then called a confidence vote, in which the communist ministers voted for the government and the remainder of the PCF parliamentary party abstained. The coalition survived, but the episode convinced leading socialists that a rupture with the communists sooner or later would be 'inevitable'.[64]

They would not have to wait long. When, in late April, a Trotskyite-inspired strike broke out at the Renault factory in Boulogne-Bilancourt, the communist-dominated trade union confederation (CGT), after unsuccessfully trying to quell the strike, found itself forced to come out in favour of the strikers' wage demands. Ever since the liberation, the CGT, in an effort to showcase the communists' good faith, had done all in its power to hold back strikes. Yet in a situation of decreasing working-class living standards – by mid-1947 they were at half their 1945 levels – this had come at the price of alienating a growing part of the communist industrial clientele.[65] The Renault strike was the final straw. Faced with the prospect of losing (further) control of the working class, the communists revoked their support of the government's wage restraint policies. Ramadier did not wait long to call a new confidence vote, which he won handsomely, but in which the communist ministers, along with the PCF parliamentary party, voted against their own government. In an extraordinary session of the Council of Ministers on 4 May 1947, the prime minister expelled the communist ministers from his government – bringing an end to the tripartite experiment in post-war France.

The question of how to proceed divided the SFIO. Among socialist ministers and parliamentarians, there was strong support for moving ahead with a centrist government of the SFIO, the MRP, and the RGR. A majority in the Mollet-led SFIO Directorate, however, wanted Ramadier to resign and the SFIO to press for a new single-party socialist government. To resolve the matter, an extraordinary session of the SFIO's National Council was called for 6 May. Opening the session, Mollet reiterated the foremost argument that had won him the party leadership: that an exclusive socialist coalition with the MRP and the Radicals would estrange the SFIO from its working-class roots. This time around, however, that argument was trumped by the more urgent considerations put forward by Ramadier, Blum, and a series of socialist ministers. With delegates voting

---

[64] Elgey, *Histoire de la IVe République*, p. 261.

[65] In the first trimester of 1947, the CGT had seen its membership decline by 7 per cent, whereas, in the April 1947 elections to the (trade union-managed) social security organisations, the CGT had done particularly poorly in industrial regions. Phillipe Buton, 'L'éviction des ministres communistes', in Serge Berstein and Pierre Milza (eds.), *L'Année 1947* (Paris: Presses de Sciences Po, 2000), pp. 339–55, 342–3.

by 2529 to 2125 for the Ramadier government to remain in office, the National Council heeded their warnings that a socialist exit from the government would see the country descend into chaos, see inflation spinning out of control, and endanger the republic itself.[66]

This perceived danger to the republic had everything to do with General De Gaulle's return to the political scene. After his January 1946 resignation, De Gaulle had remained silent for almost six months – offering no comment on the constitutional project that was defeated in the May referendum. Following the June elections to the Constituent Assembly, however, he presented his outline for a presidential constitution at a mass rally in Bayeux. Over the next year and a half, this type of mass political gathering was to become the trademark Gaullist intervention in public life.[67] The most significant of these came in Strasbourg in April 1947, where De Gaulle announced the founding of his own political movement: the Rally of the French People (RPF). This new formation, with the aim of propelling De Gaulle to power on the wings of a new constitution, took France by storm during the first months of its existence. Within a couple of months it boasted 400,000 members, second only to the PCF. And in the October 1947 local elections it made spectacular gains: winning 38 per cent of the vote and seeing its candidates become mayor in a quarter of cities with more than 9000 inhabitants (including Bordeaux, Lille, Marseille, and Rennes). Buoyed by the result, De Gaulle called for the immediate dissolution of parliament, fresh parliamentary elections, and a revision of the constitution.[68]

To make matters worse for the government, the RPF offensive coincided with a PCF offensive. In the first months after their removal from government, communist leaders, expecting a rapid return to office, had still urged caution – seeking to restrain the strike wave of the summer of 1947 and even taking a moderately positive attitude towards the Marshall Plan when it was first unveiled. All of this changed, however, after the PCF attended the founding conference of the Communist Information Bureau (Cominform) – effectively a new Communist International for those six Eastern European and two Western European communist parties deemed

---

[66] 'Parti Socialiste – SFIO: Conseil National du mardi 6 mai 1947', FJJ. http://62.210.214.184/cg-ps/documents/pdf/cons-1947-05-06.pdf (last consulted: 27 June 2018).

[67] Apart from the rallies mentioned above, there were to be further major episodes in Épinal (September 1946), where De Gaulle denounced the constitutional compromise arrived at by the PCF, SFIO, and MRP, and, surrounding and after the establishment of the RPF, in Bruneval (March 1947), Bordeaux (May 1947), Lille (June 1947), Rennes (July 1947), and Vincennes (October 1947).

[68] Graham, *Choice and Democratic Order*, p. 374.

sufficiently significant by Stalin – in September 1947. At this secret meeting, during which the French and Italian communists came under severe attack for their 'parliamentarian illusions' and for having allowed themselves to be removed from government, the Soviets signalled the end of the national road to socialism.[69] In line with these fresh Soviet instructions, the PCF made it clear that it would not be joining any more coalition governments, while embarking on a press campaign vilifying the socialists as 'imperialist lackeys'. It was this newfound rhetorical bravado, rather than some insurrectionary design on the part of communist leaders, that led a fresh strike wave in November and December 1947 to spin rapidly out of control.[70]

Irrespective of the PCF's real intentions, though, socialist leaders certainly believed they were dealing with a communist insurrection. When the Ramadier government collapsed at the height of the strike wave, therefore, far fewer socialists had qualms about renewing the coalition with the MRP and the Radicals than six months before. In fact, the conception of 'the Third Force' – a centrist coalition of those parties committed to parliamentary democracy, simultaneously fighting off the communist challenge on the left and the Gaullist challenge on the right – was now also taken up by Mollet. In the new government under Robert Schuman (MRP), accordingly, the SFIO would cement its position as 'party of the system'. Jules Moch, the incoming socialist minister of the interior, immediately mobilised the riot police and the army against the strikers and managed to defeat the strike wave by mid-December. By restoring order, the government won a double victory: it had seen off a communist 'insurrection' and had proven to the nation that France could be governed without General De Gaulle.[71] The country thus stabilised, the Third Force coalition would remain in office until 1951.

Czechoslovakian politics entered a similarly stormy phase in the summer of 1947. For, much like their French and Italian counterparts, the Czechoslovakian communists suddenly found themselves confronted

---

[69] Silvio Pons, 'Stalin and the European Communists after World War Two (1943–1948)', *Past and Present*, 210, Supplement 6 (2011), pp. 121–38, 134.

[70] Starting in Marseille, strikes spread rapidly through the country, with more than a million workers on strike within weeks, and saw such overt acts of sabotage as the derailment of the Paris–Tourcoing express, which left fifteen dead. See, on this strike wave, Robert Mencherini, *Guerre froide, grèves rouges: Parti communiste, stalinisme et luttes sociales en France: Les grèves 'insurrectionnelles' de 1947–1948* (Paris: Syllepse, 1998).

[71] The Gaullists were among the first to realise this. As Jaques Baumel – a close ally of De Gaulle – wrote to the General in 1948: 'For the man in the street, the Rally [of the French People] has been absent from the great communist strikes, ultimately stopped by the Third Force.' Quoted in Bernard Lachaise, 'La creation du Rassemblement du Peuple Français', in Serge Berstein and Pierre Milza (eds.), *L'Année 1947* (Paris: Presses de Sciences Po, 2000), pp. 328–37, 335.

with the Soviet disavowal of the moderate line they had followed up to that point. After first having accepted an invitation to the Paris conference on the Marshall Plan, the Czechoslovakian government was forced into a humiliating retreat by Stalin personally in July 1947. At the founding conference of the Cominform, moreover, the KSČ became the object of much criticism in the slipstream of the PCI and the PCF – with one delegate going as far as arguing that the Czechoslovakian communists had already missed their chance to take power and would meet the same fate as their French comrades. In these circumstances, the KSČ leadership decided to go on the offensive in August 1947.[72]

This offensive found its first expression in the far more radical and populist approach the communists took to socio-economic questions. There was ample scope for such a politics, as, by mid-1947, the Czechoslovakian economy was stalling, the food situation worsening, and the working class becoming increasingly restless. The communists did all in their power to play to worker sentiments: instigating a series of violently anti-Semitic strikes against returning state-managed companies to their rightful Jewish owners and proposing a special 'millionaires' tax' to prevent the state-sanctioned price of grain from going up. The bitter and confrontational street campaigns that frequently accompanied these communist initiatives much alarmed the ČSSD leadership. At a meeting of the party presidium in early September, Laušman claimed that the KSČ seemed determined to follow the path already taken by the other Eastern European communist parties. ČSSD secretary general Blažej Vilím, for his part, argued that the KSČ wanted to create 'an atmosphere of fear' in order to win a majority in the May 1948 parliamentary elections. Once again, only those on the left of the party leadership struck a more conciliatory tone, attributing the recent communist excesses to a feeling of isolation to which the ČSSD had itself contributed.[73]

Even if most other leaders roundly rejected this reasoning, the ČSSD leadership did sanction three of its left-wingers to begin talks with the communists. The delegation of three – consisting of deputy prime minister Fierlinger, trade union leader Erban, and deputy ČSSD chairman František Tymeš – entered into the talks with strict instructions, though. At the very least, the KSČ had to speak out for democracy and stop the 'terror' against social democrats in factories. Any agreement between the KSČ and the

[72] Karel Kaplan, *The Short March: The Communist Takeover in Czechoslovakia 1945–1948* (London: C. Hurst & Company, 1987), pp. 71–7.
[73] Kaplan, *Das verhängnisvolle Bündnis*, p. 121.

ČSSD, moreover, had to be the extended to the National Socialists of the ČSNS. On 11 September, the two delegations reached an agreement in principle, which committed the two parties to concerted action in the 'millionaires' tax' controversy, to continued cooperation with all governmental parties, and to a revival of the wartime 'Socialist Bloc' of the KSČ, the ČSSD, and the ČSNS. Yet, before the ČSSD leadership and parliamentary group had signed off on the agreement, the KSČ published it.[74] The result was a huge backlash. The ČSNS vehemently attacked the social democrats for having succumbed to communist pressure for 'a Marxist bloc'. Minister of food Majer, the foremost leader of the ČSSD's right wing, tendered his resignation and could only be convinced to stay on by a joint plea by the entire presidium except for Fierlinger and deputy speaker of parliament Oldřich John. At the local and provincial level, moreover, several ČSSD branches began calling for Fierlinger's head.

In this atmosphere, the November 1947 ČSSD congress in Brno turned into a showdown between the left-wingers who had by and large been in charge since 1945 and those faithful to the party's pre-war traditions. The centre and the right wing of the ČSSD now united behind Laušman's bid to oust Fierlinger as party chairman. What had already become obvious at the pre-congress meetings of provincial ČSSD departments was confirmed at the congress, as Laušman defeated Fierlinger by 283 to 182 votes.[75] What was more, as Denis Healey, attending the congress as British Labour Party representative, pointed out, the incoming party presidium 'contains in a large majority supporters of an independent line to the Communists'. With the much-maligned Erban voted off the party leadership altogether, the 'only outstanding party leader' still supporting Fierlinger was John.[76]

The new ČSSD leadership, however, was at pains to stress that the personal changes would not alter the party's course.[77] During the months that followed Laušman's election, then, the social democrats stuck to the line they had pursued since the parliamentary elections: advocating cooperation with the communists as a matter of principle, but often siding with the three centre-right parties in practice. This line was soon to become untenable, though. After defeats in separate disputes about wages and land reform had already prompted the KSČ to convene mass worker and peasant meetings, the Council of Ministers of 13 February 1948 was

[74] Pernes, 'Vztahy ČSSD a KSČ', p. 31.
[75] Kaplan, *Das verhängnisvolle Bündnis*, pp. 132–6.
[76] Quoted in Heumos, *Europäischer Sozialismus*, p. 389.
[77] Kaplan, *Das verhängnisvolle Bündnis*, p. 137.

rattled by another bombshell: the communist-dominated ministry of the interior had dismissed eight borough commanders in the Prague police force for no other apparent reason than that they were not communists. As interior minister Nosek was (conveniently) ill,[78] however, the communist ministers refused to even discuss the matter. In response, the ministers of the four other parties united to pass a decree instructing the interior ministry to reinstate the commanders. When no action had been taken by 20 February, the ministers of the three centre-right parties tendered their resignations to President Beneš.

Events then started to unfold quickly. The communists pressured the social democrats to join them in a majority left-wing government. But the ČSSD refused, calling instead for reconciliation between the five parties that had governed Czechoslovakia since the liberation. Yet the KSČ was not about to throw away the tactical advantage it had been gifted by the three centre-right parties and took the governmental crisis to the streets. The communists wasted no time in calling mass meetings across the country and creating 'action committees' in factories, communities, and institutions. Within a matter of days, the press of the three centre-right parties had been paralysed, demonstrations in favour of the centre-right were forbidden, and action committees prohibited anti-communist ministers (including Majer) from accessing their own offices. Even in this atmosphere of overt intimidation, though, the ČSSD persevered in its refusal to help the KSČ to a majority for a left-wing government. On the evening of 24 February, therefore, communist activists and social democratic left-wingers occupied the ČSSD headquarters. Gottwald then presented Laušman with an ultimatum: if he did not reverse his decision, the communists would move ahead, forming a government without the social democrats. In these circumstances, Laušman capitulated. That same night, Majer's right wing was excluded from the ČSSD leadership, while Fierlinger's left wing returned with a vengeance. The following day, President Beneš accepted the resignation of the centre-right ministers and swore in a new, communist-controlled government.[79]

The 'Prague Coup', as the February 1948 events in Czechoslovakia came to be known, spelt the end for both Czechoslovakian democracy and the ČSSD. The widespread purge that followed the coup saw independent

---

[78] Igor Lukes suggests that the KSČ leadership had 'instructed' Nosek to 'come down with a case of diplomatic influenza'. See Igor Lukes, 'The 1948 Coup d'État in Prague Through the Eyes of the American Embassy', *Diplomacy & Statecraft*, 22/3 (2011), pp. 431–49, 437.

[79] This account of (the run-up to) the February 1948 events is based on Kaplan, *The Short March*, pp. 166–86.

politicians in the Czech non-communist parties replaced by communist stooges and the Slovakian Democratic Party outlawed. All legal parties then ran the May 1948 parliamentary 'elections' on a common list, which obtained 89.2 per cent of the vote. The next month, the ČSSD and the KSČ officially 'merged' into a single working-class party. With the great majority of former ČSSD members barred from the new party[80] and the KSČ not even bothering to change its name, however, the fusion is more properly described as a hostile take-over.

In post-war Poland, as we have seen, communist suppression had been a major factor in political life all along. In the wake of the rigged January 1947 parliamentary elections, there was a brief reprieve in the persecutions as more than 25,000 military and political prisoners were released under a post-election amnesty. But from May onwards, the repression returned with fresh vigour.[81] Several socialists outside the PPS, especially those who had been part of the wartime WRN underground organisation, were now actively targeted by the security services. And the clampdown on the PSL, or at least on those of its functionaries and leaders unwilling to join the newly created communist-backed 'PSL-Left' breakaway party, continued likewise. Fearing for his life, Stanisław Mikołajczyk fled Poland in October 1947.

The liquidation of the PSL as an independent political force meant that the PPS remained the only credible counterweight to the communists in Poland. This was reflected in a membership surge. After its membership had rocketed from 500,000 to 660,000 in the space of just a month and a half, the PPS even began a new membership drive under the slogan: 'PPS – party of a million'.[82] This was part of a far more self-assured attitude on the part of the socialists in the aftermath of the elections. The months following the elections, accordingly, witnessed increasing 'discussions and polemics' between the PPR and the PPS over 'political, economic and ideological problems'.[83]

These communist–socialist arguments, however, often did not run along the same lines as in Czechoslovakia. To be sure, the PPS, much like the ČSSD, called for the empowerment of parliament and for cross-party

[80] Pernes, 'Vztahy ČSSD a KSČ', p. 33.

[81] Kersten, *The Establishment of Communist Rule*, p. 384.

[82] Though this target was never met, PPS membership stood at 750,000 by the time of its December 1947 congress: Spałek, 'Między pragmatyzmem a zdradą', p. 210.

[83] Janusz Wrona, *System partyjny w Polsce, 1944–1950: miejsce-funkcje-relacje partii politycznych w warunkach budowy i utrwalania systemu totalitarnego* (Lublin: Wydawn. Uniwersytetu Marii Curie-Skłodowskiej, 1995), p. 238.

control over the security services.[84] Yet, in many ways, these were moot points: the PPR and its two vassal parties had a solid parliamentary majority and the socialists had acquiesced in Poland effectively becoming a police state during the election campaign. What still hung in the balance, though, was the economic future of Poland, and it was on this issue that major conflicts developed between the PPR and the PPS.

The 'Polish road to socialism', in its original communist-supported conception, foresaw a mixed, three-tier economy consisting of a state, a cooperative, and a private sector. By mid-1947, however, the communists set about rolling back the two sectors that did not fall directly under the control of the state. Under the guise of a government offensive against 'speculation' and 'high prices', the communist-dominated ministry of industry unleashed the 'battle for trade': a series of tax hikes and repressive measures directed at shopkeepers and tradesmen, the 'aim of which was the elimination of private wholesale trade, a drastic reduction of private retail trade, and a subjection of cooperative trade to state control'.[85]

Yet the socialists, who had considered the three-tier economy to be a permanent feature of socialist Poland and who were particularly strongly represented in the cooperative movement, quickly disowned the 'battle for trade'. In its first public rebuttal of a communist scheme since the liberation, the PPS claimed that the material shortages and high prices were to be addressed by revising investment plans rather than by curbing private trade.[86] This was part of a larger dispute between the two parties: where the communist-led ministry of industry backed heavy investment in capital goods and fast industrialisation after the Soviet model, the socialist-led Central Planning Office (CUP) had consistently favoured consumer-goods-producing medium and light industries in its funding decisions.

Of course, the balance of forces in post-war Poland was such that the socialists could never win the 'battle for trade' and, by early 1948, the communists forced the CUP leadership to resign. Yet the strength of the socialist reaction to the communist plans belies the assertion that the PPS, having turned its back on the PSL and signed a unity pact with the PPR in the run-up to the parliamentary elections, effectively surrendered to the communists. In fact, the PPS was probably at its most autonomous during

[84] On the empowerment of parliament: Pięta-Szawara, 'Socialiści w Sejmie Ustawodawczym wobec zmian ustrojowych w Polsce w 1947 roku'.

[85] Jacek Kochanowicz, 'Początki planowania w Polsce po II wojnie światowej w perspektywie porównawczej', in Alexsander Łukaszewicz, Elżbieta Mączyńska, and Jerzy Wilkin (eds.), Ekonomia i ekonomiści w czasach przełomu (Warsaw: Polskie Towarzystwo Ekonomiczne, 2010), pp. 203–22.

[86] Kersten, The Establishment of Communist Rule, pp. 373–4.

its December 1947 congress. In what was widely regarded as a rebuff of communist pressure for a merger, Josef Cyrankiewicz – who had become prime minister and PPS leader after the January 1947 elections – exhorted that 'the PPS is and will remain indispensable to the Polish nation'; in response, the congress rose to sing the party anthem.[87] Socialist leaders were confident that this line had the backing of Stalin, who, in his role as 'arbitrator' between the PPR and the PPS, had repeatedly come out in favour of the socialists.[88] They might well have been right at the time. But in the changed international context after the Prague Coup, Stalin demanded complete loyalty in his sphere of influence. Upon his return from a state visit to Moscow in March 1948, Cyrankiewicz announced that the time for a communist–socialist merger had come. Even then, socialist resistance to a fusion appears to have been so strong that the 'unification congress', originally scheduled for the summer, had to be postponed and the new Polish United Workers' Party (PZPR) could only be established in December 1948.[89]

From the Nineteenth Century to the Second World War

This discussion of the first post-war years clearly brings to light parallels and differences between the four parties that cannot be explained through the traditional Cold War narrative. From the perspective of their pre-war histories, however, the roots of these similarities and differences become much clearer. To begin with, the four parties came into being in very diverse socio-economic settings. France and the Czech lands, on the one hand, were advanced industrial economies: in the nineteenth century they had witnessed strong industrial development, rapid urbanisation, and a spectacular drop in illiteracy. Italy and (what was to become) Poland, on the other hand, by and large remained backward rural economies: industrialisation only came late and in a very uneven manner, primitive and semi-feudal farming was still the norm in agriculture, and overall illiteracy hovered around 50 per cent. These very different societal structures provide

---

[87] Quoted in Spałek, 'Między pragmatyzmem a zdradą', p. 222.

[88] Ibid., pp. 201–3; Harald Moldenhauer, '"Ihr werdet Euch dem Sozialismus ohne blutigen Kampf annähern." Kommunistische Blockpolitik und "Gleichschaltung" der Parteien in Polen, 1944–1948', in Stefan Creuzberger and Manfred Görtemaker (eds.), *Gleichschaltung unter Stalin: Die Entwicklung der Parteien im östlichen Europa 1944–1948* (Paderborn: F. Schöningh, 2002), pp. 85–122.

[89] Jan De Graaf, '"The Usual Psychological Effects of a Shotgun Wedding". British Labour and the Socialist Parties in Eastern Europe, 1945–1948', *Bohemia*, 50/1 (2010), pp. 138–62, 162.

the background for the divergent political histories of the four parties and countries between the late nineteenth century and the Second World War.

Founding Divisions

When the four parties came into being, however, these divergences were not directly obvious. In fact, each of the four parties initially modelled themselves after German social democracy in their political behaviour: theoretically and rhetorically, they were committed to a revolution and to the dictatorship of the proletariat, but, in practice, they frequently worked within the parliamentary system and with non-worker parties to achieve reformist or nationalist goals. Yet in the first decade of the twentieth century, often in an atmosphere of heightened socio-political tensions, this reformist consensus came under pressure from more radical socialists looking to press ahead with the revolution.

The early history of the Italian Socialist Party (PSI) exemplifies this trend. Established in 1892 by the reformist lawyer Filippo Turati, the PSI initially fought much the same battles as the left-liberal Radical Party: for universal suffrage, for progressive taxation, and for the eight-hour working day. The PSI urged its supporters to vote for non-socialist, centre-left candidates in run-off second ballots and repeatedly entered into (parliamentary and non-parliamentary) alliances with centre-left bourgeois parties, although both Turati (in 1903) and his fellow reformist leader Leonida Bissolati (in 1911) stopped short of accepting an offered ministerial post.[90]

But the sharp deterioration of industrial relations in the aftermath of the 1907 economic crisis strengthened the hand of socialist 'intransigents' – the intra-party minority that had rejected the reformist policy of working within the system all along. The Italo-Turkish War over Libya of 1911–12 brought matters to a head. The reformist majority split over the war, allowing the intransigents to take control at the October 1912 congress of the PSI. Those reformist leaders who supported the war (including Bissolati and the PSIUP's later nemesis Ivanoe Bonomi) were expelled from the PSI and founded the Italian Reformist Socialist Party (the precursor of the PDL). The intransigents or 'maximalists' were now firmly in charge and would remain so for the duration of the First World War.[91]

If the political context was completely different in France, the internal dynamics within its socialist movement were very similar. France having

---

[90] Martin Clark, *Modern Italy 1871–1995* (London/New York: Longman, 1996), pp. 108–12.
[91] Mattera, *Storia del PSI*, pp. 53–6.

known (male) universal suffrage since 1848 and having been a parliamentary republic with the corresponding set of constitutional rights and freedoms since the 1870s, the struggles of its socialists in many ways differed from those of their counterparts in more authoritarian systems.

Yet the question of participation in the 'bourgeois' political system divided the French socialists all the same. When, in 1899, leading socialist Alexandre Millerand took up a ministerial post in the centre-left 'Government of Republican Defence' that came to power at the height of the Dreyfus Affair, the socialist movement split into two separate parties.[92] The French Socialist Party, led by Jean Jaurès, supported alliances with bourgeois Republicans and took part in the cross-party Left Bloc coalition that won the 1902 parliamentary elections. The Socialist Party of France, in contrast, rejected any form of cooperation with non-proletarian forces, its leader Jules Guesde claiming that the proletariat would 'abandon its own struggle' if it set about defending the 'Republic of its masters'.[93] It was only after the intervention of the Second International, which prohibited reformist alliances at its 1904 Amsterdam congress, that the two parties merged into one. Established in 1905, the SFIO immediately withdrew its support from the Left Bloc government, erecting a barrier between socialism and bourgeois republicanism that was to survive well into the interwar years.

In the Czech lands, the national question added a further dimension to the struggles between moderate and radical socialists. The founding of the Czech Social Democratic Workers' Party (ČSDSD) in 1887 was the result of a compromise between the reformist and revolutionary wings of the clandestine Czech socialist movement in the Habsburg Empire. Moderation certainly prevailed within the new party, though. Even if the ČSDSD, which was an autonomous organisation within the larger setting of the Austrian Social Democratic Workers' Party at the time, did not renounce its ultimate revolutionary aims, its focus was firmly on achieving its objectives through legal means – with demands for universal suffrage once again taking centre stage. Sure enough, the ČSDSD did very well in the elections to the Habsburg Imperial Council, becoming the largest force in the Czech lands in both elections (in 1907 and 1911) that were fought on male universal suffrage.

[92] Geoff Eley provides a succinct summary of the 'Millerand affair'. See Eley, *Forging Democracy*, pp. 87–88.
[93] Quoted in Alain Bergounioux and Gérard Grunberg, *Le long remords du pouvoir: Le Parti socialiste français 1905–1922* (Paris: Fayard, 1992), p. 30.

Yet parliamentary representation presented the party with a fresh dilemma: was the ČSDSD going to cooperate with its social democratic comrades from other Habsburg nations or with its national compatriots in bourgeois Czech parties? When the ČSDSD first entered the Imperial Council in 1897, its delegates had still denounced bourgeois demands for renewed Czech statehood as an effort 'to dig up old privileges'.[94] Much like social democratic parties in other countries, however, the ČSDSD took up increasingly nationalist positions during the first decade of the twentieth century. In 1910, it even defied a Second International ruling by taking the Czech trade unions out of the unitary Austrian trade union movement – effectively breaking all ties with its Austrian mother organisation.[95]

The national question was of even greater significance in pre-war Polish socialism. Their nation still carved up as a result of the Austrian, German, and Russian partitions, the question of whether the struggle for national independence or the struggle for a proletarian revolution was to be prioritised divided the Polish socialists. The first socialist party in the Polish territories – The Proletariat (founded in 1882) – was a revolutionary organisation with links to Russian anarchist groups, but it was quickly quashed by the Tsarist authorities. When the PPS was created in 1893, accordingly, a more nationalist line was adopted. Its leader, Józef Piłsudski, ruled that Polish socialists could only cooperate with Russian revolutionaries if they supported Polish claims for independence. The result was a split with revolutionary Polish socialists (including Rosa Luxemburg), who, viewing nationalism as a diversion from the proletariat's real struggles, established the Social Democratic Party of the Polish and Lithuanian Kingdom (SDKPiL) in 1894.

The question of (non-)cooperation with Russian revolutionaries, however, was to remain the foremost bone of contention within the pre-war PPS. After the crushing of the 1905 rebellions in various Polish cities (part of the revolutionary wave that hit the Russian Empire during that year), the party split in two. The Piłsudski-led PPS–Revolutionary Fraction wanted to continue the struggle for Polish independence by terrorist and para-military means. Yet the PPS–Left, led by a group of younger socialist

[94] Quoted in: Jiří Kořalka, 'Českoslovanská Sociálně Demokratická Strana Dělnická', in Jiří Malíř and Pavel Marek (eds.), *Politické strany: vývoj politických stran a hnutí v českých zemích a Československu 1861–2004* (Brno: Doplněk, 2005), pp. 213–39, 233.

[95] According to the ČSDSD, the German trade unionists dominating the Austrian trade union movement were 'denationalizing' Czech workers. C.A. Macartney, *The Habsburg Empire, 1790–1918* (New York: Macmillan, 1969), pp. 803–4.

leaders, was looking to build alliances for an empire-wide revolution against Tsarism.[96]

Revolution and Schism

The (consequences of the) First World War intervened in a decisive manner in these divisions within the pre-war socialist movement. On the one hand, the extension of democratic rights and freedoms in a series of (newly independent) states strengthened reformist beliefs about the need to work within the system. On the other, the existence of the Soviet Union provided the revolutionaries with a clear focal point and model to emulate. In these circumstances, a schism between the two wings of the socialist movement became all but inevitable.

The Italian case demonstrates this clearly. By all accounts, the PSI emerged from the war as a revolutionary party. Taking its lead from developments in the Soviet Union, the radical PSI leadership called for the immediate creation of a socialist republic and the dictatorship of the proletariat.[97] There certainly seemed to be ample appetite for radical social change: the PSI became the largest party by far in the November 1919 parliamentary elections with 32.4 per cent of the vote, and the *biennio rosso* (two red years) of 1919–20 saw widespread factory and land occupations.

As it turned out, however, the PSI's revolutionary rhetoric was not matched by commensurate action. For one thing, there was a deep rift between the revolutionary slogans espoused by the PSI leadership and the reformist beliefs of many socialist parliamentarians and trade unionists. But even the more radical leaders, educated in the classical Marxist notion that a proletarian revolution would develop spontaneously, 'had no idea how to lead a revolution'.[98] At the January 1921 PSI congress in Livorno, therefore, the extreme left pressed for the PSI to become a vanguard communist party in the Leninist sense. Yet a majority rejected Lenin's Twenty-One Conditions of admission to the Communist International (Comintern), which demanded the expulsion of 'proven reformists' like Turati. The left wing broke away immediately to form the PCI. In October 1922, the reformists followed suit to found the Unitary Socialist Party

---

[96] These two paragraphs are based on Anita Prazmowska, *Poland: A Modern History* (London/New York: I.B. Tauris, 2010), pp. 44–60.

[97] Eley, *Forging Democracy*, p. 170.

[98] Clark, *Modern Italy*, p. 212.

(PSU). Just as fascism was in the ascendancy, then, the socialist movement split three ways.

The back story to the schism within the SFIO is completely different. Unlike their Italian counterparts, who had consistently voted against war credits, the French socialists had supported the French war effort all along – even participating in the government for the first three war years. After the war ended, moreover, socialist leaders, far from embracing revolutionary rhetoric, tried to restrain strikes and focused fully on the upcoming parliamentary elections. Yet the November 1919 elections, in which the SFIO gained votes but lost seats, were a bitter disappointment for the socialists. The resulting disillusionment with parliament contributed to the balance within French socialism swinging 'sharply to the left'.[99] At its December 1920 congress in Tours, accordingly, the SFIO became the only major European socialist party to vote for adhesion to the Comintern.

The (moderate) minority at Tours broke away and continued as the SFIO. Even if the party was now devoid of its most radical elements, it did not fundamentally change its attitude towards (peacetime) governmental participation. To be sure, the socialists entered into victorious electoral coalitions with the Radicals in 1924 and 1932, but these coalitions never saw the socialists taking ministerial responsibility. It would take a perceived fascist challenge to the republic for the SFIO to abandon its 'refusal of power' in the mid-1930s.[100]

The interwar ČSDSD, in contrast, very much became a party of government. Its nationalist wing having taken control over the party leadership during the war, the ČSDSD supported Tomáš Garrigue Masaryk – Czechoslovakia's 'founding father' – in his quest for national independence and participated in the provisional Czechoslovakian government that came to power in November 1918. The first post-war ČSDSD congress formulated a set of reformist demands, including the nationalisation of large companies and the introduction of universal health care. Yet the governmental coalition with bourgeois parties was denounced by the ČSDSD's emerging Bolshevik wing. Unity was just about preserved until the April 1920 parliamentary elections,[101] which saw the ČSDSD becoming the largest party by far with 25.7 per cent of the vote.

[99] Tony Judt, *Marxism and the French Left: Studies on Labour and Politics in France, 1830–1981* (New York: New York University Press, 2011), p. 122.

[100] Bergounioux and Grunberg, *Les ambitions et les remords*, pp. 13–122.

[101] Ladislav Cabada, 'Vztahy sociálních demokratů a komunistů v období první a druhé Československé republiky', in Hynek Fajmon, Stanislav Balík, and Kateřina Hloušková (eds.), *Dusivé objetí: historické a politologické pohledy na spolupráci sociálních demokratů a komunistů* (Brno: Centrum pro Studium Demokracie a Kultury, 2006), pp. 14–24, 18.

When the ČSDSD renewed its coalition with bourgeois parties after the elections, however, the Bolsheviks went into open opposition: refusing to vote for the programme of the incoming coalition government under the social democrat Vlastimil Tusar and pressing for the acceptance of Lenin's Twenty-One Conditions. Moderate leaders now seriously feared they would lose control to the Bolsheviks at the September 1920 party congress. Eleven days before the congress was supposed to take place, therefore, the ČSDSD left the government and postponed its congress until December. The Bolsheviks then called their own congress, at which they founded the party that was to become the KSČ. The schism severely weakened the ČSDSD: the party lost a third of its parliamentarians and most of its working-class membership, and dropped to 8.9 per cent of the vote in the 1925 parliamentary elections.[102] Yet after returning to government in September 1921, the ČSDSD cemented its role as one of the five parties ruling interwar Czechoslovakia – but for a three-year spell between 1926 and 1929, the party was to remain in government until 1938.

Newly independent Poland saw rival communist and socialist parties emerge too. For at least two reasons, though, its communist–socialist struggles lacked the salience of those in the three other cases. Firstly, the Polish socialist movement had already split before the war. The PPS–Revolutionary Fraction changed its name back to PPS in 1913, while the PPS–Left and the SDKPiL merged to form the Polish Communist Party (KPP) in 1918. Secondly, the Polish-Soviet war of 1919–21, during which the Polish army under Józef Piłsudksi eventually fought off the Red Army, 'ensured that an overwhelming majority of Poles rejected emphatically the blandishments of Bolshevism for the remainder of the interwar period'.[103]

Unhampered by a bruising internecine fight, then, the interwar PPS practised moderation right from the outset. The socialists were fully committed to a democratic and parliamentary road to socialism and presented reformist demands: the nationalisation of some industrial and agricultural sectors, universal access to education, and state pensions.[104] Even though Piłsudski cut all ties with the PPS in his effort to present himself as standing above the parties, the socialists initially supported his

[102] Jan Kuklík, *Československá Sociálně Demokratická Strana Dělnická'*, in Jiří Malíř and Pavel Marek (eds.), *Politické strany: vývoj politických stran a hnutí v českých zemích a Československu 1861–2004* (Brno: Doplněk, 2005), pp. 683–709, 687.
[103] Peter D. Strachura, *Poland, 1918–1945: An Interpretive and Documentary History of the Second Republic* (London/New York: Routledge, 2004), p. 62.
[104] Roman Bäcker, *Problematyka państwa w polskiej myśli socjalistycznej lat 1918–1948* (Toruń: Wydawnictwo Uniwersytet Mikołaja Kopernika, 1994), p. 92; Strachura, *Poland*, p. 60; Prazmowska, *Poland*, p. 110.

May 1926 military coup. It was only when Piłsudski subsequently installed a dictatorship that the PPS began to reconsider the reformist politics it had pursued up to that point.

Facing Fascism

During the interwar years, parliamentary democracy came under right-wing pressure in each of the four countries. This pressure was uneven: whereas Italy and Poland succumbed to fascist or authoritarian dictatorships in the 1920s, parliamentary democracy survived in interwar Czechoslovakia and France. Yet the (perceived) fascist challenge to democracy prompted all four parties to seek allies on the left. This process received a strong boost when the Comintern adopted its popular front strategy in 1934, leading communist parties across the continent to abandon their earlier sectarianism and seek broad-based anti-fascist alliances with socialist and centre-left parties. The coalitions formed in the second half of the 1930s, then, foreshadowed the governments that would rise to power after the Second World War.[105]

Fascism had its origins in Italy. If the radicalism of the *biennio rosso* had not ushered in a proletarian revolution, it had certainly frightened the Italian middle and upper classes. Among these groups, there was an increasing desire for a return to industrial and rural order. Exactly this was offered by Benito Mussolini's fascist 'squads', the para-military groups, often led by ex-servicemen, that viciously broke strikes, intimidated landless rural labourers, and burnt down local socialist offices. The squads' October 1922 'March on Rome' propelled Mussolini to power. In the April 1924 parliamentary elections, which saw overt terrorisation and massive fraud, his National Fascist Party (PNF) won a smashing victory. After Giacomo Matteotti, the PSU's leader, spoke out against the electoral abuses, he was murdered, probably at Mussolini's behest. In the aftermath of the 'Matteotti crisis', which repulsed many of Mussolini's erstwhile centre-right allies, Mussolini proceeded to set up a full dictatorship.[106] By 1926, all opposition parties had been outlawed, their press organs banned, and many of their leaders were languishing in prison.

---

[105] On the socialist response to the rise of fascism: Gerd-Rainer Horn, *European Socialists Respond to Fascism: Ideology, Activism, and Contingency in the 1930s* (Oxford/New York: Oxford University Press, 1996).
[106] Clark, *Modern Italy*, pp. 215–28.

Those socialists who managed to escape reconstituted their parties in French exile. Convinced that the labour movement's split had much weakened the Left vis-à-vis fascism,[107] PSI leader Pietro Nenni set about reconciling its warring factions. In July 1930, the PSI and the PSU merged. This was followed in August 1934 by the Unity of Action Pact with the PCI, which was to remain in force until the liberation. Post-war Italian socialism's 'unitarian' outlook received its final impulse from the PSI's August 1943 merger with Lelio Basso's clandestine Movement of Proletarian Unity (MUP) – resulting in the creation of the PSIUP.

The 1930s likewise saw the French Left pull together. The Radical-SFIO coalition that had won the May 1932 elections proved very unstable. With the two parties advocating opposite policies in the face of the Great Depression, governments fell in rapid succession. Worse, several leading Radicals became embroiled in a corruption scandal, sparking a series of increasingly violent demonstrations by extra- and anti-parliamentary right-wing leagues. These culminated in 'the February 1934 crisis': a right-wing riot in Paris that left fifteen death and hundreds wounded. Widely interpreted by the French Left as a fascist coup attempt,[108] the crisis prompted its three major parties to join forces. The anti-fascist 'vigilance committees' formed in the wake of the crisis had already brought together communist, socialist, and Radical intellectuals. In July 1934, the PCF and SFIO leaderships followed by entering into a Unity of Action Pact. The next year, communists, socialists, and Radicals agreed a common electoral programme. The resulting Popular Front won the May 1936 parliamentary elections. Having emerged as the largest party in both votes and seats, the SFIO entered a peacetime government for the first time – its leader Léon Blum becoming prime minister.

In spite of its impressive list of social reforms, the Popular Front government brought the socialists many 'disillusions'.[109] The communists, offering only parliamentary backing, refused to join the government and quickly began attacking Blum over a string of domestic and international policies.[110] What was worse, facing a right-wing majority in the Senate,

---

[107] Alexander De Grand, '"To Learn Nothing and to Forget Nothing": Italian Socialism and the Experience of Exile Politics', *Contemporary European History*, 14/4 (2005), pp. 539–58, 541.

[108] The historiographical consensus is that, while some fascist groups were active, it was probably not. See e.g. Philip Morgan, *Fascism in Europe, 1919–1945* (London/New York: Routledge, 2002), pp. 102–9.

[109] Bergounioux and Grunberg, *Le long remords du pouvoir*, pp. 148–54.

[110] The PCF was scathing about the government's non-intervention in the Spanish Civil War and 'severely criticised the government on its left' over Blum's 1937 'pause' in reform. See Stéphane Courtois and Marc Lazar, *Histoire du Parti communiste français* (Paris: Aubier, 1992), pp. 147–54.

Blum was unable to address France's economic problems. After the upper house had blocked his strongly interventionist investment programme, Blum resigned in April 1938. The Radicals subsequently formed a new government with right-wing backing, which reversed many of the Popular Front's social reforms. Having long been a dead letter, moreover, the communist–socialist Unity of Action Pact came to a definite end upon the announcement of the Nazi-Soviet pact in August 1939. In the 'phoney war' after the subsequent German invasion of Poland, the SFIO played a much-diminished role in French politics. The depth of socialist despondency at their defeat and isolation became obvious after the fall of France, when the great majority of SFIO deputies present at the National Assembly's session in Vichy on 10 July 1940 voted in favour of suspending the Third Republic's democratic constitution and according General Philippe Pétain dictatorial powers to produce a new one – thereby contributing to the creation of the collaborationist Vichy France.

The threat of fascism did not lead to rapprochement between communists and social democrats in interwar Czechoslovakia. From 1935 onwards, the KSČ did make some overtures towards a united or popular front with the ČSDSD and the National Socialists of the ČSNS. Yet, compared with communist outreaches elsewhere, these overtures were half-hearted at best and dismissed as a ruse by the social democrats and National Socialists. In fact, the ČSDSD always viewed the ČSNS, with which it formed the left wing of the five-party coalition that governed Czechoslovakia for most of the interwar period, as its 'natural ally in the effort to preserve the democratic character of Czechoslovakia'.[111]

As the 1930s progressed, Czechoslovakia's democratic character came under pressure from both within and abroad. The Great Depression hit the Sudetenland particularly hard, fuelling nationalist resentments among its majority-German population. In the 1935 parliamentary elections, the radical nationalist Sudeten German Party (SdP), financially backed by Nazi Germany, became the second strongest party in Czechoslovakia. The following years witnessed the SdP and Hitler formulate an ever-increasing set of demands upon the Czechoslovakian government. This campaign culminated in the September 1938 Munich Conference, where British and French governments sought to appease Hitler by effectively signing over the Sudetenland to Germany. The loss of the Sudetenland, followed quickly by further territorial concessions to Hungary and Poland, spelt the end for the First Czechoslovakian Republic. In the short-lived Second

---

[111] Cabada, 'Vztahy sociálních demokratů a komunistů', p. 23.

Republic, the ČSDSD and the left wing of the ČSNS merged into the National Labour Party, conceived mainly as a bulwark against the increasingly authoritarian tendencies of the appeasing right-wing government that had taken office after Munich. But it was to no avail. In March 1939, Hitler first forced Slovakia to declare independence and then ordered his troops to march into the Czech lands – thus creating the Protectorate of Bohemia and Moravia.

In interwar Poland, parliamentary democracy had collapsed long before the Nazis imposed their will upon the country. Presenting itself as a national revival against a dysfunctional and corrupt parliamentary system, Piłsudski's 1926 coup was part of a broader European backlash against parliamentarism.[112] The PPS initially welcomed the coup, expecting that its erstwhile leader would enact radical socio-economic reforms. But Piłsudski had no such intentions. In fact, his Sanacja (purification) regime quickly won the backing of landowners and industrialists by ruling out any further land reform and clamping down forcefully on strikes. In the face of the government's rightward thrust and its increasingly repressive nature, the PPS joined forces with peasant and Christian democratic parties to form the Centrolew (centre-left) parliamentary opposition group in 1929. Yet in the run-up to the November 1930 parliamentary elections, prominent Centrolew leaders, six of them socialists, were arrested on trumped-up conspiracy charges. In 'an atmosphere of intimidation', the Sanacja then won a majority in the elections, while the Centrolew leaders were convicted in a show trial.[113]

Their defeat at the hands of what had now become a full-fledged dictatorship prompted many PPS leaders to move away from their reformist convictions. Over the course of the 1930s, the socialists embraced a more leftist agenda. In economic terms, the PPS drew a sharp line between the 'worker control' enshrined in socialisations and the 'state capitalism' represented by nationalisations. Such 'young Turks' as Oskar Lange and Julian Hochfeld, who would be among the foremost socialist theorists during the post-war years, no longer viewed the parliamentary road to socialism as viable, moreover. Even if most socialists still rejected their viewpoints, the new PPS programme of 1937 did allow for a temporary dictatorship of the proletariat.[114] This opened the way for an alliance with

---

[112] In this respect, Anita Prazmowska draws parallels between Piłsudski's coup and Mussolini's March on Rome and Primo de Rivera's military coup in Spain (1923). See Prazmowska, *Poland*, pp. 119–20.

[113] Prazmowska, *Poland*, pp. 123–4

[114] Bäcker, *Problematyka państwa*, pp. 98–9.

the communists and, from the mid-1930s, the PPS leadership set aside its objections to 'limited cooperation' with the KPP in a popular front.[115]

Conclusion

The four parties thus embarked upon 'the national road to socialism' with widely divergent back stories. In large part, these divergences went back to their very different experiences with 'bourgeois' parliamentary democracy during the interwar years. For the Italian and Polish socialists, on the one side, parliamentary democracy within the framework of bourgeois capitalism had proven itself to be very fragile indeed. The advent of fascism, explained PSIUP Directorate member Sandro Pertini at the party's April 1946 congress, had 'shown that freedom, if it does not have those social reforms associated with socialism at its core, can be obliterated in the space of an afternoon'.[116] For the Czechoslovakian social democrats and the French socialists, on the other side, parliamentary democracy had proven itself to be the best guarantee for personal rights and freedoms. The broader political consensus around these freedoms, which included non-proletarian centrist parties, convinced them that it was possible to work for socialist change from within the 'bourgeois' political system.

It was not merely these conflicting political 'lessons' from the interwar years guiding the four parties on their post-war trajectories, however. The socialists also drew wider implications from their countries' longer-term socio-economic development. For each of the four parties, as we will discuss in far greater detail in the three chapters on political reconstruction, based their political views on historically informed perceptions of the societies they operated in. Before we move on to these questions, however, we will turn our attention to socio-economic reconstruction, starting with the immediate concerns among rank-and-file (socialist) workers. In their struggle for everyday survival, after all, such 'political' concepts as democracy took on a wholly different, and strongly subsistence-related, connotation.

---

[115] Prazmowska, *Poland*, p. 127.
[116] 'Al Congresso di Firenze' (April 1946), in Simone Neri Serneri, Antonio Casali, and Giovanni Errera (eds.), *Scritti e Discorsi di Sandro Pertini. Volume I, 1926–1978* (Rome: Presidenza del Consiglio dei Ministri, Dipartimento per l'Informazione e l'Editoria, 1992), pp. 78–9.

CHAPTER 2

Bread, Butter, and Egalitarianism

As the Second World War drew to a close, worker grumbles about the material situation began to sound louder. During a May 1944 meeting of the *comité social* – the shop floor body created by the Vichy regime to guarantee cordial worker–management relations – at the Lever soap factory in Lille, several workers filed a complaint about the meals being served in their canteen. They were unhappy about the insufficient rations of potatoes, as they did not like the split peas which had been served in lieu of them that day. But the committee chairman made it quite clear that 'the current circumstances no longer allow for such abundance as to satisfy all the tastes', calling on workers to resign themselves 'to eating whatever can be found'.[1]

Such demands for appetising food would indeed seem increasingly presumptuous once the occupation had made way for renewed freedom. Contrary to a widespread popular belief that working-class living standards would improve dramatically after the war had come to an end, the material conditions actually grew worse for many workers during the first post-war years, as various factors combined to their disadvantage. In the first place, the chaos reigning in the run-up to and aftermath of the liberation brought industry to a standstill across continental Europe. Secondly, the destruction of infrastructure and the paucity of natural resources seriously affected supply lines even after industrial production had been resumed. Thirdly, the devastation of machinery and the severe shortage of (skilled) labour kept overall industrial output well below pre-war levels until the late 1940s. All of this was compounded still further by the two brutally cold winters of 1945–46 and 1946–47, which drove the working class to the edge both physically and mentally. In these circumstances, workers were

---

[1] 'Compte rendu de la réunion du Comité Social du 5 mai 1944', Archives Nationales du Monde du Travail, Roubaix, Fonds CGT Lever à l'usine de Haubourdin, 2001 005 0001.

often completely preoccupied with the quest for such scarce commodities as food, coal, or clothing.

This chapter aims to illustrate how the post-war hardships affected the political views taken by (socialist) workers in Lille, Łódź, Milano, and Plzeň. It will explore the endless list of complaints that ordinary workers levelled against their political leaders: about their utter failure to improve working-class living standards, their powerlessness in the face of rampant inflation, their inability to clamp down on the flourishing black market, and their general disinterest in the everyday predicament of their own rank and file. In doing so, it not only demonstrates that the bread-and-butter demands formulated at the socialist grassroots were fundamentally at odds with the political goals pursued by socialist leaders (which we will deal with in far greater detail in Chapter 3). It also lays bare how the face of the industrial working class had changed over the interwar and war years. In fact, the loudest protests often came from relative newcomers to the working class: women, rural migrants, and those employed in the state sector. The failure to come to terms with, or even to take seriously, the grievances expressed by such newcomers did much damage to socialist efforts to regain control over the working class.

The Supply Side

The extent to which lacking access to basic necessities trumped all other considerations among the post-war European working class is borne out by the concepts dominating their vocabulary. Worker discourses in post-war Lille, Łódź, and Milano were packed with demands for a better *ravitaillement, aprowizacja,* and *alimentazione,* respectively – designating either 'supply' or simply 'food' in each case. In Plzeň, the material situation was initially more tolerable,[2] with the ČSSD daily claiming victory in the battle for bread by the autumn of 1945.[3] But even with food more readily available, workers increasingly complained about excessive *drahota* – the prohibitively high prices at which first necessities had to be bought. It was

---

[2] This was due mostly to the fact that the Czech lands came out of the Second World War in a better material situation than virtually all other formerly German-occupied areas. In the first place, the Nazis had initially sought to win over the working class in the Protectorate of Bohemia and Moravia, whose effort was crucial to the German war industry, by making economic concessions – food and clothing rationing was even introduced later in the Protectorate than in the Reich itself. Secondly, its position right at the centre of the German empire shielded the Protectorate from Allied bombing until late 1944. See Hugh Agnew, *The Czechs and the Lands of the Bohemian Crown* (Stanford, CA: Hoover Institution Press, 2004), pp. 211, 214.

[3] 'Otázka chleba už je u nás vybojována', *Nový Den*, 30 September 1945.

this combination of severe shortages and dwindling purchasing power that tormented, unnerved, and more and more outraged workers. For despite socialist leaders' promises to the contrary, things were not getting better for their rank and file as the first post-war years went by.

It was not long before it dawned on the working class that the sufferings of the occupation were to continue into the post-liberation era. If food and fuel were already hard to come by during the final months of the war, they were in even shorter supply after the fighting had ended. At first, this still seemed to be related to the direct exigencies of the ongoing war and of troop movements. In the north of France, the liberation was reported to have been a 'hard awakening' for those people who had expected their problems to disappear and *ravitaillement* to renormalise. It had taken the German Ardennes counter-offensive for them to realise that the war was still ongoing and that equipping the frontline remained the number one priority.[4] In Plzeň, meanwhile, there was widespread worker concern and discontent about the American Army (the city was liberated by General George Patton's Third US Army in May 1945) moving food out of the city to supply their forces.[5] But as direct hostilities receded further into the background, it became clear that these difficulties were not of a momentary nature. By July 1945, Milanese workers were taking to the streets in a hunger march, carrying signs with such slogans as 'reduction of the cost of living', 'bread and work', 'our children are hungry', 'price control', 'we want an immediate devaluation', 'protect our interests against those starving the people', and 'struggle with the black market'. Patience with those in power (including socialists) was already running thin, the local PSIUP press reported, as 'all things human have a limit'.[6]

But it quickly emerged that the new rulers were unable to deliver upon even the most basic demands of the working class. In the Łódź region alone, there had been twenty strikes protesting the terrible state of *aprowizacja* by August 1945.[7] At a meeting of socialist workers in the city's public transport shops that month, one worker lamented that the reigning

---

[4] Commissaire du Police to Directeur des Reseignements Generaux (Réunion du Parti Socialiste à Escaudin), 17 January 1945, Archives Departmentales du Nord, Lille (hereafter ADN), Commissariat Régional de la République (hereafter CRR), 19 W 37108 2.

[5] 'Zápis schůze Národního Výboru dne 28. května 1945 v Plzni', Archiv Města Plzně, Plzeň (herafter AMP), Zápisy o schůzich Národniho Výboru a rady Okresního Národního Výboru a Místního Národního Výboru statutárního města Plzeň 1945.

[6] 'Manifestazione di protesta di popolo e di lavoratori per la rivendicazione dei diritti dell'ora', *Sesto Proletaria*, 7 July 1945.

[7] XXVI Kongres (August 1945), Archiwum Akt Nowych, Warsaw (hereafter AAN), Polska Partia Socjalistyczna (hereafter: PPS), 235/1-12, fo. 91.

chaos demonstrated the government was not up to its task. After all, winter was approaching fast and still the working class had not been supplied with coal. Demanding compensatory payments to fill up the holes in his household budget, another worker illustrated his predicament graphically. Where his new-born should be a source of parental joy, he argued, it was quickly developing into 'a tragedy'. As his entire income was swallowed up by buying baby food on the free market, 'what should he and the rest of his family live on?'[8] Similarly, local socialists in Roubaix were soon to voice their discontent about their own party's minister for provisions in the first De Gaulle government – Paul Ramadier.[9] So meagre were the rations handed out by his ministry that he was rapidly nicknamed 'Ramadan' or 'Ramadiète' across the region.[10]

This pattern of rank-and-file workers reproaching their leaders for failing to provide for their everyday necessities would repeat itself over and over again during the months and years to follow. The common charge was that political and trade union leaders were so immersed in high politics and macro-economic management now that they were finally in (shared) power that they had lost sight of the real problems besetting the very people they were representing. And these problems were real enough. Not only did the insufficient supply of food, coal, and clothing cause starvation and freezing, but the prices of those few goods that were available were spiralling dangerously out of control. In these circumstances, workers were often at a loss as to why their wages were held back or even dropping.

In fact, working-class living standards had been falling right from liberation. In each of the four cities, workers complained bitterly that wages and prices were completely out of balance and getting worse. In Lille, a popular saying went that 'whereas salaries take the staircase, prices take the elevator',[11] as the cost of living had risen by 35 per cent and wages only by 25 per cent.[12] In Plzeň, there was strong criticism of the Supreme Pricing Authority, which calculated the prices for a whole range of everyday

[8] 'Protokoł zwyczajnego Koła P.P.S. przy Zarzadzie Miejskim, Wydziale Technicznym, Oddziale Pómiarow' (16 August 1945), Archiwum Panstwowe w Łodzi, Łódź (hereafter APŁ), DK PPS Śródmieście Prawa, 10, fos 5–6.
[9] Commissaire de Police to Commissaire Central Chef du Sous-District de Roubaix (Réunion de la Section de Roubaix du Parti Socialiste), 26 February 1945, ADN, CRR, 19 W 37108 2.
[10] Martine Pottrain, *Le Nord au cœur: historique de la Fédération du Nord du Parti Socialiste, 1880–1993* (Lille: SARL de Presse Nord-Demain, 1993), p. 87.
[11] 'Note des renseignements d'une importante réunion privée d'information (d'arrondissement) organisée par le Parti Socialiste SFIO, à Cambrai' (3 February 1947), ADN, CRR, 30 W 38630 8.
[12] L'Officier de Police Judiciaire to Commissaire Central Chef du Sous-District du Tourcoing (Compte rendu d'une réunion politique), 18 October 1946, ADN, CRR, 28 W 38454 2.

necessities. Based upon its estimates, the government had increased wages in December 1945, but reality had quickly caught up. With incessant price rises wiping out the entire increase within a matter of months, workers in the metal sector faulted the body both for setting its projections too low and for failing to include the prices of water, electricity, and gas in its calculations.[13] Whereas the combination of relentless price increases and static (or rising-below-inflation) wages caused serious anxieties among the Milanese working class as well,[14] the situation was arguably worst in Łódź. There were repeated testimonies of wages either coming down or being paid belatedly in the face of unbridled price hikes.[15] In that situation, even vital necessities were often beyond the reach of workers, with coal and foodstuffs all but impossible to acquire on an average salary.[16]

Small wonder, then, that workers were demanding something far-reaching to change this state of affairs. According to the internal commission (the elected shop floor trade union representation in Italian factories) at Milano's tram-manufacturing and -repairing Teodosio, the continuous hikes in the cost of living had made the food situation so precarious that workers were no longer able to work productively. In these circumstances, a 10 per cent salary increase would not do anymore – the trade unions should instead aim for a 40 per cent raise.[17] Such generous pay packages were, however, not forthcoming. Quite the contrary, in their efforts to break the vicious cycle of wage and price rises, governments in each of the four countries increasingly relied on wage restraint. There was much resentment over unfulfilled promises regarding pay increases and bonuses among such diverse groups as miners in Plzeň,[18] tyre makers in Milano,[19] and functionaries in Łódź.[20]

[13] 'Ceny a mzdy musí být v souladu', *Nový Den*, 19 April 1946.

[14] CI Alfa Romeo to Camera del Lavoro, 25 August 1946, Archivio del Lavoro, Milano (hereafter AdL), Camera del Lavoro, Class. 5.2.2.4., Fasc. 1.

[15] 'Protokół z nadzwyczajnego zebrania Koła Miejscowego' (2 June 1945), APŁ, DK PPS Śródmieście Prawa, 10, fo. 3; 'Protokół z zebrania Koła PPS przy PPT-EP Oddz. Łódź' (4 March 1947), APŁ, DK PPS Śródmieście Prawa, 10, fo. 43; 'Protokoł z zebrania Kola PPS przy PZPB Nr. 15 w Lodzi' (22 May 1947), APŁ, DK PPS Górna, 7, fo. 20.

[16] 'Protokół spisany z zebrania członkow P.P.S. przy Panstwowych Zakładach Przemysłu Wełnianego Nr. 40 w Łodzi' (28 October 1947), APŁ, DK PPS Fabryczna, 8, fos 82–3; 'Protokoł z zebrania Polskiej Partji Socjalistycznej na terenie przedzalni Ksziezy Młyn' (3 March 1947), APŁ, DK PPS Fabryczna, 8, fo. 53.

[17] CI Teodosio to Camera del Lavoro, 10 July 1946, AdL, Camera del Lavoro, Class. 5.2.2.4., Fasc. 1.

[18] 'Horníci naléhají', *Nový Den*, 1 August 1945.

[19] CI Pirelli to Ministro del Lavoro, Camera del Lavoro Milano, and Confederazione Generale del Lavoro, 8 August 1945, AdL, Camera del Lavoro, Class. 5.2.2.4., Fasc. 1.

[20] 'Protokół sporządzony na zebraniu Koła Prac. Umysł. przy Polskiej Partii Socjalistycznej' (13 November 1946), APŁ, DK PPS Tramwaje, 13, fos 39–40.

But the issue was most thorny in France, where salaries were blocked
for a prolonged period in 1946 while the cost of living kept going up. At a
regional meeting of the SFIO in Cambrai, emotions over the government's
price and incomes policy ran high. Where the delegate from Lille's Santes
commune was still polite, describing the control of wages and not prices as
'a mistake' and calling for an attack on profit margins instead, his colleague
from Pérenchies condemned the party for not living up to socialism while
branding the salary policy 'criminal'. The representative from Tourcoing
summed up the general mood, demanding that not the franc but the purchasing power of workers be defended.[21]

In all four countries, the newly unified trade union movement had been
charged with the task of defending working-class interests in questions of
living standards and wages. But as workers in the four cities were soon to
find out, trade union leaders toed the government line rather than vice
versa. Although the Central Council of Trade Unions (ÚRO) tried its best,
an editorial in the Plzeň ČSSD press argued, 'we would be lying if we were
to say that its interventions with the president, the government, and the
political parties have made much of a difference'.[22] In the north of France,
at the same time, a growing number of workers were refusing to pay their
monthly membership dues to the CGT. It is clear, one of them lamented,
'that the directives of the CGT leadership make it impossible for us to have
a go at some of our demands'. Where trade union officials kept harping on
about the need for sacrifices to rebuild the country, 'it must not be the case
that all sacrifices are made by workers'.[23]

Local socialists often used such worker grievances as a stick with which
to beat communist trade union leaders. A brochure published by the SFIO
sections in Denain and Bouchain criticised the communists for 'their complete disinterest vis-à-vis the trade union movement at the sole benefit of
a political party'. During the last strike at the Cail furnace works, 'political arrivals' had ordered strikers to make up for lost hours. Since when,
the brochure asked, 'were struck hours recovered? Where was the time
that trade union leaders demanded the integral payment of lost hours as
a precondition for a return to work?'[24] Similarly, local social democrats
in Plzeň accused their Provincial Trade Union Council (KOR) of only

[21] 'Note de Renseignements' (Activité du Parti Socialiste SFIO (réunion privée)), 16 September 1946,
    ADN, CRR, 28 W 38453 2.
[22] 'Kdo za to odpovídá?' Nový Den, 19 February 1946.
[23] 'Note de Renseignements' (Mécontentement d'une partie des ouvriers vis-à-vis de l'action des
    délégués ouvriers), 26 February 1946, ADN, CRR, 27 W 38337 1.
[24] 'Honte aux faux frères' (September 1946), ADN, CRR, 28 W 38453 2.

fighting the KSČ's political struggles. Rather than staging factory walkouts on such partisan issues as the 'lenient' sentences handed to the collaborationist leaders of the wartime Protectorate government (see Chapter 4) or the re-election of Plzeň's communist mayor (see Chapter 7), it should redirect its energies towards the cost of living crisis.[25] For many workers were complaining that the KOR was doing all sorts of things that could easily be left to political parties, while forgetting what really dominated working-class concerns – the question of *drahota*.[26]

Not that socialist leaders were beyond grassroots reproach for their attitudes towards trade unionism. Reflecting upon the subordinate role played by trade unions, local socialists in Sesto San Giovanni (the industrial district on the outskirts of Milano) pointed to their national leaders. Where they might have the best of intentions towards the trade union movement, 'the road to hell is paved with good intentions'. Concrete support was needed, as trade unions had grown into the 'Cinderella' of present-day Italy. Never publishing any articles dealing with 'trade unions, their function, and above all their indispensability', the national PSIUP newspaper *Avanti!* (run by the party leadership) was severely criticised. After all, workers would happily forsake all treatises on political processes to finally read something that related to their vital problems. Was it 'impossible to clear out half a column' for that?[27]

Far from empowering the trade unions, however, socialist (and communist) leaders increasingly employed them as transmission belts for government policy.[28] Workers were quick to identify their unions with the authorities and worse. Claiming that everyone who spoke out against the fact that the collective agreements had only been to the benefit of the industrialists was censured, one Milanese socialist argued that it had been exactly these types of injustices that had created worker discontent with and distrust towards the fascist unions.[29] The negotiating positions taken by trade union bodies were also a major source of dissatisfaction among Łódź socialists. Complaints focused on such diverse issues as the unfairness of collective agreements for the most needy workers,[30] on union inability

---

[25] On the tribunal: 'Právní řád nebo anarchie', *Nový Den*, 4 August 1946. On the Plzeň mayoral election: 'To že má býti demokracie?' *Nový Den*, 29 June 1946.

[26] 'Aktuální otázky', *Nový Den*, 9 August 1946.

[27] Gandi, 'Quattro Parole sui Sindacati', *Sesto Proletaria*, 12 July 1945.

[28] On how trade unions were used to serve the productivist goals of the Italian and Polish governments: Serneri, *Resistenza e democrazia dei partiti*, p. 420; Kenney, *Rebuilding Poland*, pp. 61–9.

[29] R.R., 'Risposta a Gandi', *Sesto Proletaria*, 19 July 1945.

[30] 'Protokuł z zebrania Koła PPS przy Łodzkich Zakładach Przemysłu Czesankowego' (7 August 1945), APŁ, DK PPS Górna, 6, fo. 3.

to reach collective agreements in the first place,[31] and on union support for a prolongation of the working day.[32] By mid-1946, socialist workers in Łódź's textile industry were wondering where the trade unions were, asking who was fighting their corner, and petitioning trade unionists to show some interest in their lives.[33] Less than a year later, their counterparts in the city centre concluded that trade unions were powerless in questions of pay drops.[34]

Feeling abandoned by its traditional organisations, the working class increasingly took matters into its own hands. Agitations, (wildcat) strikes, and theft were the order of the day in industry, as workers were desperate to improve their standard of living. Out of the four cities, the situation was definitely least volatile in Plzeň,[35] but even here there were several agitations demanding a pay increase to cope with unbearable *drahota*.[36] Łódź, on the other hand, was the strike capital of Poland and possibly Europe, with over 500 strikes between 1945 and 1948. Not only were the overwhelming majority of these inspired by economic concerns, but even those strikes that historiography describes as 'political' quickly developed a bread-and-butter character.[37] Although the big strike wave that swept the city in September 1947 had its origins in a workplace conflict over the introduction of multi-machine work at the I.K. Poznański cotton mill, its rowdy meetings were marked by claims that life was harder now than it had been before the war or even during the occupation. And while officially an outcry against the alleged maltreatment of Poznański strikers by the authorities, the solidarity strikes that subsequently broke out across the city had strong subsistence overtones as well. Especially among Łódź's large

[31] 'Protokół zebranie członkow P.P.S. Dzielnica Tramwaje Miejskiej' (25 July 1946), APŁ, DK PPS Tramwaje, 13, fos 28–9.
[32] 'Protokół' (28 August 1947), APŁ, DK PPS Śródmieście Lewa, 14, fo. 12.
[33] 'Protokół z zebrania członkow P.P.S. koła fabrycznego przy Panstw. Zakł. Włokiem. daw. K. Scheibler i I. Grohmann' (25 May 1946), APŁ, DK PPS Fabryczna, 8, fos 9–10.
[34] 'Protokół z zebrania Koła PPS przy PPT-EP Oddz. Łódź' (4 March 1947), APŁ, DK PPS Śródmieście Prawa, 10, fo. 43.
[35] Though there were some strikes in Czechoslovakia during 1945 and 1946, the country only really saw widespread industrial unrest emerge after the economic downturn of 1947 – with 103 strikes in 1947 alone and a further 218 strikes between 1948 and 1953. See: Peter Heumos, 'Zum industriellen Konflikt in der Tschechoslowakei 1945–1968', in Peter Hübner, Christoph Kleßmann, and Klaus Tenfelde (eds.), *Arbeiter im Staatssozialismus: Ideologischer Anspruch und soziale Wirklichkeit* (Cologne: Böhlau, 2005), pp. 473–98, 475, 478.
[36] Ladislav Cígler, 'Ceny musí býti sníženi!' *Nový Den*, 14 July 1946.
[37] Out of the 1220 strikes that hit 'People's Poland' between 1945 and 1948, Łukasz Kamínski reckons that 84.43 per cent had an economic, 13.23 per cent a political, and 2.34 per cent a mixed basis. But this classification includes the strike at I.K. Poznański (see below) among the politically motivated strikes. Łukasz Kamínski, *Polacy wobec nowej rzeczywistości, 1944–1948: formy pozainstytucjonalnego, żywiołowego oporu społecznego* (Toruń: A. Marszałek, 2000), pp. 115, 141.

female workforce, many complained about low earnings, bread tasting like clay, children starving, and the threat of tuberculosis.[38]

Theft from the workplace, which was 'endemic' in several post-war European industrial centres,[39] was a further manifestation of worker despair. A worker at Milano's tractor-producing Motomeccanica called upon the government to no longer hand orders to firms laying off workers, as in the current situation of mass unemployment even 'honest people become black marketers, thieves, etc. to feed themselves and their families'.[40] Similarly, one socialist employed in the Łódź public transport system remarked that the theft of coal by railway workers was a sign of their bitterness. The worker, he argued, demanded 'that something was done for him', for the 'sad reality' was that the worker was 'treated like a beggar' by 'his own comrades in leading positions'.[41]

Grassroots socialists in the north of France likewise berated their leaders for simply not comprehending the ordeal the working class went through. When, at the first post-war congress of the SFIO's Northern Federation, its leader and SFIO Executive member Augustin Laurent identified the constitutional question as the most urgent problem of the day, denounced the strike movement as 'motiveless', and admonished socialist workers to play a more positive role in the run-up to the next elections, a local delegate swiftly rebuked him. While he agreed with Laurent on the importance of drawing up a new constitution, there were 'other problems' to which SFIO ought to devote its attention. Above all, this concerned the problem of *ravitaillement*, which formed the central concern for the bulk of the electorate and to the amelioration of which the party should immediately commit itself.[42]

If the disregard socialist leaders seemed to show for the woes tormenting their rank and file initially met with such constructive criticism, the mood at the grassroots rapidly soured. While still expressing understanding for the fact that their government was completely immersed in the business of post-war reconstruction, miners in Plzeň were already warning that it would be hard for them to make their peace with further delays to promised improvements in pay and food provision by mid-1945.[43] In the

---

[38] Henryk Wachowicz to CKW PPS, 6 October 1947, AAN, Polska Partia Socjalistyczna, Sekretariat Generalny, Wydz. Ekonomiczno-Przem. – Strajki, 1946–48, 2291, 235/xv-86, fos 18, 22.

[39] Pittaway, *The Workers' State*, p. 72. See also Kenney, *Rebuilding Poland*, pp. 91–3.

[40] B. Filippo to Camera del Lavoro, 15 October 1946, AdL, Camera del Lavoro, Class. 5.2.2.4., Fasc. 1.

[41] 'Protokoł zwyczajnego Koła P.P.S. przy Zarzadzie Miejskim, Wydziale Technicznym, Oddziale Pómiarow' (16 August 1945), APŁ, DK PPS Śródmieście Prawa, 10, fos 5–6.

[42] 'Congrès de la Fédération du Nord du Parti Socialiste SFIO' (August 1945), ADN, CRR, 19 W 37108 2.

[43] 'Horníci naléhají', *Nový Den*, 1 August 1945.

north of France, meanwhile, local socialists were much bewildered at the SFIO's acquiescence to the economic policies implemented by liberal minister René Pleven – at that time combining both the finance and national economy briefs in the first De Gaulle government. Fingered by grassroots socialists as a representative of those notorious '200 families' that had dominated inter-war France,[44] Roubaix's socialist mayor Victor Provo condemned Pleven for 'nothing but copying the measures that [Raymond] Poincaré [the conservative who served three terms as France's prime minister in the 1920s] had adopted in 1925'. As this could only lead to 'public debt rising and living standards dropping every day', it was about time that Pleven devised some new fiscal measures that would hit the rich.[45]

Socialists in Milano expressed a similar exasperation with the same old laissez-faire economics. Franco Mariani, the foremost socialist trade unionist in the region, declared in 1946 that it had been a 'fundamental mistake' for the government to sacrifice every form of market discipline at the altar of free trade. In the face of severe problems with *alimentazione*, ministers had 'preferred to do nothing', expecting the issue 'would solve itself'. The opposite had been the case and therefore it was imperative to arrive at 'a controlled economy'.[46]

But even under more interventionist regimes, workers found ample cause for dissatisfaction. When the SFIO's André Philip took over the finance and national economy brief in the Gouin government, his efforts to clean up the nation's finances by exerting tight control over prices and wages created considerable turmoil in socialist ranks. If socialist workers were already disgruntled about the government-warranted price hikes of tobacco and coal,[47] matters came to a head over the 25 per cent wage increase suddenly demanded by the CGT in the run-up to the June 1946 parliamentary elections. While it was brushed aside by socialist leaders as no more than a communist election stunt, rank-and-file party members saw more merit in the proposal. At a meeting of the local SFIO section in Cambrai, grassroots socialists castigated the party leadership for its 'passivity' and 'procrastination' in questions of prices and wages.[48]

---

[44] Commissaire de Police to Directeur des Renseignements Generaux (Réunion de la section du Parti Socialiste SFIO à Helemmes), 19 January 1945, ADN, CRR, 19 W 37108 2.

[45] Commissaire de Police to Commissaire Central, Chef du Sous-District (Réunion publique d'information de la section de Wattrelos du Parti Socialiste SFIO), 19 April 1945, ADN, CRR, 19 W 37108 2.

[46] Interview Leonardi with Franco Mariani, AdL, Camera del Lavoro, Class. 5.1.3., Fasc. 4.

[47] 'Le Parti Socialiste: Département du Nord' (reference date: 28 February 1946), ADN, CRR, 19 W 37108 1.

[48] 'Note de Renseignements' (Congrès d'arrondissement du Parti Socialiste SFIO à Cambrai), 22 July 1946, ADN, CRR, 28 W 38449 1.

Had the socialist press organs really 'considered it appropriate to inter-view workers and almost have them say that a 25% raise would be unwelcome'?[49]

This form of patronising was all the harder to accept from parties and governments claiming to rule in the name of the working class. The last thing workers needed, an editorial in the Plzeň social democratic press read, was 'prestige or flattery – that they are spoken about as if they have power and dominate the situation'. What the working class did require was an improvement in their living standards: cheap clothing and shoes for their children, new homes and furniture for their youngsters, all those things they 'put off buying for six years'. The clothing reserves had reached rock bottom: 'we need to return to the living standards of the last years of the First Republic as soon as possible'.[50]

As the longed-for amelioration in the supply situation failed to materi-alise, grassroots socialists invoked the memory of the interwar years, for better or (more often) worse, with increasing frequency. Addressing the social ills of post-war Poland, one Łódź socialist compared current times to the period when the country was ruled by the Sanacja dicta-torship.[51] The Sesto San Giovanni PSIUP expressed similar sentiments in an open letter to the national PSIUP leadership in August 1946. After giving an exposition of all the causes underlying the miserable living conditions of the working class, it concluded: 'The worker is patient and has been waiting for a year and a half for someone or some-thing to change this state of affairs. Nothing! Like before, worse than before. We cannot continue like this.' In devoting all their energies to the peace negotiations, which were going to be decided by the imperi-alist powers anyway, political leaders had ignored 'the harsh realities of our internal situation, the truth about the conditions of the working masses'. They should take an interest in the concerns of the working class and remember that there was 'a certain limit where people stop reasoning, close their eyes, and vent the anger that has been brewing in their hearts'.[52]

---

[49] 'Note de Renseignements' (Activité du Parti Socialiste SFIO (réunion privée de la section de Cambrai)), 6 July 1946, ADN, CRR, 28 W 38449 I.

[50] 'Myslíme to dobře', *Nový Den*, 16 March 1946.

[51] 'Protokół sporządzony na zebraniu Koła Prac. Umysł. przy Polskiej Partii Socjalistycznej' (13 November 1946), APŁ, DK PPS Tramwaje, 13, fos 39–40.

[52] Esecutivo PSIUP Sesto San Giovanni to Direzione PSIUP, Vice Presidente del Consiglio dei Ministri Nenni, and Gruppo Parlamentare PSIUP, *Sesto Proletaria*, 28 August 1946.

The Dark Side

More than anything, this grassroots resentment concerned their leaders' seeming diffidence in the face of the sinister forces seeking to profit from working-class misery. With so many shortages, the widespread opportunities to make a quick gain often proved irresistible for those people with access to scarce goods and services. The black market was not just about peasants selling off their surpluses at outrageous prices – it was a vast system encompassing entire businesses or sectors, frequently in connivance with either the authorities or the workforce, committing massive frauds. Nor was speculation the only wrongdoing that caught the worker's eye. From the shameless incompetence, indifference, and wastefulness at the top to the nepotism that saw some workers getting more than their fair share at the bottom, there were all sorts of scandals that beggared working-class belief. One common theme clearly emerges, though: that of the honest and diligent worker suffering at the hands of those having only personal gain on their minds.

In order to guarantee an equitable division of first necessities, all four countries adopted a rationing regime. In reality, however, workers frequently complained that rations were neither even-handed nor sustainable. There were several protestations that workers or other vulnerable groups were short-changed in or even excluded from the distribution of various goods. Socialist workers in Łódź's city centre argued that their provision of coupons did not suffice. Bread had been rationed, but the worker also needed cereals, peas, and other foodstuffs. Moreover, despite personal hygiene being crucial in the struggle against diseases, workers had been left out of the allotments of soap altogether.[53] Similarly, socialist workers in Cambrai expressed their bemusement that already better-off peasants received additional supplements of butter, oil, and sugar.[54] In Plzeň, finally, there were many complaints that, unlike workers, tradesmen, artisans, students, and housewives taking care of young children, the ill as well as pensioners had not been awarded with 'P3' coupons for bread, fats, and meat by the ministry for food. Josef Janouš – the ČSSD spokesman for

---

[53] 'Protokoł z zebranie komórki P.P.S. odbytego w dniu 25 października 1945 r. w Łodzi' (25 October 1945), APŁ, DK PPS Śródmieście Prawa, 10, fos 9–10.
[54] 'Note de Renseignements' (Congrès d'arrondissement du Parti Socialiste SFIO à Cambrai), 22 July 1946, ADN, CRR, 28 W 38449 1.

supply in the city council – recommended intervening with Prague so that every household would at least have one of these coupons.[55]

Even if coupons were forthcoming, however, workers had plenty of grievances about the abuses of rationing and distribution. First of all, these concerned the size of rations. Socialists in the north of France initially blamed their government's passivity for small rations. Once Paris came to grips with *ravitaillement* and finally cracked down on the distributional organisms of Vichy, the rations could certainly be enlarged.[56] But such improvements were often a long time in coming. By the summer of 1947, socialist city guards in Łódź were still arguing that their coal rations were insufficient. Winter was approaching again and 'nobody cares whether guards have something to keep them warm after they return from service'.[57]

Secondly, what little supplies workers received in return for their coupons were often of questionable and decreasing quality. The combination of severe ingredient shortages for and substantial profit margins on everyday essentials led to the widespread diluting of foodstuffs. Among Milanese workers, there was intense unease about the dropping nutritional value of bread. While workers understood that the paucity of flour made a return to higher sifting levels impossible, they demanded that the new 80 per cent level would be observed. This was part of a more general indignation over the 'dilution' of several vital necessities, especially the sugars indispensable for babies. If the city authorities were not going to live up to their protective duties in this respect, it was imperative that 'special surveillance squads' were formed to exert a 'capillary control' over the distribution process 'in the interest of the more upright part of the Milanese population'.[58]

Thirdly, rations were sometimes entirely fictitious, as workers were unable to cash in their coupons. In Plzeň, *drahota* had turned into such a problem by April 1946 that countless workers on low wages, pensioners, and families with many children could not afford to buy all the products they were entitled to according to the rationing system. As a consequence, workers earning below the average working-class income of 2000 crowns a month often failed to meet the state-prescribed daily calorie intake.[59]

---

[55] 'Schůze rady okresního národního výboru v Plzni' (27 August 1945), AMP, Zápisy o schůzich Národního Výboru a rady Okresního Národního Výboru a Místního Národního Výboru statutárního města Plzeň 1945.

[56] 'Note de Renseignements' (Réunion du parti socialiste à Mortagne du Nord), 23 June 1945, ADN, CRR, 19 W 37108 2.

[57] 'Protokuł' (22 August 1947), APŁ, DK PPS Śródmieście Lewa, 14, fos 52–3.

[58] Comitati direttivi di organismi dei massa della Motomeccanica to Prefetto della Provincia di Milano, 19 July 1946, AdL, Camera del Lavoro, Class. 5.2.2.4., Fasc. 1.

[59] Ladislav Cígler, 'Ceny musí býti sníženi!' *Nový Den*, 14 July 1946.

How, then, the local ČSSD press asked, were these people supposed 'to pay for clothing, shoes, and rent'?[60] But even when the worst cost-of-living problems were in the past, some workers still felt cheated by rationing outcomes. Across the Plzeň region, women workers complained bitterly about shops being empty by the time they had finished their shifts. The preferential permits that had awarded working women a 'right to buy' were no good, as shopkeepers had chosen to ignore these and to allow their stocks to sell out. Instead, women trade union representatives called for no new satin coupons to be handed out until all women had spent theirs and for those queuing up in front of stores to be subjected to controls.[61]

Finally, distribution centres were often hotspots for all sorts of tampering with rations and coupons. This was especially true for the rations provided by the United Nations Relief and Rehabilitation Administration (UNRRA) that was active in three of the four cities (Łódź, Milano, and Plzeň). As its aid packages were frequently dispersed to factories before being passed on to workers, those presiding over the issue of rations were in a position that was at the same time crucial and corruptible. In Plzeň, there were ČSSD misgivings about several factory council members, whom they accused of deliberately withholding UNRRA allotments in their personal interest.[62] If the Plzeň social democrats wanted (part of) the factory council out of the UNRRA distribution process, the Łódź socialists wanted it in. Its cross-party nature, socialist textile workers argued, was the only guarantee that the raffles of UNRRA allocations would not be 'won' exclusively by PPR members.[63] Such charges of party-political favouritism were likewise levelled at local communists in the north of France. In communes under communist direction, the allegation went, 'T-coupons' designated for blue-collar workers had been granted to white-collar workers and even to young girls.[64]

This is indicative of the considerable power wielded by those able to get their hands on products at some point in the distribution chain. Grassroots activists in each of the four cities much resented the countless middlemen taking a cut between the production and consumption of goods for

[60] 'Ceny musí dolů!' *Nový Den*, 25 April 1946.
[61] 'Zápis z plenární schůze KOR v Plzni' (14 December 1947), Všeodborový Archiv – ČMKOS, Prague (hereafter VA), Krajské Odborové Rady 1945–1960, Karton 1, Inv. j. 16 – KOR Plzeň 1947.
[62] 'Dodatky ke schůzi rady MNV' (17 December 1945), AMP, Zápisy o schůzích Národního Výboru a rady Okresního Národního Výboru a Místního Národního Výboru statutárního města Plzeň 1945.
[63] 'Protokół z zebraniu Koła P.P.S. przy P.Z.P.B. Nr. 4 w Łodzi' (19 July 1947), APŁ, DK PPS Fabryczna, 8, fos 66–9.
[64] 'Note de Renseignements' (Congrès d'arrondissement du Parti Socialiste SFIO à Cambrai), 22 July 1946, ADN, CRR, 28 W 38449 1.

driving up prices. During a meeting with Edward Osóbka-Morawski, a delegation of the Łódź provincial PPS pressed their prime minister on the question of trade controls and returned with assurances that 'abuses and speculation' would be halted.[65] Similarly, workers in Milano demanded that 'the illegal trafficking of goods, artificial price hikes, and the smoke-screen around products' would come to an end.[66] Socialists in the north of France, for their part, identified 'the disappearance of the intermediaries between producers and consumers' as a prerequisite for the 25 per cent price drop championed by their national leaders.[67]

But the adverse effects of distribution go-betweens were undoubtedly most keenly felt in Czechoslovakia. Petitioning ÚRO to intervene with the government against 'all parasites in our economic life', Plzeň railway workers claimed their living standards had been hit twice by these 'distribution mooches'. Not only did their cut add further to the already excessive costs of living, but their lavish spending on luxury items also pushed up inflation still higher.[68] In a similar vein, Ladislav Cígler, the foremost ČSSD trade unionist in the region, protested against the 'absurdity' of fruit needlessly going bad during its prolonged storage at 'collection points'. If swift action was not taken, he concluded, Plzeň might well follow in the footsteps of Slovakia, where the 'added value' of official distribution intermediaries had got so out of control that beef and eggs were cheaper on the black market than at state-licensed shops.[69]

Workers certainly never felt they were getting a bargain when having recourse to the black market. As much as they resented having to deal with the 'vampires' operating on this shady scene,[70] however, it was often the only way to add sufficiently to that being provided via official channels (both rations and the products sold on the free market) for their families to get by. The authorities' inability to root out the countless abuses of the black market, then, caused more widespread disillusionment among workers than shortages, prices, and wages ever did. For unlike the force majeure of war and reconstruction associated with the problems on the

---

[65] 'Protokul z posiedzenia Egzekutywy WK. PPS' (28 August 1945), AAN, Fonds Henryk Wachowicz, 5 WK PPS.

[66] 'L'operaio Valboretti nell'Esecutivo della Camera del Lavoro Milano. Cosa ha fatto e cosa farà l'organizzazione sindacale' (15 August 1945), AdL, Camera del Lavoro, Class. 5.1.3., Fasc. 4.

[67] 'Meeting du Parti Socialiste à Brunemont' (21 July 1946), ADN, CRR, 28 W 38449 1.

[68] 'Železničáři protestují proti drahotě', *Nový Den*, 23 October 1946.

[69] Ladislav Cígler, 'Ceny musí býti sníženi!' *Nový Den*, 14 July 1946.

[70] 'L'operaio Valboretti nell'Esecutivo della Camera del Lavoro Milano. Cosa ha fatto e cosa farà l'organizzazione sindacale' (15 August 1945), AdL, Camera del Lavoro, Class. 5.1.3., Fasc. 4.

supply side, there was no excuse for failing to protect the working class against those growing rich at their expense.

At a base level, worker grievances about the black market constituted a backlash against peasant ascendancy across post-war Europe. Their direct access to food not only shielded peasants from the hunger so often suffered by the urban working class, but also gave them a powerful economic tool if they managed to keep their produce out of the official distribution channels. Indeed, the most common accusation workers brought against peasants was that of subverting or withholding food earmarked for the city, with a view to selling it at a much-inflated price on the black market. Whereas factory workers in Sesto San Giovanni held peasants responsible for their starvation,[71] local socialists in Łódź noted how peasants 'exploited the moment' by not sending to the city those 'first necessities for which the worker was languishing'.[72] Accordingly, there were many calls for more thorough controls over the rural economy. As statistics clearly demonstrated that the production of milk had not dropped since the liberation, a leader in the Plzeň ČSSD press suggested the city authorities implement a broad range of measures to guarantee 'that milk coupons can be abolished and that there will be sufficient quantities of butter for our children'.[73] Socialists in the north of France went one further, favouring 'exemplary sanctions' against those peasants defaulting on their obligations to provide milk at the new state-regulated price.[74]

It was, however, not just such immediate subsistence concerns that underlay working-class hostility towards the peasantry. There was a distinct feeling that the balance between worker and peasant, as well as between urban and rural interests, badly needed redressing. During the war, argued a ČSSD representative in the Plzeň city council, the collection of milk had still proceeded in an orderly fashion. But in the freedom that had accompanied liberation, many in the countryside had 'spotted an opportunity to loosen discipline'. From various villages and communities, milk was either arriving in a miserable state or not reaching the city at all.[75] Similarly, socialist textile workers in Łódź wondered why villages were still being equipped with limitless supplies of textiles. Had the assumption not been

[71] X, 'La rivoluzione continua', *Sesto Proletaria*, 19 July 1945.
[72] 'Protokół z ogólnego zebrania Koła PPS w Panstwowej Fabryce Nr. 2, Ł.Z.P.W' (7 May 1947), APŁ, DK PPS Śródmieście Lewa, 14, fo. 40.
[73] Dr. Kotyk, 'Hospodaření mlékem. Nízké dodávky mléka měly by se zvýsit', *Nový Den*, 3 August 1945.
[74] 'Le Parti Socialiste: Département du Nord' (reference date: 28 February 1946), ADN, CRR, 19 W 37108 1.
[75] 'Schůze Národního výboru' (8 June 1945), AMP, Zápisy o schůzích Národního Výboru a rady Okresního Národního Výboru a Místního Národního Výboru statutárního města Plzeň 1945.

that providing the peasantry with indispensable industrial goods would be met with a commensurate price drop for agricultural products?[76] If Łódź socialists were bemused that peasants received something for nothing, their counterparts in Cambrai were outraged when the French government proposed a 'revalorisation' of wheat and milk. Amid several claims that peasants were 'exploiters', who had emerged enriched from the war, one delegate illustrated the contrasts between worker 'misery' and peasant 'opulence' vividly. 'Before the war', he declared, 'there were men and pigs. Now there are pigs and men: the former eat wheat, the latter bran.'[77]

The black market did not stop at peasants taking advantage of worker desperation, though, but quickly drew in wide sections of post-war society. By late 1945, Mariani lamented that 'the most shameless speculation and profiteering has permeated all groups'.[78] What is more, products often found their way to the black market via an intricate web involving several of these groups. If bakers in Monza closing their shops at 11 am after selling all of their bread on the black market might still have been working on their own,[79] the same could certainly not be said for those people diverting raw materials or finished products from industrial sites. The Plzeň ČSSD press repeatedly called upon workers to keep their eyes open for the defrauding of goods from their factories – workers, after all, 'definitely did not work for some to grow rich easily off their labour'.[80] But, as time went by, it became increasingly clear that pockets of the working class were embroiled neck-deep in the illicit trails of goods. Whether it was those truckers shipping 59 cubic metres more coal than indicated on their bill of lading[81] or that factory council allowing thousands of metres of textile to disappear to Slovakia,[82] some workers certainly seemed to have a stake in keeping the black market up and running.

Things were exactly the other way around in Milano, where employers were accused of facilitating the speculative practices of their workforce. The internal commission at Pirelli castigated the 'immorality' of other

---

[76] 'Protokół zebrania informacyjnego koła P.P.S. przy Łodzkich Zakładach Przemysłu Czesankowego' (24 July 1945), APŁ, DK PPS Górna, 6, fo. 2.

[77] 'Note de Renseignements' (Congrès d'arrondissement du Parti Socialiste SFIO à Cambrai), 22 July 1946, ADN, CRR, 28 W 38449 I.

[78] Interview Robert Hadfield with Franco Mariani (1945), AdL, Camera del Lavoro, Class. 5.1.3., Fasc. 4.

[79] CI Breda to Prefetto di Milano, 11 December 1946, AdL, Camera del Lavoro, Class. 5.2.2.4., Fasc. 1.

[80] 'Dvojí druh černého obchodu', *Nový Den*, 11 August 1946.

[81] 'Falknovské doly podporují šmelinu s uhlím. Směšné tresty ONV a ZNV šmelinářům. – Na Plzeňsku dvě tajné koželužny. – Sláva pánů z Prahy a práce Pizcňáků', *Nový Den*, 10 January 1947.

[82] Ladislav Cígler, 'Závodní rady', *Nový Den*, 11 January 1947.

local companies' failure to observe new regulations restricting the working week to forty hours. Overtime being paid in kind, this measure had been put in place to stem the flow of products to the black market. Yet, far from reducing hours, some firms had prolonged the working week to sixty or even seventy-two hours – giving their workers products with a street value of between 700 and 800 lire in return.[83]

While the black market might have enabled a segment of the working class to 'squander not inconsiderable sums' gambling in bars,[84] it constituted a horrible aberration for the great majority of workers. 'Illegal trade', a socialist in the Łódź textile sector argued, should be forbidden for it allowed 'elements who never work' to 'live well'.[85] The contrasts between the sumptuous lifestyles afforded by speculators and the daily anguish of the working class were an affront to many workers. A conference of ČSSD factory organisations from Plzeň district demanded that the 2 per cent living off the black market be made to work. 'Filling bars' and 'spending dizzying amounts', after all, their behaviour 'provokes others, i.e. those who strive for fulfilment of the government's Two Year Plan'.[86] More and more, this toxic combination of black market extortion and speculator extravagance drove workers to extremes. Calling for 'a firm BASTA to the wild and greedy speculation that is running rampant and could lead us to wholly unintended actions', a resolution adopted by socialist trade unionists at Milanese train manufacturer TIBB already seemed to hint at retributive action.[87]

What rank-and-file activists really wanted, however, was for their leaders to finally bring the full force of the law to bear upon the black market. Observers noted a strong upswing in satisfaction among socialists in the north of France after François Tanguy-Prigent, the SFIO's new minister for agriculture, launched a campaign wishing 'death on the bloodsuckers of the black market'. But even with slogans like that, there was a distinct feeling that the party faithful wanted to 'go further still than their representatives in terms of the reforms to enact'.[88]

[83] CI Pirelli to Camera del Lavoro, 7 August 1946, AdL, Class. 5.2.2.4., Fasc. 1.

[84] 'Constatazione', *Sesto Proletaria*, 7 July 1945.

[85] 'Protokół spisany z zebrania członkow P.P.S. przy Panstwowych Zakładach Przemysłu Wełnianego Nr. 40 w Łodzi' (28 October 1947), APŁ, DK PPS Fabryczna, 8, fos 82–3.

[86] 'Proti drahotě, černému obchodu a lenošení. Konference závodnich politických organsací čs. sociální demokracie na ochranu zájmů lidu', *Nový Den*, 4 September 1946.

[87] Gruppo sindacale socialista TIBB to Camera del Lavoro Milano, 18 April 1947, AdL, Camera del Lavoro, Class. 5.2.2.4., Fasc. 3. Emphasis in original.

[88] 'Le Parti Socialiste: Département du Nord' (reference date: 31 January 1946), ADN, CRR, 19 W 37108 1; 'Le Parti Socialiste: Département du Nord' (reference date: 28 February 1946), ADN, CRR, 19 W 37108 1.

In fact, grassroots socialists frequently berated their national leaders for failing to follow through on their hawkish rhetoric regarding the black market. Despite official government propaganda being full of militaristic hyperbole of battles with high prices, speculators, and the like, socialists in Łódź found that the Commission to Combat Abuse and Economic Sabotage, created in the context of the 'battle for trade', left much to be desired.[89] To add insult to injury, workers were unpleasantly 'surprised' by that same government raising train fares right in the middle of the campaign.[90] Milanese socialists were likewise left disillusioned by anti-speculative measures that had looked promising on paper. When 'our party ... had sensed the overriding need to squeeze prices, to sort out the flow of raw materials, and to take action against the black market' in its economic programme, the local PSIUP in Sesto San Giovanni wrote, 'workers had enjoyed a moment of confident satisfaction'. But once they realised that 'the proposals did not have an adequate application in practice', workers had 'shaken their heads revealingly'.[91]

Local socialists often attributed the ineffectiveness of such initiatives to the leniency that the authorities showed profiteers. According to Robert Coutant, who played a key role in the rebuilding of local SFIO sections in the north of France, many of the continuing *ravitaillement* problems were due to the fact that there had been no thorough crackdown on the distributive organisms of the Vichy regime – notorious for their involvement in the black market during the war. '[S]ome examples' should have been set at the moment of liberation, he told a meeting of socialists in Pecquencourt, by handing its high functionaries 'criminal rather than administrative penalties'.[92] Whilst Milanese workers demanded a more 'drastic' approach to the black market as well,[93] the outrage over caught black marketeers getting away with a slap on the wrist was definitely greatest in Plzeň. Reports in the ČSSD press repeatedly decried the sentences pronounced by the provincial authorities as a joke – receiving a 1000 crown fine for making

[89] 'Protokół z plenarnego posiedzenia Rady Wojewódzkiej Polskiej Partii Socjalistycznej w Łodzi' (27 September 1947), APŁ, Wojewódzki Komiet PPS w Łodzi, 2, fos 28–39.
[90] 'Protokół zebrania Fabrycznego Koła P.P.S. przy P.Z.P.B. nr II' (27 June 1947), APŁ, DK PPS Górna, 7, fo. 27.
[91] Esecutivo PSIUP Sesto San Giovanni to Direzione PSIUP, Vice Presidente del Consiglio dei Ministri Nenni, and Gruppo Parlamentare PSIUP, *Sesto Proletaria*, 28 August 1946.
[92] 'Réunion d'information socialiste à Pecquencourt', 23 July 1945, ADN, CRR, 19 W 37108 2. For the outrage caused by the numerous *ravitaillement* scandals in wartime and post-war France: Fabrice Grenard, *Les scandales du ravitaillement: détournements, corruption, affaires éttouffées en France, de l'Occupation à la Guerre Froide* (Paris: Payot, 2012).
[93] 'L'operaio Valboretti nell'Esecutivo della Camera del Lavoro Milano. Cosa ha fatto e cosa farà l'organizzazione sindacale' (15 August 1945), AdL, Camera del Lavoro, Class. 5.1.3., Fasc. 4.

a 12,000 crown profit on the black market would 'only make the prof-
iteer crave further frauds'.[94] The hunt for speculators, moreover, seemed
to be systematically obstructed from above. Local social democrats were
baffled as to why the police action to detect speculators and put them to
work was going to be stopped, why arrested speculators were not named
and shamed, and how factory managers sanctioned for fraud could be
rehired.[95] When another factory manager got an already small fine halved,
fingers pointed towards the KSČ. 'How many people … in Prague' was he
'cooperating with'?[96]

Increasingly, then, workers were left with the impression of a ruling class
primarily concerned with closing ranks on itself. This was borne out by the
various scandals revealing those in responsible positions simply not to care
about the plight of the working class. There were instances of shocking
negligence: the burning of great quantities of wheat and shoes in Limoges,
while 'a part of the French population cannot feed and clothe itself properly'.[97] There were cases of deliberate market manipulation: industrialists in
Milano stockpiling their goods pending further inflation[98] and employers'
organisations calling on those few businesses that had lowered prices to
re-raise them in Czechoslovakia.[99] And there was blatant cronyism: despite
the housing situation being 'tragic' in Łódź,[100] occupancy controls on the
homes of industrial directors were being blocked by the PPR.[101] All things
considered, those with 'money as only motherland' definitely seemed to be
running the show yet again.[102] Or, as workers at Škoda put it: 'We know

---

94   'Zastavte neodpovědné zvyšování cen. Ve Falknově zahálejí prázdné vagony. – Manka zdrojem
     černých příjmů a zdražení. – Nedostatky trestání provinilých šmelinářů. – Šmelináři se i s
     rozumem', Nový Den, 5 December 1946.
95   'Proti drahotě, černému obchodu a lenošení. Konference závodních politických organsací čs.
     sociální demokracie na ochranu zájmů lidu', Nový Den, 4 September 1946; 'Kdo to jsou oni zatčení
     šmelináři?' Nový Den, 22 December 1946.
96   'Ruce pryč od šmelinářů! Cvrkovina musí být potrestána, nesmí být kryta', Nový Den, 16
     February 1947.
97   'Note de Renseignements' (Réunion organisée par le Parti Socialiste à l'occassion du 40ème
     Anniversaire de fondation de la Fanfare Ouvrière de Saint-Amand), 25 August 1946, ADN, CRR,
     28 W 38451 2.
98   Esecutivo PSIUP Sesto San Giovanni to Direzione PSIUP, Vice Presidente del Consiglio dei
     Ministri Nenni, and Gruppo Parlamentare PSIUP, Sesto Proletaria, 28 August 1946.
99   'Snižování cen nesmí býti bráněno', Nový Den, 6 August 1946.
100 'Protokół ogólnego zebrania członkow Dzielnicy P.P.S. Tramwaje Miejskie w Łodzi' (15 November
     1945), APŁ, DK PPS Tramwaje, fos 18–24.
101 Henryk Wachowicz to Sekretariatu Generalnego CKW PPS, 5 October 1946, AAN, Polska Partia
     Socjalistyczna, Sekretariat Generalny, Wydz. Ekonomiczno-Przem. WK Łódź, 1946–48, 2291/6,
     235/XV-44, fos 38–9.
102 Interview Robert Hadfield with Franco Mariani (1945), AdL, Camera del Lavoro, Class. 5.1.3.,
     Fasc. 4.

very well that within certain groups in our country, thanks to the unscrupulous price hikes, a new capitalist class is growing.'[103]

The Other Side

To halt this development, the post-war working class demanded a levelling of the playing field first and foremost. There had been a widespread expectation that income inequalities would decrease or wither away under democracy, a concept workers frequently associated with economic equality at least as much as with political freedom. Where elections might have propelled the Left into (shared) political power with relative ease, however, making good the economic imbalances between rich and poor proved a much harder task. Increasingly restless about the static or even widening gap between the haves and have-nots of post-war society, rank-and-file activists began questioning their leaders. How could those enriched by war be let off lightly, while the working class was bearing the brunt of post-war reconstruction? Why were the better-off able to profit from government social schemes, whereas workers on the state's payroll got a terrible deal? But working-class egalitarianism went far beyond a mere resentment of business fat-cats. For even within the working class, there were all sorts of jealousies. Whether it was workers in other factories, sectors, or regions bringing home more, the grass always seemed to be greener on the other side.

Right from the liberation, local socialists made it quite clear where the funds for reconstruction ought to be found. The SFIO's deputy federal secretary for Pas-de-Calais, for example, told socialists in Avion that the 280 billion deficit in the government's budget should be made up for by the confiscation of the great fortunes amassed during the war. If the government continued to refuse this, he went on under loud applause, 'the working class will find itself forced to take to the streets'.[104] 'Taking the money there where it is' quickly became a recurring theme in socialist rhetoric across the north of France, as the party was not about to make 'the underlings' pay.[105] Similarly, a socialist worker in Sesto San Giovanni

---

[103] 'Škodováci proti vysokým cenám', *Nový Den*, 31 October 1946.
[104] Commissaire du Police to Directeur des Reseignements Generaux (Réunion organisée par le Parti Socialiste à Avion), 20 February 1945, ADN, CRR, 19 W 37108 1.
[105] Commissaire du Police to Directeur des Reseignements Generaux (Réunion d'information du Parti Socialiste à Douai), 25 February 1945, ADN, CRR, 19 W 37108 2; Commissaire du Police to Directeur des Reseignements Generaux and Direction Générale de la Sûreté Nationale (Meeting Socialiste à Lambersart (Nord)), 17 March 1945, ADN, CRR, 19 W 37108 2.

insisted the inevitable sacrifices that lay ahead for liberated Italy should be shouldered in a proportional manner. The working class would contribute its sweat to the reconstruction effort, but he who had amassed 10 million should give at least half of that to the state.[106]

In both countries, however, calls for a requisition of (war) profits were largely in vain. By late 1946, a worker at Motomeccanica was still demanding state controls over 'excess profits', for it could not be the case that the worker was paying for 'a war wanted by capital [while] capitalists were making billions each month'.[107] Socialists in the north of France, for their part, were soon to bemoan not only the fact that 'the working masses have paid, are paying, and will be paying the costs of war',[108] but also the half-hearted nature of those expropriation measures the government did enact. They widely denounced the nationalisation of the mines as a 'caricature', falling well short of what workers had expected.[109] Allowed to keep receiving their dividends and to stay on as finance directors, former owners certainly appeared to be hanging on to 'their share of the spoils'.[110]

Where confiscations and nationalisations at once cut deeper and took a broader scope in post-war Eastern Europe, relations between workers and management were hardly transformed overnight. In fact, concerns that nothing much had changed were already voiced during an August 1945 meeting of the Łódź provincial PPS. While one delegate questioned the gap between the 190 points (which could be traded for goods in the rationing system) earned by managers at the Horak textile factory and the 47 points their workforce received, another pointed out that railway directors addressed their workers in a language reminiscent of the pre-war reaction.[111]

Both in form and in substance, then, despised capitalist practices proved far more persistent than workers had anticipated in the wake of liberation. Workers in Plzeň repeatedly vented their frustration at managerial abuses past and present, which their trade unions seemingly

---

[106] Un Operaio, 'L'ancora c'è', *Sesto Proletaria*, 12 July 1945.
[107] B. Filippo to Camera del Lavoro, 15 October 1946, AdL, Camera del Lavoro, Class. 5.2.2.4., Fasc. 1.
[108] Commissaire du Police to Chef Regional du Services des Renseignements Generaux (Réunion du Parti Socialiste à Anzin), 31 December 1944, ADN, CRR, 19 W 37108 2.
[109] Commissaire du Police to Directeur des Reseignements Generaux (Réunion de la section du Parti Socialiste SFIO à Mons en Baroeul), 29 January 1945, ADN, CRR, 19 W 37108 2; 'Congrès de la Fédération du Nord du Parti Socialiste SFIO' (August 1945), ADN, CRR, 19 W 37108 2.
[110] Commissaire du Police to Directeur des Reseignements Generaux (Réunion du Parti Socialiste à Escaudin), 17 January 1945, ADN, CRR, 19 W 37108 2.
[111] 'Sprawozdanie z konferencji przewodniczacych i sekretarzy Komitetów Powiatowych Miejskich P.P.S. Województwa Łódzkiego' (20 August 1945), AAN, Fonds Henryk Wachowicz, 5 WK PPS w Łodzi.

condoned. While workers at the Willy Geyer garment factory disputed KOR's acquiescence in the return of an 'asocial' pre-war owner to management,[112] their counterparts at Škoda called upon ÚRO and the government to go after those 'without a conscience who had made millions off the labour of their employees' since 1945.[113] Even party leaders acknowledged that such unrepentant self-indulgence on the part of those in charge of now-nationalised industry had bred much bad blood. Speaking in the PPS Central Committee, party chairman Kazimierz Rusinek listed the reasons for working-class opposition to the government. In his view, little had changed since the war – the administrative apparatus in industry was distrusted and while industrial managers had made no concessions regarding their living standards, workers got nothing.[114]

In each of the four cities, therefore, rank-and-file activists demanded the divide separating rich and poor be narrowed one way or another. Many at the grassroots favoured income levelling. Signalling how much bitterness the huge varieties in earnings generated among the working masses, one socialist representative in the Łódź area wondered what had happened to the PPS. Having always struggled for income equalisation, after all, the party seemed to have 'ignored' the question since liberation.[115] In a similar vein, social democrats in Plzeň called on those standing at the helm of public institutions or nationalised companies to set the right example. As nobody could argue the working class was living in prosperity, those on 'fairy-tale' salaries should show some 'sobriety' too.[116]

Apart from such moral appeals to parties or individuals, rank-and-file activists also urged their governments to use the levers at their disposal in a more progressive manner. Internal commissions across Milano united to prevent their city authorities from retrieving a new 'family tax' from workers on fixed wages. Branding it 'immoral and anti-social' that the burden of post-war reconstruction fell almost exclusively on the shoulders of the working class, they called for a tax on 'every form of luxury and extravagance' instead.[117] Socialists in the north of France went even further,

[112] 'Referáty z 28. Schůze rady místního národního výboru statut. Města Plzně' (25 February 1946), AMP, Zápisy o schůzich rady Místního Národního Výboru statutárního města Plzeň 1946/1.

[113] 'Škodováci proti vysokým cenám', *Nový Den*, 31 October 1946.

[114] 'Protokół posiedzenia C.K.W. P.P.S.' (30 November 1945), AAN, PPS, Centralny Komitet Wykonawczy (hereafter CKW), 2037, 235/III/2, fos 9–18.

[115] 'Protokół z plenarnego posiedzenia Rady Wojewódzkiej Polskiej Partii Socjalistycznej w Łodzi' (27 September 1947), APŁ, Wojewódzki Komiet PPS w Łodzi, 2, fos 28–39.

[116] 'Nelze-li dobře platit dole, musíme byt střízliví nahoře', *Nový Den*, 10 January 1947.

[117] CI Sindacato Bancari, Banca Commerciale Italiana, Banca d'America e d'Italia, Banca Popolare, Banco di Napoli, Banca Commercia Serico, Piccolo Credito Bergamasci, Cassa di Risparmio della P.P.L.L.. Rhodiacata, Elettrotoce, Edison, Innocenti, Falck, Bemberg, Telegrafo Centrale,

proposing income tax, 'which hits workers above all', be scrapped altogether and replaced with a levy on 'fortunes and enrichment'.[118]

If rank-and-file socialists would occasionally applaud their leaders' initiatives to soak the rich,[119] however, they far more frequently derided government interventions for coming up short in redistributive intent. The ČSSD in Plzeň joined its counterpart from Brno in opposing the strong shift from direct to indirect taxation in the government's 1947 budget. Making no difference between rich and poor, the government was reminded, indirect taxes on daily necessities had always been contested 'by socialists of all colours when the bourgeoisie still held a majority before Munich'.[120]

What social policy was introduced by the state, moreover, activists often condemned for favouring the rich at least as much as the poor. Socialists in Cambrai remonstrated against the plan to provide all consumers with 300 grams of bread at a rate fixed by income and a further amount of bread at a higher price. 'It is workers', one of them exhorted, 'who are the largest consumers of bread and who would, once again, be bearing all the costs were the Council of Ministers to pass this measure.'[121] Łódź workers found the system stacked against them to an even greater extent. Denouncing the fact that all sorts of allowances of bonuses were available to senior officials while 'the lower functionary was starving', a worker in the city's public transport shops pointed to 'the intelligentsia'. Having shed its blood for the freedom of the motherland, he argued, it should be the working class receiving such assistance. But the intelligentsia had exploited all the 'old habits', forcing the worker to 'renounce everything'.[122]

More contentious still than the perks bestowed upon white-collar workers, though, was the preferential treatment (allegedly) meted out to segments of the working class. First of all, there was much rancour that some workers seemed to be better off by virtue solely of where they lived. These questions often revolved around rural dwellers coming into the city

Alfa Romeo, Officine Bossi, Motomeccanica, Brill, Credito di Francia, Feltrinelli, and Siemens to Camera del Lavoro, 28 March 1947, AdL, Camera del Lavoro, Class. 5.2.2.4., Fasc. 2.
[118] 'Note de Renseignements' (Réunion publique organisée par la section socialiste de Trith St-Leger), 18 October 1946, ADN, CRR, 28 W 38454 2.
[119] Among rank-and-file socialists in the north of France, there was much satisfaction about the special tax, introduced by André Philip, on wartime enrichment. 'Le Parti Socialiste: Département du Nord' (reference date: 28 February 1946), ADN, CRR, 19 W 37108 1.
[120] 'Nesouhlasíme s ministrem financí', Nový Den, 30 November 1946.
[121] 'Note de Renseignements' (Activité et position du Parti Socialiste S.F.I.O. – et réunion extraordinaire de la section de Cambrai), 14 August 1946, ADN, CRR, 28 W 38451 2.
[122] Protokoł zwyczajnego Koła P.P.S. przy Zarzadzie Miejskim, Wydziale Technicznym, Oddziale Pómiarow' (16 August 1945), APŁ, DK PPS Śródmieście Prawa, 10, fos 5–6.

to work. On the one hand, the extras granted to workers already taking home an urban wage to a place where the costs of living were much lower needed explaining.[123] It was perfectly understandable, the urban workforce at the Falck metal plant in Sesto San Giovanni argued, that workers commuting from the surrounding villages were favoured in the distribution of bicycle shelters. But why had workers living in villages, where supply was 'much easier and less costly', not been excluded from the distribution of food packages?[124]

On the other hand, workers from outside the city frequently felt penalised just for residing in the countryside. Workers dwelling beyond the Łódź borders repeatedly questioned why they were left out of food or coal rations.[125] In the north of France, meanwhile, there was much anger that the wartime distributive distinctions between rural and urban communities remained in force. The socialist section in rural Paillencourt passed a motion stressing the discontent caused by the smaller rations accorded to its workers. After all, many rural communities had not been blessed with potato seeds, while gardens were often larger in urban communities. It would even happen that 'in the same factory … at the same table, urban workers do have potatoes for dinner whereas "rurals" do not'.[126]

If such inequalities within one and the same factory generated much worker spite, colleagues did unite over the fringe benefits enjoyed by workers at other industrial sites. Miners' representatives in the Plzeň region complained that, while miners at the Stříbro pits had been receiving food and tobacco supplements, their counterparts at Křimice had not. Such discriminating practices would certainly lead to discontent and discord, 'for miners desire all to be measured by the same standards'.[127] Expressing their surprise at the raise awarded to the workforce at nationalised gas companies, socialists in Cambrai voiced similar objections. If there was

---

[123] This was actually used as an argument to remove the wartime distinctions between (higher) urban and (lower) rural wages in Plzeň. According to an article in the local ČSSD press, such wage levelling constituted the only way to stop the exodus of much-needed rural labourers to the city. Jiří Kíncl, 'Jednotné mzdy', *Nový Den*, 4 November 1945.

[124] 'Girotondo', *Sesto Proletaria*, 7 July 1945.

[125] 'Protokoł z zebranie komórki P.P.S. odbytego w dniu 25 października 1945 r. w Łodzi' (25 October 1945), APŁ, DK PPS Śródmieście Prawa, 10, fos 9–10; 'Protokół ogólnego zebrania członkow Dzielnicy P.P.S. Tramwaje Miejskie w Łodzi' (15 November 1945), APŁ, DK PPS Tramwaje, fos 18–24.

[126] 'Note de Renseignements' (Activité du Parti Socialiste SFIO), 6 July 1946, ADN, CRR, 28 W 38449 1.

[127] 'Horníci naléhají', *Nový Den*, 1 August 1945.

'a subsistence minimum for them', they insisted, 'the same advantages'
should be extended 'to all other categories'.[128]

Such demands notwithstanding, workers at smaller plants remained
particularly vulnerable to being overlooked in the distribution of
advantages. Asking why they had not been provided with cheap shoes,
workers at a 72-employee Łódź factory were told that scheme only applied
to establishments employing at least 250.[129] Workers at Milano's Amilcare
Pizzi printing shop felt neglected in favour of larger enterprises as well.
Despite announcements regarding the distribution of food, clothing, or
shoes in *Avanti!* or *Unità* (the PCI daily), the internal commission wrote,
smaller factories were left in the dark about the specifics. It urged the trade
union authorities to also inform companies without a canteen of pending
hand-outs, in order not to disillusion 'those who, plagued by need, believe
in finding help [but] end up with a fistful of flies'.[130]

The single worst-off group in each of the four cities, however, did not
work in industry, nationalised or otherwise. It was the blue-collar workers
employed by the state, such as railway workers, road builders, or postmen,
who got the worst deal by far. Public sector workers often pointed out
how bad their pay and conditions were in comparison with those of
their counterparts in factories. In a memorandum to the ČSSD and the
ČSL, manual labourers for Plzeň province demanded their wages and
contributions be levelled with those of industrial workers. It was beyond
belief, after all, that 'the physically exhausting work of constructing and
maintaining highways was valued disproportionally lower than far lighter
work in warm factory halls'.[131] Socialist city workers in Łódź likewise raised
the question of 'unequal pay for the same work in different institutions'.
After one worker lamented that the family allowances received by city
workers were up to five times lower than elsewhere, another condemned
the practice of handing out different types of coupons to different workers
for creating 'two categories of citizens'.[132] So dire was the material situation

[128] 'Note de Renseignements' (Activité et position du Parti Socialiste S.F.I.O. – et réunion extraordinaire de la section de Cambrai), 14 August 1946, ADN, CRR, 28 W 38451 2.
[129] 'Protokół zebrania ogólnego robotników i pracowników Państwowej Fabryki Nr. 22 z udziałem
przedstawicieli P.P.S. i P.P.R.', APŁ, DK PPS Fabryczna, 8, fos 56–57.
[130] CI Amilcare Pizzi to Camera del Lavoro, 25 November 1946, AdL, Camera del Lavoro, Class
5.2.2.4., Fasc. 1.
[131] 'Zaměstnanecká rada veřejné služby technické při ONV Plzeň-venkov usnesla se na Memorandu'
(28 February 1947), Státní Oblastní Archiv v Plzni, Plzeň (hereafter SOA Plzeň), Fonds Krajský
Výbor KSČ Plzeň (hereafter KV KSČ Plzeň), 534.
[132] 'Protokół z zebrania członków Koła P.P.S. przy Gazowni Miejskiej' (15 October 1947), APŁ, DK
PPS Fabryczna, 8, fos 79–80.

of public sector workers that even their opposite numbers in industry wanted something to be done. Calling attention to the 'absolute remunerative inferiority' of state employees, especially railroad and postal workers, socialists at TIBB insisted the entire working class should show solidarity with public sector workers in their negotiations with the Italian government.[133]

Public sector workers certainly needed all the support they could get, for they often felt utterly deserted by their political and union leaders. State employees in the Milano area warned that the 'inconceivable abandonment' of and the 'congenial disinterest' in their cause on the part of regional trade union leaders was about to drive them 'into open struggle' with the trade union authorities.[134] Governments, too, were frequently accused of taking their own people for granted. There were reports of 'a serious discontent' among socialist public sector workers in the north of France, who claimed that 'their spirit of discipline had been abused to make them bear heavy sacrifices'.[135] Plzeň social democrats likewise underlined public employees' dedication to the republic at liberation. Witnessing 'the pomp' of official cars, banquets, and foreign travel relished by the mushrooming civil service, however, they increasingly came to view the official reasons for holding back their wages as 'mere excuses and evasions'.[136] These disparities between the happy few at the top of the state apparatus and the needy many at its bottom, also deplored in the north of France,[137] caused much bewilderment, given that they were coming from governments boasting their democratic and egalitarian character. While lambasting ÚRO for its lack of interest in their ordeal, a meeting of Plzeň region road builders noted how they had been disappointed in their belief that 'the lowest categories of workers' would be helped out first and foremost 'in a democratic state under popular government'.[138]

In their protests against the remaining inequalities of post-war society, workers drew increasingly on such allusions to the state's own rhetoric. A government 'calling itself democratic', public sector workers in Sesto San Giovanni argued, could not afford to disregard 'one of our most sacred rights, the right to life'.[139] But workers often understood democracy to

---

[133] Gruppo sindacale socialista TIBB to Camera del Lavoro Milano, 18 April 1947, AdL, Camera del Lavoro, Class. 5.2.2.4., Fasc. 3.

[134] Croce Anselmo, 'Statali e parastatali chiedono giustizia', *Sesto Proletaria*, 24 July 1946.

[135] 'Le Parti Socialiste: Département du Nord' (1946), ADN, CRR, 19 W 37108 1.

[136] H., 'Veřejní zaměstnanci', *Nový Den*, 11 December 1946.

[137] 'Note de Renseignements' (Activité du Parti Socialiste SFIO (réunion privée)), 16 September 1946, ADN, CRR, 28 W 38453 2.

[138] 'Silničním zaměstnancům se musí dostati pomoci', *Nový Den*, 7 December 1946.

[139] Croce Anselmo, 'Statali e parastatali chiedono giustizia', *Sesto Proletaria*, 24 July 1946.

mean much more than merely such elementary rights. A worker in Łódź asked how it could be justifiable 'in a democratic system' that a manager earned 120 per cent of what his subordinates made.[140] The claim that 'Poland [was] now a democratic country' was used by workers elsewhere in the city to attack the 'especially privileged' position of Jews. Everyone being equal in a democracy, there could be no 'superior citizens', who, by virtue of the 'special grants' meted out by 'the Jewish community' and their strong representation in trade and industrial management, were able 'to drive limousines and dine in the best restaurants'.[141]

Such manifestations of luxury were particularly poignant in the 'popular' democracies of Czechoslovakia and Poland, as they flew directly in the face of government slogans. In view of the official state propaganda that there was no longer a bourgeoisie in 'People's Poland', one socialist worker wondered who it was 'driving around in limousines at Piotrkowska [Łódź's main shopping street] and buying all the luxurious products that a worker can only dream of'.[142] Further west, however, workers faulted governments for not delivering upon their egalitarian premises all the same. Calling for an end to the 'injustice' of rural and urban communities, socialists in the north of France reminded their leaders 'that, amongst the three words that symbolise the Republic, there is EQUALITY!'[143]

For many rank-and-file activists, then, the post-war state had failed on its own terms. To be sure, the Left was in (shared) power, but many of the expectations of what that would entail, raised and cultivated during the interwar and war years, had been disappointed. As early as August 1945, one worker commented to the Milanese trade union authorities that the hopes of the liberation – including the levelling of the most evident income inequalities and the provision of state employees with a wage sufficient to avoid starvation – had not been realised. Seeing prices multiply relative to wages every day, moreover, it was an affront to the working class to witness countless people still living in luxury.[144]

---

[140] 'Protokół sporządzony na zebraniu Koła Prac. Umysł. przy Polskiej Partii Socjalistycznej' (13 November 1946), APŁ, DK PPS Tramwaje, 13, fos 39–40.

[141] 'Protokół z zebranie komórki P.P.S.' (25 October 1945), APŁ, DK PPS Śródmieście Prawa, 10, fos 9–10. The resolution adopted at this meeting has strong anti-Semitic overtones throughout, including the bizarre claim that 'the Jewish people did not suffer larger losses during the war than the Polish people' and 'therefore cannot be specifically protected'.

[142] 'Protokół spisany z zebrania członkow P.P.S. przy Panstwowych Zakładach Przemysłu Wełnianego Nr. 40 w Łodzi' (28 October 1947), APŁ, DK PPS Fabryczna, 8, fos 82–3.

[143] 'Note de Renseignements' (Activité du Parti Socialiste SFIO), 6 July 1946, ADN, CRR, 28 W 38449 1. Emphasis in original.

[144] 'L'operaio Valboretti nell'Esecutivo della Camera del Lavoro Milano. Cosa ha fatto e cosa farà l'organizzazione sindacale' (15 August 1945), AdL, Camera del Lavoro, Class. 5.1.3., Fasc. 4.

If these remarks, accompanied as they were by an appeal to the government to do more, might yet be read as constructive criticism, there was more resignation in a retrospective commentary carried by the Plzeň ČSSD press in October 1946. 'When we wrote incendiary articles and rebelled against the economic order during the economic crisis', it reminisced, 'we imagined a time would come when the small man ... was to receive a proper and fair wage for his work.' Talking to workers today, the commentary went on, an altogether different reality revealed itself: 'We have shortages, we live badly. We understand that we emerge from a horrible war and that everything cannot be changed overnight. We do not begrudge anyone, and we have suffered the necessary sacrifices, but we regret that these sacrifices have not been distributed evenly over everyone.'[145]

Conclusion

We have seen in this chapter that conditions and concerns on the ground in the four cities were roughly similar. To be sure, the material situation in post-war Plzeň was initially slightly better, meaning that worker protests there lacked the sense of utter desperation they often exhibited in Lille, Łódź, and Milano. But these were differences in degree rather than kind and, after the supply situation in Czechoslovakia took a turn for the worse in 1946, grassroots discourses in the four cities became almost indistinguishable in their denunciations of the shortages or unaffordability of everyday necessities, of the shameless profiteering by so many with access to food, and of the remaining inequalities in post-war society.

On a broader level, this chapter has offered further evidence of how the war had weakened the social position of the working class. After a war of attrition fought predominantly in cities, hungry workers often found themselves at the mercy of peasants or various middlemen and speculators. The liberation had thus certainly not ushered in the longed-for improvements in the everyday lives of the working class. As speculators were able to continue their sinister work unimpeded and the state lost any semblance of control over the rural economy, (socialist) workers quickly grew disillusioned with the course steered by their leaders in national government. What was worse, the massive economic disparities that had outlived the war left the working class, which had expected so much more of democracy, with a sense of deep injustice. In these circumstances, the political arguments put forward by party leaders met with an increasingly

---

[145] 'Škodováci proti vysokým cenám', *Nový Den*, 31 October 1946.

hostile reception among ordinary workers. This became very clear during the 'extremely stormy' shop floor meetings that communists and socialists organised in the run-up to the October 1945 factory council elections in Łódź. 'A strong turmoil erupts when a female worker takes to the stage and begins to shout that her children are hungry', noted a report of one of these meetings; 'then a more general cry develops ... "we are fed up with political talk, we want to eat".'[146]

It was of course no coincidence that women played such a prominent role in post-war industrial protest. Charged with procuring and preparing food, women experienced first-hand that 'the politics of food *were* politics in the first post-war months'.[147] Yet, as women were quick to find out, socialist leaders had precious little to offer on this front. In fact, many of the newcomers to the industrial working class felt that their interests were being overlooked. Whether it was the rural commuters who had entered factories in large numbers during the war or the manual labourers in the expanding public sector, newcomers of all stripes complained that they found themselves at a disadvantage vis-à-vis the traditional working class. Far from reaching out to these groups, however, socialist elites often took an actively hostile attitude towards the newcomers and their demands. For their message, as we will see in the following chapter, was still tailored almost exclusively to the 'aristocracy of labour' of skilled workers in the large industrial complexes.

[146] Quoted in Wojciech Górecki, 'Strajki robotnicze w Łodzi w latach 1945–1947', in Jerzy Eisler and Krystyna Kersten (eds.), *Polska 1944/45–1989: studia i materiały* II (Warsaw: Instytut Historii Polska Akademia Nauk, 1997), pp. 93–121, 98.
[147] Donna Harsch, 'Public Continuity and Private Change? Women's Consciousness and Activity in Frankfurt, 1945–1955', *Journal of Social History*, 27/1 (1993), pp. 29–58, 30.

CHAPTER 3

Discipline, Sacrifice, and Production

Upon a February 1946 visit to Plzeň, ČSSD minister of industry Bohumil Laušman championed the 'new social order' that was under construction in post-war Czechoslovakia. He argued that the state was moving ahead both socially and economically – the hunger still suffered by many across large parts of the country after liberation having been overcome and exports picking up. To be sure, there were complaints about prices and wages. Nobody was perfect and the government might have made mistakes, but its monetary reforms had secured the purchasing power of the currency, the crown, and averted the dreadful inflation running rampant in other countries. However 'terrible' it might have been to slash departmental budgets by 35 billion crowns, it had been the only way to prevent the nation from becoming 'a beggar'. The nationalisation of banking and industry, moreover, had laid the groundwork for a flourishing economy. Now all that was needed was *'work, work, and more work!'*[1]

In a nutshell, this sums up how socialist leaders countered the grievances among their rank and file. Sure enough, times were hard and were going to remain so for the foreseeable future. But the austerity packages introduced by each of the four governments had been absolutely necessary to stave off the looming disasters of mounting debt and spiralling inflation. What made these rounds of cuts different from the ones implemented to such catastrophic effect before the war, furthermore, was that they were based upon a sustainable economic model. The short-term sacrifices demanded of the working class, then, would come to the rescue not of capitalists, but of the reconstruction effort, the nation, and ultimately workers themselves. In order for these sacrifices to be worth their while, however, it was imperative that workers should not engage in self-defeating agitations against the very institutions that were fighting their corner. Rather than

---

[1] 'Vždy věrni demokracii a socialismu. Cesta k novému společenskému řádu', *Nový Den*, 1 March 1946. Emphasis in original.

constantly finding fault with their unions, parties, and governments, they were to abide by the labour movement's discipline and produce to the full extent of their abilities.

This chapter endeavours to reveal just how strong this productivist ethos was within post-war European socialism's leading circles. Party leaders often presented more production as the answer to all the bread-and-butter woes of the working class, whether concerning shortages, price hikes, or wage restraint. But as working-class living standards kept dropping, party leaders' promises that workers would soon reap the fruits of their discipline and sacrifice began sounding more and more hollow. It was not just exhaustion and exasperation, however, that pitted the working class against the production campaigns propagated with increasingly militaristic rhetoric by their leaders. The entire premise that seemed to lie behind the drive to raise industrial output – that the working-class contribution to the reconstruction effort somehow fell short and that it was workers who had to walk the extra mile yet again – caused deep resentment at the grassroots. To make matters worse, the means by which governments sought to achieve their production targets often flew right in the face of worker egalitarianism, adding further weight to the perception of an elite utterly out of touch with the aspirations of its rank and file.

Discipline and Sacrifice

Historians have often suggested that the post-war European socialist parties were considerably softer on manifestations of worker discontent than their communist counterparts. They tend to contrast the extremely harsh view that communist leaders took of the unrest at their grassroots – denouncing strikes as 'a weapon of the [capitalist] trusts'[2] and scolding workers for absenteeism, theft, and their unwillingness to work[3] – with the supposedly more sympathetic attitudes socialist parties assumed towards the plight of their rank and file.[4] Yet, like so many of the academic claims about

---

[2] This often-quoted remark was made by veteran communist CGT secretary Gaston Monmousseau. Quoted in Donald Sassoon, *One Hundred Years of Socialism: The West European Left in the Twentieth Century* (London/New York: I.B. Tauris, 1996), p. 103.

[3] For various examples of provincial and national communist leaders denouncing workers in this manner: Kenney, *Rebuilding Poland*, pp. 85–99; Tom Behan, ' "Riding the Tiger": The Italian Communist Party and the Working Class of the Porta Romana Area of Milan, 1943–1948', *The Italianist*, 10 (1990), pp. 111–50, 137–40.

[4] See e.g. Eric Mechoulan, 'Le SFIO et les grèves', in Serge Berstein, Frédéric Cépède, Gilles Morin and Antoine Prost (eds.), *Le Parti socialiste entre Résistance et République* (Paris: Publications de Sorbonne, 2000), pp. 205–22; Reynolds, 'Communists, Socialists and Workers'.

the post-war socialist parties and the working class, such assertions tend to be based more on anecdotal evidence (e.g. socialist support for individual strikes and agitations) than grassroots research. A more systematic analysis of grassroots–elite relations within the four parties under review in this book reveals how socialist leaders frequently found themselves at loggerheads with their rank and file too.

To be sure, socialist leaders often showed a remarkable deal of understanding towards manifestations of worker despair. A worker who has to spend double his income to survive, PPS Trade Union secretary Lucjan Motyka declared, will arrive at the conclusion that he has to steal – 'we put him on that road of demoralisation'.[5] Far be it from party leaders, therefore, to take too harsh a view of the disenchantment among their rank and file. It was very easy, PSIUP minister of industry Rodolfo Morandi told a crowd in Milano, to tell the masses that their impatience was not going to change 'the iron limits of reality'. Nor was it difficult for those not affected by 'the mortifications' of the working class to dispassionately calculate the costs and time of post-war reconstruction. But behind such 'accusations and criticisms' all too often levelled against workers was 'a mind without understanding, a heart without a pulse'.[6]

For all of their compassion for the predicament of their rank and file, however, socialist leaders frequently claimed there was precious little they could do to improve the lot of the working class. They often claimed that only time could heal the severe disruptions wrought by war. Speaking to local socialists in Valenciennes, Augustin Laurent acknowledged that people had expected better from liberation. But he was quick to dissociate any 'inefficiencies' or 'ineptitudes' on the part of the authorities from this 'deception' – the 'fifth column' of former Vichyists still perceived to dominate the state apparatus was 'not as pernicious as some want us to believe'. 'The true evil' was that 'we are lacking wagons, locomotives, flatboats, lorries, that our ports are destroyed'. Natural resources, moreover, were 'notoriously insufficient', meaning that 'even if collection was organised well, our rations would still not suffice'.[7] Motyka also stressed that there

---

[5] 'Posiedzenie Rady Gospodarczej PPS' (27 February 1946), AAN, Polska Partia Socjalistyczna, Sekretariat Generalny, Wydz. Ekonomiczno-Przem, Rada Gospodarcza, 1946–47, 2291/3, 235/xv-23, fo. 17.

[6] 'Discorso pronunciato dal Ministro Rodolfo Morandi al Teatro Nuovo' (16 March 1947), Istituto Nazionale per la Storia del Movimento di Liberazione in Italia, Milano (hereafter INSMLI), Fondo Lia Bellora, Fasc. 6.

[7] Commissaire du Police to Directeur des Reseignements Generaux (Exposé de M. Augustin Laurent, Ministre des P.T.T., devant la section socialiste de Valenciennes), 5 February 1946, ADN, CRR, 19 W 37108 2.

were no quick fixes for governments to contrive their way out of their socio-economic woes. While readily conceding that much of working-class opposition was the result of the government's economic plan to return production to profitability 'in a very short period', he immediately underlined that even 'the most wise, the most thought-through plan could not come to terms with the resistance of popular nerves'.[8]

The common response to such worker nervousness was that party leaders could not work miracles. Socialist leaders warned workers not to listen to those suggesting the new governments were at fault for the absence of material improvements. The local PSIUP weekly in Sesto San Giovanni drew socialists' attention to the fact that many of the people bemoaning how much worse things were now than under fascism had been collaborating with the Germans during the war.[9] Politicians promising the earth were likewise to be distrusted. Contrary to what some politicians were pretending, socialists in the north of France were told, everything could not be ameliorated 'by the wave of a magic wand'. Instead, the measures taken 'without fear of unpopularity' by André Philip represented the only way out of the 'very critical situation' in which the country found itself.[10]

More and more, however, socialist leaders felt workers themselves needed a reality check. Working-class demands, local and national party leaders lamented with increasing frequency, showed no appreciation whatsoever of the daunting task facing those at the helm of the reconstruction effort. Ivan Hollman, the ČSSD's social affairs and repatriation spokesman in the Plzeň city council, derided how 'many people' reverted to 'excessive simplifications' in economic issues. Apparently convinced that 'the flick of a magic wand' could see 'machines repaired and replaced, the flow of raw materials restored, and markets opening up to our products', they 'reduced the problems of managing enterprises to the question of wage adjustments'.[11] A local chairman of the Łódź PPS likewise told off socialist workers complaining about the lack of coal and high prices. Urging workers not to 'exaggerate about small matters', he described such hardships as 'a victory for the country'. In any case, the new government could hardly be

---

[8] 'Posiedzenie Rady Gospodarczej PPS' (27 February 1946), AAN, Polska Partia Socjalistyczna, Sekretariat Generalny, Wydz. Ekonomiczno-Przem, Rada Gospodarcza, 1946–47, 2291/3, 235/XV-23, fo. 16a.

[9] Decio, 'Siamo peggio di prima! …' *Sesto Proletaria*, 19 July 1945.

[10] 'Note de Renseignements' (Réunion organisée par le Parti Socialiste à l'occasion du 40ème Anniversaire de fondation de la Fanfare Ouvrière de Saint-Amand), 25 August 1946, ADN, CRR, 28 W 38451 2.

[11] Ivan Hollman, 'Více pomáhat než požadovat', *Nový Den*, 10 August 1945.

blamed for working-class sorrows, as it had only been in office for a short period and had inherited a country in ruins.[12]

The Milanese trade union authorities also invoked the 'immense ruins we face' to dispel worker illusions that 'everything was possible'. It would be absurd, a declaration underwritten by communist, socialist, and Christian democratic union representatives insisted, for those who had for years cheered on fascism's criminal war politics to now think that trade union bodies could perform 'the miracle of multiplying bread'. If labour representatives were going to ask employers to contribute more towards the economic recovery and to show more humanity towards the misery of the masses, it continued, 'we also have to be able to say *no* to workers when we think that is necessary'.[13]

It was definitely in questions of wages that socialist leaders turned down their workers most often. Even if party leaders agreed that some groups were hit disproportionally hard in the post-war state's social settlement, they were still reticent to countenance wage increases for fears of a domino effect. This was very much the case for the demands put forward by the more bereaved public sector workers. Although he admitted that some, if not all, railway workers were worse off than others in the state's employment, Jules Moch cautioned against giving in to their biddings. Should the government award railway workers a raise, after all, 'we will be bombarded with demands of the same order by mine, gas, and electricity workers, and after that the private sector'.[14] In a similar vein, ČSSD chairman Zdeněk Fierlinger expressed his delight that the Czechoslovakian government had been able to close ranks against fresh wage demands made by public sector workers. If these had become the subject of 'a new party fight', he argued, there would have been a real danger of 'restlessness' among factory workers feeling they were entitled to a pay rise as well. That would 'mean a further increase of all economic indices, a considerable hindrance for our export, and we would have been in a chaotic situation'.[15]

Pietro Nenni also sketched a descent into chaos when he discussed 'the terrible problem of salaries' in the PSIUP Central Committee. Under the threat of a general strike, he informed his fellow party leaders,

---

[12] 'Protokuł z zebrania Koła PPS przy Łodzkich Zakładach Przemysłu Czesankowego' (7 August 1945), APŁ, DK PPS Górna, 6, fo. 3.

[13] 'Disciplina Sindacale' (1 August 1945), AdL, Camera del Lavoro, Class. 5.2.2.9., Fasc. 1. Emphasis in original.

[14] OURS, CD SFIO, 29 January 1947.

[15] 'The Mission of Social Democracy in the New State' (November 1947), Archiv Narodního Muzea, Prague (hereafter ANM), Fonds Zdeněk Fierlinger, Karton 40, Sjezd soc. dem. v Brne.

the government was negotiating a wage increase for state workers. An agreement binding the government to spending an extra 36 billion lire on those in its employment seemed within reach, but Nenni remained far from convinced. Not only did he fear that this was no more than a makeshift solution to be 'eaten up' by price hikes within a matter of weeks, but he also worried about the wider repercussions. What if private sector workers were encouraged to go on strike too? That could set off a 'chain reaction', in which 'we lose control over money and risk moving towards an inflation of the German type'.[16]

Socialist leaders constantly raised the spectre of inflation to defend their socio-economic records. An SFIO propaganda brochure, published at the time of the salary blockade, described inflation as 'a mortal danger for the country'. The document went on to list the 'calculation-defying' price situation in early 1920s Germany, where bread had been sold for 95 billion Reichsmark one day, only for its price to rise still further to 120 billion the next. The sole groups that stood to gain in such a situation were 'merchants and traders who retain goods, industrialists who possess equipment and raw materials, and speculators who have gold'. For workers and small rentiers, on the other hand, inflation signified 'the disappearance, pure and simple, into total misery'.[17]

Much more than low wages or living standards, then, party leaders cited inflation as the true enemy of the working class. The PSIUP leadership repeatedly associated inflationary economics with right-wing politics. During the cross-party negotiations on the composition of the second De Gasperi government, the socialist delegation made it quite clear that it was opposed to the reinstatement of the 'definitely inflationist' liberal Epicarmo Corbino as treasury minister.[18] But labour representatives were in the firing line for acquiescing to inflation-boosting measures all the same. Ludovico d'Aragona, for example, soon to be named the PSIUP's minister of labour and social security in the same government, questioned the general 10 per cent raise agreed by industrialists and trade unions for interfering with the deflationary politics of the government.[19]

[16] 'Comitato Centrale' (17 October 1945), Archivio Centrale dello Stato, Rome (hereafter ACS), Carteggio Nenni, Busta 87, Fasc. 2189.

[17] 'Les prix et les salaires', Arguments et Ripostes, Bulletin Intérieur du Parti Socialiste (S.F.I.O.), 15 April 1946, OURS.

[18] 'Riunione della Direzione' (10 July 1946), ISRT, Fondo Foscolo Lombardi, Partito Socialista Italiano, Direzione Nazionale, Busta 4, Fasc. 20.

[19] 'Riunione della Direzione' (9 July 1946), ISRT, Fondo Foscolo Lombardi, Partito Socialista Italiano, Direzione Nazionale, Busta 4, Fasc. 20.

Such across-the-board pay increases, especially those mechanically connected to the price level, were almost universally counselled against by socialist leaders. A 'mechanical' wage rise would not see working-class well-being improving, socialist workers in Łódź were told, for it would be accompanied by just as 'automatic' a price hike. And for the 'misfortunes' inflation caused the worker, one only had to look at the development of working-class wages and living standards after the First World War.[20]

That did not stop workers from demanding that their salaries be linked to the prices of daily necessities, though. Speaking in the SFIO Executive, under-secretary of state for the national economy Albert Gazier identified the need to 'detoxify' those 'comrades who are not making our task easier'. The party should not commit itself to the 'sliding scale' of wages and prices, he continued, for wage increases were the number one reason for the inflation that had hit France since the liberation.[21] By the same token, ČSSD leaders credited their rejection of a premature price-matching wage raise with seeing off the threat of inflation in post-war Czechoslovakia. If the government had heeded calls to link wages to prices in the immediate aftermath of liberation, Laušman explained to a ČSSD provincial congress in Olomouc, inflation would certainly have followed suit. But because the government had chosen to 'swim against the tide' and 'settle the monetary question' first, wages could now be brought into line with prices.[22]

Safeguarding the value of the national currency by balancing the books was indeed part and parcel of socialist leaders' efforts to keep inflation down. For if spiralling prices on the domestic level were bad already, worse still was the progressive incapacitation of the procurement of vital raw materials, machinery, and consumer goods from abroad on account of a weak exchange rate.

SFIO leaders were particularly adamant that achieving budget equilibrium and stabilising the currency provided the only way out of the woes of the working class. According to Moch, at that time minister of transport and public works in the Ramadier government, the rescue of the franc was a precondition 'for the amelioration of *ravitaillement*'.[23] Speaking at a socialist rally in Lille, SFIO secretary general Guy Mollet likewise identified fiscal consolidation with working-class interests. Calling on

---

[20] 'Protokół z zebrania Koła P.P.S. przy Wiedza' (13 December 1947), APŁ, DK PPS Śródmieście Lewa, 14, fo. 71.
[21] OURS, CD SFIO, 7 June 1946.
[22] 'Vláda bude řešit otázky cenové a mzdové', *Nový Den*, 13 November 1945.
[23] OURS, CD SFIO, 29 January 1947.

rank-and-file activists 'to restore the truth' about the unpopular measures taken by the government, he argued that 'only a return to budget equilibrium and the rescue of the Franc' could 'prevent a bankruptcy from which the working classes would be the first to suffer'.[24] At the height of the strike wave that would bring an end to *tripartisme*, Philip set out what that would mean in practice. After lamenting the 'complete rift' between 'public opinion' and 'the reality of the situation', he described the huge balance-of-payments deficit as 'the supreme reality' in France. With two-thirds of the country's gold reserves already projected to be in foreign hands by the end of the year, a wage rise would destroy any hope of getting a loan from the International Bank for Reconstruction and Development – which would leave France 'forced to accept the political and economic conditions of the Americans'. The accompanying inflation, moreover, would amount to 'the total suicide of the working class'. For while the situation may have been 'tragic' in France, it was 'catastrophic ... where they have let things go' in inflation-ridden Hungary and Italy. 'We have to prevent our comrades', Philip concluded, from embarking upon that 'dangerous road'.[25]

That Italy was 'heading for a catastrophe' was something that Morandi fully acknowledged. Addressing the PSIUP Directorate in March 1947, he painted an extremely grim picture of the country's economic outlook. There were 'neither hopes nor illusions about the possibilities of curbing the costs of living, of reducing unemployment, [and] of improving the conditions of workers'. But giving in to the sweeping pay rises demanded by workers offered no solution, as these would spark 'severe inflation' for which workers would end up 'also paying the price'. Quite the contrary, if the PSIUP were to carry 'the full responsibility of government' it would 'have to draw up a plan that subjected the working classes to a rigorous discipline'.[26]

The problem for each of the four parties, of course, was that they did not run single-party governments. And as the hardships of post-war life certainly did not meet working-class expectations of socialism, socialist leaders felt a distinct need to reassure workers that their coalitions were still on course to a brighter tomorrow. 'We need to give the worker some perspectives', Motyka declared, by talking about 'those achievements that

---

[24] 'Fête populaire socialiste à Lille' (30 December 1946), ADN, CRR, 28 W 38457 2.
[25] OURS, CD SFIO, 30 April 1947.
[26] 'Riunione della Direzione' (27 March 1947), ISRT, Fondo Foscolo Lombardi, Partito Socialista Italiano, Direzione Nazionale, Busta 4, Fasc. 21.

are in the nearest future'.[27] Lelio Basso, at that time deputy PSIUP secretary, was more elaborate. The masses, he argued, wanted to know 'for
what and for whom they were working and suffering'. If there was going
to be yet 'another winter of misery, of cold, and of hunger', it should be
made plain to the working class what would follow after that. 'It is for a
general directive that the country is waiting … it is a political motto that
could cause the psychological *shock* required for the masses to overcome
the deadlock of the situation.'[28]

The changed political context was one such incentive for the working
class to endure hardships. That it would not be possible for workers to
enjoy 'a full bowl at home' and that their 'sitting rooms were going to be
cold', a ČSSD leader of the Plzeň KOR wrote, represented 'a test' of their
'mental maturity'. It would be 'very harmful for our democracy', which
was now built upon 'healthy foundations', if the working class failed to
appreciate that such 'renunciations' still lay ahead and disturbed 'the
normal functioning of companies for trivial reasons'.[29] While asking their
rank and file for patience in socio-economic questions, PSIUP leaders in
Sesto San Giovanni likewise alluded to newfound democracy. Being both
the 'inheritors' and the 'insolvency practitioners' of 'the bankrupt fascists',
after all, the popular parties could not 'perform miracles'. A 'single miracle'
'could and should be hoped for': the election of 'the Constituent Assembly,
from which alone working people can expect the resolution of their most
urgent problems'.[30]

More frequently, however, socialist leaders justified the sacrifices they
demanded of the working class with reference to the transformed socio-
economic relations. The state having assumed a far greater role in economic
life, they often claimed, the proceeds of worker sufferings would henceforth fall to the working class itself. Insisting that the case against wage
increases was temporal rather than absolute, Mollet called for SFIO party
propaganda 'to accentuate the planned economy to make workers accept
sacrifices'.[31] With the economy not only planned but also largely in the
state's hands in post-war Eastern Europe, socialist leaders there went further in their affirmations that the adversity the working class was currently

[27] 'Posiedzenie Rady Gospodarczej PPS' (27 February 1946), AAN, Polska Partia Socjalistyczna,
Sekretariat Generalny, Wydz. Ekonomiczno-Przem, Rada Gospodarcza, 1946–47, 2291/3, 235/XV-
23, fo. 17.
[28] Lelio Basso, 'Espedienti o soluzioni', *Avanti!*, 19 September 1945. Emphasis in original. www
.leliobasso.it/documento.aspx?id=6c9c65ef2df3c28d35883209f0732a80 (last consulted: 27 June 2018).
[29] Frant. Filip, 'Do vlastních řad', *Nový Den*, 17 October 1945.
[30] 'IVᵃ Assemblea Generale del P.S.I.U.P.', *Sesto Proletaria*, 1 November 1945.
[31] OURS, CD SFIO, 29 January 1947, OURS.

living through served an altogether different purpose than their pre-war hardships. Speaking at the first post-war PPS congress, under-secretary for labour and social security Eugenia Pragierowa declared that 'the knowledge' that 'he is working for himself and not for someone else's private gain' certainly constituted 'a moral boost' for the worker.[32] Laušman likewise insisted that both 'the function' and the 'moral purpose' of work had changed fundamentally from the liberal-capitalist period. 'If we therefore have to talk about what we have done for the working man', he told a conference of ČSSD factory organisations, 'we actually have to explain what the working man has done for himself'.[33]

The nation itself constituted a final cause to which party leaders urged workers to sacrifice their immediate needs. Milanese trade union leaders, according to Franco Mariani, were doing all in their power to instil 'a spirit of sacrifice for the salvation of Italy' among their working-class constituents.[34] Calling on miners to raise production and refrain from strikes, SFIO minister of industrial production Robert Lacoste likewise pointed to the national interest. The lack of coal represented 'a veritable national danger', he argued, meaning miners' diligence was crucial 'for France to live'.[35]

As we have seen, though, such appeals to workers were largely unsuccessful, as agitations and wildcat strikes continued to hit industrial centres. Socialist leaders were quick to bemoan the pointless and ultimately self-defeating character of these worker protests. Laurent complained that workers, by not allowing their national leaders 'a day of respite', were repeating their pre-war mistakes – when Léon Blum's incoming Popular Front government had struggled with an unremitting strike movement.[36] Such internal discord within the labour movement, after all, could only benefit its right-wing and capitalist enemies. In this respect, Frantisek Macháček, the ČSSD's education, health care, and hospitals spokesman in the Plzeň city council, warned workers of those 'collaborators of the deceased plutocracy' now taking 'tremendously radical' attitudes.

---

[32] XXVI Kongres (August 1945), AAN, PPS, 235/1-12, fo. 121.

[33] 'Projev na konferencí závodních politických oragnisací' (15 September 1946), Narodní Archiv, Prague (hereafter NA), Fonds Bohumil Laušman, III Pisemnosti související s ústřední, veřejnou a politickou činnosti B. Laušmana, Karton 26, Projevy B. Laušmana 1940–1947.

[34] Interview Robert Hadfield with Franco Mariani (1945), AdL, Camera del Lavoro, Class. 5.1.3., Fasc. 4.

[35] Quoted in Hannah Diamond, 'Miners, Masculinity and the "Bataille du Charbon" in France 1944–1948', *Modern & Contemporary France*, 19/1 (2011), pp. 69–84, 72.

[36] 'Congrès de la Fédération du Nord du Parti Socialiste SFIO' (August 1945), ADN, CRR, 19 W 37108 2.

Deliberately inciting the working class to 'struggles … for perpetual wage increases, for the reduction of working hours, for all possible perks' they knew full well nationalised companies could not grant, these elements were seeking to bring the nationalised sector into such dire straits that it would 'collapse' and 'former capitalists would be called in as saviours'.[37]

Despite such occasional references to the sinister forces at play in worker protests, however, both the ČSSD and the SFIO by and large interpreted spontaneous agitations and strikes as a socio-economic problem. It was only when the communists started backing and fomenting strikes over the course of 1947 that the two parties began viewing worker unrest as a political challenge to their governments and democracy itself.[38]

For PPS and PSIUP leaders, on the other hand, there had been political connotations to manifestations of worker discontent all along. PPS leaders felt particularly strongly about strikes. Jan Stefan Haneman, one of the socialist architects of the Lublin government, lashed out at a congress delegate from Poznań who had claimed that 'there was no other choice' for workers but to strike. The working class, Haneman admonished, should understand that they were now 'producing for themselves, for the country, for the motherland, [and] for democracy'. In these circumstances, it was 'a crime' for workers to strike, just like it was 'a crime for party members not to oppose' strikes.[39]

Making no sense from the perspective of the working class, therefore, strikes were often interpreted by PPS leaders as an attempt at undermining popular democracy by the remnants of the pre-war 'reaction'. Its 'access to the democratic press', argued Edward Osóbka-Morawski at a joint meeting of the PPS and PPR leaderships, allowed 'the reaction' to stir resentments over all sorts of alleged inequities in industrial life.[40] Henryk Wachowicz – the leader of the Łódź PPS – subsequently pointed out just how successful

---

[37] Fr. Macháček, 'Boj o socialisaci se teprve začíná', *Nový Den*, 7 November 1945.

[38] The ČSSD leadership already condemned the communist 'abuse' of strikes in March 1947. The direct cause was the violent, overtly anti-Semitic, and communist-instigated strike of that month in Varnsdorf (on the German border), which prompted Laušman to offer his resignation as minister of industry (he retracted it under pressure from the ČSSD presidium). Communist-backed strikes continued unabated into the summer and autumn of 1947, however, and formed an integral part of the 'atmosphere of fear' that ČSSD leaders accused the communists of trying to create. For the French socialists, the turning point came with the 'insurrectionary' strikes of the autumn of 1947, which the national SFIO newspaper described as a communist mobilisation 'against the Republican regime'. See Kaplan, *Das verhängnisvolle Bündnis*, pp. 93, 117–21; Mechoulan, 'Le SFIO et les grèves', p. 217.

[39] xxvi Kongres (August 1945), AAN, PPS, 235/I-12, fos 179–81.

[40] 'Protokół z wspólnego posiedzenia CKW PPS i KC PPR' (28 September 1945), AAN, PPS, CKW, 235/III/6, fo. 4.

these efforts had been. Caused by 'reactionary forces' active in the area, he informed the meeting, the recent strikes in Pabianice (near Łódź) had assumed a political character and were 'targeted at the government'. That even the Scheibler and Grohmann textile factory, 'the pride of the Łódź PPR', had been hit by strikes offered further 'evidence' of 'the political substrate of strikes'.[41]

The PSIUP leadership was likewise obsessed with the political fallout of agitations at its grassroots. Though the majority of party leaders rejected suggestions that wildcat strikes had somehow been concocted by adherents of the neo-fascist Front of the Common Man,[42] they were constantly at pains to remind the working class that 'uncoordinated' agitations would seriously compromise the political struggles being fought out in their name. In this context, socialist leaders often invoked the lessons of 1919, when the radicalism enshrined in strikes and factory occupations had split the labour movement and driven the horrified middle class straight into the open arms of fascists. 'Rash blows, uncontrolled and unadvised actions, [and] isolated and sporadic agitations', warned an article urging Sesto San Giovanni socialists to show 'trade union discipline', carried a double risk. While offering 'the bourgeoisie vast possibilities for reinforcement' and 'counter-manoeuvring', the concomitant 'dysfunctional disagreement' within the working class could 'lead to tragic situations like in 1919'.[43] Addressing a rally in Torino, Nenni likewise impressed on workers that they should have 'the courage' not to strike. For even if the motives for workers to stage a walkout were 'profoundly felt to be in defence of their own interests', strikes still constituted a 'distraction' from the 'battle for power' in which the working class was involved. The recent strike at Fiat's Mirafiori plant had been 'wrong', accordingly, because it had 'threatened to exacerbate our relations with other classes, which are already difficult enough by themselves'.[44]

Behind the closed doors of the PSIUP Central Committee, Nenni explained just how crucial it was that relations with the party's non-proletarian coalition partners would not be pushed past the tipping point.

[41] Ibid., fo. 17. Despite a 'widespread belief' to the contrary, Łukasz Kamiński found no fundamental differences between PPS and PPR attitudes to strikes in his extensive research on industrial action in post-war Poland. Middle- and higher-level PPS activists, he explains, were just as active in 'liquidating protests' as their communist counterparts and 'also accused reactionary forces of stirring them'. See Kamiński, *Polacy wobec nowej rzeczywistości*, pp. 129–30.

[42] 'Riunione della Direzione' (4 April 1947), ISRT, Fondo Foscolo Lombardi, Partito Socialista Italiano, Direzione Nazionale, Busta 4, Fasc. 21.

[43] Eugenio Sighinolfi, 'Disciplina Sindacale', *Sesto Proletaria*, 24 July 1946.

[44] 'Seduta pomeridiana' (18 October 1945), ACS, Carteggio Nenni, Busta 87, Fasc. 2189.

'If we go and talk to workers at Fiat in the capacity of men of government and tell them that they must not abuse strikes, that they have to wait for certain situations, because that constitutes the only way to preserve for their parties the possibility to arrive at the Constituent Assembly and give the country a democratic solution', he insisted, 'we are listened to today.' But should the Left be forced to leave government and change its rhetoric, he continued, 'we would be heading for a situation reminiscent of 1919, with strikes ... multiplying from week to week ... creating an infernal situation'. That was a prospect 'to despair of', he concluded, to be accepted 'only once every other solution has been ruled out'.[45]

So overwhelming was its fear of losing control over the situation yet again that the PSIUP leadership remained extremely wary of strikes and agitations even after the party had been removed from government. As the political temperature rose during the autumn of 1947, several leaders began sounding alarm over grassroots agitations 'discredit[ing] the labour movement'. Basso lamented that there were 'communists and socialists who behave like there will be a revolution within fifteen days'. In reality, they had allowed themselves to be 'manoeuvred by Scelba onto a terrain that he prefers'. According to Vannuccio Faralli, who had been the PSIUP's under-secretary for industry in the third De Gasperi government, the situation in industry was 'grave' too. Workers were 'not being paid', causing 'violent strikes' to erupt. If this was 'not remedied', he declared, 'we will be faced with more serious cases'. In such circumstances, former minister for the postal service Luigi Cacciatore noted, it was unfortunate that neither the socialists nor the communists had a clear 'objective'. Rather than getting 'carried away by the situation', he concluded, 'we need to dominate it and impose discipline upon the socialist masses'.[46]

It was this purported lack of discipline that accounted for socialist leaders' growing disillusionment with their own rank and file. Already during the massive rally celebrating the decrees for the nationalisation of Czechoslovakian industry in October 1945, Fierlinger had pointed out that popular democracy had accorded workers 'important duties' alongside 'important rights'. Among those duties were the need to 'maintain working discipline everywhere' and the improvement of 'working morale'.[47] As the months and years went by, however, party leaders increasingly found

[45] 'Comitato Centrale' (17 October 1945), ACS, Carteggio Nenni, Busta 87, Fasc. 2189.
[46] 'Riunione Direzione' (5 December 1947), ISRT, Fondo Foscolo Lombardi, Partito Socialista Italiano, Direzione Nazionale, Busta 4, Fasc. 21.
[47] 'The Mission of Social Democracy in the New State' (November 1947), ANM, Fonds Zdeněk Fierlinger, Karton 40, Sjezd soc. dem. v Brne.

working-class discipline and morale to be on the wane rather than on the rise. By November 1946, Laurent was deploring 'the absence of political maturity and moral awareness' within the working class, who were showing 'neither a sense of effort nor trade union spirit'.[48] In the aftermath of the big Łódź strike wave of September 1947, Wachowicz came to an even harsher verdict on the working class. 'Over the last two weeks', he recalled, 'the whole party had to be mobilised to convince the worker that he is not allowed to strike, because strikes always have a political character and are directed against the government and the system.' Even though the strikes had ended, however, there was no escaping the fact that workers' 'attitude to work was often dismissive'. In view of 'these weaknesses within the working class', he lamented, 'we cannot say that the majority … wants to work honestly'.[49]

The Battle for Production

Party leaders condemned low morale and poor discipline with such exasperation because of their detrimental effects on the productivist campaigns that socialist parties co-launched and co-championed in three of the four countries. Socialist leaders in Czechoslovakia, France, and Poland constantly stressed that working harder, longer, and in a more targeted manner represented the only way to improve the lot of the working class. In case workers themselves were unable to muster the resolve to achieve that, they were to be encouraged by all sorts of monetary bonuses and other inducements. But the disparities these created, both between skilled and unskilled labour and between well-supplied and poorly supplied industries, were the cause of much resentment among workers. The 'battle for production', consequently, quickly developed into a clash between two conceptions of socialism: an egalitarian conception held at the grassroots and a more performance-based conception held by party leaders.

The leaders of the PSIUP, conversely, rarely talked about production. This was due in part to the altogether different set of socio-economic problems facing post-war Italy. Instead of being so short of manpower that its government had to overburden the workforce with demands, it was desperately seeking to prevent mass unemployment among ex-servicemen and

---

[48] OURS, CD SFIO, 13 November 1946.
[49] 'Protokół z plenarnego posiedzenia Rady Wojewódzkiej Polskiej Partii Socjalistycznej w Łodzi' (27 September 1947), APŁ, Wojewódzki Komiet PPS w Łodzi, 2, fo. 30.

those formerly earning their living in the war industry. But the PSIUP's lack of interest in productivism was also inspired by reasons more peculiar to Italian socialism. After all, the basic productivist argument – that more production would greatly assist economic recovery – held for postwar Italy too. Both communist and Christian democratic (trade union) leaders, accordingly, repeatedly banged the drum for productivism.[50] For socialist leaders, however, economic problems always played second fiddle to political problems.[51] Much like its efforts to restrain strikes, then, the PSIUP's endeavours to mobilise workers to go and work where the state needed them most were motivated more by concerns over the political stability than over the economic prosperity of the nation.

For the other three parties, though, political and economic concerns often converged in productivism, as production itself was increasingly politicised. The Plzeň ČSSD, as well as the other parties forming the local coalition, called upon its supporters to herald the launch of the Two Year Plan by sacrificing a free Sunday to come and assist in the harvest of potatoes and sugar beets in October 1946.[52] Addressing socialist textile workers at Łódź's I.K. Poznański factory, PPS Central Committee member Marian Rybicki similarly defined the socialist 'role in the reconstruction of the motherland' by work. The 'difficult economic circumstances', he declared, 'force us to intensive labour, to give the maximum, and to be an example for others'.[53] But it was the French socialists who came closest to formulating a full-fledged ideology of production. 'The production effort', an official organ of the SFIO's Northern Federation wrote, 'takes on an authentically revolutionary value in these decisive days.' As it was not possible 'to build socialism until the forces of production were in full swing', it was crucial 'for socialism … to reconstitute these forces as soon as possible'.[54]

---

[50] Luigi Ganapini, *Una città, la guerra: Lotte di classe ideologie e forze politiche a Milano, 1939–1951* (Milan: F. Agneli, 1988), pp. 238–9.
[51] This found its reflection in the attitudes of some of the foremost PSIUP leaders. Nenni was notoriously uninterested in economic problems, repeatedly affirming his maxim of *politique d'abord* ('politics above all else') and insisting that such political issues as the institutional question trumped all other considerations. Basso, for his part, was more concerned with abstract schemes of working-class unity than with day-to-day economics. See Degl'Innocenti, *Storia del PSI*, p. 50.
[52] Krajský Sekretariát ČSSD Plzeň to Ústřední Sekretariát ČSSD, 16 September 1946, Archiv České Strany Sociálně Demokratické, Prague (hereafter Archiv ČSSD), Fond 71, Část II, Karton 200, fo. 541.
[53] 'Protokół z zebrania koła P.P.S. przy P.Z.P.B. Nr. 2' (25 October 1947), APŁ, DK PPS Śródmieście Lewa, 14, fo. 59.
[54] 'Le Parti Socialiste: Département du Nord' (reference date: 28 February 1946), ADN, CRR, 19 W 37108 1.

Accordingly, party leaders frequently propagated increased production as a panacea for the problems of both the working class and their governments. The 'basic source' of high prices, a commentary in the Plzeň ČSSD press read, 'is the imbalance between national income and national production'. That meant that all manpower that was 'expendable elsewhere' had to be directed towards productive work. Whereas it had been 'a good thing' under the occupation for people to avoid deportation to the Reich by taking refuge in office work, things were 'different today'. What was needed at present was for all available hands 'to go where new goods, new objects, new products, [and] new commodities are actually being created, because that is the only way for the nation to grow richer'.[55]

In emphasising 'the imperious necessity to produce',[56] the SFIO also identified the everyday concerns of workers with national interests. 'If we want to regain a *high standard of living* and effectively place ourselves in *international competition*', a party brochure on production argued, 'we have to … *produce*, and *produce* more.' Both the '*problem of ravitaillement*' and the '*financial problem*' were linked to the '*problem of production*', after all, and 'as long as the latter has not been resolved, the two others cannot be resolved either'. 'The state has to secure the working class a decent standard of living', the brochure concluded, 'but, in return and to allow France to recover and re-take its place among the great nations, the working class has the duty to put all of its productive forces at the service of the nation.'[57]

More and more, however, socialist leaders felt that workers were failing to keep up their end of the bargain. According to Stanisław Szwalbe, the vice-president of the PPS Central Committee, efficiency was lacking in Poland's productive apparatus. While he acknowledged that this was due in part to the ills of popular supply, he also lambasted labour discipline. In the Łódź industry, for example, the number of workers not showing up for work had reached 20 per cent. The 'unprofessional attitude' many workers displayed towards both the shop floor and raw materials, moreover, had

---

[55] 'Aktuální otázky', *Nový Den*, 9 August 1946.
[56] 'Manifeste du Parti Socialiste aux peuples de France et de l'Union Française', Arguments et Ripostes, Bulletin Intérieur du Parti Socialiste (S.F.I.O.), 1 May 1946, OURS.
[57] 'La nécessité de produire', Arguments et Ripostes, Bulletin Intérieur du Parti Socialiste (S.F.I.O.), 1 May 1946, OURS. Emphasis in original. Serge Berstein points out that the 'conviction that economic recovery was the prerequisite for any return to "power"' was 'widely shared' among political parties in post-war France. On the SFIO in particular, he argues that it was its 'obsessive preoccupation with economic reconstruction' that prompted the party to demand a reduction of the military budget – ushering in the political row that was to lead to General De Gaulle's resignation in January 1946. See Serge Berstein, 'French Power as seen by the Political Parties after World War II', in Josef Becker and Franz Knipping (eds.), *Power in Europe: Great Britain, France, Italy, and Germany in a Postwar World, 1945–1950* (Berlin/New York: De Gruyter, 1986), pp. 163–84, 171–2.

turned into an 'epidemic'. In order to prevent production in nationalised and cooperative factories from worsening and becoming more expensive, he admonished, factory management, factory councils, and trade unions should make sure of three things. Firstly, they had to ascertain 'that there was no excess of manpower within their factories', as the desolate 'Recovered Territories' in Western Poland were crying out for workers, and that labour was more properly organised. Secondly, they had to 'control labour efficiency, i.e. to rule on the shop floor'. Thirdly, they had to use piece rates 'so extensively that initiative and productivity on the part of the individual worker are genuinely and seriously rewarded and the lack thereof punished'.[58]

It was these three guiding principles – that labour had to be deployed in accordance with the nation's socio-economic requirements, that workers had to be chastened into giving the reconstruction effort their utmost, and that performance counted for more than anything – that shaped party leaders' attitudes towards the working class during the battle for production.

Socialist leaders frequently defended those measures directly related to the reconstruction effort as a necessary but temporal evil. This was the case for the extra hours they ordered workers to put in. The ČSSD struggled to honour its long-standing pledge to reduce the Saturday shift in the mines to six hours. By December 1946, its parliamentary party put forward a proposal to cut back the miner's working week to forty-six hours on average over a four-week period. The 'exceptional economic circumstances' in which the country found itself, though, warranted that this would entail three eight-hour Saturdays followed by one free Saturday for the foreseeable future.[59] Where the French socialists had delivered substantial improvements in labour conditions during the interwar period, the demands of the reconstruction effort forced them to backtrack too. Nowhere was this more painful than with the suspension of that flagship social policy of the Popular Front government – the law guaranteeing the forty-hour working week. But 'the ruins, the lack of food, [and] the shortage of clothing and various provisions' wrought by war, Laurent told socialists in Cambrai, had left the government with no other choice. 'We have to produce above all', he argued, and that was why 'we find ourselves under the obligation, for the sake of rebuilding the country, to demand forty-eight hours of labour from workers'. The 'law of forty hours'

[58] xxvi Kongres (August 1945), AAN, PPS, 235/1-12, fo. 52.
[59] 'Zaručte horníkům v sobotu šest hodin práce', *Nový Den*, 14 December 1946.

remained 'an immutable principle', however, that would 'enter into force again as soon as the circumstances allow it'.[60]

Party leaders tended to describe the piece rates and other performance-related bonuses that made up an increasing part of the working-class wage package as being of a purely transitory nature too. For socialist leaders, though, there were also more properly ideologically motivated considerations at play in this context. Stakhanovism, the Soviet-born movement of challenging workers to outperform and rewarding them for outperforming their norms in 'competitions of labour', was always a delicate issue for socialists, because of its obvious communist connotations. But party leaders were certainly never proponents of the blanket egalitarianism, which understood socialism to mean no income differences whatsoever, that many at their grassroots demanded. Even leading Italian socialists appeared to agree here, as PSIUP trade union secretary Fernando Santi attested to upon his return from a visit to the Soviet Union. Noting how the basic wage of the Soviet worker could be supplemented with a whole range of bonuses if production targets were met, he concluded that income levelling in the Soviet Union had definitely not reached the proportions that 'many fear and some naively hope'.[61]

Out of the three parties that were engaged in the battle for production, the PPS was certainly most enthusiastic about Stakhanovism. The government was 'on its way to a better future', Rybicki told socialist textile workers in Łódź, and 'to that end' it was organising 'labour competitions and a whole series of other noble rivalries'.[62] Several speakers at the second post-war PPS congress stressed that it was imperative for socialist workers to partake in labour competitions. As a revolutionary vanguard party, Central Committee secretary Włodzimierz Reczek declared, the PPS 'should participate prominently in labour competitions'. That 'movement', after all, 'will decide not only over our living standards, but also over the direction of our politics'.[63] Justice minister Henryk Świątkowski likewise underlined just how much was at stake in labour competitions. The party wanted its

---

[60] 'Note des renseignements d'une importante réunion privée d'information (d'arrondissement) organisée par le Parti Socialiste SFIO, à Cambrai' (3 February 1947), ADN, CRR, 30 W 38630 8.
[61] 'Prime impressioni sull'Unione Sovietica', AdL, Camera del Lavoro, Class. 5.1.3., Fasc. 4. And indeed, the Italian Left did increasingly accept the introduction of piece work from late 1945 onwards, although Tom Behan argues that this 'was due more to the urgent need to raise wage levels to compensate for high inflation' than to 'complete agreement with the system of piece work itself'. See: Behan, *The Long Awaited Moment*, p. 181.
[62] 'Protokół z zebrania koła P.P.S. przy P.Z.P.B. Nr. 2' (25 October 1947), APŁ, DK PPS Śródmieście Lewa, 14, fo. 59.
[63] XXVII Kongres (December 1947), AAN, PPS, 235/1-25, fo. 146.

members to 'prevail' in labour competitions, he argued, 'to execute the Three Year Plan ... increase the strength and democratic sovereignty of our Polish state, and thereby also raise the living standards of the working class'. 'The labour race for Poland', then, represented 'the only way' for party members 'to increase the prestige of the PPS, [and] reinforce its historic role in the construction of People's Poland, a free and fair Poland'.[64]

The ČSSD took a more ambiguous attitude towards the exclusively target-based production methods so common to Stakhanovism. Evaluating the first five months of the Two Year Plan at a conference of ČSSD managers of nationalised companies, Laušman deplored the fact that targets were too often being fulfilled at the expense of the standard and marketability of the produce. 'It makes no sense', he declared, 'to stockpile one's warehouses with goods [while] having no idea whether and where these will be sold' or 'to strive to execute the plan in terms of quantity and at the same time compromising quality'. Yet Laušman quickly qualified this statement for those industrial sectors vital to the reconstruction effort. In the production of coal, energy, and iron, he argued, 'we must today still execute the plan in terms of quantity and forgive shortcomings in quality'.[65]

It was in such heavy industries that social democrats did seem to favour Stakhanovite production. Ladislav Cígler revelled in the 'amazing performance' of individual miners in Ostrava, who had managed to fill up to twenty-four wagons of coal a shift.[66] An article in the Plzeň ČSSD press sang the praises of Stakhanovism more explicitly. The significance of Stakhanovite production in mining and manufacturing, it insisted, went well beyond the increased output generated by workers actually outperforming their norms. Not only had their example often 'encouraged others to higher performances', but the experiences of the Soviet Union also taught that 'Stakhanovists often came up with new techniques of labour, with new ideas, with minor or major improvements in the workflow'. The 'key issue in our production', it continued, 'lies in increasing the average performance'. And 'one of the means' to that end was 'performance competition, a race, [to decide] who produces more, produces more than the others, produces more than another company'.[67]

[64] Ibid., fo. 231.
[65] 'Projev s. ministra průmyslu B. Laušmana na konferencí soc. demokratických ředitelů a námestků nár. podniků' (29 June 1947), NA, Fonds Bohumil Laušman, III Pisemnosti souviseljící s ústřední, veřejnou a politickou činnosti B. Laušmana, Karton 26, Projevy B. Laušmana 1940–1947.
[66] Ladislav Cígler, 'O pracovní moralku', *Nový Den*, 21 November 1945.
[67] 'Pod čarou: O stachanovicich a průměrném výkonu', *Nový Den*, 19 February 1946.

The SFIO, on the other hand, was officially opposed to Stakhanovism. According to Robert Coutant, the performance bonuses that the MRP and the PCF wanted to include in the wage package of public sector workers were 'wrong'. The SFIO had 'always fought against this principle', he argued, which was 'likely to cause dissensions among functionaries'. To adopt this method would amount to embarking on 'a road paved by Lenin: Stakhanovism'.[68] Touring the north of France in October 1946, SFIO Executive member Suzanne Charpy repeatedly condemned Stakhanovism too. Her criticisms were directed at the communists and 'their great slogan of production' above all.[69] Unlike the PCF, she professed, the SFIO was opposed to 'production at any price'. 'We socialists', after all, 'are against piecework, which requires a continuous human effort that risks wearing down health; we are, furthermore, adversaries of the system of individual performance bonuses, which inevitably constitute a divisive factor and create a toxic climate among workers.' It was important for party members 'to shed light on these practices inspired by Russian methods'.[70]

But it is worth noting that these and other attacks on the Stakhanovite dispositions of the SFIO's political rivals were all made during the campaign for the November 1946 parliamentary elections.[71] As we will see, moreover, Charpy was far from a typical socialist leader. Other party leaders, operating in different contexts, took a more positive view of performance bonuses. Philip, having returned as minister of the national economy after the elections, explained how living standards could not rise until production picked up and concluded that 'there remains only one solution: increasing production by all means, especially by collective performance bonuses'.[72] The about-face would be complete after the PCF had been removed from government, with socialist leaders seeking to make a greater part of working-class wages performance-dependent in the face of communist opposition. By September 1947, the then minister of labour Daniel Mayer informed the SFIO Executive that, 'under the pressure of the CGT', the government had been forced to drop planned performance

---

[68] 'Note de Renseignements' (Réunion organisé à Cambrai par le Parti Socialiste SFIO, avec le concours de Mr Daniel Mayer), 7 October 1946, ADN, CRR, 28 W 38454 2.

[69] 'Note de Renseignements' (Réunion organisée par le Parti Socialiste SFIO, à Anzin), 25 October 1946, ADN, CRR, 28 W 38454 2.

[70] 'Conférence du Parti Socialiste à Douai', 7 October 1946, ADN, CRR, 28 W 38454 2.

[71] 'Note de Renseignements' (Réunion publique organisée par la section socialiste de Trith St-Leger), 18 October 1946, ADN, CRR, 28 W 38454 2; 'Note de Renseignements' (Réunion électorale tenue par le Parti Socialiste SFIO à Feignies), 29 October 1946, ADN, CRR, 28 W 38454 2.

[72] OURS, CD SFIO, 29 January 1947.

bonuses. A general 11 per cent salary increase had come in the place of 'two provisions of a revolutionary character'.[73]

Whatever the theoretical exactitudes of their parties' attitudes towards Stakhanovism, though, the bulk of the socialist rank and file resented the practical consequences of the introduction of more performance-based production methods. Firstly, this concerned the human costs of the incessant demands placed upon the working class. There was much anxiety over working conditions. SFIO groups in the mines wanted security to be improved, as deadly accidents were 'frequent'.[74] The chairman of Škoda's factory council expressed similar worries upon welcoming communist minister of labour and social welfare Jozef Šoltész to the plant. While there had been thirty accidents per million worked hours at the height of the occupation, he pointed out, the commensurate number, even though nobody was being chased to work anymore, had now risen to forty-six. He concluded that nationalised companies desired 'that attention would be devoted to maximum protection at work'.[75]

Workers often associated the absence of such proper safeguards with Stakhanovite or other productivist campaigns. It could not be the case, a PPS factory circle leader in Łódź declared, that the labour race led to 'the murderous destruction of machine and man'.[76] Writing in the propaganda leaflet of the SFIO group in the Ledoux mines (near Valenciennes), a socialist miner's delegate was more elaborate. In an article entitled 'From Production … to the Cemetery', he railed against 'scientific' production methods 'that pay very little attention to the health of our miner comrades'. The 'longwall' mining method, enabling miners to excavate much longer faces of coal by means of a conveyor belt, resulted in 'poor ventilation, the heating of the site so harmful to health, bad gasses and the accumulation of dust, which can cause explosions and carbon monoxide poisoning'. The 'Bedeau[x] system' of meticulously calculated individual performance bonuses had to be replaced by collective pay, moreover, which was 'more humane for allowing the weak to eat like the strong'.[77]

The disparities that piece rates generated between workers were the second main protest levelled against performance-based production.

---

[73] OURS, CD SFIO, 24 September 1947.
[74] OURS, CD SFIO, 5 March 1947.
[75] 'Ministr Šoltesz mezi škodováky v Plzni', *Nový Den*, 4 April 1946.
[76] 'Protokół spisany z zebrania członkow P.P.S. przy Panstwowych Zakładach Przemysłu Wełnianego Nr. 40 w Łodzi' (28 October 1947), APŁ, DK PPS Fabryczna, 8, fos 82–3.
[77] Gaston Guislain, 'De la production … au cimitière. Peut-on demander encore plus aux mineurs?' *Le Marteau Piqueur: Feuille de propagande du Groupe socialiste des Mines de Ledoux*, February 1947.

Workers often complained that whether or not they were able to meet their targets depended on a whole range of factors beyond their reach. The workforce in Plzeň-area sugar refineries turned down ÚRO's offer of wage supplements to be paid upon 'outperformance', arguing that there was 'no question of outperformance in their sector because of the shortage of materials'.[78] This was also 'the terrible objection' to the collective performance bonuses frequently championed by the SFIO leadership, as Moch readily acknowledged. As production increases were linked to the supply of raw materials, he noted, it was 'not possible to favour one industrial sector without that being to the detriment of another'.[79]

Still more grievous, though, were discrepancies in the equipment and supply among colleagues. There was particular anger over the preferential treatment of the first Stakhanovists in Łódź.[80] Textile workers in the city's Ruda Pabianicka district went on strike when factory management started sequestering power from their spinning machines in order to facilitate two Stakhanovite 'volunteers' who had accepted multi-machine work. These measures, the district PPS wrote, had come at the 'wrong moment' completely, as the inadequate electricity supply already had 70 per cent of spinners sitting idly by. Nevertheless, the arriving trade union officials threw their full weight behind factory management.[81]

The state prioritising performance over working-class well-being and living standards at least as much as the capitalist, then, workers rapidly lost the will to make sacrifices towards the new economic order. Though condemning strikes and strikers, Mollet called upon his fellow party leaders to take heed of 'the profound dissatisfaction' in worker communities, where 'misery, difficulties, and a sentiment of injustice' reigned. Worse still was that 'workers have the impression that the [state-]directed economy requires all efforts on their part without the government having the possibility to demand the same efforts of other segments of the population'.[82] An editorial in the Plzeň ČSSD press likewise voiced misgivings over what had developed in the place of 'the capitalist production anarchy'. 'We have to be watchful', it admonished, 'that the system [capitalism] that caused unemployment and the waste of forces and values could not return under

---

[78] 'Zápis ze schůze tajemníků Krajské odborové rady' (15 March 1946), VA, Organizační oddělení ÚRO, Karton 11, Inv. j. 78, z Zápisy z schůzi KOR 1946, fo. 3.
[79] OURS, CD SFIO, 2 May 1947.
[80] Kenney, *Rebuilding Poland*, pp. 122–3.
[81] Dzielnicowy Komitet P.P.S. Ruda Pabianice to Wojewodzki Komitet P.P.S. Łódź, 15 September 1947, APŁ, DK PPS Ruda Pabianicka, 5, fo. 48.
[82] OURS, CD SFIO, 30 April 1947.

the pretext that other experiments have not worked, that it is the only possible production system.' Thus far, after all, 'the worker profits little from the invocation of his power'.[83]

In such circumstances, workers would find it harder and harder to summon the productivist enthusiasm demanded by their party leaders. A report on the maltreatment of electric welders at the railways in Plzeň flagged this up. Having seen promised improvements in labour conditions come to nothing and their hourly wage supplements cut, they had complained to their factory council. But not only did the factory council give them no explanation whatsoever and hint at even further supplement reductions, a welder who pointed out that no one would be willing to undertake heavy labour against such conditions was thrown out of the meeting and fired within a matter of days. 'Electric welders', the report insisted, 'are fully aware of their duties and their desired performance, and want to work for the reconstruction of the Republic, sometimes even harder than lies within their power.' In order for them to fulfil their duties, however, welders were entitled both to 'a just salary' and to being treated 'like colleagues'. 'If we ask workers to increase performance', after all, it was a 'necessary precondition' that they were 'at peace and satisfied at work'.[84]

In very similar terms, at the first post-war PPS congress a delegate from Łódź expressed his disgust at claims that workers did not want to work. As a worker's party, he argued, 'we know our workers, we know that they are patriotic … that the Polish worker does everything to raise labour productivity, [and] gives the state his all'. Yet 'the other side of the medal' was that nationalised factories were 'very frequently' still being led by those pre-war owners who did 'not understand the new reality'. 'How is it possible to demand enthusiasm of the worker', he wondered, 'if the attitude the manager takes towards the worker has not changed one jot'? More than that, those in charge of the state sector locally also seemed to have retained their friends in high places. 'One Mr Géra', the delegate lamented, had been removed from high office by the local authorities for embezzlement, only for him to 'return two days later with an even greater mandate from the ministry [of industry]'.[85]

The constant allegations of wanting labour morale also left rank-and-file workers feeling frustrated. The 'persistent talk of the lack of labour morale' should stop, a resolution adopted by the Assembly of the West

[83] H., 'Myslíme to dobře', *Nový Den*, 16 March 1946.
[84] 'Neutěsené poměry elecktrických svárecú v dílnách státnich drah v Plzni', *Nový Den*, 18 April 1946.
[85] XXVI Kongres (August 1945), AAN, PPS, 235/1-12, fos 198–9.

Bohemian ČSSD avowed, as it had been 'established that the vast majority of workers work diligently and completely dependably'. The shortcomings in certain industrial sectors, hence, had not been caused by aversion upon the part of the working class, 'but rather by the unwillingness to remove those ailments that burden performance'.[86] Among those ailments were such technical problems as the excess of people involved in non-productive work and the deficient organisation of economic life,[87] but crucially also the state's failure to stand up for workers. The fact that some roads remained untravelled in the struggle to lower prices, Cígler pointed out to the Czechoslovakian National Assembly, 'does not create an atmosphere conducive to a rise in labour morale'. People found it 'incomprehensible', for example, that the government appeared unable 'to crack down on the black market'. There would be 'much more enthusiasm and dedication towards work', he declared, if the government clamped down relentlessly on 'all those hampering the economic construction of our republic'.[88]

Coutant likewise affirmed that the state had to come through for the working class first and foremost, rather than the other way around. 'Miners are often criticised for the lack of coal', he told socialists in the north of France, 'but we do not take into account that they are malnourished.' The 'efforts demanded of the working class', he maintained, should be matched by 'a struggle against the financial and economic oligarchies' thus far 'insufficient'.[89]

For many at the grassroots, then, the battle for production only served to highlight everything that was unfair about the post-war state: while governments constantly squeezed workers to do more for less in deteriorating conditions, they seemingly left the better-off in peace. What was worse, their national leaders gave the impression of not being bothered by inequality. The disagreement over ÚRO and the Czechoslovakian government's unanimous decision to pay out a flat Christmas bonus to all workers in the public, nationalised, and private sectors illustrated the rupture between local and national perspectives. While the government indicated it considered income levelling 'undesirable',[90] Cígler, on behalf of the Plzeň KOR, faulted the decision for 'ignor[ing] the weakest in

---

[86] 'Hlas západočeské sociální demokracie: Resoluce, přijatá konferencí krajského zastupitelstva československé sociální demokracie v Plzni', *Nový Den*, 5 November 1946.
[87] Ladislav Cígler, 'Ceny musí býti sníženi!' *Nový Den*, 14 July 1946.
[88] 'Parlamentní řeč posl. s. Cíglera o palčivých problémech doby', *Nový Den*, 20 September 1946.
[89] 'Réunion d'information socialiste à Pecquencourt' (23 July 1945), ADN, CRR, 19 W 37108 2.
[90] 'Národní fronta doporučila vánoční výpomoc', *Nový Den*, 30 November 1946.

society'.[91] Such income differences within the working class were indeed often the hardest to swallow. The wage increases meted out to workers in some companies, admonished Josef Janouš to the Plzeň city council, risked repeating the 'wage terms' of the occupation. These had generated 'different categories' of workers, with some being 'supplemented' and others 'marginalised'. There had been, he remembered, 'a wilful promotion of dissension'.[92]

Yet party leaders proved quite prepared to put labour movement harmony on the line to reward workers willing or able to be mobilised for the reconstruction effort. Socialist leaders were often at pains to stress that far too many person hours were wasted on non-productive or non-essential work. Whereas Osóbka-Morawski called for the 'de-bureaucratisation' of the Polish state apparatus by directing superfluous public servants to productive work,[93] Moch bemoaned the difficulties in relocating French workers 'from dormant industries to more active industries'.[94]

But the shortage of productive and skilled labour was definitely greatest in Czechoslovakia, and the lengths to which its political and economic elites went to address this shortage certainly bred most bad blood among the working class too. Firstly, this concerned the outrageous remunerations for those contributing their scarce skills to the reconstruction effort. The Plzeň ČSSD press ran an angry article about 'the not isolated case' of bricklayers. Already earning 2000 crowns per week, the same as the average worker brought home each month, bricklayers had often been lured away from Plzeň with promises they could get double that amount in the deserted regions on the Hungarian border. No longer welcome at their former firms when such promises fell through, however, they did not take another, lower-paid job. Instead, 'they form the so-called "reserve of scarce crafts" and wait until they find a Maecenas ... who provides them with a royal wage'. The article called upon the Office for Labour Protection to take a look not only at the 'black wage' thus earned by bricklayers, but also at the employers able to pay such wages.[95]

---

[91] 'Zápis z plenární schůze Krajské odborové rady v Plzni' (17 November 1946), VA, Organizační oddělení ÚRO, Karton 11, Inv. j. 78, 2 Zápisy z schůzi KOR 1946, fo. 7.

[92] 'Zápis schůze Národního Výboru dne 28. května 1945 v Plzni', AMP, Zápisy o schůzích Národního Výboru a rady Okresního Národního Výboru a Místního Národního Výboru statutárního města Plzeň 1945, 42.

[93] 'Protokół z wspólnego posiedzenia CKW PPS i KC PPR' (28 September 1945), AAN, PPS, CKW, 235/III/6, fo. 4.

[94] OURS, CD SFIO, 2 May 1947.

[95] 'Odstraňte černé mzdy zedníků', *Nový Den*, 4 October 1946.

If the authorities were sent for in this instance, though, they were the driving force behind some of the other grievances over the preferential treatment given to those lending themselves to the government's productivist campaigns. This was the case for the 'brigades', made up of workers from various sectors, that were sent to the mines to assist in the production of coal. Miners complained bitterly that they required permanent rather than temporal reinforcement and that brigadiers' labour morale left much to be desired. What seemed to frustrate miners most, though, was that brigadiers had immediately gained access to their generous and hard-fought social security system. More than anything, this left them with the impression that brigadiers 'did not come to help, but to devour their bread'.[96]

If the Czechoslovakian programmes to circulate labour still presupposed voluntarism, the Italian socialists allowed their workers no such luxury. Mariani, for example, was adamant that 'all bricklayers, carpenters, navvies, [and] peasants owning land' were obliged 'to leave plants to go and work there where manpower is in demand'. 'All those having the possibility to survive otherwise (merchants, small proprietors, artisans, etc.)', moreover, had to vacate factory jobs or lose every state subsidy. Mariani's main concern, however, was not so much to raise output as to offset the worst effects of looming mass unemployment. With the spectre of joblessness rearing its ugly head now that the post-liberation ban on dismissals was drawing to an end, he noted, it was imperative to 'make all those workers absorbed by the war industry in exceptional times return to their original crafts'.[97] The jobs opening up as a result would go some way towards not only shielding the established workforce from redundancy but also reintegrating those proletarians who had left industry altogether during the war. It was this latter group, consisting of ex-servicemen, former resisters, and returning prisoners of war, that PSIUP leaders feared most. Mindful as always of the lessons of the interwar years, Nenni agonised over what lay ahead for those several millions of partisans and veterans experiencing so many difficulties accommodating to post-war life. 'Here unfortunately', he warned the PSIUP Central Committee, 'is a human repository that could lend itself to new adventures of a squadrist character'.[98]

[96] 'Zápis č. 3 ze schůze krajské odborové rady' (9 March 1947), VA, Organizační oddělení ÚRO, Karton 32, Inv. j. 144.

[97] Interview Robert Hadfield with Franco Mariani (1945), AdL, Camera del Lavoro, Class. 5.1.3., Fasc. 4.

[98] 'Relazione Nenni al Comitato Centrale' (7 January 1946), Carteggio Nenni, Busta 87, Fasc. 2190.

Conclusion

We have seen in this chapter that the attitudes socialist leaders took towards the working class were very similar across the four countries. To be sure, the PSIUP did not glorify production in the same manner that the ČSSD, the SFIO, and the PPS did, but this had more to do with the specific Italian socio-economic situation and the political preoccupations of its leaders than with any greater receptiveness towards the concerns among its rank and file. In fact, whether in terms of performance-related pay or of labour mobilisation, the Italian socialists placed much the same demands on workers as their Czechoslovakian, French, and Polish counterparts.

Behind the many parallels between the four parties that this chapter has exposed, however, the contours of some of the divergences that will grow far more pronounced over the following chapters are already emerging. These divergences have manifested themselves primarily in the four parties' contradictory interpretations of strikes, agitations, and other examples of worker indiscipline. ČSSD and SFIO leaders viewed such expressions of industrial discontent, however untimely or self-defeating, as socio-economic problems first and foremost. The PPS and PSIUP leaderships, on the other hand, tended to explain uncontrolled worker ferments as a direct political challenge to newfound democracy. None of this, though, supports the claim that the post-war European socialist parties were in any way 'soft' on the working class. Much like their communist counterparts, socialist leaders in each of the four countries took a very dismissive attitude towards the grievances at their grassroots – castigating workers for failing to understand what was in their own interest, for their shocking indifference towards the reconstruction effort, and for being very unruly.

A more fruitful way of looking at grassroots–elite relations in the four cities would be to focus on the two questions that divided socialist leaders from ordinary workers. The first concerns the disconnect between socialist elites and the newcomers in industrial life. For many of the criticisms that socialist leaders levelled against workers were actually coded attacks on these newcomers: on the inflationary demands formulated by public sector workers, on the predominantly female workforce on strike in Łódź, or on the peasants with land who were holding down factory jobs in Milano. This increasingly left the newcomers with the impression that the socialist parties were only there for skilled workers, who stood to benefit from production bonuses or could declare themselves free agents altogether. The second concerns the mismatch between local and national perspectives. After national government had all but disintegrated during the final years of the war, many workers had come to identify with their local communities first and foremost. As we have seen, however, national (and provincial) socialist leaders had no time for grievances framed around the local community. In the run-up to the first post-war PPS congress, Osóbka-Morawski warned local socialist representatives that their 'small problems' should not blind them to the bigger picture. Especially among those new to the party, he argued, many did 'not appreciate the current situation [and] think that the most important problems are the small problems of the local area'. That was not what the party congress was supposed to be about. 'The point is that we consider the general problem that besets us, the problem of reconstruction.'[99]

---

[99] 'Sprawozdanie stenograficzne z obrad Rady Naczelnej P.P.S.' (28 June 1945), AAN, Polska Partia Socjalistyczna, Rada Naczelna, 235/11/4, fo. 35.

CHAPTER 4

The Moral of the Story

In his leader's address to the first post-war congress of the PPS, Edward Osóbka-Morawski discussed what 'the abomination' of fascism had left behind in post-war Poland. Even though 'we have survived the great disease, one might say epidemic, of fascism', he declared, it had taken 'the horribly bloody sacrifices' of the Second World War for 'people to understand the criminal goals and methods of fascism'. That people were now turning away from fascism, moreover, did not mean 'that we have cured this cursed disease completely'. For if Hitlerism and fascism might 'lie in ruins … still much fascist venom remains in the hearts and minds of the people'. It was up to socialists to 'destroy and exterminate this venom', as 'it may spread again like an epidemic to the detriment of humanity'. The 'full moral reconstruction of society', therefore, 'just like the [material] reconstruction of the devastated country, constitutes one of the most important issues of the peacetime era'.[1]

The moral and psychological state in which European societies found themselves following the liberation has attracted increasing scholarly attention in recent years. For the experience of war and occupation had left deep scars on public consciousness. In a situation where lawlessness reigned and extreme material shortages bred a spirit of self-preservation, lines between right and wrong were often blurred. This is what the French called the *système D* – the D standing for *débrouillard*, or resourcefulness – a system of mostly illegal exchanges and survival mechanisms that had come into being under the Vichy regime and continued into the post-war years.[2]

---

[1] xxvi Kongres (August 1945), AAN, PPS, 235/1-12, fos 34–5.
[2] Shannon Lee Fogg, *The Politics of Everyday Life in Vichy France: Foreigners, Undesirables, and Strangers* (Cambridge: Cambridge University Press, 2009), p. 6.

These were problems that governments across continental Europe were faced with, from the 'moral strike' which Italian society went on in the aftermath of the liberation[3] to the widespread looting that took place in post-war Poland.[4] Most of the academic work on the theme, however, has addressed the post-war moral crisis from the perspective of (restoring) public order.[5] Insofar as political movements are dealt with at all in such accounts, the moral reconstruction effort is associated rather with conservative and Christian forces than with such proverbial 'progressives' as socialists.[6]

This chapter aims to demonstrate that post-war reconstruction carried strong moral connotations for socialist parties all the same. According to socialist leaders in each of the four countries, the war had generated a profound moral crisis. This crisis came in many shapes and forms. In the first place, it had motivated many people to throw in their lot with fascists. Secondly, it had disoriented those social constituencies, women and youngsters in particular, with little or no experience of democratic politics. Thirdly, it had destroyed any form of (national) solidarity among a working class preoccupied with day-to-day survival. For all of their essentially similar laments about moral decay, the four parties actually understood fundamentally different things by moral reconstruction. For the Italian and Polish socialists, moral reconstruction carried acute political significance. In their view, only a ruthless purge of all those associated with fascism and a thorough moral re-education of society would do to prevent their countries from succumbing to fascism once again. If the Czechoslovakian social democrats and French socialists were far more relaxed about the overall political morality of their populations, they were certainly not about the unsavoury social and economic habits that the occupation had left within their societies. The chief purpose of moral reconstruction, from their perspective, was for socialists to regain control over the working class and roll back communist influence in public life in doing so. At the crossroads of socio-economic and political reconstruction, the question of moral reconstruction thus begins to reveal what really divided the four parties.

---

[3] Renzo De Felice, *Rosso e nero* (Milan: Baldini & Castoldi, 1995), p. 43.

[4] Marcin Zaremba, *Die grosse Angst. Polen 1944–1947: Leben in Ausnahmezustand* (Paderborn: Ferdinand Schöning, 2016), pp. 213–44.

[5] Richard Bessel, 'Establishing Order in Post-War Eastern Germany', *Past and Present*, Supplement 6 (2011), pp. 139–57.

[6] See e.g. Pieter Lagrou, *The Legacy of Nazi Occupation: Patriotic Memory and National Recovery in Western Europe, 1945–1965* (Cambridge: Cambridge University Press, 1999), pp. 144–56.

The Reckoning

For socialist leaders, the point of departure for the moral reconstruction effort was the purge of those people they held responsible for the lapse of morals in the first place. Among the parties represented within the post-war coalition governments, the socialists were frequently the most strenuous advocates of a full-fledged purge of all those associated with interwar fascism and/or the occupational regimes. This purge had to take place on three levels. First of all, it was to affect the socialist movement itself, with the past behaviour of party members or those seeking to (re-) join having to be beyond any conceivable reproach. Secondly, it was to bring to justice both fascist and collaborationist leaders and their underlings who had thus far managed to escape punishment. Thirdly, it was to usher in a sweeping clean-up of the state apparatus, where all those who had sustained the authoritarian, fascist, or occupational regimes had to be removed. While the four parties departed from a similar set of principles, though, differences between them quickly emerged, as the purge did not always proceed according to plan.

These differences were due in part to the fact that the shake-up at the top of public life was at the same time more severe and more widespread in post-war Eastern Europe. Many of the region's foremost collaborators decided not to await the arrival of the Red Army and to leave for the West in the final days of the war. Millions more ethnic Germans or Hungarians, whose ancestors had often lived in this part of Europe for centuries, were caught up in the forced population movements out of Czechoslovakia and Poland. And a significant number of those with nowhere to go fell prey to the 'wild retribution' that the new rulers did so little to stop during the first weeks and months of freedom.[7] On the face of it, therefore, the purge was swift as well as comprehensive in post-liberation Czechoslovakia and Poland.

The same could certainly not be said of retributive action in France and Italy. It did not take long for socialists in both countries to start expressing their perplexity at the sluggish pace and narrow scope of the purge. Little more than two months after the liberation of Milano, a letter to the local socialist press wondered 'which are the obscure forces that hinder the purge and justice'. Some of the 'prime culprits, instigators, and agents' of fascism,

---

[7] Benjamin Frommer, *National Cleansing: Retribution Against Nazi Collaborators in Postwar Czechoslovakia* (Cambridge: Cambridge University Press, 2005), pp. 33–62.

after all, had been able to 'escape scrutiny' and 'save their face' solely by virtue of having disowned Mussolini after the Allied landings of 1943.[8]

The redemption of those who only turned their back on fascism at the eleventh hour likewise caused profound commotion within the post-war SFIO. To 'repeated applause', SFIO Executive member Louis Noguères railed against those 'bastards who have voted for the Vichy Government [but] presently call themselves resisters' at a party meeting in Avion. The appointment as minister of state in the first De Gaulle government of Jules Jeanneney, the Radical who had been the speaker of parliament during the early stages of the occupation, attracted his particular condemnation. He criticised De Gaulle for claiming that all that counted was what people thought today, not what they had thought on 10 July 1940 – when a parliamentary majority had granted Phillippe Pétain full powers. 'I will never tolerate them [erstwhile Vichy supporters]', Noguères concluded, 'because they have committed treason and should be removed from French political life.' That was 'a point on which we cannot compromise'.[9]

This intransigence about eliminating all those tainted by fascism from political office was one question on which socialists leaders and their rank and file did see eye to eye. The 'problem of the purge', Daniel Mayer explained to the first post-war congress of the SFIO, 'is a problem that distresses us all'. Socialist leaders, therefore, had warned the government that there was 'a barrier between the government and the people of this country, and that barrier has been there for too long: it concerns this entire Vichy administration which still remains in its place within certain ministerial departments'.[10]

Having refused to join the second Bonomi government, the Italian socialists went further in their denunciations of the purge. Bonomi himself, already 'compromised by fascism' (when he served as prime minister in 1921–22, Bonomi had given the fascist squads free rein), Lelio Basso pointed out, was hardly 'the man most suitable' for making 'a clean break with the fascist past'. Worse, 'the reactionary clique of [Raffaele] De Courten [one of the foremost navy commanders under Mussolini, who went on to serve as post-fascist Italy's navy minister between 1943 and 1946] and [Giovanni] Messe [who had been Mussolini's field marshal during the Second World

---

[8] Jaurey Capiluppi, 'Chi sono?' *Sesto Proletaria*, 12 July 1945.

[9] Commissaire du Police to Directeur des Reseignements Generaux (Réunion organisée par le Parti Socialiste à Avion), 20 February 1945, ADN, CRR, 19 W 37108 1.

[10] 'Parti Socialiste – SFIO: Congrès national extraordinaire des 9, 10, 11 et 12 novembre 1944', FJJ, p. 29. http://62.210.214.184/cg-ps/documents/pdf/cong-1944-11-09.pdf (last consulted: 27 June 2018).

War, and was appointed chief of staff of the Allied 'Co-Belligerent' Army shortly after the 1943 Italian armistice]' had made abundantly clear its 'intentions not to take a single step towards democracy, not to take seriously the purge, [and] to still tolerate fascism in many of its aspects'. This tolerance had not only allowed many former fascist leaders to 'continue to live undisturbed', but had also resulted in the 'very slow' and 'negligible' renewal of the diplomatic corps and the maintenance of 'a large part of the bureaucratic-police apparatus of fascism'.[11]

That the purge had to stretch well beyond the fascist elites and affect all foot soldiers who had placed themselves at their service was a principle that all four parties could agree on in theory. Yet they quickly parted company when it came to the practical implementation of this principle. For the PPS and the PSIUP, on the one hand, only a thorough cleansing of political life and the state apparatus would suffice, even if that meant violating due constitutional process in the short term. The ČSSD and the SFIO, on the other hand, increasingly came to view the purge itself as the problem, abused as it was by the communists to fight personal and political vendettas.

This divergence between the two sets of parties already manifested itself in the attitudes they took towards their own organisations. To be sure, socialist leaders in each of the four countries were adamant that there was no way back for members who had in any way collaborated with fascists. The SFIO expelled all ninety socialist parliamentarians who had voted for Pétain in 1940, even those who built up an impeccable Resistance record later on,[12] while also showing no mercy to popular local leaders who had initially thrown in their lot with Vichy.[13] The argument for excluding numerous pre-war socialist leaders, united in the WRN Resistance organisation, from the post-war PPS went back even further. Their 'crimes' originated in the interwar years, when they had failed to mobilise against the 1926 Piłsudski coup d'état and acquiesced in the authoritarian 1935

---

[11] Lelio Basso, 'Atene e Roma', *Avanti!*, 10 January 1945. www.leliobasso.it/documento.aspx?id=0b0bd 04f656ede422e35133bb6b38305 (last consulted: 27 June 2018).

[12] For discussions of the various 'cases', see the protocols of the November 1944 extraordinary SFIO congress: 'Parti Socialiste – SFIO: Congrès national extraordinaire des 9, 10, 11et 12 novembre 1944', FJJ, pp. 256–80. http://flipbook.archives-socialistes.fr/index.html?docid=49328&language=fra&use rid=0 (last consulted: 27 June 2018).

[13] During a reunion of the SFIO in Lille's Mons-en-Baroeul district, a 'clamour' developed after the declaration that one Mr De Goedt had been excluded from the party. The meetings's president was implacable, however, reading out a March 1941 letter in which De Goedt had praised Pétain. Commissaire du Police Godec to Commissaire Regional de la République à Lille, 26 January 1945, ADN, CRR, 19 W 37108 2.

Constitution. The 'fundamental criterion' by which the post-war PPS ought to condemn WRN leaders, insisted Henryk Wachowicz therefore, was that they had 'collaborated with Polish fascism'.[14]

But if socialist leaderships were united in their desire to take resolute action against (former) party representatives blemished by collaboration, however short-lived or atoned for, the political purge quickly took on a different meaning for the four parties. PPS and PSIUP leaders remained essentially inward-looking, obsessed with keeping anyone whom they considered a former fascist or collaborator from their parties. The PSIUP initially barred all erstwhile members of Mussolini's PNF from joining – a truly 'draconian' measure given that membership in that organisation had almost become a prerequisite for finding a job in the latter days of fascism.[15] PPS leaders likewise made it quite clear that 'we do not want to see people who have placed themselves at the service of Hitlerism in our ranks',[16] as repeated campaigns to 'verify' the past allegiance of party members attested to.[17]

The Czechoslovakian social democrats and the French socialists had far fewer qualms about the political righteousness of their own rank and file, but rapidly started worrying about the kind of people their communist rivals took in. As early as June 1945, Vincent Auriol – the socialist speaker of the French National Assembly – warned his colleagues in the SFIO Executive that the PCF was recruiting 'intensively' and 'indiscriminately', quoting examples of former *pétainistes* or *miliciens* (members of the para-military militias upon which the Vichy regime had relied to fight the Resistance) bribing their way into the shelter of PCF membership.[18] Similar reports were reaching the ČSSD leadership. In what was certainly not an isolated case,[19] there was much discontent over communist protection of and support for 'some bad people' in rural Bořetice (near the Austrian border) – even prompting a dozen or so local communists to defect to the ČSSD.[20]

---

[14] 'Protokół posiedzenia Komisje Programowo-Statutowej' (15 June 1945), PPS, xxvi Kongres, 295/1-7, fos 3–7.

[15] Mattera, *Storia del PSI*, pp. 133–4.

[16] 'Zebrania Koła P.P.S. przy f-mie Scheibler i Grochman' (27 April 1947), APŁ, DK PPS Śródmieście Lewa, 13, fo. 35.

[17] See the reports of the party's 'Commission for Verification' at both the 1945 and 1947 congresses of the PPS: xxvi Kongres (August 1945), AAN, PPS, 235/1-12; xxvii Kongres (December 1947), AAN, PPS, 235/1-25.

[18] OURS, CD SFIO, 14 June 1945.

[19] For even in parliament the KSČ found itself accused of sheltering former collaborators. See Frommer, *National Cleansing*, p. 320.

[20] Župní Sekretariát ČSSD Brno to Blažej Vilím, 1 September 1946, Archiv ČSSD, Fond 71, Karton 200, fo. 456.

Nowhere were such 'bad people' more prominent, as far as the ČSSD and the SFIO were concerned, than in the communist-controlled security forces doing the dirty work of purging. The French socialists were particularly apprehensive of the so-called 'patriotic militias', armed Resistance bodies that had outlived the war, attracted many 'belated "resisters"', and carried out searches, arrests, and even executions.[21] At the first post-war SFIO congress, several speakers complained bitterly about the patriotic militias. Having seen their ranks swell exponentially through the post-liberation entry of 'fifth columnists', of former members of the fascist French Popular Party, and of erstwhile Gestapo informants, the militias had in many places grown into 'no more than a bunch of gangsters'. What was more, the communist command of these gangs often rendered them 'an instrument in the hands of a political party'.[22] In unison with their non-communist coalition partners, therefore, the socialists insisted that the militias be disbanded and give way to a regular police force under state control.

Even if the security services were firmly under state control in post-war Czechoslovakia, the ČSSD found itself facing the same problems in many ways. For under the iron rule of communist interior minister Václav Nosek, the police force was slowly but surely being purged of all non-communist officers and increasingly being employed to fight the political battles of the KSČ. Much like the French socialists, the Czechoslovakian social democrats were thus quick to grow wary of those communist-led forces, containing all sorts of unreliable people, that were in charge of the purge. Defending his record at the November 1947 ČSSD congress, Zdeněk Fierlinger conceded that the National Security Corps (SNB), the umbrella organisation under which both the regular police and the infamous political police operated, had initially been made up of a motley crew of employees of the pre-war and Protectorate security services, former partisans and ex-servicemen, as well as a variety of 'adventurers'. Yet his protestations that the SNB had now been cleansed of those 'unwanted elements who had frequently entered it with the help of their party cards' seem to have fallen on deaf ears.[23] For the ČSSD annual report for 1947,

[21] Jean-Jacques Becker, *Histoire politique de la France depuis 1945* (Paris: A. Colin, 1996), p. 7.
[22] See the speeches of Daniel Mayer (p. 30), Gaston Defferre (pp. 53–4), Fournier (p. 80), Espinasse (p. 101), and Brourdet (p. 103), at the November 1944 extraordinary congress of the SFIO: 'Parti Socialiste – SFIO: Congrès national extraordinaire des 9, 10, 11 et 12 novembre 1944', FJJ. http://62.210.214.184/cg-ps/documents/pdf/cong-1944-11-09.pdf (last consulted: 27 June 2018).
[23] 'The Mission of Social Democracy in the New State' (November 1947), ANM, Fonds Zdeněk Fierlinger, Karton 40, Sjezd soc. dem. v Brne.

published after the party congress had ousted Fierlinger as secretary general, concluded that the 'complaints that keep piling up' about the 'excessive political manipulation' and 'the abuse of the security apparatus' were 'unfortunately justified'.[24]

If the Czechoslovakian social democrats and French socialists felt that public security left much to be desired, their countries were still islands of peace compared with the utter lawlessness that reigned supreme in post-liberation Italy and Poland. The historiography of both countries tends to describe the period between roughly 1943 and 1947 as a civil war, during which communist-led forces took on various nationalist and/or rightist groupings in bloody struggles fought primarily outside the main urban centres.[25] In these civil wars, the allegiance of the PPS and PSIUP lay squarely with the communist camp. In fact, for the Italian and Polish socialists, the threat to public security emanated first and foremost from the Right.

The PSIUP often identified this threat with the state security forces. Already in July 1944, Pietro Nenni had expressed his concerns at 'reactionary' efforts to place the police and the army at the service of the monarchy and the Right. And even when the Italian Left was at the height of its power under the Parri government, Nenni had to acknowledge that it remained 'very difficult to completely eliminate certain forces that have survived the fascist disaster: the army, policemen, etc.'.[26] Once the Left started to lose ground over the following years, these fears seemed to be confirmed. As former partisans were systematically driven out of the state security services after Mario Scelba had taken over as interior minister in February 1947, the Italian socialists increasingly came to see the police as an arm of the DC – especially in the rural south. In the run-up to the April 1948 elections, Sandro Pertini complained that the police had done nothing when a Popular Front rally in Brindisi had been drowned out by a loudspeaker that was 'spouting insults' from the local DC headquarters. Apparently, he noted, 'the police only intervenes to protect the rallies of government parties'. Worse, there was a pattern of police intimidation in the Puglia region, of which Pertini had gathered 'direct knowledge' during his stay in Brindisi. Following up 'in an absolutely disproportionate

---

[24] *Zpráva o činnosti Československé Sociální Demokracie k XXI. řádnému sjezdu v Brně 14.–16. XI. 1947* (Prague: Československá Sociální Demokracie, 1947), p. XLVIII.

[25] On Poland: Anita Prazmowska, *Civil War in Poland 1942–1948* (Basingstoke: Palgrave Macmillan, 2004). On Italy: Claudio Pavone, *Una guerra civile: saggio storico sulla moralità nella Resistenza* (Turin: Bollati Boringhieri, 1991).

[26] 'Comitato Centrale' (17 October 1945), ACS, Carteggio Nenni, Busta 87, Fasc. 2189, p. 18.

manner' on arrest warrants that were issued all the way back in October and November 1947, he recounted, 'hundreds and hundreds of policemen' had been 'forcing doors with the butt of their rifles' without having so much as a search warrant. The city of Gravina, one of the Left's strongholds in the south, found itself 'in a state of siege'. But 'terror' was reigning across the region, leaving people with 'the impression of being confronted with punitive fascist expeditions'.[27]

PPS leaders were much alarmed too by the 'intimidating situation' created by 'terrorist gangs' roaming the forests and countryside of post-war Poland.[28] This often denoted the anti-communist organisations that had their roots in the wartime Polish underground, most notably Freedom and Independence (WiN) and the National Armed Forces (NSZ), and were engaged in guerrilla warfare with Polish and Soviet security forces. Much like the PSIUP, the PPS was quick to identify these organisations with its right-wing political rivals. '[R]eactionary-fascist elements', read a March 1946 resolution of the party's Central Executive Committee, were striving 'to anarchise economic life and political relations and thereby undermine the foundations of the democratic system in Poland'. Some of these 'illegal reactionary-fascist organisations', it went on, were now throwing their weight behind the PSL. The NSZ and the WiN, for example, had declared 'their backing and support for the PSL in the elections, instructing their members in that spirit, [and] organising special terrorist gangs to that end'.[29]

Unlike their Italian counterparts, though, PPS leaders did view the state security services as an ally in the struggle against this purported fascist danger. That the security services in post-war Poland indulged in abuses far greater than those in Czechoslovakia or Italy, including mass round-ups, torture, and summary executions, was a price they were willing to pay. To be sure, there was criticism that the security forces were dominated by communists, were frightening the population by chasing non-existent conspiracies, and were creating discontent by arresting workers.[30] On the whole, however, the PPS leadership justified the violent and repressive methods that the security services used as a necessary evil. In a congress

[27] 'Comitato Centrale d'intesa per la libertà elletorale' (10 March 1948), Fondazione Nenni, Rome (hereafter FN), Carteggio Nenni, Busta 47, Fasc. 2034.
[28] 'Protokół z posiedzenia CKW-PPS' (2 March 1946), AAN, PPS, CKW, 235/iii/2, fo. 28.
[29] 'Uchwała Centralnego Komitetu Wykonawczego' (2 March 1946), AAN, PPS, CKW, 235/III/2, fos. 30–5.
[30] 'Protokół z wspólnego posiedzenia CKW PPS i KC PPR' (28 September 1945), AAN, PPS, CKW, 235/III/6, fo. 28.

speech that won the special acclaim of the party leadership, PPS Supreme Council member Kazimierz Dębnicki bemoaned the 'oppositional relics' that still shaped the attitudes that rank-and-file socialists took towards the security services. 'We know that there are transgressions [and] crimes, that there are improper [and] irresponsible people [within the security services]', he acknowledged, 'but we must not lose sight of the most important issue: that there is not only the reaction in Poland, that there are not only malcontents, but that the counter-revolution is around us.' Instead of complaining about the security services, therefore, local and provincial party branches 'should send activists, capable people' to reinforce their ranks. For the security apparatus constituted 'a critical protection of our young people's democracy'.[31]

The PPS leadership hoped to promote grassroots participation not only in the struggle with but also in the prosecution of the enemies of 'People's Poland'. During a meeting with representatives of the Łódź provincial PPS, prime minister Osóbka-Morawski responded positively to a request for popular tribunals to be convened, indicating that he had already instructed the ministry of justice to draw up the relevant decrees.[32] The PSIUP shared this preference for popular tribunals. In late 1944, Nenni wrote that the popular masses desired 'justice more than bread'.[33] Thus far, however, the 'bureaucratic organisation' of the purge had allowed King Victor Emmanuel to 'spend his days in peace' and Pietro Badoglio to 'play bocce ball in Rome'. According to Nenni, Italy would do better to follow the example of France in this regard, where post-war retribution lay in the hands of revolutionary 'people's courts' – a reference to the makeshift popular tribunals, the members of which had often been hand-picked by the communist-dominated liberation committees, that handed out so many death sentences during the 'wild purge' that engulfed France in the immediate aftermath of the liberation. For while he acknowledged that the whims of such courts might result in the occasional innocent man spending a couple of days or weeks in prison, that was still better than 'a Nazi-fascist criminal' being at large.[34]

If the Italian and Polish socialists relished the prospect of popular tribunals, the Czechoslovakian social democrats and French socialists rapidly grew disenchanted with the reality of popular involvement in

---

[31] XXVI Kongres (August 1945), AAN, PPS, 235/1-12, fos 233–4.
[32] 'Protokul z posiedzenia Egzekutywy WK. PPS' (28 August 1945), AAN, Fonds Henryk Wachowicz, 5 WK PPS.
[33] Pietro Nenni, 'La volontà del paese', *Avanti!*, 26 October 1944.
[34] Pietro Nenni, 'Lezione di un processo', *Avanti!*, 23 December 1944.

the purge. As early as April 1945, Robert Coutant was pointing towards 'defects' in the newly created Courts of Justice – which had come into being in the autumn of 1944 to replace the revolutionary people's courts, but the juries of which were still (co-)selected by the liberation committees. Juries 'know nothing of the case before them', he lamented, 'and they are overly influenced by the testimonies of "resisters", which … have often been bought, and by the arguments of counsel.' After citing local examples of juries adopting 'a wrong opinion' on cases, he called for the establishment of military courts 'to mitigate this shortcoming'.[35]

The Czechoslovakian social democrats were likewise quick to develop second thoughts about the Extraordinary People's Courts, the popular tribunals that had been established in the wake of the liberation to prosecute 'Nazi criminals, traitors, and their accomplices'. Operating at the regional level, the decisions of these courts were repeatedly challenged by such communist-dominated bodies as factory councils or national committees. When the mandate of the Extraordinary People's Courts came up for renewal in May 1946, the ČSSD parliamentary group was already voicing reservations about popular justice. It agreed to vote for the mandate of the courts to be extended by a year, therefore, 'only under the condition that this would definitely be their final term and that all unfinished cases will be referred to ordinary courts'.[36] And after popular retribution had in fact come to an end by May 1947, much against the wishes of the communists, an editorial in the national ČSSD weekly observed that it was 'high time already' for the Extraordinary People's Courts to be wound down.[37]

This desire to return to judicial normality as quickly as possible must be seen in the light of communist endeavours to politicise the legal settlement of the purge. The ČSSD expressed serious misgivings over the communist-inspired agitations and strikes after the National Court, established to prosecute the most prominent Czech collaborators, handed lenient sentences to five former protectorate ministers in July 1946. For even if the social democrats had 'made no secret' of their feelings that the sentences were 'disproportionally low', they could not agree with attempts 'to overturn a verdict of the National Court by means of demonstrations'. The National Court, after all, was 'a popular tribunal' too, 'in which six lay judges, all

---

[35] Commissaire de Police to Directeur des Reseignements Generaux (Réunion socialiste à Marly), 6 April 1945, ADN, CRR, 19 W 37108 2.

[36] *Zpráva o činnosti*, p. XL.

[37] Jiří Veltruský, 'Očista, která nebyla ještě provedena', *Cíl*, 23 May 1947.

victims of Nazi persecutions, were represented alongside one professional judge'. Its verdict, moreover, was in line with the Great Retributive Decree that the Czechoslovakian government had adopted in the revolutionary period immediately after the liberation. To 'tread upon revolutionary laws that we have enacted ourselves', the ČSSD warned, 'could jeopardise the further effectuation of the purge as no one would dare to become member of a tribunal ... when its decisions are not respected.'[38]

In remarkably similar terms, the French socialists denounced the PCF's response when the communists failed to get their way in the trial of several Vichy admirals that took place over the summer of 1946. Cases against the ministers and high functionaries of the Vichy regime were tried by the High Court of Justice, the juries of which were selected from parliamentarians. After the charges against one of the admirals were dropped on account of his poor health, however, communist deputies began boycotting jury selection in protest. As the law that had instituted the High Court of Justice stipulated that all of its juries were to reflect the parliamentary balance of power in a proportional manner, this rendered jury selection impossible altogether – leaving its socialist president, Louis Noguères, with no choice but to release all defendants under the Universal Declaration of Human Rights. At the August 1946 SFIO congress, Noguères hit back at the anti-socialist press campaign that the PCF unleashed over this affair. 'The party and me', he argued, 'consider it wrong not to respect a law one has voted for.' What was to 'become of the regime in France and of democracy', after all, 'when a party does not respect a law it has accepted'? The 'truth' was that the communist attitude was 'purely fascist'. For 'it is fascist to refuse to respect a law, to refuse to apply the law, and to want to impose another'.[39]

This point goes right to the heart of the distinction between the two sets of parties when it came to the purge. For the Czechoslovakian social democrats and the French socialists, on the one side, the reality of the purge quickly blurred the lines between fascism and communism. Both in the people they attracted and in the attitudes they adopted, the two ideologies increasingly came to represent two sides of the same coin in the opinion of the ČSSD and the SFIO. Yet, if the war had brought fascism to its knees, the two parties considered the threat posed by the anti-constitutional excesses that the communists were committing on a daily basis very real. For the Italian and Polish socialists, on the other side, the purge was part of

---

[38] *Zpráva o činnosti*, pp. xxxv–xxxvi.
[39] 'Parti Socialiste SFIO: 38ème Congrès national, 29, 30, 31 août et 1er septembre 1946', FJJ, pp. 297–8. http://62.210.214.184/cg-ps/documents/pdf/cong-1946-08-29.pdf (last consulted: 27 June 2018).

a much broader and ongoing struggle against fascism. In this struggle, they regarded the communists, with their armed forces and their revolutionary fervour, as an indispensable partner. To be sure, the PPS and the PSIUP granted that the communists often overstepped constitutional boundaries during the purge, but in the civil wars that were raging in their countries the constitution was out of the window anyway. The point was rather to broaden and democratise the anti-fascist struggle by animating as many ordinary people as possible to participate in it.

Reorienting the Disoriented

A similar set of beliefs informed the widely divergent approaches that the four parties took towards the second task they set themselves in the moral reconstruction effort: to straighten out and take by the hand those social constituencies that had been left disoriented by the fascist experience. In this respect, socialist leaders fretted about 'declining morals' among two groups in particular. In the first place, they often lectured women for having their priorities all wrong. Secondly, they repeatedly scolded youngsters for their depraved behaviour. Behind these essentially similar laments, however, went entirely different motivations for wanting to reorient women and youngsters. The Italian and Polish socialists, on the one hand, were driven primarily by broader political concerns. They hoped to strengthen democracy by immunising these vulnerable and impressionable groups against the temptations of the anti-democratic Right. The Czechoslovakian social democrats and the French socialists, on the other, were driven largely by more narrow electoral concerns. They were not so much striving to win women and youngsters for democracy as to make them vote for their parties. What accounted for the divergence between the two sets of parties, then, were deeper-seated beliefs about the social foundations upon which fascism had been built.

Women presented (overwhelmingly male) socialist leaders with a challenge in more than one way. We have already seen how women often dominated industrial protest during the first post-war years and how socialist leaders grappled with the bread-and-butter agenda that female workers formulated. This chasm between socialism and women was all the more problematic as the social consequences of the Second World War had handed women the key to election outcomes. For the much higher death toll among men as well as the predominantly male dislocation caused by military conscription and forced labour in the Reich meant that women significantly outnumbered men across post-liberation Europe.

The preponderance of women formed a major cause of concern for socialist leaders, who, all of their historical struggles for (male) universal suffrage notwithstanding, had often been ambivalent at best about female suffrage. In the late nineteenth and early twentieth centuries, many leading socialists had still dismissed female suffrage on the ground that women were irrational creatures, who stood under the influence of clerics and would be easy prey for Catholic and conservative parties come polling day.[40] Although socialist parties did embrace the cause of female suffrage during the first decades of the twentieth century, it remained anything but a priority and even France, with its proud republican traditions, only gave women the vote in 1945.[41] In fact, with women now fully enfranchised, lingering anti-women prejudices were quick to resurface among post-war socialist leaders. During a November 1944 meeting of the SFIO Executive, André Le Troquer, who was to become minister of the interior in the Gouin government, counselled his colleagues against calling elections any time soon for fears of the unpredictability of women voters. 'Without the counterweight of male prisoners [of war] and deportees', he warned, 'the female vote … might provide us with the greatest of surprises.'[42]

When the first post-war elections did not deliver the anticipated successes for socialists, accordingly, party leaders often pointed the finger at female voters. The Italian socialists attributed the Christian democratic victories in the 1946 and 1948 parliamentary elections to the pernicious influence that the Catholic Church exerted upon women.[43] Worse, the national daily of the SFIO, *Le Populaire*, repeatedly showed a 'barely disguised contempt' for female voters.[44] After the French socialists had suffered yet another disappointing result in the November 1946 parliamentary elections, for

[40] See e.g. James McMillan, *France and Women, 1789–1914: Gender, Society and Politics* (London/ New York: Routledge, 2002). On the prejudicial views on the role and place of women that Czech social democrats took during this period: Vít Strobach and Jan Mareš, 'Třída dělníků i žen? Proměny chápání genderových vztahů v českém dělnickém hnutí (1870–1914)', *Střed: Časopis pro mezioborová studia Střední Evropy 19. a 20. století*, 2 (2012), pp. 34–68. On how many of these views survived into the interwar years, see the essays in Helmut Gruber and Pamela M. Graves (eds.), *Women and Socialism, Socialism and Women: Europe between the Two World Wars* (New York: Berghahn Books, 1998).

[41] Italy likewise only introduced female universal suffrage after the Second World War. In Czechoslovakia and Poland, by contrast, women had already gained the vote after the First World War.

[42] OURS, CD SFIO, 22 November 1944.

[43] Anna Rossi-Doria, 'Italian Women Enter Politics', in Claire Duchen and Irene Bandhauer-Schöffmann (eds.), *When the War Was Over: Women, War and Peace in Europe, 1940–1956* (London/ New York: Leicester University Press, 2000), pp. 89–102, 95.

[44] Joan Tumblety, 'Responses to Women's Enfranchisement in France, 1944–1945', *Women's Studies International Forum*, 26/5 (2003), pp. 483–97, 488.

example, an editorial in the newspaper lamented that 'elections today hardly seem to interest anyone, especially women who, mostly, do not know what it is all about'.[45]

For socialist leaders, the female voter thus often represented the epitome of the misguided constituent, whose single-minded obsession with bread-and-butter issues had blinded her to the bigger political picture. In explaining the defeat of the yes camp in the May 1946 constitutional referendum, for instance, Mayer drew a sharp line between male and female no-voters. For whereas 'many men in rural areas' had voted no because they believed the political falsehoods that the no camp had been spreading about the constitution, he told an SFIO meeting in Cambrai, women who had rejected the constitution did so frequently because they were 'dissatisfied about *ravitaillement*'.[46]

The PPS leadership likewise observed that 'not all arguments that convince men strike a chord with the female psyche', listing education, care for mothers and children, social welfare, and labour protection for women among the 'issues which interest them above all'.[47] Yet socialist leaders had precious little to offer on such socio-economic questions as long as government funds had to be diverted primarily towards the reconstruction effort. Much like local and provincial leaders had done when confronted directly with the bread-and-butter grievances of (female) workers, therefore, national party leaders pointed women to the political achievements that supposedly made up for low living standards. In a mission statement that is very revealing about the way party leaderships thought about the kind of demands that women often put forward, the ČSSD undertook to politicise women. For 'if the woman has to decide over the fate of the state with her ballot paper, she must be politically conscious, deprived of all pettiness – then will she choose for democracy and for the path of socialist progress'.[48]

If each of the four parties set out to politicise women, though, their aims and methods in doing so were very different. For the Czechoslovakian social democrats and French socialists, it was all about broadening the appeal of their own parties. They were after the female vote first and

[45] Quoted in Claire Duchen, *Women's Rights and Women's Lives in France, 1944–1968* (London: Routledge, 1994), p. 36.

[46] 'Note de Renseignements' (Meeting organisé à Cambrai par le Parti Socialiste SFIO, avec le concours de Mr Daniel Mayer), 7 October 1946, ADN, CRR, 28 W 38454 2.

[47] 'Sprawozdanie na XXVII Kongres we Wrocławiu, 14–17 grudnia 1947 roku', AAN, PPS, XXVII Kongres, 235/1-27, fo. 43, p. 83.

[48] *Zpráva o činnosti*, p. 150.

foremost, and tailored their efforts to that end. After both of its election defeats in 1946, the SFIO leadership committed to stepping up its efforts to attract female voters by including more women on its electoral lists and reorganising socialist women's groups.[49] Such electoral concerns also took centre stage in the women's politics pursued by the ČSSD. Whereas the activity report that the party leadership put before its November 1947 congress much lauded the social democratic women's movement for its endeavours to make sure that female party members were to be found in 'all associations, corporations, companies, offices', it was quick to question the contribution that these endeavours had made to the overall fortunes of the ČSSD. For not only did it note that '[t]he results of this well-organised extra-party work are yet to be translated into party work', it also warned that such endeavours 'can never come at the expense of party work'.[50]

The objective of such party work among women was to portray socialism as the unrivalled champion of the female cause. In doing so, the Czechoslovakian social democrats and French socialists often dwelled on the successes that their parties had achieved during their interwar heyday. Speaking to local party members in Escaudain, Rachel Lempereur, the leader of the Socialist Women in the north of France, argued that women should vote for the SFIO because of its 'proven' track record on social affairs. 'It is thanks to the action of socialism that workers have gained certain ameliorations', she declared, quoting the law of forty hours, collective bargaining, and paid holidays as examples.[51] In the same vein, the post-war ČSSD made much of its interwar struggles to make the Czechoslovakian civil code more female-friendly, which had resulted in the right of divorce being granted in 1919. The next step was for women to become economically independent by enrolling in the labour force.[52] For that reason, the social democrats promised that women would be 'guaranteed the possibility of finding a job' in new legislation.[53]

For the Italian and Polish socialists, the socialist outreach to women was to serve altogether different than purely electoral purposes. In fact, the PSIUP leadership denounced as 'little socialist' the dismissive attitudes

---

[49] OURS, CD SFIO, 13 November 1946; 'Parti Socialiste SFIO – Conseil national du Palais de la Mutualité 9 juin 1946', FJJ.

[50] *Zpráva o činnosti*, p. 150.

[51] Commissaire du Police to Directeur des Reseignements Generaux (Réunion du Parti Socialiste à Escaudain), 17 January 1945, ADN, CRR, 19 W 37108 2.

[52] Melissa Feinberg, *Elusive Equality: Gender, Citizenship, and the Limits of Democracy in Czechoslovakia, 1918–1950* (Pittsburgh, PA: University of Pittsburgh Press, 2006), pp. 196–7.

[53] 'Ceny životních potřeb musí být lépe propočítány: Čs. sociální demokracie po pořádek ve státním hospodaření a pro zvýšení životní úrovně mešta i venkova', *Nový Den*, 5 February 1947.

that 'too many male comrades' took towards 'the participation of women in the political struggle'. All too often, it noted, 'the female contribution to that struggle is viewed only in function of the ballot paper'.[54] The prime aim for socialists, conversely, was to free women from political isolation by encouraging their direct involvement in grassroots participatory bodies. According to Basso, for example, socialist factory cells constituted a 'school of politics and socialism' for those women who did not dare to join their local PSIUP section 'for fear of the priest's reprisal'.[55] Far from instructing the rank-and-file activists in charge of this educative effort to harp on about the party's achievements, however, he urged them to take a 'nonsectarian' approach. For 'like we cannot expect to immediately make an illiterate appreciate *Divine Comedy* [Dante's most famous poem]', it could not be expected that hitherto 'apolitical' women would 'immediately convert to socialism'.[56]

The PPS also noted how 'work among women' encountered 'a series of obstacles, both technical [the difficulties in drawing women, as homemakers, into party meetings outside of working hours] and those stemming from the centuries of women's exclusion from political and social life'. Alongside the more traditional objectives of organising women within the party and addressing their most urgent social needs, therefore, the PPS Women's Council also set itself the goal of ensuring 'the most active participation of women in the build-up of a socialist system'. This involved not only 'the political and organisational education of women by means of discussion clubs', but also 'the promotion through women of the education of the youth in a socialist spirit'.[57]

The post-war morality of youngsters caused socialist leaders still more profound misgivings than that of women. For if the fascist and occupational regimes had merely prolonged the political disorientation of women, they had actively targeted the youth for indoctrination. At the local level, socialist activists and leaders frequently sounded the alarm over how the experience of dictatorship, war, and occupation had corrupted the young.

---

54 'Relazione sull'organizzazione femminile' (March 1947), Fondazione di Studi Storici Filippo Turati, Firenze (hereafter FFT), Partito socialista italiano (Psi) – Direzione nazionale, Serie 2: Circulari, Busta 1, fos 42–7.

55 Lelio Basso, 'Formazione dei quadri', *Avanti!*, 6 November 1945. www.leliobasso.it/documento.asp x?id=124c9327c1edc63b4e79a02654719c2e (last consulted: 27 June 2018).

56 Lelio Basso, 'Per una coscienza democratica', *Avanti!*, 29 August 1945. www.leliobasso.it/documento .aspx?id=1fb14f1db3eb10586206df1cbf448089 (last consulted: 27 June 2018).

57 'Sprawozdanie na XXVII Kongres we Wrocławiu, 14–17 grudnia 1947 roku', AAN, PPS, XXVII Kongres, 235/1-27, fo. 44, p. 84.

Fascism 'has polluted the conscience of youngsters', a socialist from Sesto San Giovanni wrote to the local PSIUP weekly, by 'diverting the minds of young people from the path of good sense and of humility'. This purported lack of morals found its reflection in the long list of perversions that local socialists in each of the four countries identified with the young, including alcohol abuse,[58] marauding,[59] prostitution,[60] and an attitude of desire for easy gain.[61] For that reason, party leaders should 'look after our youth', as one Łódź socialist put it, 'which is demoralised after the war'.[62]

If socialists in each of the four countries agreed that the war had brought on a serious moral crisis among youngsters, they were very much at variance over the depth of the political imprint that fascism had made on young minds. For the Czechoslovakian social democrats and French socialists, the ultimate democratic dependability of the youth was never really in question. To be sure, the SFIO leadership bewailed its losses among the young in the November 1946 parliamentary elections, but was quick to accept responsibility for these. The SFIO, after all, had failed to entice young voters with a proper offer, while 'the mystique' of working-class unity, which had still been a strong socialist attribute in the 1936 elections, had driven many youngsters to the communists this time around.[63]

For the Czechoslovakian social democrats, Fierlinger also affirmed that the youth was of sound political convictions. 'The occupier', he explained, 'has tried to subvert the spiritual foundations [of our youth] at the roots … to eradicate from Czech culture and history everything that binds us to the national tradition, to poison our youth with fascist venom, and to make of it a characteristic minion of the regime.' But this plan 'to Nazify the Czech youth', he insisted, had failed. For 'our youth has proven by its actions' – both by partaking in large numbers in the anti-German Prague uprising of May 1945 and by making up a significant part of the labour brigades that were deployed during the battle for production – 'that it has retained its healthy core'.[64]

[58] Jař. Průcha, 'Otevřte oči!' *Nový Den*, 30 August 1946.
[59] Kz, 'Není lehké být kacířem!' *Nový Den*, 3 April 1946.
[60] 'La section du Parti Socialiste de Marville et son action dans le domaine de la moralité publique' (2 August 1945), ADN, CRR, 19 W 37108 2.
[61] 'Note de Renseignements' (Réunion organisée par le Parti Socialiste à l'occasion du 40ème Anniversaire de fondation de la Fanfare Ouvrière de Saint-Amand), 25 August 1946, ADN, CRR, 28 W 38451 2.
[62] 'Protokól zebranie Koła PPS przy Państwowych Zakladach Przemysłu Wełnianego Nr. 1' (11 March 1947), APŁ, DK PPS Czerwona, 11, fo. 60.
[63] OURS, CD SFIO, 13 November 1946.
[64] 'My 46' (19 March 1946), ANM, Fonds Zdeněk Fierlinger, Karton 20, Projevy 1946.

All of their laments about moral degeneration among youngsters notwithstanding, therefore, the Czechoslovakian social democrats and French socialists very much believed that their democracies could build upon the young. The point was, then, to win over the youth to socialism in general and to their parties more specifically. In both countries, this involved strong competition with the communists, who dominated much of youth politics through such (officially non- or cross-party) transmission belt organisations as the Czechoslovakian Youth Union (ČSM) and the Union of the Republican Youth of France (UJRF). According to the Czechoslovakian social democrats, the ČSM had stood in the way of attempts to redress the 'weak position' among young voters from which the social democrats had suffered in the parliamentary elections of May 1946.[65] In fact, the ČSSD's Youth Commission complained that the guidelines of the ČSM, declaring a whole range of activities to be the special realm of that organisation, constituted an impediment to the creation of a proper social democratic youth movement and petitioned the ČSSD congress to address this question.[66]

Not bound by membership in any cross-party youth organisation, the SFIO had more latitude to pursue its own agenda among youngsters. As so often, its propaganda to this end took a distinctly anti-communist shape. The official youth organisation of the SFIO, the Young Socialists (JS), lent itself perfectly to this task. For the JS was led by radical activists of frequently Trotskyite inspiration, who took a very negative view of the moderation that the communists had practised in the wake of the liberation. To be sure, when a speaker of the JS addressed a pre-election rally in Feignies (on the border with Belgium), he attacked both the MRP youth organisations for serving the 'politics ... of the clergy' and the 'essentially communist' UJRF for placing 'the designs of a party ahead of the interests of the youth'. Yet it was only on the communist betrayal of the youth that he elaborated. Education should be free of cost until the age of eighteen, he explained, and should include a period of professional apprenticeship. The communists, however, were opposed to apprenticeships because they wanted 'to throw youngsters into the battle for production as quickly as possible without caring for their health and their faculties'. For that reason, he concluded, 'reasonable people agree with the socialists in condemning Stakhanovism'.[67]

[65] 'Čs. ústav pro výzkum veřejného mínění: Neúspěch sociální demokracie v květnových volbách' (1946), ANM, Fonds Zdeněk Fierlinger, Karton 40, Neúspěch soc. dem. ve volby, p. 6.

[66] *Zpráva o činnosti*, p. 151.

[67] 'Note de Renseignements' (Réunion électorale tenue par le Parti Socialiste SFIO à Feignies), 29 October 1946, ADN, CRR, 28 W 38454 2.

For the Italian and Polish socialists, on the other hand, the moral crisis afflicting youngsters was but a symptom of their political unsteadiness. Basso repeatedly mentioned women and youngsters in the same breath as social constituencies that had been left disoriented by the fascist experience.[68] Even among those youngsters flocking to the PSIUP, he lamented, there was 'a high percentage that certainly does not have an adequate class consciousness'. This included youngsters 'still paying involuntary tribute' to their fascist formation 'in the form of anti-communism', youngsters who had arrived at anti-fascism 'through sentimental impulses or vague humanitarian aspirations', and youngsters blind to the class antagonisms underlying political struggles.[69] In a similar vein, Nenni warned young workers in particular that the war-induced bankruptcy of fascism did not mean that the capitalist interests it had served had also been defeated. 'We have to foil', he declared, attempts to have people believe that 'fascism, from 1922 to 1939, represented a genuine effort of reconstruction ... and an endeavour to solve the problems of our country on the national and international level.'[70]

The leadership of the PPS was extremely concerned too about the fertile ground that fascism had supposedly found among youngsters. 'The bitter experience of five years has taught us', an outgoing secretary of one of the PPS youth organisations told the August 1945 party congress, 'that the youth can be a wing and a bulwark of fascism.'[71] When confronted with youth protests, therefore, the Polish socialists were very quick to attribute these to 'reactionary' stirrings. After the student demonstrations of 3 May 1946, on what had been the Constitution Day national holiday in pre-war Poland and was to become the focal point of anti-regime protests in 'People's Poland', Józef Cyrankiewicz expressed alarm at 'the mass base' that 'reactionary groups of students' had formed within 'schools, the scouts, etc.'. In its current state, he warned 'the academic youth could

[68] Lelio Basso, 'Per una coscienza democratica', *Avanti!*, 29 August 1945. www.leliobasso.it/documento. aspx?id=1fb14f1db3eb10586206dfcbf448089 (last consulted: 27 June 2018); Lelio Basso, 'Dall'unità antifascista all'unità democratica', Socialismo, July–December 1947. www.leliobasso.it/documento. aspx?id=71f4bb9f46ba9a75a822ea3d0197a90f (last consulted: 27 June 2018).

[69] Lelio Basso, 'Rifare il partito', *Quarto Stato*, 30 January 1946. www.leliobasso.it/documento.aspx?id =59ecaea94815ae9ec663887f321c04e4 (last consulted: 27 June 2018).

[70] 'Discorso Nenni, Segretario del Partito Socialista Italiano', ACS, Carteggio Nenni, Busta 87, Fasc 2186.

[71] XXVI Kongres (August 1945), AAN, PPS, 235/1-12, fo. 149.

provide us with a cadre of judges and prosecutors of the pre-war type'. It was necessary, therefore, to intervene vigorously in higher education: all academics that had participated in the demonstrations were to be expelled from universities and new professors should henceforth be appointed by the Senate only.[72] Such measures notwithstanding, the PPS leadership remained deeply anxious about youngsters' political mindset. The new order in Poland, Lucjan Motyka still had to concede at the December 1947 congress of the PPS, often met 'with much greater opposition among the youth than the older generation'. This was due, he argued, to 'the influence of nationalist-reactionary education in the pre-war and war years and a significant emotional deference to pseudo-patriotic platitudes'.[73]

The key to the widely divergent attitudes that the two sets of parties took towards women and youngsters thus lies in the severity of their countries' dictatorial experience. For the Italian and Polish socialists, on the one side, the moral and political re-education of women and youngsters, who had never or hardly known anything but dictatorship, was going to be a drawn-out process. Already in the 1930s, Basso had written that 'we must accomplish a long and slow penetration of ideas and of moral re-education, especially among the young'.[74] The PPS leadership, for its part, explained how the 'serious havoc' that the occupation had wrought on 'the morality and mental robustness of Polish society' was all the deeper as the Nazis had been thriving in the 'fertile ground prepared by the long years ... of the depraved methods of the Sanacja clique'.[75] For the Czechoslovakian social democrats and the French socialists, on the other side, the moral disorientation among women and youngsters was merely an unfortunate and temporary by-product of the occupation. There was no reason, therefore, to start from scratch in re-educating these groups. Whereas the SFIO insisted that 'the Third Republic has accomplished admirable work as regards schools',[76] after all, Bohumil Laušman even argued that 'the Czechoslovakian school has always been our pride'.[77]

---

[72] 'Protokuł posiedzenia Centralnego Komitetu Wykonawczego P.P.S.' (14 May 1946), AAN, PPS, CKW, 235/III/2, fo. 45.
[73] xxvii Kongres (December 1947), AAN, PPS, 235/1-25, fo. 180.
[74] Lelio Basso, 'Il Partito, ma in Italia', *Quaderni di Giustizia e Libertà*, June 1933. www.leliobasso.it/documento.aspx?id=c24f46ce9c7327085f4845df72727e26 (last consulted: 27 June 2018).
[75] 'Projekt Uchwała Programowa xxvi Kongresu', AAN, PPS, xxvi Kongres, 295/1-7, fo. 16.
[76] 'Programme d'Action du Parti Socialiste 1946', FJJ, p. 61.
[77] 'Protokol xx. Manifestačního Sjezdu Československé Socialní Demokracie', Archiv ČSSD, Fond 71, Část II, Karton III, p. 235.

The Morals of Labour

Up to this point, we have primarily discussed moral reconstruction from a political perspective. In this respect, there was a clear fault line between the two sets of parties. The PPS and PSIUP, on the one side, were deeply concerned about the vestiges that the experiences of authoritarianism and fascism had left in the hearts and minds of their populations. The ČSSD and SFIO, on the other, were far more sanguine that the social fabric of their countries had been able to withstand the fascist challenge. Things were often the other way around, however, when it came to the social and economic morals that fascism had instilled among ordinary workers. To be sure, each of the four parties insisted that the spirit of selfishness engendered by the wanton oppression and exploitation of the war years had to be replaced by a national solidarity as quickly as possible. Yet they found themselves much at odds over the origins and depth of socio-economic demoralisation. The Czechoslovakian social democrats and French socialists increasingly came to reproach the industrial working class for pursuing a narrow and self-interested agenda. For the Italian and Polish socialists, conversely, the moral crisis remained a middle-class phenomenon first and foremost. This was part of a broader debate about the social constituencies upon which democracy and socialism could draw, which will continue into the next chapters.

The socialist leaders who had spent the war in exile or foreign internment were often left much disillusioned by the societies they found upon their return. In the first major speech that Léon Blum delivered in post-liberation France, he stressed that 'the significance of the moral clean-up of this country cannot be overstated'. In the mere eight days that he had now spent in France, he had grown 'full of disappointment and concern in this regard'. For Blum had not found what he had expected. In fact, he was under the impression of finding himself in a 'corrupted' atmosphere. 'I get the feeling of a sort of tired convalescence, nonchalance, [and] laziness', he lamented, 'which constitutes an environment conducive to the development of all sorts of infections.'[78] According to the broader SFIO leadership, the divisive effects of the occupation were at the root of these moral shortcomings. For not only had the occupation dispersed the French population over a vast geographical area, it had also seen both 'virile' and 'reprehensible' habits leave their 'footprint on individuals'. If

---

[78] Léon Blum, *Les devoirs et les tâches du socialisme: Discours prononcé à la Conférence des Secrétaires de Fédérations Socialistes Paris, le 20 Mai 1945* (Paris: Éditions de la Liberté, 1945).

'the liberation has bit by bit brought together separated brethren', there-fore, 'the moral unity between them has not yet been re-created'.[79]

One of the worst manifestations of this lack of moral unity was what socialist leaders frequently described as 'regional selfishness'. With national steering all but non-existent during the final months of the war and the first months following the liberation, local and/or regional administrations had become the focal point of many vital provisions and services. Crucial as their activities may have been in keeping the population fed and produc-tion going, however, socialist leaders quickly came to resent the engrained localism or regionalism of such administrations as they struggled to enforce a national distribution system. Speaking about *ravitaillement* to socialists in the north of France, Coutant deplored 'the impervious walls' that prefects had erected between departments and called for sanctions against those 'not acting for the good of the collective'.[80] For the Plzeň ČSSD, meanwhile, Ivan Hollman complained that 'the required solidarity' was 'lacking altogether' among some local administrations. With 'narrow selfishness, indiscipline, [and] a view to [strengthening their] appeal', he argued, these administrations sought 'to improve supply in the area under their jurisdiction at the expense of other regions'.[81]

But the problems of regional selfishness definitely had their most lasting impact in post-war Italy. Even by mid-1946, Franco Mariani was still insisting on the need 'to combat regional and provincial egoism'. In the provision of milk, for example, some provinces did not have to ration at all, whereas a city like Genova was so desperately short of supply that, for three days every week, it could 'only give milk to the old and to babies, and many times [in the form of] half milk and half water'.[82] Such regional selfishness, moreover, was hardly confined to the unpurged provincial authorities. For even those grassroots bodies that sprang directly from the wartime Resistance, i.e. the revolutionary liberation committees and fac-tory councils that had taken over local and industrial administration in the wake of the war, often put the local ahead of the national. At the first congress of liberation committees in Milano province, Rodolfo Morandi attacked such grassroots bodies, otherwise much cherished by the Italian

---

[79] 'Le bilan de la situation à la libération', Arguments et Ripostes, Bulletin Intérieur du Parti Socialiste (S.F.I.O.), 1 May 1946, OURS.

[80] 'Réunion d'information socialiste à Pecquencourt' (23 July 1945), ADN, CRR, 19 W 37108 2.

[81] Ivan Hollman, 'Vyživovací věci', *Nový Den*, 31 January 1946. How much of a pan-European problem 'regional selfishness' was becomes still more clear by comparison with post-war Austria, where ministers repeatedly accused provincial governments of deliberately failing to fulfil their supply obligations. See: Lewis, *Workers and Politics*, p. 118.

[82] Interview Leonardi with Franco Mariani, AdL, Camera del Lavoro, Class. 5.1.3., Fasc. 4.

socialists (see Chapter 7), for acting as if their 'community and factories are separate entities'. Circumstances 'momentarily benefiting' the inhabitants of a local community or the workforce of a factory, he admonished, 'can worsen the living standards of the collective if they nullify the efforts aimed at restoring a common standard within society'. Morandi went on to list a long series of local infractions upon these efforts: 'allowing breaches in rationing discipline within communes because there are stocks, selling workers factory products under their price, and … a large company producing chemical fertilisers bartering in grain that should be delivered to the masses'. Liberation committees and factory councils, he concluded his criticism, 'have to consider themselves factors in the national reconstruction, elements of a unitary system in the interest of the people, not aggregates that isolate themselves from the collective'.[83]

As we have seen in Chapter 3, this desire to shift the orientation of the post-war working class away from their local community and towards the national collective united the four parties. Beyond the question of regional selfishness, however, they often took widely divergent views of the moral degeneration in social and economic life. These were linked intimately to their broader political outlook.

For the Czechoslovakian social democrats and French socialists, the post-war moral crisis often found its embodiment in the social and economic indiscretions of the working class and their local (communist) representatives. In a February 1946 article in the ČSSD national daily, Laušman gave the communist-dominated factory councils (see Chapter 7) a stark dressing-down. He insisted that the factory councils had to do more to make clear that there was a world of difference between the pre-war capitalist economy and the post-war nationalised economy. For workers in the nationalised sector had to understand that their economic well-being was linked to the prosperity of their firm. 'We have to approach the new social order as pristine, more sincere, and more virtuous people', he argued, and certainly not as 'liars, cowards, jerks, [or] pushovers'. Of late, however, the demeanour of the industrial working class had given him 'cause for concern'. Laušman went on to list five examples where factory managers and workers had placed their own sectional interests ahead of the collective good. These included the management of an unprofitable factory inciting its workforce to go on strike against a government decision to close the plant, bosses placed under government surveillance for mismanagement

[83] '1° congresso dei CLN Prov. di Milano' (1945), INSMLI, Fondo CLN Regionale Lombardia, Busta 17, Fasc. 94, p. 51.

urging their personnel to start a protest action, and anti-fraud inspectors being banished from a factory on the command of a 'political official' (frequently used as code for 'communist'). The 'new social order', concluded Laušman, 'requires respect for the law right from the minister of industry through any managing director and up to the last worker'. [84]

The SFIO often berated the working class for losing sight of the common good too. What its leaders described as 'corporatism', small groups of workers seeking sectional gain at the expense of the collective, became an increasing problem as the communist-dominated trade unions abandoned their erstwhile moderation over the course of 1947. Here too, employers often seemed willing to make common cause with worker corporatism, especially if it might serve their longer-term interests. [85]

Many of these factors played a part when Parisian press operators went on strike in February 1947, demanding that their salaries be linked to inflation. Already before the strike broke out, SFIO Executive member André Ferrat counselled forcefully against giving in to the demands of the press operators. 'We cannot allow', he insisted, 'that a tiny segment of the working class, whose wages are already high, is more concerned with its personal corporative interest than with that of the working masses.' He also warned his fellow party leaders 'that big business encourages the demands of press operators in order to take control of the press, particularly of the socialist press which is in danger [as it was experiencing severe financial difficulties]'. [86] When the strike did occur, accordingly, the SFIO leadership was unanimous in denouncing it as 'unjustified'. Mayer was especially scornful of the rank-and-file socialists who had partaken in the strike. 'Because they are members of the Socialist Party', he argued, 'they have additional duties.' But rather than seeking the counsel of the SFIO Executive before going on strike, they had undermined 'worker's action and the labour movement [by] impeding the [anti-inflationary] politics of the Government'. The (socialist) press operators, Mayer concluded, had demonstrated 'their inability to rise to the level of the Nation. They are not practising syndicalism, but corporatism.'[87]

[84] Bohumil Laušman, 'Slovo do pranice, ale …', *Právo Lidu*, 17 February 1946.
[85] This is what Victor Provo, member of the SFIO Executive and mayor of Roubaix, seemed to suggest when, after complaining about corporatism and noting how employers and trade unions were in agreement that performance bonuses should be increased, he argued that there was now 'a set of circumstances to defeat [the government's] politics of a price drop'. OURS, CD SFIO, 16 June 1947.
[86] OURS, CD SFIO, 29 January 1947.
[87] OURS, CD SFIO, 19 February 1947.

If the Czechoslovakian social democrats and French socialists regularly decried workers for their self-centredness, the Polish and Italian socialists identified this trait first and foremost with the (lower) middle classes. According to the PPS leadership, these groups had exhibited 'a particularly low level of social awareness' in failing to understand that their 'objective' interests united them with other groups 'opposed to the capitalist system'. What is more, middle-class 'aversion to productive work', their 'search of an easy income through secret trade or scalp', and their 'pointless, malignant, and thereby detrimental criticism of the social efforts to rebuild the state apparatus', were all 'characteristic phenomena of the current moral crisis'.[88]

The PSIUP was very much alive to the political implications of such artificial socio-economic barriers between the classes. For fascism might have been the 'the political superstructure of the interests of monopolistic capitalism', Nenni wrote, 'the typical fascist ... is the educated supervisor horrified at the idea of being a white-collar proletarian who firmly believes in the paternalistic function of the middle classes'.[89] With such people continuing to resist their inevitable proletarianisation, he approvingly quoted Action Party theorist Guido Dorso, the dictatorship of the proletariat had now become a necessity from a Marxist point of view.[90]

The ČSSD, conversely, was soon to grow wary of the dictatorial action that the proletariat was undertaking against middle management. Six weeks into the liberation, Laušman called for 'peace' to 'finally' return to factory life. The purge, he insisted, 'must come to an end in order for labour, which has to turn the Republic into a happy home for all working people, to become a joy'.[91] What seems to have underlain this desire to halt the industrial purge so abruptly was the party's growing belief that it was being abused by workers and their communist enablers. In Plzeň, for example, the ČSSD objected to the KOR's proposal to remove one engineer, Josef Šmolík, from the management at the city's waterworks. The complaints against him, as the KOR readily acknowledged, were 'not of a political nature', but concerned his 'aggression and morbid ambition'. Josef Janouš refused to accept these as sufficient grounds for dismissal, however. 'The current purge of traitors and occupiers from all companies does not mean', he remonstrated, 'that those people who are not guilty of

[88] 'Projekt Uchwała Programowa XXVI Kongresu', AAN, PPS, XXVI Kongres, 295/1-7, fo. 16.
[89] Pietro Nenni, 'Le classi nella lotta per la democrazia', *Avanti!*, 11 August 1944.
[90] Pietro Nenni, 'Paura borghese', *Avanti!*, 4 February 1945.
[91] 'Ministr průmyslu dr. Laušman: V závodech musí býti již konečně zjednán klid. Očišťovací akce musejí už jednou skončit', *Nový Den*, 22 June 1945.

anything, but have been appointed as director and are forced to execute various commands, should also go.' Instead of 'benefiting it', after all, that would 'only hurt the public economy'.[92]

Although the SFIO did call for a more strenuous cleansing of the industrial apparatus, its main focus, as per usual, was to attack the communists for undermining these efforts. 'The purge of the mines has been compromised by the communists', Augustin Laurent told a party meeting in Cambrai, 'who have given important posts to formerly collaborationist engineers.'[93] During the October 1946 election campaign, this row went public, as Laurent exchanged open letters with Léon Delfosse, the communist leader of the CGT in the mines of the north. After Delfosse had accused Laurent's 'very close friend' Francis-Louis Closon – appointed by De Gaulle as regional commissioner of the Republic for the north of France after the liberation – of saving several 'less marked' collaborators from the purge, Laurent hit back at the communist role in the inadequate purge of the mines. '[M]ore than Closon', he argued, 'Marcel Paul [the PCF's minister of industrial production], [Auguste] Lecoeur [the PCF's under-secretary of state for the mines], [and] Delfosse [alongside his trade union role also the vice-president of the nationalised mines in the Nord-Pas-de-Calais region] … are the masters of the situation.' But 'not only do they not purge', they wanted to place 'culprits … in the highest posts in the hierarchy of the most important nationalised sector'.[94]

For the Italian socialists, though, the industrial purge had to cut far deeper than that. Writing to Nenni, PSIUP parliamentary deputy Giovanni Tonetti recounted the indignation among workers in his Veneto constituency over the leniency meted out to thirty-two of their collaborationist colleagues. This group, which included former squad members, had first been suspended with pay and now, under new dispositions, had to return to the workforce. 'Workers say', Tonetti wrote, 'at [the ministry of] justice there is Togliatti, at [the Commission for] the Purge we have Nenni, [and Mauro] Scoccimarro [the PCI's finance minister in the Parri and first two De Gasperi governments] is there for the confiscation of the profits of the [fascist] regime, and yet nothing concrete and satisfactory has been done thus far.' It 'is all fine to tell [workers] that our comrades in Government do what they can, not what they would want, that the

---

[92] 'Schůze Národního výboru' (19 July 1945), AMP, Zápisy o schůzich Národního Výboru a rady Okresního Národního Výboru a Místního Národního Výboru statutárního města Plzeň 1945.
[93] 'Note de Renseignements' (Activité du Parti Socialiste SFIO (réunion privée)), 16 September 1946, ADN, CRR, 28 W 38453 2.
[94] Augustin Laurent, 'Ma réplique à une "Lettre ouverte"' (October 1946), ADN, CRR, 28 W 38454 2.

presence of representatives of the bourgeois reaction in Government [and] the obstructionist action of the intact bureaucratic apparatus creates a situation in which the socialist and communist presence in Government does not allow for the positive work of repressing fascism, but is limited to preventing the installation of a reactionary capitalist-militaristic regime', he continued, 'but they remain perplexed'.[95]

Conclusion

We have seen in this chapter that post-war reconstruction had a strong moral dimension for each of the four parties. Yet the parties had a fundamentally different understanding of the aims and content of moral reconstruction. For the Italian and Polish socialists, on the one side, moral reconstruction was crucial from a political point of view. In their view, the purge had to be severe and the re-education of disoriented groups thorough to fully cleanse post-war society of everything associated with fascism. If the working class, or the political parties representing the working class, were forced to take recourse to radical or even violent measures to see this cleansing effort through, that was to be accepted. For the Czechoslovakian social democrats and French socialists, on the other side, moral reconstruction was mainly of social and economic significance. They were by and large confident that their societies, after an initial purge of the foremost collaborators, could pick up where they had left off before the occupation. For this to happen, though, the socio-economic vices that had outlived the war and that were being fostered by the increasingly unruly communists had to be eliminated as soon as possible.

On a broader level, the three chapters on social and economic reconstruction have dispelled some of the more persistent myths about the post-war continental socialist parties. There is still a tendency in much work to take a romantic view of the continental socialists, who, programmatically and rhetorically at least, were much to the left of the communists during the crucial period between 1944 and 1947. Softer on the working class yet sterner on the purge, the socialist parties were then more in tune with the radical spirit supposedly engulfing Europe in the aftermath of the Second World War. The last three chapters have clearly demonstrated that such claims are based in large part on anecdotal evidence and come undone under closer scrutiny. As we have seen, after all, there was often a deep gulf between socialist elites and their grassroots in the very approach to

[95] Tonetti to Nenni, 1946, FN, Carteggio Nenni, Busta 44, Fasc. 2025.

the reconstruction effort: national versus local, performance-based versus egalitarian, and high politics versus everyday concerns. Far from being uniquely in step with the popular masses, moreover, the socialist parties managed to alienate many of the newcomers to industrial and political life. It was the lack of support among these groups that accounts for much of the socialist weakness in post-war continental Europe.

If the four parties experienced similar difficulties in coming to terms with post-war society in general and the post-war working class more specifically, the contours of their very different remedies have already become clear. For the Italian and Polish socialists, on the one side, the impetus for industrial, moral, and ultimately democratic renewal had to come from the bottom up. In their view, the key to the regeneration of society, after decades of dictatorship had ushered in widespread apathy, lay in more direct popular participation in political struggles. To that end, the two parties set out to draw as many ordinary workers and rank-and-file party members (or sympathisers) as possible into participatory structures at the local level. The Czechoslovakian social democrats and French socialists, on the other side, conceived of social and economic reconstruction as a top-down process. Their prime aim was to ensure a rapid return to industrial and political normality: ordinary workers had to know their place and their duties, and it had to be made clear to voters that socialism had their best interests at heart. To achieve this, the two parties became increasingly convinced that they had to confront head-on the poisonous influence that the communists were exerting at the factory and local level. These divergences between the two sets of parties were closely linked to their conceptions of democracy, to which we will now turn our attention.

CHAPTER 5

The Lessons of the Past

By late 1945, the schism that would tear post-war Italian socialism apart was beginning to take shape. Having been accused by some of the party's future secessionists of subordinating the PSIUP to the PCI, Pietro Nenni rejected their claims that 'Italy would be the only country in Europe where there is no great socialist party'. It was all fine for Giuseppe Saragat to argue that the socialists led the government in Belgium, he told the PSIUP Executive, '[b]ut that was also the case before the war and they have regained a position that is in certain respects analogous to that'. In fact, across the continent 'we are witnessing a resumption of situations that already existed before. In Norway, the socialists were in power and have returned. In Sweden, they were in power and have remained'. It could not be held against the PSIUP, he argued, that 'the situation [for socialist parties] is more favourable in other countries'. For the Italian socialists, after all, the sole frame of reference remained '1919–20, when we were the only party of the working class, when the impetus of the entire working class was behind us, and when, despite all that, we not only failed to resolve certain problems, but even failed to frame them'.[1]

Such historically informed perceptions of national vicissitudes were more than once a decisive factor in socialist attitudes towards political reconstruction. The past had taught the four parties a plethora of political lessons: what form democracy should take, which social constituencies could be relied upon, and which political parties to work with. Yet these lessons varied considerably from country to country and from party to party. The PPS and the PSIUP, on the one hand, were haunted both by their countries' dictatorial pasts and by their own role in the demise of democracy in the 1920s. To counter the still omnipresent 'fascist' threat, the working class had to present a united front this time around. The ČSSD and the SFIO, on the other, were confident of their countries'

---

[1] 'Seduta pomeridiana' (18 October 1945), ACS, Carteggio Nenni, Busta 87, Fasc. 2189, pp. 5–7.

democratic traditions and of the broad political consensus around them. For the parties to finally prevail in the democratic contest, however, it was crucial that socialism broke free from its historical working-class ghetto and reached out to other social groups.

This chapter seeks to retrace how the widely divergent lessons the four parties drew from their respective national histories shaped their approach towards rebuilding democracy. There are two dimensions to this. In the first place, the experience of party-political rivalry and cooperation during the interwar years pulled the parties in opposite directions. Whereas the ČSSD and the SFIO had found democracy to be in safe hands with the centrist and centre-right parties, the PPS and the PSIUP concluded that a close-knit alliance between communists and socialists represented the only hope for democracy. Secondly, history had left the parties with polarised impressions of the democratic maturity of their people. While the ČSSD and the SFIO felt that centuries of freedom struggles had instilled democratic beliefs among wide sections of their societies, the PPS and the PSIUP despaired that their recent pasts had demonstrated that there was no popular bulwark of democracy beyond the working class. It was these widely divergent historical lessons that lay at the root of the two sets of parties' strongly divergent conceptions of democracy, which we will outline in the extended conclusion to this chapter.

Unity and Disunity

At the moment of liberation, none of the four parties advocated simply reverting to the pre-war ways of doing politics. Even the ČSSD, which had participated in governments almost throughout the interwar First Republic, insisted that Czechoslovakia 'cannot and must not return to 1938'. Instead, it was to 'implement a radical transformation in its political, economic, social, and cultural system'.[2] The concept of unity frequently played a key role in such considerations. Each of the four parties agreed that the political disunity and party fragmentation of the interwar years, particularly on the left, had contributed a great deal to their inability to achieve a socialist transformation. By the war's end, accordingly, they all found themselves in some sort of partnership with the communists. Working with a party of questionable democratic credentials, which was competing for the same voters, quickly proved a challenge, however.

---

[2] 'Program akčního výboru Československé sociální demokracie', Archiv ČSSD, Fond 71, Část II, Karton III, p. 5.

Whether the communist alliance outlasted the heady days following the liberation, therefore, depended on how the four parties assessed their historical experience of surviving on their own.

In the immediate aftermath of the war, the impetus for working-class political unity emanated chiefly from the socialists. Uninhibited by Moscow-ordered moderation, it was they much more than the communists who banged the drum for the single working-class party.[3] 'Aware of the irresistible strengths that the working class will draw from its union', a PSIUP resolution of August 1943 read, 'the Socialist Party intends to realise the fusion of socialists and communists in a single Party based on a clear understanding of the revolutionary purposes of the proletarian movement.'[4] For the time being, however, the communists preferred national to working-class unity, as the PSIUP was to find out the hard way when the PCI 'seriously compromised' the two parties' Unity of Action Pact by entering the second Bonomi government without the socialists.[5]

These dynamics were to repeat themselves in other countries. During the final stages of the war, several ČSSD leaders called for a merger with the communists in the near future, with Bohumil Laušman even going so far as to claim that the ČSSD had 'fulfilled its historical mission as a reformist party' and that it would be 'impossible to reconstitute it in the long run'.[6] Yet fusion was not on the agenda of the Muscovite KSČ leadership at that time. The uncoordinated September 1944 merger of the underground organisations of communists and social democrats in Slovakia, hence, came as 'an untimely [and] unpleasant surprise' for communist leaders – one to which they would later partially attribute their electoral setbacks in Slovakia.[7]

---

[3] Alongside a post-liberation revolutionary 'euphoria', tactical considerations may well have played their part in the socialists' 'fusionism' too. Peter Heumos, for example, argues that the Eastern European socialist parties hoped to outflank the communists among the working class by preaching 'greater socio-political radicalism'. As for the French socialists, Wilfried Loth claims that their endeavours to achieve 'working-class unity' were inspired in large part by their desire to benefit, by association, from the prestige that the communists had gained as the driving force of the French Resistance. See Peter Heumos, 'Arbeiterschaft und Sozialdemokratie in Osteuropa 1944–1948', *Geschichte und Gesellschaft*, 13 (1987), pp. 22–38, 30; Wilfried Loth, 'Die französische Linke und die "Einheit der Arbeiterklasse" 1943–1947', *Vierteljahrshefte für Zeitgeschichte*, 35/2 (1987), pp. 273–88, 275.

[4] 'Dichiarizione politica del partito socialista' (25 August 1943), *Orientamenti: Bollettino di Commento e di Indirizzo Politico*, 18 January 1948, p. 4.

[5] Lelio Basso, 'Atene a Roma', *Avanti!*, 10 January 1945. www.leliobasso.it/documento.aspx?id=obobd 04f656ede422e35133bb6b38305 (last consulted: 27 June 2018).

[6] Quoted in Kaplan, 'Tschechoslowakische Sozialdemokratie', p. 296f.

[7] Ibid., p. 282. With approximately 40 per cent of the vote, the communists did spectacularly well in the Czech lands during the May 1946 parliamentary elections. Yet, in Slovakia, in spite of the fact that the party landscape there was basically limited to two parties, they only managed 30 per cent against the 61 per cent for the nationalist and centre-right Democratic Party.

In its efforts to further the cause of working-class unity, the SFIO like-wise met with initial communist reluctance. Still during the clandestine period, the socialists had approached the PCF with a proposal to form a 'Committee of Understanding' that was to 'study the problems of worker unity, thereby paving the way for it'. 'What an example for France and for the world [it would be]', the proposal concluded, 'if we could one day say that … the two parties of the working class have, in the underground struggle, laid the groundwork for the unity of tomorrow!' Though it was regrettable that the communists had rejected that proposal, Daniel Mayer told the November 1944 SFIO congress, 'I believe the congress will be almost unanimous in saying that the offer we made back then has not lapsed, that … we have the right and the duty to repeat it publicly to the Communist Party at this forum'.[8]

The communists did accept this time around and the Committee of Understanding met for the first time in December 1944. In fact, even though the single working-class party was to remain elusive, all four parties eventually managed to tie themselves to the communists in an offi-cial alliance: the PSIUP and the PCI agreed a new Unity of Action Pact in October 1943, the ČSSD, the KSČ, and the National Socialists of the ČSNS established a Socialist Bloc in June 1945, and the PPS and the PPR formed a United Front in November 1946.

The practical experience of cooperating with the communists both in such partnerships and in national government, however, would quickly dampen the four parties' enthusiasm for a speedy unification of the two wings of the labour movement. Before long, the socialists were striking an altogether different tone about the timeliness of a united working-class party. 'We must not keep the problem of the fusion and of the new party at the centre of our discussions', Nenni told the PSIUP Central Committee in October 1945, 'because that is not the problem of the moment.'[9]

In the SFIO leadership, meanwhile, the opponents of a single party, among them Augustin Laurent, André Le Troquer, and André Philip, had gradually gained the upper hand over such initial advocates of an (even-tual) socialist–communist merger as Daniel Mayer or Jules Moch. After a majority within the SFIO Executive had already voted down a plan to run the upcoming local elections on a common platform with the communists

[8] 'Parti Socialiste – SFIO: Congrès national extraordinaire des 9, 10, 11, et 12 novembre 1944', FJJ, p. 27. http://flipbook.archives-socialistes.fr/index.html?docid=49328&language=fra&userid=0 (last consulted: 27 June 2018).
[9] 'Comitato Centrale' (17 October 1945), ACS, Carteggio Nenni, Busta 87, Fasc. 2189, p. 25.

in March 1945,[10] the socialist representatives to the Committee of Understanding took the question of 'organic unity' off the table altogether by June of that year.[11]

The PPS more and more veered towards party-political autonomy from the PPR too. To be sure, the programme that socialist leaders put before the August 1945 PPS congress had still envisioned future 'organisational-political unity',[12] and the communists made sure that a commitment to a single working-class party formed part of the United Front agreement that the PPS and the PPR entered into in November 1946. In the face of ever-increasing communist pressure for a merger over the year that followed the creation of the United Front, however, the socialists did everything in their power to obstruct and postpone unification.[13]

In view of their later trajectories, the four parties actually articulated remarkably similar misgivings about their communist allies. In the first place, these concerned what they experienced as the roundly disloyal attitudes of the communists towards their socialist partners. Looking back on the campaign for the May 1946 parliamentary elections, Zdeněk Fierlinger lamented how the ČSSD had come under attack not only from the right, 'where the initiative we showed in the implementation of the great socialist reforms and nationalisation was naturally not received sympathetically', but also from the left, where the communists resented 'the idea of an existing strong Social Democratic Party'. In Slovakia, for example, the communists had accused the social democrats of 'splitting the socialist forces' after the resurrection of the Slovakian wing of the ČSSD in January 1946. As the elections neared, Fierlinger declared, such 'conflicts within the workers' ranks' had only grown deeper.[14]

The French socialists were likewise incensed by communist tactics vis-à-vis their party. After a series of PCF press attacks upon the SFIO, tensions between the two parties reached boiling point by the turn of 1945. For many within the SFIO Executive, the time for an ultimatum had come: if

---

[10] OURS, CD SFIO, 13 March 1945.

[11] OURS, CD SFIO, 14 June 1945.

[12] 'Projekt Uchwała Programowa XXVI Kongresu', AAN, PPS, XXVI Kongres, 295/1-7, fo. 12a.

[13] In April 1947, for example, the PPS rejected out of hand a PPR proposal to announce the unification of the two parties during the May Day celebrations. And at the December 1947 PPS congress, Julian Hochfeld presented a set of programmatic theses that foresaw a PPS-PPR merger only as the end result of a pan-European process of communist–socialist rapprochement. See De Graaf, ' "The Usual Psychological Effects of a Shotgun Wedding" ', p. 149; Kersten, *The Establishment of Communist Rule*, pp. 425–28.

[14] 'The Mission of Social Democracy in the New State' (November 1947), ANM, Fonds Zdeněk Fierlinger, Karton 40, Sjezd soc. dem. v Brne, pp. 18–19.

the communists were to continue their attacks the socialists would walk out of the Committee of Understanding. Philip summed up the general mood, arguing that the socialists had to either '[make] peace or [wage] war' with the communists, for 'we seem to be victims of an inferiority complex by continuously acting in accordance with the attitude of others'.[15] It is indicative of how exasperated even the erstwhile supporters of socialist–communist unity were that Mayer largely echoed Philip's sentiments during the following reunion of the Committee of Understanding. He told the communists that the meeting would be 'decisive': 'either we maintain the Committee of Understanding and develop fraternal relations or we suppress it and choose war, but the ambiguity has to stop'.[16]

Albeit in far more veiled terms, PPS leaders also admonished their PPR counterparts not to turn socialist–communist cooperation into a one-way street. 'When one speaks of "unity" [but] seeks to impose supremacy', socialist minister of labour and social security Jan Stańczyk told a joint PPS-PPR plenum, 'unity can collapse'.[17] And even the Italian socialists, in many ways blessed with the most moderate communist party in post-war Europe,[18] complained about communist animosity. Palmiro Togliatti's recent equation of the PSIUP with 'those struggling against the PCI', Nenni told a post-election gathering of the two party leaderships in June 1946, 'has had a negative backlash within socialist circles'. The Unity of Action Pact, he continued, had to be 'adapted ... to the present situation, stripped of ideological content, and brought to the level of concrete action'.[19]

Such ideological concerns were the second main reason for socialist parties to abandon their initial fusionism. All of the communists' affirmations that they were now committed to a multi-party system and a national road to socialism notwithstanding, lingering apprehensions over their democratic sincerity and their international allegiances were quick to resurface among the socialists. In Eastern Europe, as we have seen, such apprehensions had their basis in everyday practice. But even in Western

---

[15] OURS, CD SFIO, 26 December 1945.
[16] OURS, CD SFIO, 9 January 1946.
[17] 'Protokół z wspólnego posiedzenia CKW PPS i KC PPR' (28 September 1945), AAN, PPS, CKW, 235/III/6, fo. 28.
[18] Out of all the post-war European communist leaders, PCI secretary general Palmiro Togliatti is generally regarded to have been most genuinely committed to a 'national road to socialism'. For even at the height of the First Cold War, he kept insisting on 'using peaceful and legal means to further the development of Communism in Italy', doing so 'despite – and not because of the existence of the Cominform'. See Silvio Pons, 'Stalin, Togliatti, and the Origins of the Cold War in Europe', *Journal of Cold War Studies*, 3/2 (2001), pp. 3–27, 16.
[19] 'Riunione Direzione e Comitato Sindacale' (28 June 1946), ISRT, Fondo Foscolo Lombardi, Partito Socialista Italiano, Direzione Nazionale, Busta 4, Fasc. 20.

Europe, where the communists did by and large play by the democratic rulebook during the first post-war years, socialist leaders had all sorts of misgivings.

When the French communists published their outline for a single working-class party in June 1945, the so-called 'Charter of Unity', Vincent Auriol was quick to identify worrisome trends. At face value, he told the SFIO Executive, the communist text might appear acceptable, but that was 'not the same after an intensive study'. Stalin and Lenin, after all, 'are presented as the heirs of Marx, the dictatorship of the proletariat is not surrounded by guarantees, [and] there is no clarification regarding demo-cratic centralism'. In the final analysis, he declared, 'the communists have not changed and their tactics are the same in all countries: in Belgium, in Italy ... and in Yugoslavia where Tito has suppressed the [non-communist] parties'.[20]

Though not going as far as that, Nenni certainly questioned whether the communists had really changed. During a June 1945 meeting of the DC and PSIUP leaderships, he assured his interlocutors that 'tactical' rather than 'ideological' motivations had been 'decisive' in the socialists' decision to enter into the Unity of Action Pact. 'We are no longer the only party of the working class', he explained, 'and have by our side a communist party which has worked harder [in the anti-fascist Resistance] and which benefits from the prestige of Stalin and of the popular sympathies for the Soviet Union.' With regard to ideology, the PSIUP could only hope: 'Have the communists definitively moved away from the totalitarian ideology or not? Is the dissolution of the Comintern real?' The answers to those questions had 'not yet been given'.[21]

If each of the four parties quickly backtracked on the idea of a single working-class party, however, the question of their broader relations with the communists remained wide open. And here, for all of their essen-tially similar experiences with and reservations about the communists, the socialists were to move in opposite directions. Whereas the ČSSD and the SFIO concluded that there was no basis for continuing their formal partnership with the communists, the PPS and the PSIUP both renewed their unity pacts with the communists in October 1946. Much more than their post-war relations with the communists, it seems to have been the

---

[20] OURS, CD SFIO, 14 June 1945.
[21] 'Relazione sul convegno socialista – democratico cristiano' (1 June 1945), ACS, Carteggio Nenni, Busta 87, Fasc. 2188, p. 9.

four parties' conflicting appraisals of whether history offered socialism any alternative to the communist alliance that determined this outcome.

For the Italian and Polish socialists, on the one hand, the foremost lesson of the past was that disunity among the Left would only benefit the authoritarian Right. In their view, the socialist–communist splits of the early 1920s, placing the two parties on a war footing for the best part of the following fifteen years, had paved the way for the reaction, for dictatorship, and ultimately for fascism. The 'infighting' between communists and socialists after their 1921 schism, read the political report that the PSIUP Directorate presented to the party's April 1946 congress, 'was not the least cause of the advent of fascism'. On a broader level, moreover, 'the experience of the last quarter of a century serves to demonstrate how, when communists and socialists struggle between themselves, [it] is never in the interest of the proletariat, of the popular and middle classes, of democracy, but in the exclusive interest of the reaction, in its worst forms, fascism, Nazism, [and] Falangism'.[22]

PPS leaders similarly attributed their country's descent into right-wing dictatorship to the interwar divisions on the left. During a December 1946 international conference of Central and Eastern European socialist parties, Kazimierz Rusinek reproached the Austrian delegate for claiming that 'the unity of the proletariat' had 'practically been realised within the socialist party' in his country. 'Before the last war', he exhorted, 'the Polish socialists were of the same opinion and, unable to find common ground with the communists as a consequence, had left the initiative to the parties of the Right; the result was the Piłsudski dictatorship.'[23]

At the root of these fatal divisions, both parties agreed, lay the extreme positions that had characterised working-class politics for most of the interwar period. According to Rusinek two 'recipes' for taking power had existed, 'and both were wrong'. The communists, on the one side, had 'preached the dictatorship of the proletariat as the only solution possible'. The socialists, on the other, had 'believed that "the expropriation of the expropriators" would be realised automatically' and had taken a 'strictly defensive' attitude towards the bourgeoisie as a result. With the 'victory of fascists', he declared, the proletariat had 'paid the price ... for the political

---

[22] 'Relazione political della direzione del partito per il XXIV congresso nazionale'(15 February 1946), *Orientamenti: Bollettino di Commento e di Indirizzo Politico*, 18 January 1948, p. 27.
[23] 'Bericht über die Konferenz der sozialistischen Parteien Zentral- und Osteuropas in Prag von 7.–9. Dezember 1946', in Heumos (ed.), *Die Konferenzen*, p. 58.

mistakes of the socialists and the orthodoxy of the communists, both knowing only one "recipe" without taking into account the objective and specific conditions of each country'.[24] In similar terms, Nenni lamented the two interwar 'degenerations of Marxism': a 'reformist' degeneration that saw 'socialism as the natural outcome of bourgeois democracy' and a 'sectarian' degeneration that 'lumped the entire bourgeois world together'. It was exactly these two currents that had dominated interwar socialism and communism, he argued, 'with disastrous consequences in Germany and Italy'.[25]

For the sheer magnitude of its impact, the Italian and Polish socialists frequently cited the fate of Weimar Germany as the ultimate vindication of their alliance with the communists. 'If there had been a united front [in interwar Germany]', PPS international secretary Stanisław Dobrowolski explained, 'Hitler would not have risen to power.' And the united front was 'a life-and-death question for the Polish working class', too, for without it, the country would 'unquestionably' be governed by 'the reaction'.[26] Nenni likewise defended socialist–communist unity of action with reference to 'the Weimar tragedy'.[27] 'We do not want to give an encore to the Weimar Republic', he told a September 1944 PSIUP convention, 'which was still-born because it was established on the basis of civil war between socialists and communists.'[28]

If the PPS and PSIUP divided the blame for the interwar socialist–communist struggles in their own countries more or less evenly over the two parties, they attributed the socialist–communist conflict in Weimar Germany almost entirely to the social democrats of the SPD. Their progressive 'embourgeoisement' by their non-proletarian coalition partners, the Italian and Polish socialists insisted, had not only alienated their party from its working-class roots but effectively turned it into an ally of 'the reaction'. It was for these reasons that the PPS and PSIUP remained very suspicious of working with non-proletarian parties.

As early as January 1946, Sandro Pertini warned that government collaboration with right-wing parties had unleashed a 'neo-opportunist tendency' within the post-war PSIUP. He was adamant that socialist leaders, although in coalition with bourgeois parties, should 'never forget the

[24] Ibid., p. 71.
[25] Pietro Nenni, 'Socialisti e communisti', *Avanti!*, 11 July 1944.
[26] xxvi Kongres (August 1945), AAN, PPS, 235/1-12, fo. 224.
[27] 'Relazione Nenni' (September 1944), ACS, Carteggio Nenni, Busta 87, Fasc 2186.
[28] 'Discorso Nenni, Segretario del Partito Socialista Italiano' (4 September 1944), ACS, Carteggio Nenni, Busta 87, Fasc 2186.

purpose of the working class; they must not forget that they are socialists and that, for every measure they take, they have to ask themselves whether it benefits the working class or not; otherwise they only bring harm to the Party'. 'The shadow of [Gustav] Noske [Weimar's social democratic defence minister in 1919–20, who played a key role in the suppression of the 1919 left-wing uprisings]', he warned, 'hangs over our comrades in government.' If 'a situation like the current one were to continue for a long time', after all, 'we will one day realise that we have deprived our Party of every revolutionary content, of every class and socialist content, to have gentrified it'.[29]

Speaking at the March 1946 PPS Supreme Council, Stanisław Szwalbe likewise raised strong objections to cooperation with the centre-right. 'If you meet people saying that we should not cooperate with the PPR and should join forces with the PSL [instead]', he warned party representatives, 'that means they want to push us into the arms of the reaction again.' The post-war PPS, he concluded, 'has its revolutionary line and will not let … power slip from its hands'.[30]

For both parties, thus, the most important political lesson of the past was that socialists and communists had to close ranks in order for the working class to prevail. History taught them that equidistance to the political extremes on the left and the right often amounted to surrendering to 'the reaction'. In October 1945, Nenni still gladly noted that 'there is nobody [within the post-war PSIUP] suggesting a centrist politics … based on the old slogan: neither revolution, nor reaction'. By simultaneously fighting the communists on the left and the reaction on the right, after all, the PSIUP 'would suffer the same fate as German social democracy, i.e. we would bit by bit be absorbed into the reactionary orbit'.[31] By late 1947, however, PPS Central Committee member Julian Hochfeld was lamenting that the 'fatal and tragic mistakes' made by interwar PPS leaders – 'who talked of the unity of the working class to be sure, but [only] under the banner of the PPS' – were being repeated by 'some socialists in Western Europe'. In the face of 'a big reactionary offensive', he explained, they had come up with the doctrine of the Third Force – '[positing] that neither the communists, nor the bourgeoisie are any good, only we ourselves'.[32]

[29] 'Relazione al Comitato Centrale' (January 1946), in Neri Serneri, Casali and Errera (eds.), *Scritti e discorsi di Sandro Pertini*, pp. 68–75, 74.
[30] Rada Naczelna (31 March 1946), AAN, PPS, 235/II-6, fo. 3.
[31] 'Seduta pomeridiana' (18 October 1945), ACS, Carteggio Nenni, Busta 87, Fasc. 2189, p. 12.
[32] XXVII Kongres (December 1947), AAN, PPS, 235/I-25, fo. 216.

That was of course a barely disguised attack upon the SFIO and its participation in a centrist 'Third Force' coalition committed to fighting off the perceived communist and Gaullist threats to democracy simultaneously in France. Indeed, after the party had acquiesced in the removal of the PCF from the French government in May 1947, the post-war SFIO increasingly came to replace the interwar SPD in the rhetoric of the PPS and the PSIUP. Socialist leaders in Poland pointed out that the subsequent developments in France, above all the 'insurrectionary' strikes of the autumn of 1947, proved that 'their policy of collaboration with the Communists is not only hypothetically but categorically the right one'.[33] In reference chiefly to the situation in France, accordingly, Józef Cyrankiewicz told the December 1947 PPS congress that the Polish socialists were 'wiser than the West European socialists by a whole historical period'.[34]

Nenni, for his part, questioned the entire premise behind the Third Force. 'We cannot make any concessions to the doctrine of the Third Force', he told the January 1948 PSIUP congress, 'because that is a doctrine that goes against all of our ideologies, against all of our positions.' The truth was, he continued, that there was 'no plurality of forces' – 'there are only two ... on the one side the bourgeoisie and on the other the working class'. Those socialists who believed that the bourgeoisie was fighting communist 'excesses' rather than the labour movement as a whole, therefore, were making a fatal mistake. For history taught that, when push came to shove, the bourgeoisie did not distinguish between communists and socialists. 'In 1934 Austria [when the socialist-led Republican Defence League rose up against the increasingly authoritarian tendencies of the conservative government]', after all, 'there was no communist party [as the government had already outlawed that party]; only the [Austrian] Social Democratic Party.' But that had not stopped 'the Austrian bourgeoisie' from fighting the social democrats 'with canons and rifles, massacring unarmed workers'.[35] By the same token, he went on, there was 'only one communist' in 'the Spanish parliament elected in 1931' and there were 'no more than twenty communists' in 'the Spanish parliament elected in 1936'. Yet 'the police fought the Spanish socialists, much like it is fighting the communists in some countries today,

[33] This was how Denis Healey described it in his report of the December 1947 PPS congress. Labour History Archive and Study Centre, Manchester (hereafter LHASC), Labour Party Archives (hereafter LPA), International Department (LP/ID), Box 13.

[34] Quoted in De Graaf, '"The Usual Psychological Effects of a Shotgun Wedding"', p. 153.

[35] As the para-military wing of the Austrian Socialist Party, the Republican Defence League did of course have weapons. On the 1934 events in Austria and their broader impact upon the interwar international socialist movement, see Gerd-Rainer Horn, *European Socialists*, pp. 122–7.

by means of violence, oppression, [and] the physical destruction of working-class militants and workers' organisations'.[36]

If the interwar experiences of such countries as Austria and Spain closely resembled those of Italy and Poland, however, they certainly were nothing like those of Czechoslovakia and France. In fact, centre-left and centrist bourgeois parties had been the closest allies of the ČSSD and the SFIO for most of the interwar period. It was these more positive experiences with centrist alliances and with democratic politics in general that account for the two parties' increasingly centrist orientation when democracy found itself under mounting pressure during the post-war years.

Not that the Czechoslovakian social democrats and French socialists were overflowing with affection for their centrist coalition partners. In the first place, they accused the bourgeois and Catholic parties of being disloyal to and using all sorts of dirty tricks against socialism, especially at election time. The ČSSD leadership charged the ČSNS with targeting 'Goebbels-like propaganda' at social democracy during the campaign for the May 1946 parliamentary elections.[37] Its 'spurious flyers', claiming that a merger of communists and social democrats would follow after the elections, had 'deliberately created an atmosphere of uncertainty' around social democracy.[38] SFIO leaders, for their part, often complained bitterly about the MRP – the charges including its 'vicious' attacks upon the SFIO[39] as well as its 'desertion' and 'betrayal' of the yes camp in the May 1946 constitutional referendum.[40]

In ideological and socio-economic terms, moreover, the gap between socialism and the centrist parties seemed to have widened rather than narrowed. The ČSSD noted how the ČSNS, under the influence of bloc-building in international politics, had taken up the role of 'mouthpiece of the Right in Czechoslovakia'.[41] Insofar as the ČSNS was 'the sewer to which all of the reaction converged', as Laušman put it, these tactics had

[36] 'Partito socialista italiano. Congresso nazionale "Roma 19–22 gennaio 1948"', FFT, Partito socialista italiano (Psi) – Direzione nazionale, Serie 20: Congressi nazionali e internazionali, Sottoserie 1: Congressi Nazionali, pp. 379–82. www.archivionline.senato.it/scripts/GeaCGI.exe?REQSRV=R EQSEQUENCE&ID=151050 (last consulted: 27 June 2018).

[37] 'Volby a čs. sociální demokracie' (1946), NA, Fonds Bohumil Laušman, III Pisemnosti související s ústřední, veřejnou a politickou činnosti B. Laušmana, Karton 34, Souvicejíci činnosti v soc. dem. 1928–1948, p. 8.

[38] *Zpráva o činnosti*, p. xxviii.

[39] OURS, CD SFIO, 9 January 1946.

[40] OURS, CD SFIO, 7 May 1946.

[41] *Zpráva o činnosti*, p. xiii.

been a success.[42] The SFIO likewise observed how the 'Radical Socialists' (after the official name of the Radical Party: the Republican, Radical, and Radical Socialist Party) of times past had increasingly become the 'Radical Reactionaries' after the war. 'Since the liberation', after all, the Radicals had 'demonstrated ... that, for them, the defence of the Republic amounted to no more than defending the last privileges of the bourgeois Third Republic.'[43] The MRP, finally, remained an enigma for the socialists.[44] To be sure, it had supported the nationalisations and other structural reforms in the economy, but the party's 'solutions for social and economic problems appear to put it on the road of paternalism and corporatism more than on that of social progress'.[45]

What was never really in doubt for both the ČSSD and the SFIO, though, was the ultimate democratic reliability of their centrist and centre-right coalition partners. And, as post-war unity began giving way to socio-political polarisation, that more and more outweighed the misgivings the two parties held about their bourgeois coalition partners' economic policy preferences. According to Philip, 'capitalism ... as we have known it', of the type that had historically carried the support of the centre-right, would be 'incapable of reconstituting itself' anyway. 'We are in a transitory regime', he told the August 1946 SFIO congress, 'which will lead ... either to democratic Socialism or to an authoritarian and technocratic collectivism, taking the shape of a national Socialism or of a national Communism.' It followed that 'the principal enemy at the present moment is no longer only capitalism as we have known it, [but] totalitarianism, in every form that it manifests itself, and authoritarianism'.[46]

For the ČSSD, deputy secretary general Vojta Erban was increasingly playing up the democratic over the economic attributes of socialism as well. 'We are above all ... aware', he wrote in October 1946, 'that socialism and democracy are essentially the same thing, because socialism not only has an economic side but ... is based on the rule of a free people.' Yet

---

[42] 'Volby a čs. sociální demokracie' (1946), NA, Fonds Bohumil Laušman, III Pisemnosti související s ústředni, veřejnou a politickou činnosti B. Laušmana, Karton 34, Souvicejíci činnosti v soc. dem. 1928–1948, p. 7.

[43] 'Les Radicaux-Socialistes sont aujourd'hui des "Radicaux-Réactionnaires"', Arguments et Ripostes, Bulletin Intérieur du Parti Socialiste (S.F.I.O.), 5 October 1946, OURS.

[44] On the relations between the SFIO and the MRP during the post-war period, see also Bruno Béthouart, 'Le MRP, un nouveau partenaire', in Serge Berstein, Frédéric Cépède, Gilles Morin and Antoine Prost (eds.), Le Parti socialiste entre Résistance et République (Paris: Publications de Sorbonne, 2000), pp. 257–68.

[45] 'Discours d'Information Générale: Le Parti Socialiste et les problèmes de l'heure', Arguments et Ripostes, Bulletin Intérieur du Parti Socialiste (S.F.I.O.), 20 October 1946, OURS.

[46] 'Parti Socialiste SFIO: 38ème Congrès national, 29, 30, 31 août et 1er septembre 1946', FJJ, pp. 240–1. http://62.210.214.184/cg-ps/documents/pdf/cong-1946-08-29.pdf (last consulted: 27 June 2018).

the social democrats also knew 'very well', he continued, 'that socialism was, and is to this day, sometimes understood as a mechanic collectivism, which does not respect the individual and therefore means subjugation and dictatorship'.[47]

In the face of these dictatorial collectivisms, it was imperative that the political centre pulled together against the formation of extremist left-wing or right-wing blocs. The ČSSD always counselled against Left–Right polarisation. After the May 1946 parliamentary elections in Czechoslovakia, Laušman was quick to dispel press reports that 'a Marxist camp', consisting of the KSČ and the ČSSD, now held a two-seat majority over 'a non-Marxist camp', encompassing all other parties. '[I]f we divide the nation in two blocs', he declared, 'we will come to political and civil struggles, and that would be the beginning of the end.'[48] And even Fierlinger, the main leader of the ČSSD's left wing, by no means advocated exclusive cooperation with the communists. Defending his ill-fated Unity Pact with the communists at the November 1947 ČSSD congress, he claimed that the pact had never been intended 'to be limited to two parties only' but was always 'to be enlarged to a third party, i.e. the National Socialist Party'. There had been 'no question of forming some kind of left-wing bloc', he insisted, 'but rather of preventing the creation of a right wing one. Nor do we want to isolate any of the other political parties as far as they want to work with us at all.'[49]

The SFIO was constantly at pains to avoid fuelling polarisation too. For that reason, the party refrained from responding directly when, immediately after the new constitution was finally voted through in the October 1946 referendum, the MRP went public with demands for a revision. It would be 'a mistake', insisted SFIO deputy secretary general Yves Dechezelles, to 'rally the Right behind De Gaulle and create an anti-Marxist bloc' by taking these demands, however unacceptable, head-on.[50]

---

[47] Voita Erban to Okresní sekretariát Čs. soc. demokracie, Praha VII, 31 October 1946, Archiv ČSSD, Fond 71, Část II, Karton 200, fos 609–10.

[48] 'Volby a čs. sociální demokracie' (1946), NA, Fonds Bohumil Laušman, III Pisemnosti související s ústřední, veřejnou a politickou činnosti B. Laušmana, Karton 34, Souvicející činnosti v soc. dem. 1928–1948, p. 12.

[49] 'The Mission of Social Democracy in the New State' (November 1947), ANM, Fonds Zdeněk Fierlinger, Karton 40, Sjezd soc. dem. v Brne, p. 45. In view of the role Fierlinger later played both during the Prague Coup and in the subsequent merger of the ČSSD and the KSČ, these comments must of course be seen in the light of his (unsuccessful) efforts to retain the ČSSD Chair after his September 1947 Unity Pact with the communists was engulfed in a wave of intra-party indignation. Yet, the very fact that he chose to play up alliances with centrist parties in these efforts tells us much about the sentiments within the ČSSD at that time.

[50] OURS, CD SFIO, 16 October 1946.

A similar rationale was behind socialist leaders' lukewarm response to communist overtures to establish 'vigilance committees', reminiscent of the anti-fascist bodies that had been constituted during the February 1934 crisis, in the wake of the creation of the Gaullist RPF in April 1947. For fear of providing De Gaulle with an easy target in the form of 'a socialist-communist bloc', the SFIO instead opted 'to unite all republican energies and ... to invite the Communist Party, the Radical Party, and the MRP to make contact with it'.[51]

By that stage, however, some party leaders were already pointing out that it would be a 'challenge' or even 'paradoxical' to 'defend the Republic' and 'struggle against dictatorship side by side with the communists'.[52] And come the time of the August 1947 SFIO congress, Paul Ramadier was no longer mentioning the PCF among the parties involved in 'the work of Republican defence'. Instead, he urged party members to set aside any qualms about the 'clerical tendencies of the MRP' or the 'conservative tendencies of certain members of the [Radical] RGR'. Those were 'secondary preoccupations', he declared; 'the only thing that matters is to know whether we agree on the essential point; i.e. the Republican struggle'.[53]

In his address to the November 1947 ČSSD congress, which would vote him in as party leader, Laušman likewise placed the defence of the democratic republic front and centre. After providing a lengthy exposé of how the party had prospered since its democratic wing had prevailed over its revolutionary wing in the 1880s, he proceeded with a thinly veiled attack on the Soviet inspirations of the KSČ. 'Czechoslovakian social democracy will always be on the watch', he argued, 'that nobody anchors foreign ideas and tendencies in our nation, which would be in conflict with the deep-seated democratic, moral, and progressive sentiments of the citizens of the republic and with its socialist foundations.' It was 'substantiated by our national history', after all, that the 'violent introduction of foreign models only brings unnecessary and heavy harm to socialist endeavours ... and impedes the road to socialism'. For that reason, 'we must never allow that our politics are influenced by foreign interests, irrespective of whether these come from the Left or the Right, interests that are uncongenial or even run counter to our spirit, which diverge from our manifesto'.[54]

[51] OURS, CD SFIO, 23 April 1947.
[52] OURS, CD SFIO, 18 April and 23 April 1947.
[53] 'Parti Socialiste – SFIO: 39ème Congrès national des 14 au 17 août 1947 (partie 2)', FJJ p. 101. http://62.210.214.184/cg-ps/documents/pdf/cong-1947-08-16.pdf (last consulted: 27 June 2018).
[54] 'Zahajovací projev předsedy XXI. sjezdu čsl. sociální demokracie Bohumila Laušmana' (14 November 1947), Archiv ČSSD, Fond 71, Část II, Karton 112, pp. 10–11.

Much the same arguments underlay the SFIO's embrace of the Third Force doctrine in late 1947. In a propaganda brochure making the case for this new type of coalition, the party claimed that the authoritarian designs espoused on the leftmost and rightmost extremes of the political spectrum contravened a national democratic spirit. There were 'millions of republicans, democrats, socialists, [and] trade unionists', it insisted, who 'do not accept and do not want to accept either the solution of personal power desired by the RPF or the solution of Stalinist dictatorship, both of which would inevitably result in the destruction of democratic institutions and the suppression of political liberties'. The brochure cited the German, Italian, and, crucially, Soviet experiences as proof that dictatorship 'cannot provide the slightest solution for the problems posed by the evolution of modern society in its fundamental relations with the economical, the political, and the exigencies of freedom and democracy'. The 'necessity of a Third Force' sprang 'fatally from that observation'; it was 'a historical necessity for our country and for the world, at risk of sinking into chaos'.[55]

Internal Soul-Searching

The four parties traced national democratic traditions not only to their historical experiences with party alliances, however. At least as important as the party-political lessons of the past were the lessons history had taught them about their respective societies. These two lessons were interconnected in many ways, as the socialists' historically informed perceptions of democratic and anti-democratic social constituencies fed into their party-political decisions. The fact, then, that the industrial working class represented the only truly democratic constituency for the PPS and the PSIUP was one further reason for close cooperation with the communists. Yet their strong proletarian orientation left little room for genuine outreach to other (disadvantaged) social groups. The ČSSD and the SFIO, by contrast, were far more confident of the sound democratic beliefs of the middle-class voters who had historically backed centrist and centre-right parties. In order to win these groups over to their parties, though, it was imperative that socialism lose its sharp proletarian edges.

In fact, for each of the four parties, the first post-war years represented a period of soul-searching about their identity as proletarian organisations.

---

[55] 'La troisième force: Ou la 3e force nationale et internationale, ou le 3e guerre mondiale', Arguments et Ripostes, Bulletin Intérieur du Parti Socialiste (S.F.I.O.), December 1947, OURS.

In the post-war context, after all, that identity was doubly problematic. In the first place, the socialists were acutely aware that the industrial proletariat formed a minority of the electorate in each of the four countries and was going to remain so for the foreseeable future. After the yes camp's defeat in the May 1946 constitutional referendum, Mayer had to conclude that even the combined political forces of the working class represented 'less than one half of the country'. '[E]specially in times of economic reconstruction and redirection', he declared, 'it is impossible ... to govern without the consent or the benevolent neutrality of those broad segments of the population that are called middle classes, but who make up the social majority of the nation in France'.[56]

According to ČSSD secretary general Blažej Vilím, this message had too frequently been lost upon interwar social democracy. 'We have to ... frankly acknowledge', he told the October 1945 ČSSD congress, that, in most European countries, socialist parties had 'overestimated the strength of the industrial proletariat' and 'underestimated the significance of other strata of the nation'. The 'development of the political situation in the First Republic' presented 'an example' of this. The failure of the Left 'to become a decisive factor' in interwar Czechoslovakia, after all, had been due not to only of 'the fragmentation of our socialist movement' but also to the resilience of 'a series of right-wing parties leaning on farmers and the middle classes'.[57]

Secondly, a significant part of this working-class minority had abandoned socialism in favour of communism. In October 1945, Nenni noted how the great bulk of the Italian working class now backed the PCI, with 'the ratio between us and the communists 1 to 10, if not 1 to 15 or even 1 to 20' in many industrial zones.[58] The ČSSD and the SFIO, for their part, often alluded to the defection of the working-class vote to communism as one

---

[56] 'Parti Socialiste SFIO: 38ème Congrès national, 29, 30, 31 août et 1er septembre 1946', FJJ, p. 74. http://flipbook.archives-socialistes.fr/index.html?docid=51052&language=fra&userid=0 (last consulted: 27 June 2018).

[57] 'Protokol xx. Manifestačního Sjezdu Československé Socialní Demokracie', Archiv ČSSD, Fond 71, Část II, Karton III, p. 127.

[58] 'Comitato Centrale' (17 October 1945), ACS, Carteggio Nenni, Busta 87, Fasc. 2189, pp. 21–2. Figures for the Milano area, where the socialists had historically been strong, indeed show a huge swing towards the PCI among industrial workers – though not as big as Nenni outlined here. In the elections to the provincial FIOM– the Italian metalworkers' union, which contained more than a third of all unionised workers in the province – approximately 70 per cent of the votes cast in some of the main factories of Milano's industrial Porta Romana district went to communist candidates against a mere 20 per cent and 8 per cent for PSIUP and DC candidates, respectively. See Behan, *The Long Awaited Moment*, pp. 191–3.

of the causes for their post-war electoral woes.[59] And although it is difficult, in the absence of free and unfettered elections at both national and
factory level, to measure the exact balance of power between communists
and socialists among the working class, the PPR had certainly grown from
a tiny sect into a mass working-class party.[60]

Socialist leaders identified various reasons for their setbacks and the
communists' gains among the working class. Addressing the PSIUP Central
Committee in January 1946, Nenni listed a series of 'factors', including the
prominent role the communists had played in the anti-fascist Resistance,
the prestige the Soviet Union had acquired by its military victories, and the
'Rome or Moscow' scare campaigns of the Mussolini regime, which had
created an apparently clear-cut choice between fascism and communism.
Above all, however, he pointed to the 'in many respects unfair judgement
… that reformism [i.e. the Italian brand of reformism practised by Filippo
Turati and other PSI leaders in the first decades of the twentieth century]
paved the way for [Italian] fascism like [German] social democracy for
National Socialism'.[61]

The survey that the ČSSD commissioned from the Czechoslovakian
Institute for Public Opinion Research to analyse its poor showing in the
May 1946 parliamentary elections came to similar conclusions. In general
terms, its report, for which more than 1000 voters representative of the
electorate as a whole were interviewed, pointed out that the ČSSD had
lost out to the KSČ because voters were 'grateful' to the Soviet Union
and the Red Army for the liberation of Czechoslovakia, because voters
saw the KSČ as the more radical option in a post-war 'tendency to the
left', and because it had not been sufficiently clear what the ČSSD stood
for. Yet those criticisms that seemed to emanate directly from workers
often concerned the history of the ČSSD. While in government under the
First Republic, as the report summarised such charges, 'the party had not
achieved … what it could and should have achieved': it was reproached
for having broken promises, for having 'always betrayed workers during
strikes', for having 'done nothing for workers', and for having teamed

[59] OURS, CD SFIO, 27 November 1946; 'Volby a čs. sociální demokracie' (1946), NA, Fonds Bohumil
Laušman, III Pisemnosti související s ústřední, veřejnou a politickou činnosti B. Laušmana, Karton
34, Souvicející činnosti v soc. dem. 1928–1948, p. 10.

[60] In 1942, the PPR had a mere 4000 members. By 1947, that number had rocketed to 872,000
members. See Gary N. Marks, 'Communist Party Membership in Five Former Soviet Bloc
Countries, 1945–1989', *Communist and Post-Communist Studies*, 37/2 (2004), pp. 241–63, 253f.

[61] 'Relazione Nenni al Comitato Centrale' (7 January 1946), ACS, Carteggio Nenni, Busta 87, Fasc.
2190, p. 2.

up with the right-wing Agrarian Party. One respondent complained that the ČSSD, when in power, had not done everything in its power for the working class, whereas another went as far as to attribute the party's losses to the 'reactionary' behaviour of its interwar leaders.[62]

If the four parties faced similar challenges to their working-class identity, however, the concomitant soul-searching processes produced very dissimilar results. The PPS and the PSIUP, on the one hand, reaffirmed their proletarian character and strove to carve out a niche for themselves in the working-class movement. The ČSSD and the SFIO, on the other, sought to broaden their platform to include all 'working people' and tailored their message to that end. The lessons of the past, this time on whether there was any popular stronghold of democracy between the working class and 'the reaction', once again proved a crucial factor in determining these opposite outcomes.

For the PPS and the PSIUP, these lessons were very clear: there were 'no bourgeois democrats' in their countries.[63] For all of its lofty rhetoric about rights and freedoms, the two parties insisted, the interwar years had shown the bourgeoisie more preoccupied with its own selfish interests than with the future of the nation or democracy. Pointing out how there had been no 'luxury citizens' among those defending his home town of Gdynia against the Germans in 1939, Rusinek was adamant that the Polish bourgeoisie had 'always in history' valued 'its own life' more highly than 'freedom and the life of the nation'.[64] Lelio Basso was more elaborate. Its profit margins having been destroyed by the consequences of the First World War, he explained, the interwar bourgeoisie was no longer able to offer the working class the 'reformist and paternalistic' concessions it had used to 'blunt the revolutionary desire of the masses' before 1914. The only way for the bourgeoisie to restore its 'shaky economic predominance', then, was to forcibly squeeze salaries and recover the costs of war from the working class. In order to halt the accompanying process of class awakening among the proletariat 'conservative forces, capitalist classes, reactionaries, [and] monarchists have instigated and supported the fascist reaction in Italy,

[62] 'Čs. ústav pro výzkum veřejného mínění: Neúspěch sociální demokracie v květnových volbách' (1946), ANM, Fonds Zdeněk Fierlinger, Karton 40, Neúspěch soc. dem. ve volby, p. 5.
[63] 'Internationale socialistische bijeenkomst te Parijs tot herstel der Internationale' (18 August 1947), International Institute of Social History, Amsterdam (hereafter IISH), Archief Partij van de Arbeid, Map 2680, p. 2; Heumos (ed.), Europäischer Sozialismus, pp. 26–7.
[64] XXVI Kongres (August 1945), AAN, PPS, 235/I-12, fo. 129.

Germany, Spain, Hungary, etc.'. It followed that a new 'bourgeois restoration' in Europe 'would only mean new dictatorships, new fascisms, [and] new wars'.[65]

In the alleged absence of bourgeois democrats, the PPS and the PSIUP regarded the industrial proletariat as the sole group on which a democratic state could be built. To be sure, the two parties were well aware that the working class found itself in a numerical minority vis-à-vis other social groups, and they certainly talked a lot about the need for alliances between the proletariat and other underprivileged constituencies. Yet any overtures towards such groups always sprang from a doctrinaire position. Socialist leaders in both countries often spoke with contempt about the utter 'political backwardness' of peasants, who failed to see that their 'objective' interests lay with socialism – a topic to which we will return in far greater detail in the next chapter.

Even more contentious than reaching out to peasants, who, for all of their mistakes, were at least still manual labourers, was reaching out to the (lower) middle classes. It was this question that often dominated the debates between the supporters and the opponents of communist–socialist unity of action within the PSIUP. Giuseppe Saragat, the leader of the party's anti-communist wing that would break away at the January 1947 PSIUP congress, strongly advocated a genuine socialist outreach to the (lower) middle classes. These groups, he reasoned, had been the backbone of interwar fascism and it was crucial for democracy to keep them out of the hands of the Right in post-war Italy.[66]

Yet the supporters of the communist alliance remained extremely wary of attempts to create 'middle-class socialism'.[67] They feared that the PSIUP, in seeking to tailor to the preferences of the (lower) middle classes, would compromise its proletarian character. 'It is often claimed', argued Basso, 'that we can abandon our unitarian line to make room for … all those middle classes who have proletarianised or are in the process of proletarianisation, but who do not join our party because they are afraid of

---

[65] Lelio Basso, 'Per una politica socialista', *Quarto Stato*, 15 February 1946. www.leliobasso.it/documento.aspx?id=5704117d2290635b3b02e18da9f1c6b8 (last consulted: 27 June 2018).

[66] SFIO international secretary Salomon Grumbach was probably right when he noted, after the PSIUP had split, that both the pro-communist and the anti-communist camps were 'obsessed' with the legacy of the early 1920s: '[Nenni] is obsessed by the memory of the [communist–socialist] split when Mussolini came to power. Saragat is obsessed with the role played by the middle classes during the same period.' OURS, CD SFIO, 5 February 1947.

[67] This was how Nenni denounced Saragat's conception of socialism at the April 1946 PSIUP congress in Firenze. Quoted in Di Scala, *Renewing Italian Socialism*, p. 56.

communism.' But the 'rhetoric', he continued, that there was 'only one socialism and that all working people are equal' was fundamentally flawed. For if 'we know that the worker and the peasant, who possess nothing and live only from selling their labour ... are instinctively revolutionary ... and instinctively realise that their emancipation is a class problem', the same could certainly not be said of the (lower) middle classes. '[F]or the petit-bourgeoisie, for the professional, and often for the state employee too', after all, 'the problem of emancipation' remained 'a problem of individual emancipation'. The only way for these groups to 'acquire a proletarian conscience' was for them to be 'firmly guided by a strong working class'. That was not going to happen, however, if the PSIUP alienated the industrial workers in its ranks by forsaking upon socialist–communist unity. Doing that, insisted Basso, could only result in the 'denaturalisation' of the party. For by 'throwing wide open the entrance to the middle classes ... we will simultaneously throw wide open the exit for workers and peasants'.[68]

PPS leaders were likewise adamant that their party was a proletarian organisation first and foremost. '[D]espite our mass nature', Włodzimierz Reczek told the December 1947 PPS congress, 'nobody can deny that we have a pronounced class profile'. That, he argued, 'is our strength'. The 'example of those socialist parties that diluted their working-class composition [and] descended into the bourgeoisie', after all, 'teaches how adversely that affects their politics, how that blunts militancy, and distorts ideologically'.[69]

That was surely another taunt aimed at the SFIO, which, as we have seen, increasingly became the epitome of all that was wrong with anti-communist (Western) European socialism for the PPS. In defence of their party's proletarian orientation, PSIUP leaders similarly raised the spectre of France. Even Alberto Jacometti – by no means the most ardent pro-communist within the PSIUP leadership[70] – was on message in this respect. Orienting the PSIUP towards the middle classes, he warned the April 1946 party congress, carried the 'danger' of following in the footsteps of the SFIO. For while the SFIO had 'gained in the north [of France] and in the belt around Paris, not a single worker has voted for the Socialist

---

[68] 'xxiv Congresso del Partito Socialista Italiano di Unità Proletaria, 12 aprile 1946, seduta pomeridiana', ACS, Carteggio Nenni, Busta 88, Fasc 2193, pp. 73–6.

[69] xxvii Kongres (December 1947), AAN, PPS, 235/1-26, fo. 82.

[70] Jacometti, after all, would later oppose running the April 1948 parliamentary elections on a common list with the PCI. And in the backlash following the PSIUP's abysmal performance in these elections, he replaced Basso as Secretary General on an 'autonomist' ticket.

Party in the southern band stretching from the Pyrenees to the Alps. All the votes of workers [in that area] have gone to the Communist Party. We cannot allow that to happen in Italy.'[71]

In their efforts to (re-)gain support among all segments of the 'working people', however, the French socialists often felt that they had no choice but to distance themselves from the communists. Already in late 1944, Roger Priou-Valjean warned the SFIO Executive that the party risked losing the 'great current of sympathy' it had garnered among 'middle classes, proletarianised white-collar workers, artisans, peasants, etc.' by aligning itself too closely with the PCF.[72] And as election results confirmed the considerable working-class swing towards communism, the SFIO's focus increasingly shifted to recovering what had historically been, as Moch described it, its 'classic clientele' – public sector workers.[73] In dealing with the demands of public sector workers, the group frequently hit hardest by the anti-inflationary policies of post-war governments, Guy Mollet instructed his fellow party leaders not to 'forget about the political repercussions'. The 'world of public sector workers' constituted 'the essential bedrock of the Party', after all, with teachers making up 'our best recruiters'. Yet there was 'a real discontent' at the grassroots, which was 'exploited by the Communist Party'. While it was still impossible to give in to all their material demands, therefore, Mollet insisted that 'in the form and on the moral level all reassurances are given to public sector workers'.[74]

In the face of an even more significant working-class surge towards communism, the ČSSD similarly opted to reach out to non-proletarian constituencies. That was the foremost rationale behind the ČSSD dropping the designation 'Worker' from its name at the party's October 1945 congress. According to Vilím, the name change would help 'unite … the industrial working class' and 'other strata of working people'. For the party had 'shown too little interest in other strata of the nation' before the war, he claimed, 'especially in peasants, who were ultimately left with no choice but to join the Agrarian Party, thereby strengthening the power of the reactionary landowning clique within that party'.[75] Evžen Erban, the ČSSD's secretary general of ÚRO, likewise declared that the new party wanted

---

[71] 'xxiv Congresso del Partito Socialista Italiano di Unità Proletaria, 13 aprile 1946, seduta antemeridiana', ACS, Carteggio Nenni, Busta 88, Fasc 2193, p. 15.

[72] OURS, CD SFIO, 21 December 1944.

[73] OURS, CD SFIO, 4 June 1946.

[74] OURS, CD SFIO, 29 January 1947.

[75] 'Protokol xx. Manifestačního Sjezdu Československé Sociální Demokracie', Archiv ČSSD, Fond 71, Část ii, Karton iii, pp. 127–8.

not to 'restrict itself to the working class only' but to 'become a party of the working people of city and countryside, of salaried workers, and of the self-employed'. Though he was adamant that '[t]he party should lead the middle classes and not the middle classes the party', he conceded that '[t]he working class cannot win its struggle if it does not obtain other strata of the working people as an ally'. The ČSSD, accordingly, had to 'clarify to the working class that the victory of socialism urgently requires the winning over of the middle classes, which we must not repel with an insular politics of class containment'.[76]

This far greater willingness, by comparison with the Italian and Polish socialists, to reach out to non-proletarian social constituencies had its roots in a fundamentally different understanding of national history and national traditions on the part of the ČSSD and the SFIO. The past had taught the two parties that the great majority of their populations, including the middle classes, were committed to freedom and democracy.

For SFIO leaders, this went right from the wartime Resistance all the way back to the French Revolution. The 'struggle for national liberation and democratic liberation', declared SFIO Executive member and later interior minister Édouard Depreux at the party's first post-war congress, demonstrated

> that France has remained the country of 1789 and 1792 [when the First French Republic had come into being], the country that has taught the world the use of freedom and democracy and, with that sense of the universal that characterises the genius of our people, has proclaimed the Declaration of the Rights of Man and of the Citizen, that imperishable charter of politically emancipated mankind.[77]

ČSSD leaders traced back the democratic traditions of Czechoslovakia even further than that. In what must be seen as another warning to the communists, Laušman elaborated on a nineteenth-century nationalist narrative concerning the alleged "'natural democraticality" of the Czechs'[78] to point out that dictatorship was inimical to the national spirit. 'Our nation may be small', he told the November 1947 ČSSD congress,

---

[76] Ibid., p. 133.
[77] 'Parti Socialiste – SFIO: Congrès national extraordinaire des 9, 10, 11 et 12 novembre 1944', FJJ, p. 6. http://flipbook.archives-socialistes.fr/index.html?docid=49328&language=fra&userid=0 (last consulted: 27 June 2018).
[78] According to Robert Pynsent, this notion has been 'an essential element of [Czech] national mythology at least from the late 1830s onwards'. Robert B. Pynsent, 'Misoteutonic Myths: Lopping Noses in Hussite Nationalism and Love's Sweet Cure', in Alexander Wöll and Harald Wydra (eds.), *Democracy and Myth in Russia and Eastern Europe* (New York: Routledge, 2008), pp. 98–121, 108.

[but] it has always stood out in its spiritual fortitude [and] the strength of its convictions … Our endeavours were always thoroughly humane, our ideas always progressive and, and this I want to stress, socialist. Remember the Hussites [the followers of the fifteenth-century religious reformer Jan Hus, who, during their wars with the papal armies of the Holy Roman Empire, founded an egalitarian commune in Bohemian Tábor]! Remember the democratic theories of state that guided us in the Middle Ages [and] found their personification in our great [fifteenth-century] King George of Poděbrady, remember the teachings of [seventeenth-century educational reformer John Amos] Comenius and the exploits of [nineteenth- and twentieth-century national independence partisans Karel] Havlíček and [Tomáš Gariggue] Masaryk!

This was how 'the whole world' knew Czechoslovakia, insisted Laušman, and how it would remain known 'for eternity'. For the country, he continued, had 'never as a whole nor in any significant part succumbed to … reactionary frenzies or anti-democratic temptations'. Instead, it had always been 'freedom-loving, humane, tolerant, and progressive'. The implications for post-war Czechoslovakia were clear. It was 'self-evident', Laušman claimed, that 'it never was possible, that it is not possible, and that it never will be possible in our nation to cultivate a politics foreign to these national feelings and beliefs, to our innate worldview'. Every attempt to introduce 'violent and dictatorial methods', therefore, 'would have to fail. Our nation cannot simply be enslaved, because freedom and democracy are in its blood and are its whole life.'[79]

If a predilection towards freedom and democracy was shared across the classes, however, socialist beliefs certainly were not. And for all of their rhetoric about guiding the middle classes towards socialism, the ČSSD and the SFIO more frequently found themselves reassuring non-proletarian constituencies regarding their intentions. The desired outreach to the middle classes, then, often came at the price of abandoning socio-economic radicalism. For if those 'small proprietors, artisans, [and] small shopkeepers who are the Republican spirit', as Auriol put it, 'c[a]me to the proletariat when freedom [and] the Republican institutions are under threat', they 'moved to the right' when their 'interests are affected [and] uncertainty is knocking at the door'.[80]

---

[79] 'Zahajovací projev předsedy xxi. sjezdu čsl. socialní demokracie Bohumila Laušmana' (14 November 1947), Archiv ČSSD, Fond 71, Část II, Karton 112, p. 7.

[80] 'Partit Socialiste SFIO: Conseil national 3 et 4 décembre 1946', FJJ, p. 147. http://62.210.214.184/cg-ps/documents/pdf/cons-1946-12-03.pdf (last consulted: 27 June 2018).

It was crucial for the two parties, accordingly, not to deter the middle classes from socialism by adopting revolutionary and leftist positions. 'The grandest left-wing politics', warned ČSSD Central Committee member and chairman of the party's Commission for Tradesmen Pavel Sajal, would hardly be 'a magnet' attracting such groups. The middle classes, he argued, 'are not opposed to socialism, but … demand democracy, the rule of law, and order within and profitability of nationalised firms'.[81] Above all, however, the middle classes wanted guarantees that their long-term position would be safe under socialism, insisted the report that the Commission for Tradesmen submitted to the November 1947 ČSSD congress, amid fears that the 'independence' they had been promised in the 1945 government programme was 'limited by time'.[82]

The SFIO sought to assuage similar fears in a propaganda brochure directed at artisans and small businessmen. '[F]ar from wanting to destroy the middle classes', it insisted, the party had 'always and everywhere come to their defence'. Jean Jaurès had written, after all, that 'socialism is not opposed to small business. It does not concern itself with the proletarians of a single class, because, if that were the case, it would simply be replacing a tyranny with a tyranny, an oppression with an oppression.'[83]

Conclusion

We have seen in this chapter that the two sets of parties drew widely divergent lessons from their national and Europe's interwar history. For the PPS and the PSIUP, on the one hand, history painted a very grim picture indeed. In this picture, both the working class and its political representatives were completely isolated in their struggles for democracy and socialism. Time and again, after all, the interwar bourgeoisie had decided to throw in its lot with dictators in order to safeguard its economic interests. It followed that class struggle would be an inevitable feature of post-war society, requiring the working class to pull together and present a united front.

For the ČSSD and the SFIO, on the other hand, history offered an altogether more reassuring picture. In this picture, the working class and the socialist parties had always found non-proletarian social constituencies and centrist parties on their side when democracy came under pressure.

---

[81] 'Protokol xx. Manifestačního Sjezdu Československé Socialní Demokracie', Archiv ČSSD, Fond 71, Část II, Karton III, p. 161.

[82] *Zpráva o činnosti*, p. 137.

[83] 'Le Parti socialiste, les artisans et les petits commerçants', Arguments et Ripostes, Bulletin Intérieur du Parti Socialiste (S.F.I.O.), 15 October 1946, OURS.

The main lesson of the past, accordingly, was that democracy would survive as long as the political centre ground held. And in the increasingly polarised post-war world, that lesson warranted the search for new alliances across class boundaries.

The significance of historical lessons, however, stretched far beyond the mere question of alliances – whether political or social. They also crucially shaped the four parties' attitudes towards the key dimension of political reconstruction: the rebuilding of democracy. For each of the four parties, democracy had both political and economic connotations. In political terms, it was to guarantee the rights and freedoms we still associate with democracy today: free and fair elections, freedom of speech, conscience, and association, and the checks and balances between executive, legislative, and judiciary powers. In economic terms, it was to usher in 'structural reforms' in the economic system: the nationalisation of the commanding heights of the economy, land reform, and/or genuine worker participation in industrial decision-making. If the four parties agreed on the overall objective of establishing both political and economic democracy, however, they certainly did not on the prioritisation of one over the other or on the methods with which best to achieve this goal.

For the Italian and Polish socialists, the institution of economic democracy had to precede the reintroduction of political democracy. In their view, it was pointless to resurrect political democracy without first destroying the economic power structures upon which bourgeois domination rested. For that reason, the PPS and the PSIUP were proponents of what they called 'popular democracy' (they also used 'new democracy' and 'socialist democracy' to describe this phenomenon): a system in which the working-class parties would temporarily be guaranteed a dominant position in government even if the electoral arithmetic did not allow for that. During this transitional period, the government could implement structural economic reforms, while building up a system of direct grassroots participation in public life. It was only after the thorough political re-education that came with the experience of participation that their backward and disoriented electorates would be equipped to face up to the temptations of political democracy again.

Both parties were very much aware that 'popular democracy' involved overstepping the confines of political democracy in the short run. But their history had taught them that that was the only way to achieve freedom in the long run. The programmatic motion that the leadership of the clandestine PSIUP in northern Italy – which included Basso, Morandi, and Pertini – adopted in November 1944 makes this point very clearly. 'The

Party knows', it proclaimed, 'that true freedom will be given to the Italian people not by the Anglo-Saxon armies, not by the CLN, not by a government of concentration, nor by a Constituent Assembly if that is not an Assembly of workers.' True freedom would rather be realised, it continued, 'by the abolition of the privileges that derive from property, by the forfeiture of the right that sanctions [these privileges], and by the destruction of the economic system upon which bourgeois domination is based'. And that was not going to happen as the result of a negotiated process. 'The freedom of the people cannot come from alliances with groups that, even if they talk of socialism and are willing to make concessions today, want to salvage capitalism in its substance; nor can it be assured by any electoral majority that does not lead to the elimination of the interests that stand in the way of [freedom]'. Quite the contrary, '[f]reedom can only be achieved in a new order proclaimed by the people and constituted outside of existing legality, which is a protection and a shield for the supremacy of a class'.[84]

For the Czechoslovakian social democrats and French socialists, on the other hand, abidance by the rulebook of political democracy was a precondition for the establishment of economic democracy. In this respect, even though they would not admit to supporting 'bourgeois' democracy, socialist leaders in both countries very much fostered the political legacy of the interwar bourgeois-liberal state. It was electoral majorities that had to decide about governmental outcomes and any attempt to subvert this process would obliterate the freedom that was at the very core of socialism. Only once political democracy had been achieved could economic democracy be built following a parliamentary and constitutional trajectory.

Far from advocating the overthrow of existing legality, therefore, the ČSSD and the SFIO always insisted on working within the confines of political democracy. It is very telling that the two parties always spoke of extending political democracy with economic democracy rather than the other way around.[85] That was because their history had taught them that political democracy could not only survive within the framework of bourgeois capitalism, but also make the capitalist system increasingly social. It was this belief more than anything – that liberal capitalism, for all of its

[84] 'Mozione programmatica del Comitato Centrale per l'Alta Italia' (November 1944), *Orientamenti: Bollettino di Commento e di Indirizzo Politico*, 18 January 1948, p. 10.

[85] See e.g. 'Program československé sociali demokracie', Archiv ČSSD, Fond 71, Část II, Karton III, pp. 13–14; Guy Mollet, 'Examen de conscience', *La Revue Socialiste*, December 1946, pp 557–662, 661.

economic injustices, did guarantee 'personal and civic rights'[86] and could be transformed from within – that set the Czechoslovakian social democrats and French socialists apart from their Italian and Polish counterparts.

The question dividing the two sets of parties with regard to political reconstruction, then, was whether socialism could be achieved within the existing institutional structures and by legal means. The next two chapters will delve far deeper into the four parties' responses to this question. First, we will compare their attitudes towards the three principal institutions of 'bourgeois' democracy. Subsequently, we will contrast their views on the participatory structures that were at the heart of socialist conceptions of 'popular democracy'.

---

[86] That was at least how the 1945 programme of the ČSSD's Action Committee put it. 'Program akčního výboru – Československé sociální demokracie', Archiv ČSSD, Fond 71, Část II, Karton III, p. 9.

CHAPTER 6

Elections, Parliaments, and Constitutions

In August 1947, an article in the ČSSD's theoretical weekly questioned the course Czechoslovakian democracy had taken since the Second World War. 'The notion of political democracy, as understood by the nineteenth-century thinkers and as formulated by T.G. Masaryk', it observed, 'has changed considerably after the Second World War and after the experience of fascism.' In place of the old slogans of freedom, equality, and brotherhood, 'that is [the watchword] "equal rights for all", which the bourgeoisie completely abused', was now the 'very narrow' slogan of 'democracy only for democrats'. But it was doubtful, the article continued, 'whether this narrowing really constitutes a step in the right direction and whether it protects democracy from abuse'. The meaning of words, after all, 'ultimately depends on who expresses them and, after the experiences with Hitler, who pretended to be the only genuine socialist and democrat, we know that it is more important ... which power gives words their actual significance'. The new slogan of democracy only for democrats, therefore, not only failed to 'provide any guarantee for democracy', but also carried within it a 'danger'. For 'one powerful group' could easily declare 'that it alone represents true democracy and that it alone is entitled to democratic freedoms, whereas all others have only the democratic obligation to keep their mouths shut'.[1]

Historians typically portray the first post-war years as the period during which (Western) European socialism unreservedly came to embrace representative democracy as 'much more than the political form adopted by the bourgeoisie within the capitalist state'.[2] For if the economic and social instability of the interwar years had still 'left important sections of Social

---

[1] V. Sajus, 'Hospodářská demokracie a nová šlechta', *Cíl*, 15 August 1947.

[2] According to Ignacio Walker, this 'process', which had its origins in the interwar years, 'took definite shape in the post-war period'. See Ignacio Walker, 'Democratic Socialism in Comparative Perspective', *Comparative Politics*, 23/1 (1991), pp. 439–58, 442.

Democracy with strong and lingering doubts about the parliamentary road to socialism', the subsequent 'years of oppression and persecution under a swastika-dominated Europe' drove the socialist movement 'towards the acceptance of pluralist democracy after 1945'.[3] In these circumstances, 'virtually all Socialists insisted political democracy was an end in itself. The concept included both respect for individual civil rights and adherence to a system of political decision-making founded on free, universal suffrage. Most Social Democrats favoured parliamentary democracy as a constitutional system.'[4]

Yet, as the above story already hints at, the experience of dictatorship (initially) also drove some socialists in the opposite direction. Far from embracing the parliamentary road to socialism, these socialists argued that 'bourgeois' democracy had failed their countries and would, if reconstituted, only usher in new dictatorships. For that reason, they advocated a radical, albeit temporary, curtailing of the franchise, the party landscape, and/or the rights and freedoms of their political rivals more generally. These anti-representative sentiments among post-war European socialists, however, have hardly received any scholarly attention. This is unfortunate, as the question of whether socialists should adhere to the democratic rulebook of bourgeois society divided the four parties under review in this book more than any other question.

This chapter aims to demonstrate this by comparing the two sets of parties' attitudes towards the three key institutions of 'bourgeois' democracy. In the first place, it will analyse their views on elections. Whereas the ČSSD and the SFIO treated election results as infallible reflections of the popular will, the PPS and the PSIUP were often dismissive of their meaning after decades of dictatorship. Secondly, it will delve into their perspectives upon parliamentary activity. If the ČSSD and the SFIO saw parliament as the chief bulwark of democracy, the PPS and the PSIUP mostly regarded parliamentarism as an outdated and overly legalistic form of doing politics. Thirdly, it will address their approaches towards constitutions and above all constitutionalism. While the ČSSD and the SFIO were adamant that the rule of law was to be upheld at all times, the PPS and the PSIUP were more willing to countenance the proletarian parties using dictatorial methods in the struggle for political power.

---

[3] Stefan Berger, 'Democracy and Social Democracy', *European History Quarterly*, 32/1 (2002), pp. 13–37, 26–7.
[4] Orlow, *Common Destiny*, p. 45.

Elections

In the wake of liberation, each of the four parties relished the prospect of elections. With the last (free) parliamentary elections dating back (almost) a decade in Czechoslovakia (1935) and France (1936) and as far as a generation in Italy (1921) and Poland (1928), socialist leaders considered a popular verdict on the state of parties to be long overdue. What is more, they fully expected elections to go their way. The 1930s Depression having discredited capitalism and the disastrous consequences of the appeasement of, or the collaboration with, fascism having tainted many on the interwar bourgeois Right, party leaders were confident that an electoral breakthrough towards socialism could finally be achieved.

Pietro Nenni was exuding such confidence when he told the September 1944 National Convention of the PSIUP that 'we have faith in the [still to be elected] Constituent Assembly', for 'we know that we have the great bulk of the people behind us'.[5] Much like their Italian and other Western European counterparts, the French socialists came out of the war considering a transition to socialism 'a dialectical near-certainty'.[6] The resolution adopted by the November 1945 Supreme Council of the PPS, for its part, emphasised that the upcoming parliamentary elections were 'to be not only a reflection of the real social-political balance of power in the country, but also a working people's trial of Polish fascism'. That the entire pre-war ruling class was subsumed under this banner became apparent from the long list of charges the resolution levelled against 'Polish fascism', which included depriving parliament of the right to control the Sanacja government, the dissolution of trade unions, and 'the alliance of the reaction and Hitler in 1934' – that is, the ten-year non-aggression pact that the Piłsudski government and Nazi Germany had entered into in January 1934. As a result of elections, the resolution concluded, the working class would finally be able to 'realise its fundamental programme'.[7]

Yet this supreme confidence in the outcome of free and unfettered elections would quickly dissipate. Within the PPS and the PSIUP, the

---

[5] 'Discorso di Pietro Nenni, Segretario del Partito Socialista Italiano' (4 September 1944), ACS, Carteggio Nenni, Busta 87, Fasc 2186, p. 21.

[6] The quote is from Marc Sadoun, who points to the similarities between socialist rhetoric – 'socialism is the master of the hour', 'we are the masters at present', and 'after Hitler us' – within the SFIO, the Labour Party, and the exiled German SPD, respectively. See Marc Sadoun, *Les socialistes sous l'occupation: résistance et collaboration* (Paris: Presse de la Fondation Nationale des Sciences Politiques, 1982), p. 269. Dietrich Orlow provides further Dutch and German examples of post-liberation socialist euphoria. See Orlow, *Common Destiny*, p. 289f.

[7] 'Uchwały Rady Naczelnej' (4 November 1945), AAN, PPS, Rada Naczelna, 235/II/5, fo. 10a.

elation initially surrounding the prospect of a popular vote made way for gloom even before the first ballot had been cast. Already at the first post-war congress of the PPS, Wincenty Stawiński – the socialist member of parliament for Pabianice (near Łódź) – counselled against calling elections anytime soon. Finding itself in power in 1918, he reminisced, the party had also called elections and lost. To entrust the Polish people with a ballot again would amount to 'the burial of the achievements of the Provisional Government. We first have to educate Polish society.'[8] Albeit in slightly less dramatic terms, Lelio Basso also warned against viewing the upcoming parliamentary elections as a cure for all of Italy's political ills. 'We would be making a very serious mistake and exposing the country to dangerous delusions', he wrote in August 1945, 'if we attribute miraculous virtues to the Constituent Assembly; if we think, following an old parliamentary mentality, that electoral rallies can resolve a crisis so profound as the one tormenting us, can give a democratic conscience to a people that never had one.'[9]

What seems to have underlain this pessimism regarding electoral outcomes among Italian and Polish socialists was a deep-seated belief that their societies were ill-prepared for the temptations of democratic politics. While almost impervious to democratic and socialist arguments, party leaders in both countries lamented, large swathes of their electorates were easily swayed by reactionary and populist solutions.

This was especially true for the two countries' large peasant majorities. All of their rhetoric about the essential community of interest between industrial proletarians and rural labourers notwithstanding, PPS and PSIUP leaders often despaired of the political acumen of the peasantry. There were repeated allusions to the utter backwardness of peasants, many of whom were lacking basic literacy skills and would believe anything their local priest told them. These were people who, in the words of leading Polish socialists, were only just 'returning to humanity', having been 'the property of counts and wealthy landowners' for centuries.[10] And whereas 'the message of socialism' had never reached the countryside, soon-to-be-elected PSIUP parliamentarian Bianca Bianchi told her party's April 1946 congress, the 'almost omnipresent' Catholic Action (the largest lay organ-isation of the Roman Catholic Church in Italy, which played a significant

[8] xxvi Kongres (August 1945), AAN, PPS, 235/1-12, fo. 196.
[9] Lelio Basso, 'Per una coscienza democratica', *Avanti!*, 29 August 1945. www.leliobasso.it/documento.aspx?id=1fb14f1db3eb10586206dfcbf448089 (last consulted: 27 June 2018).
[10] xxvi Kongres (August 1945), AAN, PPS, 235/1-12, fo. 131, 269.

role in post-war election campaigns) was 'leading women towards the DC' and 'all small villages' had 'a church denigrating socialism'.[11]

In these circumstances, the crucial peasant vote was unlikely to befall to socialism. Although PPS and PSIUP leaders did not tire of repeating that peasants' 'objective interests' lay with socialism, they had to acknowledge that peasant electoral behaviour was frequently determined by factors that were far from objective. Recounting what he had heard at the January 1948 congress of the PSIUP, Léon Boutbien informed the SFIO's International Commission that the 'many illiterates without political education' in the largely rural South of Italy would vote for 'anyone at all'. Even the PCI had been able to make considerable inroads[12] in some of the more pious districts by claiming that a vote for the communists amounted to a vote for Saint Joseph – a reference to Italy's founding father Giuseppe (=Joseph) Garibaldi, whose image adorned the emblem of the Popular Front.[13]

Basso affirmed that the political understanding of the peasantry did not exceed a very basic level. '[D]eliberately kept in a state of illiteracy and superstition', he argued, 'rural plebs' voted 'against their own interests because they are unable to "consciously" exercise their right to vote'. To be sure, when faced with such a simple yes-or-no question as 'do you approve land reform?' – one of the three questions that had been put to the Polish people in the referendum of June 1946 – peasants would overwhelmingly vote yes. But come the time of the next parliamentary elections, Basso continued, those same peasants would 'certainly vote for the candidates of the priests, i.e. for the exponents and representatives of the old feudal nobility, [who are] opposed to peasant interests and to land reform in particular'.[14] Jan Żerkowski – the PPS chairman of the Parliamentary Commission for Cooperatives, Supply, and Trade – likewise cautioned his fellow party leaders that peasant enthusiasm for specific socialist policies would not translate into electoral support for socialism. 'We know very well', he explained, 'that the small farmer and peasant do not come

---

[11] 'XXIV Congresso del Partito Socialista Italiano di Unità Proletaria', 14 aprile 1946, seduta antimeridiana, ACS, Carteggio Nenni, Busta 88, Fasc 2193, p. 29.

[12] Of course, the PCI's success in the rural areas of southern Italy – for it was in the rural south much more than in the industrial north of Italy that the communists outperformed the socialists in electoral terms – must also be attributed to the radical traditions among landless rural labourers in that region. On the PCI and the southern peasantry, see Paul Ginsborg, 'The Communist Party and the Agrarian Question in Southern Italy, 1943–1948', *History Workshop Journal*, 17/1 (1984), pp. 81–101.

[13] 'Réunion de la Commission Internationale du Parti Socialiste' (17 January 1948), Centre d'Histoire Social, Paris (hereafter CHS), Fonds Marceau Pivert, 559API42, 1948, p. 5.

[14] Lelio Basso, 'Socialismo europeo (1)', *Quarto Stato*, 15 September 1946. www.leliobasso.it/documento.aspx?id=cf99e9daef3d5143ea3b0399083d2f01 (last consulted: 27 June 2018).

to socialism.' Contrary to what the Congress of Socialist Peasants was claiming, socialism was 'not catching on with the peasant' – 'he is taken in by the cooperative movement, by the League of Peasant Self-Help, but not by socialist ideology'.[15]

Just how much of a mountain the parties had to climb in electoral terms was borne out further by election news seeping through from abroad. The results of the late 1945 elections in Austria and Hungary, both of which had returned the main Catholic centre-right party with an absolute parliamentary majority, made for particularly terrible reading. When, in late November 1945, the PPS Central Committee discussed the trajectory towards parliamentary elections in post-war Poland, several party leaders reflected on the lessons to be learned from these experiences. Józef Cyrankiewicz insisted that the Polish parliamentary elections would be 'prepared politically and organisationally, so that the PSL will not follow in the footsteps of the Smallholders in Hungary' – i.e. the Independent Smallholders' Party, which had secured 57 per cent of the vote in the Hungarian elections. Henryk Wachowicz agreed that the PPS found itself 'in a difficult situation'. 'If the PSL does not join us [the PPS and the PPR] in a common bloc', he explained, 'it will receive very many votes'. The Austrian elections, after all, were 'an example of the demagogical grasp of the reaction'.[16]

According to the Italian and Polish socialists, that grasp reached well beyond ignorant and illiterate peasants. PPS Central Committee member Stanisław Skowroński argued that 'the potential strength of the reaction in Poland' was 'exceptional', its mesmerism attracting such diverse groups as 'the petit-bourgeoisie, philistines, the clergy, [and] teachers'.[17] By October 1945, Nenni had likewise identified a broadening appeal of reactionary politics in post-war Italy. Examining the causes of 'the noteworthy intensification of reactionary activity' since the PSIUP's September 1944 National Convention, when he had still predicted a straightforward victory for the Left in democratic elections, he highlighted three phenomena. In the first place, 'all political, social and economic forces' that were afraid of 'the tidal wave emanating from below' were rallying around the monarchy. Secondly, the purge had driven a segment of the population 'to conservative or even reactionary positions'. But 'the most serious phenomenon' was

---

[15] Rada Naczelna (31 March 1946), AAN, PPS, 235/II/6, fo. 33.
[16] 'Protokół posiedzenia CKW PPS' (30 November 1945), AAN, PPS, CKW, 235/III/2, fos 9–10.
[17] 'Protokół posiedzenia CKW PPS' (14 May 1946), AAN, PPS, CKW, 235/III/2, fo. 51.

the popular misery 'creating vast groups of malcontents, who we cannot forever ask to make sacrifices, to tighten their belts, etc.'.[18]

As such misery hit the working class first and foremost, PPS and PSIUP leaders were increasingly fixated on reactionary stirrings in their traditional industrial heartlands. Franco Mariani warned of 'political speculators' preying upon legitimate worker grievances to plunge Italy into chaos before democracy could take root. The same 'reactionary and parasitical classes that have subsidised and sustained fascism', he explained, were now hoping to 'profit from unemployment and misery' by 'creating street tumults and insurrections', which would, in turn, be quashed 'by exactly those Allies [i.e. the Anglo-American troops which had assumed control over law enforcement in early post-war Italy] upon which these reactionary currents have pinned their hopes to destroy the nascent democratic structure of our country'.[19]

What was worse, there were indications that dissatisfied workers were turning their back on the Left altogether. The many votes for non-party (i.e. neither socialist nor communist) candidates in factory council elections, Wachowicz told the PPS Central Committee in November 1945, 'bears testimony to the fact that even the most conscious class, the working class, takes a hostile attitude towards us'.[20] And, as the parliamentary elections drew closer, that became an increasing cause for concern. By May 1946, Cyrankiewicz was stressing the need to 'draw up an economic plan for the working class'. For 'if positive changes [in working-class wages, living standards, etc.] have not been effected by the time of the elections', he warned, 'a surprising situation might transpire at the last minute, which we must avoid with respect to the PSL. That would deprive us of our driving force in the electoral struggle – the working class.'[21]

By contrast with the PPS and the PSIUP, the euphoria surrounding electoral outcomes lasted rather longer within the ČSSD and the SFIO. Right up to the first parliamentary elections in France (October 1945) and Czechoslovakia (May 1946), party leaders and activists in both countries had been expecting to come out on top in the democratic contest. The 'overwhelming participation' in the 'more than 5000 electoral meetings', reflected the ČSSD on its 1946 campaign, 'seduced many of our functionaries to too optimistic expectations of the election result'.[22] Bohumil

---

[18] 'Comitato Centrale' (17 October 1945), ACS, Carteggio Nenni, Busta 87, Fasc. 2189, pp. 13–14.
[19] Interview Hadfield with Franco Mariani, AdL, Camera del Lavoro, Class. 5.1.3., Fasc. 4.
[20] 'Protokół posiedzenia CKW PPS' (30 November 1945), AAN, PPS, CKW, 235/III/2, fo. 10.
[21] 'Protokół posiedzenia CKW PPS' (14 May 1946), AAN, PPS, CKW, 235/III/2, fo. 53.
[22] *Zpráva o činnosti*, p. XXVII.

Laušman, though claiming not to have been among 'the greatest of optimists' himself, also granted that the 'reports coming in from some provinces' and the assumption that 'we would be able to win two non-member votes for every party member' had made the party 'overestimate its strength by 45–50 seats' – a result that would probably have seen the ČSSD become the largest force in parliament.[23]

SFIO leaders likewise approached the elections to the Constituent Assembly with the utmost confidence. Opening his party's August 1945 congress, Gérard Jacquet – who had been the deputy secretary general of the clandestine SFIO – professed that 'times have never been more favourable to socialism'. Governments 'presided over by our friends', after all, were being installed 'around the world' and 'our Labour comrades have just secured a great success' (i.e. the Labour Party's landslide victory in the United Kingdom's 1945 general election). In France, too, 'all eyes are turning towards us'. With 'offers for collaboration' coming in 'from all walks of life', Jacquet concluded, the SFIO had 'at no moment in its history ... been as powerful as it is today'.[24]

The actual election results, then, were a harsh awakening for the SFIO and the ČSSD. Relegated into third and fifth place in parliament, respectively, behind both the communists and the main centre-right and/or Christian democratic parties, illusions of a Labour-like electoral breakthrough were rapidly dashed. Unlike their Italian and Polish counterparts, however, the French socialists and the Czechoslovakian social democrats did not attribute their electoral woes to an underdeveloped and uneducated society.

In fact, party leaders in both countries identified the ample appeal of democracy and socialism among their electorates. According to the ČSSD, the election results were proof that the interwar 'reactionary parties' (including the Agrarian Party – the strongest political force in the First Republic), which had been outlawed for their collaboration with the Protectorate authorities, no longer enjoyed significant support in Czechoslovakian society. The fact, after all, that only 'a negligible number' of voters had made use of their right to cast a blank ballot, an option introduced to allow people to register their protest at the disappearance of the party of their choice, constituted 'evidence' that the new order was backed by

[23] 'Volby a čs. sociální demokracie' (1946), NA, Fonds Bohumil Laušman, III Pisemnosti související s ústřední, veřejnou a politickou činnosti B. Laušmana, Karton 34, Souvicející činnosti v soc. dem. 1928–1948, p. 8.

[24] 'Parti Socialiste – SFIO: 37ème Congrès national des 11, 12, 13, 14 et 15 août 1945', FJJ, p. 7. http:// 62.210.214.184/cg-ps/documents/pdf/cong-1945-08-11.pdf (last consulted: 27 June 2018).

'the overwhelming majority of erstwhile followers of these parties'.[25] Guy Mollet also noted a sea change in popular attitudes in post-war France. In the aftermath of the liberation, he declared, there had been 'an immense call for socialism', reflected in 'a desire for change, a revolutionary drive'. It was 'a tragedy' that 'the SFIO has been unable to respond to that call'.[26]

The ČSSD and the SFIO identified three causes for their failure to capitalise upon this favourable Zeitgeist. In the first place, there were the countless organisational and propagandistic shortcomings which Mollet dubbed 'internal causes' for defeat at the polls.[27] After their party came a disappointing third in the October 1945 parliamentary elections, SFIO leaders listed a raft of problems in these areas. Marius Moutet – minister of Overseas France in both the Popular Front and various post-war governments – explained how the disparities in the organisational preparedness of the parties had made themselves felt in his Drôme department. Whereas the communists had put up 'a great effort' with '[local] newspapers and a profound organisation', he lamented, 'we changed our Federal Secretary during the election [campaign]' and suffered from 'a lack of organisation'.[28] Moutet's and other SFIO leaders' pleas for the creation of socialist factory groups, a better organisation of party propaganda, and the political and administrative training of the party cadre notwithstanding, however, progress was slow. By November 1946, after a third consecutive election defeat for the SFIO, Mollet was still calling for the streamlining of the party's message, for more use to be made of written propaganda, and for the reorganisation of the party's factory, women's, and youth groups.[29]

The ČSSD likewise imputed its May 1946 election defeat in large part to organisational failings. The party's Central Organisational Commission identified no fewer than twelve deficiencies in the party organisation, including the insufficient development of local and factory party organisations, an unqualified party cadre, and the insufficient agility of national and provincial party leaders.[30]

One party arm singled out for particular criticism within both the ČSSD and the SFIO was the national party press. Provincial party branches complained bitterly about the 'ideological ambiguity' of their

[25] *Zpráva o činnosti*, p. xxv.
[26] 'Parti Socialiste SFIO: 38ème Congrès national, 29, 30, 31 août et 1er septembre 1946', FJJ, p. 67. http://62.210.214.184/cg-ps/documents/pdf/cong-1946-08-29.pdf (last consulted: 27 June 2018).
[27] OURS, CD SFIO, 13 November 1946.
[28] OURS, CD SFIO, 24 October 1945.
[29] OURS, CD SFIO, 13 November 1946.
[30] 'Připomínky organisačni komise strany k volebním výsledkům' (1946), ANM, Fonds Zdeněk Fierlinger, Karton 40, Vysledek Voleb, p. 1.

national press organs,[31] about their lack of 'reflection on the party line' and of 'arguments allowing us to defend our politics',[32] and about their 'snobbish' attitude towards the everyday concerns of the people.[33] But even national party leaderships, themselves in charge of the party press, were frequently scornful of their own newspapers and periodicals. The ČSSD's Central Organisational Commission acknowledged that there were 'major weaknesses in our press': the national daily *Právo Lidu* was not answering to the 'organisational needs of the party' and the provincial ČSSD press was not being provided with 'the unified guidance it deserves'.[34] The SFIO leadership similarly found fault with the inadequate cohesion between the socialist press and socialist ministers,[35] while Édouard Depreux lamented that the party's national daily *Le Populaire* 'does not make enough of our semi-successes'.[36]

Both parties needed all the positive exposure they could get, for they struggled to leave a strong mark on their electorates. This was the second main cause to which ČSSD and SFIO leaders attributed their electoral setbacks. Squeezed between the communist and bourgeois/Christian democratic poles in the post-war coalition governments, socialist leaders in both countries often lamented that their parties lacked a clearly defined profile other than that of perpetual compromise. After the strong polarisation of the war years and the liberation struggle, compromise was hardly what voters were looking for. Zdeněk Fierlinger wrote that the ČSSD had entered the parliamentary elections in 'an unenviable position'. 'We found ourselves ... somewhere in the centre between the communists and the other parties', he explained, whereas '[d]evelopments after every war and every revolution have a tendency to move away from the centre'.[37] Mollet likewise pointed out that it was 'normal' that, after fascism, 'the great bulk of voters are attracted towards extremes'. It had been 'our mistake', he continued, 'to suggest that we were not one of these extremes'.[38]

[31] 'Prohlášení krajského výkonného výboru čs sociální demokracie v Plzni' (1946), ANM, Fonds Zdeněk Fierlinger, Karton 40, Vysledek Voleb, p. 6.

[32] 'Parti Socialiste – SFIO: 37ème Congrès national des 11, 12, 13, 14 et 15 août 1945', FJJ, p. 95. http://62.210.214.184/cg-ps/documents/pdf/cong-1945-08-11.pdf (last consulted: 27 June 2018).

[33] 'Parti Socialiste – SFIO: 38ème Congrès national, 29, 30 31 août et 1er septembre 1946', FJJ, p. 143. http://flipbook.archives-socialistes.fr/index.html?docid=51052&language=fra&userid=0 (last consulted: 27 June 2018).

[34] 'Připomínky organisační komise strany k volebním výsledkům' (1946), ANM, Fonds Zdeněk Fierlinger, Karton 40, Vysledek Voleb, p. 1.

[35] OURS, CD SFIO, 25 January 1945.

[36] OURS, CD SFIO, 9 January 1946.

[37] 'The Mission of Social Democracy in the New State' (November 1947), ANM, Fonds Zdeněk Fierlinger, Karton 40, Sjezd soc. dem. v Brne, p. 22.

[38] OURS, CD SFIO, 13 November 1946.

What is more, their key intermediary position between the communists and the centre-right, in personnel as well as policy terms, had the ČSSD and the SFIO at a disadvantage during campaign time. The two parties repeatedly stressed how they had fallen prey to their own devotion to national unity and recovery. 'Czechoslovakian social democracy ... did all in its power to secure national unity and reconcile the political forces', read the resolution that the ČSSD Central Executive Committee passed after the party's dismal showing in the May 1946 parliamentary elections, but this had come 'at the price of the greatest party-political sacrifices'.[39] As the party delivering the prime minister, after all, the ČSSD had been forced to practise the 'due restraint' that had certainly not been observed by the other parties during the election campaign.[40]

SFIO leaders similarly claimed that their 'overly loyal'[41] attitude and their 'excess of honesty'[42] had cost them dearly in elections. 'Without regard for its electoral interests', insisted a manifest the SFIO Executive published in May 1946, 'the party ... has served national interests first by demanding a massive reduction of the military budget, subsequently by delegating its people to the heaviest governmental posts ... and finally by telling the country the truth about our economic and financial problems and putting forward rigorous, but necessary, solutions towards these'.[43]

It was in the severe popular discontent about the terrible socio-economic situation that the ČSSD and the SFIO found a third major cause for their unpopularity with the electorate. If this was one electoral concern they shared with the PPS and the PSIUP, the four parties heartily disagreed about who was the main beneficiary of the bread-and-butter outrage among their voters. Rather than the 'reactionaries' pointed to by the Italian and Polish socialists, it was the communists who stood to gain most from a continued squeeze on living standards according to the Czechoslovakian social democrats and the French socialists. Even though communist leaders were co-signatories to and vociferous supporters of the austerity packages adopted by their governments, they seemed to be able to deflect the blame for the concomitant popular misery onto their socialist coalition partners. Viewed as parties of government through and through, the ČSSD and SFIO complained that they were being punished

[39] *Zpráva o činnosti*, p. XXIX.
[40] Ibid., pp. XXVIII–XXIX.
[41] OURS, CD SFIO, 4 June 1946.
[42] OURS, CD SFIO, 13 November 1946.
[43] OURS, CD SFIO, 7 May 1946.

for the hard choices their governments had been forced to make.[44] The communists, on the other hand, had managed to portray themselves as the great outsiders. They represented, in the words of SFIO deputy secretary general Jacques Arrès-Lapoque, 'the dissatisfied'.[45]

This, the ČSSD and SFIO claimed, had everything to do with the communist tendency to play on popular grievances with demagogical campaigns. Time and again, the two parties accused their communist coalition partners of making false claims or completely unfeasible demands, often in direct contradiction to government policies they had supported before, to appeal to a particular electoral constituency. This was the case with the millionaires' tax controversy, which rattled Czechoslovakian politics in the autumn of 1947 and constituted the catalyst for the defeat of Fierlinger's pro-communist wing at the November 1947 congress of the ČSSD. The controversy revolved around the way in which peasants, who had been hit by a severe drought in the summer, were to be compensated for their losses. On the same day that Václav Majer – the ČSSD's minister of food – proposed to raise state-sanctioned grain prices, the communists blind-sided their coalition partners by putting forward an extraordinary levy on millionaires instead. After all other coalition parties voted this down as unworkable, the communists went on the offensive, branding the ministers who had voted against the levy 'defenders of millionaires' in their press and exploiting their domination of the (officially non-party) trade union movement to organise workers' meetings demanding that the levy be adopted. Far from bullying the party into submission, however, these attacks only made the ČSSD more combative. If the communists wanted 'a dirty campaign', the party leadership concluded, 'they can have it'.[46]

The French socialists described their experiences with the communists in very much the same terms. When the PCF, after its November 1946 election victory, published an outline for a 'governmental programme', the SFIO leadership concluded that the communists were far more interested in scoring political points than in solving France's problems. During a meeting of the SFIO Executive, several socialist leaders derided the communist programme for being 'demagogical', for containing

---

[44] After the party's abysmal performance in the May 1946 parliamentary elections, ČSSD presidium member Frantisek Nový argued that 'public opinon … condemns us as an accomplice for all the bad things the communists have done'. Quoted in Kaplan, 'Tschechoslowakische Sozialdemokratie', p. 299f. SFIO leaders, for their part, partly attributed their electoral losses to the fact that the electorate had closely identified their party – unlike the PCF and the MRP – with *tripartisme*. OURS, CD SFIO, 13 November 1946.

[45] OURS, CD SFIO, 13 November 1946.

[46] Quoted in Kaplan, 'Tschechoslowakische Sozialdemokratie', p. 289.

'flagrant contradictions', and for lacking 'any means of realisation'. The PCF, argued Oreste Capocci, 'continues to view the French people as a bunch of *moujiks*' – after the backward serfs in pre-revolutionary Russia.[47] Ministerial solidarity, moreover, seemed a concept foreign to the PCF. After his first six months as minister of the national economy, André Philip dubbed his dealings with the communists 'cruel'. '[I]t is very difficult to govern with the communists', he told the SFIO's August 1946 congress, 'because they do not bring ... the minimum of intellectual honesty to the table'. In governmental negotiations, after all, 'they take positions geared exclusively towards the next elections [and] put forward demagogical propositions with the sole purpose of making their colleagues reject them'. For these and other reasons,[48] Philip concluded, the SFIO 'should have the courage to state that we no longer want permanent unity of action with the communists'.[49]

The four parties, then, attributed their (anticipated) electoral woes to widely divergent causes. The Italian and Polish socialists, on the one hand, felt they were destined to lose out in democratic elections. Having hardly known democracy and still imbued with decades of unchallenged right-wing propaganda, they argued, their impressionable electorates were always more likely to vote for 'reactionary' candidates backed by church and clergy than for socialists as yet unable to deliver upon socialism in material terms. The Czechoslovakian social democrats and French socialists, on the other hand, primarily blamed themselves for their poor showings in elections. Victory had been within reach, they insisted, but their parties had not been equal to their organisational task, had failed to communicate their programmes in an effective manner, and had allowed themselves to be outmanoeuvred by their rivals. These contrasting renditions of their difficulties at the polls were reflected in the four parties' approaches to elections.

The PPS and the PSIUP, believing that divisive campaigning would only disorient their electorates, opted for the broadest possible party-political unity. At first, their efforts to achieve such unity extended even to the centre-right. In the face of 'the forces and interests' hoping 'to nip democracy in the bud', Nenni wrote in July 1944, 'the most comprehensive

---

[47] OURS, CD SFIO, 27 November 1946.
[48] He mentioned two more: the communists' 'instinctive' predilection for serving the interests of the Soviet Union and their efforts to manipulate the nationalisations so as to assure 'the domination of their party over the structure of the State itself'.
[49] 'Parti Socialiste SFIO: 38ème Congrès national, 29, 30, 31 août et 1er septembre 1946', FJJ, p. 244. http://62.210.214.184/cg-ps/documents/pdf/cong-1946-08-29.pdf (last consulted: 27 June 2018).

national unity is required'. For that reason, both socialists and communists had endeavoured to 'draw the DC into the united proletarian front'.[50] But these efforts were to no avail. By October, Nenni was warning that 'the distrust' the 'parties of the centre' – this time mentioning the social-liberal Democratic Labour Party alongside the DC – were showing communists and socialists was 'bringing a civil war closer'.[51]

For the PPS, Jan Stańczyk was even more alarmist. 'If we cannot put together a bloc of six' (i.e. the projected electoral alliance between the four 'Lublin' parties – the PPR, the PPS, the SL, and the SD – and the two legal centre-right parties – the PSL and the SP – negotiations towards which broke down repeatedly in 1946), he admonished, 'we risk a revolution'. For 'if only a part of society can muster enthusiasm for us, we will definitely not be able to rely on the police to deal with the bands' – the term that Polish socialists and communists used to describe the underground groups fighting the government. Because the Soviet Union 'cannot allow that there is a revolution to the rear of its army, it will have to crush it – and then our role as government will be finished'.[52]

In the increasingly polarised post-war landscape, however, these efforts to get centrist and centre-right parties to join a communist-socialist electoral bloc would come to nothing. Worse, the first major electoral test in both countries, i.e. the parliamentary elections in Italy and the popular referendum in Poland (both held in June 1946), revealed the political strength of the Right. In these circumstances, the socialist commitment to party unity on the left only grew stronger. Come the time of the second major electoral test, therefore, the PPS and PSIUP found themselves in a united front and on a common list with the communists.

The aim of these electoral blocs was twofold. In the first place, they were to prevent the escalation of social conflicts at a time of great dangers to democracy. In this respect, Julian Hochfeld compared the challenges facing post-war Poland to those of wartime Britain. Despite the party's resolve to press ahead with forming an electoral bloc with or without the PSL, he claimed, 'the PPS is not ... principally in favour of electoral blocs in all circumstances and at all times'. Neither, of course, was the British Labour Party. But, in 1940, with the country under attack from Nazi Germany, that party had agreed to postpone the elections and enter government, because 'everyone realised that, in these circumstances, it was

[50] Pietro Nenni, 'Il "ni" della Democrazia Cristiana', *Avanti!*, 13 July 1944.
[51] Pietro Nenni, 'Non deludere il popolo', *Avanti!*, 29 October 1944.
[52] 'Protokół posiedzenia CKW PPS' (14 May 1946), AAN, PPS, CKW, 235/III/2, fo. 49.

not possible to engage in [domestic] struggles ... to fight elections on separate lists'. Poland, insisted Hochfeld, was 'now fighting a battle equal to, if not harder than, that fought by Britain in 1940'. For whereas 'the whole of British society' had been 'democratic and disciplined' during the war, 'we are a society politically far less mature'. Various issues were 'still in an explosive state' and 'should not be exacerbated'. Political unity and social peace, therefore, were 'indispensable'.[53]

For all of their mollifying effects on burning issues, though, the ultimate raison d'être of the electoral blocs the two parties entered into remained winning elections. This was less of an issue for the Polish socialists, who were well aware that the communists would never allow the real election results to see the light of day. For the PSIUP, on the other hand, the electoral significance of unity was paramount. According to Nenni, the Popular Front represented 'the only hope of an electoral victory, without which we would see a fatal return to the clerical reaction'. Oreste Lizzadri, the foremost socialist trade unionist in post-war Italy, agreed. 'The division of the popular classes on various lists creates distrust and leads to defeat', he insisted, 'whereas unity inspires confidence and constitutes a guarantee for victory.'[54]

The ČSSD and the SFIO, conversely, responded to their electoral setbacks by stressing their independence from all other parties and from the communists in particular.[55] The ČSSD, declared Laušman in the wake of the party's May 1946 election defeat, had made 'only one mistake' in its pre-electoral tactics: 'that we did not draw a stronger line of demarcation between ourselves and the communists'.[56] The SFIO likewise felt it had to disassociate itself from the communists in the struggle for the popular vote. When the PCF called for a joint communist-socialist campaign in favour

[53] Julian Hochfeld, 'Chleb i Wybory', *Przegląd Socjalistyczny*, 1 February 1946, pp. 6–7.
[54] 'Riunione Direzione' (6 November 1947), ISRT, Fondo Foscolo Lombardi, Partito Socialista Italiano, Direzione Nazionale, Busta 4, Fasc. 21, fo. 100.
[55] Especially in the Czechoslovakian case, the pre-war social democratic electorate seems to have defected to the communists in huge numbers. Jiří Sláma and Karel Kaplan note that, by comparison with the last pre-war parliamentary elections in 1935, the ČSSD lost nearly half of its voters – 'the lion's share' of which switched to the KSČ. In post-war France, the picture was more mixed. Disputing the contemporary view that the SFIO lost votes predominantly to the MRP in the June 1946 elections, Bruce Desmond Graham argues that the socialists seem to have lost to the PCF, the MRP, and even the Radicals in more or less equal measure. See Jiří Sláma and Karel Kaplan, *Die Parlamentswahlen in der Tschechoslowakei 1935–1946–1948* (Munich: Oldenbourg Verlag, 1986), p. 62; Graham, *The French Socialists and Tripartisme*, p. 180.
[56] 'Volby a čs. sociální demokracie' (1946), NA, Fonds Bohumil Laušman, III Pisemnosti související s ústřední, veřejnou a politickou činností B. Laušmana, Karton 34, Souvicející činnosti v soc. dem. 1928–1948, p. 11.

of a yes vote at the May 1946 constitutional referendum, Daniel Mayer immediately issued the SFIO's provincial federations with 'an absolute ban' on common propaganda with the communists. Amid widespread applause for the secretary general's swift response within the SFIO Executive, Charles Dumas, who had just returned from the April 1946 PSIUP congress, advocated going still further. On the basis of 'conversations with various foreign socialists', he concluded that 'not only should we not campaign together with the communists, but we should make very clear what separates them from us'.[57] The next parliamentary elections seemed to vindicate that position, with the socialists having, as Depreux noted, 'gained votes from the communists where we have emphasised the differences between them and us'.[58]

There was much more than just electoral considerations, however, to the ČSSD's and the SFIO's antipathy towards party-political unity. The two parties very much believed that democracy was best served by the resumption of 'normal' party competition. To be sure, they agreed that their countries had seen too much political fragmentation during the interwar period and that the number of parties needed to be narrowed down. But if party integration was driven to the extremes seemingly desired by some of their opponents, both ČSSD and SFIO leaders warned, democracy would emerge less rather than more stable.

This was how Fierlinger defended the decision to shelve 'the idea of one great socialist party', comprising the pre-war communist, social democratic, and National Socialist parties, that ČSSD leaders had so enthusiastically advocated in the immediate aftermath of liberation. This idea, he recounted, had been strong 'in the days of national humiliation' (i.e. the period after the dismemberment of Czechoslovakia in 1938–39) and 'in the concentration camps', where '[e]very Czech feared the return of the pre-war chaos and of the political disunity in which Fascism and Nazism grew strong'. In the end, however, the arguments for a broader, four-party political spectrum, with a communist and a social democratic party to the left and a Catholic and a nationalist party to the centre-right, won the day in the Czech lands. Just '[h]ow justified this solution was', insisted Fierlinger, became clear by comparison with the subsequent developments in Slovakia, where a 'political simplification to two parties' had been tried – a reference to the fact that, until early 1946, legal political activity in Slovakia was confined to the Slovakian Communist Party and the

[57] OURS, CD SFIO, 23 April 1946.
[58] OURS, CD SFIO, 4 June 1946.

centre-right nationalist and Catholic Slovakian Democratic Party. In view of the negative experiences with that system, he continued, 'we also had to introduce the four-party system in Slovakia'. But 'as a result of the fact that the two new parties, among them our own, are still too weak, political life in Slovakia is still prone to superfluously heavy shocks'. 'The system of four political parties', then, 'has clearly proved itself to be the better system. It remains our duty to keep it.'[59]

The French socialists were equally quick to question the unitary designs so popular during the first post-war years. As we have seen, they had serious reservations about communist overtures towards working-class unity. But their misgivings concerned the brand of national unity championed by General De Gaulle at least as much. The socialists took particular issue with De Gaulle's contemptuous attitude towards political parties while he was still prime minister. 'A true democracy', read a letter the SFIO Executive sent to De Gaulle to complain about his refusal to meet with delegations of political parties, 'cannot live without normal and regular party competition'. No doubt, it continued, political parties 'should be transformed, their number reduced, their methods of propaganda overhauled, and the tone of their polemics modified' and the SFIO had 'set the example for that effort of transformation and adaptation'. 'But a state without political parties – and we use the plural, [because the existence of] a single party is a sign of dictatorship just as much as the absence of parties – is no longer a democratic state.'[60]

Parliaments

The four parties' contrasting perspectives on the merits of democratic elections were reflected in their attitudes towards the upshot of such elections: the parliamentary balance of power. The Italian and Polish socialists, on the one hand, believing that the electoral odds were stacked heavily against their parties, viewed parliaments mostly as vehicles for bourgeois interests. The legalistic and formulaic methods of parliamentary democracy, they claimed, would never give way to socialism in backward societies like theirs. For the Czechoslovakian social democrats and the French socialists, on the other hand, who held their electorates in far

---

[59] 'The Mission of Social Democracy in the New State' (November 1947), ANM, Fonds Zdeněk Fierlinger, Karton 40, Sjezd soc. dem. v Brne, pp. 46–7.
[60] 'Lettre du Comité Directeur au Général de Gaulle' (10 February 1945), OURS, 'Procès-verbaux des réunions du Comité Directeur du congrès de Paris, 9–12 novembre 1944 au 37e congrès national, 11–15 aout 1945', p. 98.

higher esteem, parliamentary relations were always the point of departure. If socialism was going to live up to its democratic credentials, they insisted, the impetus for it should come from elected representatives.

At the root of these widely divergent attitudes towards parliamentary democracy lay opposite attitudes towards parliamentary elections and their results. The PPS and the PSIUP, after their initial post-war euphoria wore off, considered parliamentary elections a nuisance at best, a dangerous, possibly fatal experiment at worst. As early as September 1945, just months after their government had signed up to organising 'free and unfettered' elections in Poland, Stańczyk warned socialist and communist leaders against showing too much dedication to 'the form'. Hitler too, he argued, 'has risen to power by democratic means and had the great majority of the nation behind him'.[61] If not going that far, Basso was similarly scornful of parliamentary outcomes. While it was crucial for the working class to exercise power commensurate with its 'real political strength', he insisted, ' "political [strength]", mind you, does not necessarily equate, indeed almost never equates, to "parliamentary [strength]" '.[62]

For the ČSSD and the SFIO, conversely, parliamentary outcomes very much represented the real balance of political forces. As sacred expressions of the will of the people, the two parties insisted, election results were to be respected by those in power. After the ČSSD's drubbing in the May 1946 parliamentary elections, Laušman's rhetoric was all about honouring the result. '[I]f the communists ask us whether comrade Fierlinger wants to continue as prime minister', he told a ČSSD provincial conference, 'we will answer that we do not want one decagram more responsibility than the electorate has given us'. To be sure, he continued, Fierlinger was a far more suitable candidate for the post than communist leader Klement Gottwald, who 'would command the confidence of the East but less so of the West', or National Socialist leader Petr Zenkl, who 'would command the confidence of the West but less so of the East'. Yet 'the electorate has decided and that is how it has to be'.[63]

The French socialists were equally adamant that election results should be abided by. When the PCF became the largest party in the November

[61] 'Protokół z wspólnego posiedzenia CKW PPS i KC PPR' (28 September 1945), AAN, PPS, CKW, 235/III/6, fo. 25.

[62] Lelio Basso, 'Socialismo europeo (1)', *Quarto Stato*, 15 September 1946. www.leliobasso.it/documento.aspx?id=cf99e9daef3d5143ea3b0399083d2f01 (last consulted: 27 June 2018).

[63] 'Volby a čs. sociální demokracie' (1946), NA, Fonds Bohumil Laušman, III Pisemnosti související s ústřední, veřejnou a politickou činnosti B. Laušmana, Karton 34, Souvicející činnosti v soc. dem. 1928–1948, pp. 13–14.

1946 parliamentary elections, the SFIO leadership concluded that the communists should take the lead in a new government. Whatever their personal misgivings about the intentions and loyalties of the communists, therefore, most socialist leaders felt they owed it to the electorate to support PCF leader Maurice Thorez in his (ultimately unsuccessful) bid to secure a parliamentary majority for his candidacy for the prime ministry. François Tanguy-Prigent summed up the general mood within the SFIO leadership, arguing that 'the election results show that voters want a government presided over by a communist'. As a party 'abiding by universal suffrage and anxious to respect democracy', consequently, 'we must vote for a communist prime minister'.[64]

The four parties' divisions over parliaments and parliamentarism went deeper, however, than their different takes on the election results producing parliamentary outcomes. At stake was the very notion that parliaments, irrespective of their make-up, could bring about socialist change in the first place. For the Italian and Polish socialists, parliaments were inextricably linked to bourgeois society. The two parties took particular exception to the idea, widespread also within the larger European socialist movement, that democracy found its expression in freely elected parliaments. Basso bemoaned tendencies 'to confound democracy and parliamentarism'.[65] In fact, what so many of the PSIUP's sister parties called democracy constituted 'nothing more than the acceptance of constitutional legalism, of bourgeois legalism, i.e. the acceptance of a democratic formalism that has nothing in common with the substance of democracy'. The truth was, he continued, that 'society is not founded on laws: that is a fantasy of lawyers'. For laws rarely kept up with social developments. Far from 'having created modern society', after all, the Napoleonic Code had merely given the already victorious bourgeoisie its legal outlet.[66] Just as bourgeois parliamentary democracy had not been achieved by adhering to the laws of feudal society, proletarian popular democracy would never be achieved by adhering to the laws of bourgeois society. For 'every time that that democracy has made a stride ahead in history, it has been forced to turn its back on the law'.[67]

[64] OURS, CD SFIO, 27 November 1946.
[65] Lelio Basso, 'Compiti nuovi', *Quarto Stato*, 15 July 1946. www.leliobasso.it/documento.aspx?id=de8 f3eobc1ede65c4e2b659ea076de4d (last consulted: 27 June 2018).
[66] Lelio Basso, 'Sul socialismo europeo' (1948), Fondazione Lelio e Lisli Basso Isocco, Rome (hereafter FLB), Fondo Lelio Basso, Serie 15, Fasc. 6, pp. 24–5.
[67] Lelio Basso, 'Voltare le spalle al legalitarismo', *Ill Giornale dell'Emilia*, 17 February 1947. www. leliobasso.it/documento.aspx?id=e90b9808d8c6a2983ecd806716ca5f31 (last consulted: 27 June 2018).

If Basso made the theoretical case against parliamentary democracy, Wachowicz was more concrete. In his view, bourgeois parliamentary democracy only served to perpetuate social inequalities. In the United Kingdom, for example, 'the worker and the Lord ... notionally have the same right to vote [but], in reality, the Lord is in power – in other words, he who has money is in power'. Of course, in a parliamentary democracy, 'the working class can organise itself [and] elect its leaders in parliament, but modern history knows no examples of the working class succeeding in forming a government'. The Danish and Swedish social democrats who had been in government before and during the war, after all, 'only gave [the government] their name, [while] failing to implement any reforms bringing their countries closer to a democratic system'. In fact, Wachowicz went on, 'democracy must fade away in a revolutionary period'. For when 'entering into class struggle, there is no longer question of democracy, only of class victories'.[68]

Not all PPS and PSIUP leaders shared these principal objections against parliamentary democracy. In fact, there were many within both party leaderships arguing that a parliamentary road to socialism, while not an option in their countries, was perfectly viable in places like Great Britain and Scandinavia. Such leaders insisted there was no one precept for arriving at socialism – it was the social fabric and national history of a given country that determined which path to socialism it should take. It was 'pointless' to ask, argued Nenni, whether socialism would be achieved 'by the methods of Lenin or Beveridge'. For reformist or revolutionary trajectories to socialism were 'results not causes: a certain type of society produces a certain type of struggle'.[69] Welcoming the foreign delegates to the December 1947 congress of the PPS, Stanisław Szwalbe expressed similar sentiments. After emphasising that Poland's economic programme was 'a socialist programme', he expressed the hope that 'the dealings of our congress [and] the visit to our country will convince you that the PPS has chosen a proper socialist path – corresponding to the conditions of our country and the needs of our working class'.[70]

In this respect, Italian and Polish socialists frequently distinguished between two roads to socialism – one where socialism could be the end

---

[68] 'Rola stronnictw polityznych w Polsce', AAN, Fonds Henryk Wachowicz, 8, Prezmowienie, Referaty, p. 9.
[69] Pietro Nenni, 'Il terzo ladrone', *Avanti!*, 2 February 1945.
[70] XXVII Kongres (December 1947), AAN, PPS, 235/1-25, fo. 8.

result of reforms enacted by parliaments and one where the economic bases
of socialism had to be laid by extra-parliamentary means. Basso contrasted
the feasibility of parliamentary trajectories towards socialism in various
regions. In the Scandinavian countries, he explained, 'a democratic tradition has taken root, the proletariat has long since achieved a relatively high
standard of living, and, through this economic elevation, [it] has acquired
political maturity'. In these circumstances, parliamentary democracy was
'doubtless still the most effective method of socialist action'. The Eastern
European countries, conversely, were 'almost all underdeveloped industri-
ally, with a numerically scarce and profoundly immature middle class, and
with a vast mass of ignorant and often illiterate peasants'. Sticking 'purely
and simply to parliamentary methods' in such circumstances 'would mean
keeping the old plutocratic classes in power indefinitely, would mean post-
poning for centuries not only the realisation of socialism but even the mere
elevation of the material and moral living conditions of the proletariat'.[71]

Drawing on his experiences in the London wartime emigration, PPS
under-secretary for shipping and international trade Ludwik Grosfeld similarly identified two distinct roads to socialism. Especially during the war, he
recalled, 'very reformist [and] very right-wing convictions prevailed among
socialists in the West', who refused to recognise that the road the Soviet
Union had taken since the October Revolution was 'irrevocable'. Yet the
PPS had 'to realise that the Western road to socialism, although it is completely different [and] arises under different circumstances, is equally irrevocable'. There were thus 'two different systems and two different methods
of socialism, which have grown out of different economic conditions'. For
all of its 'hidden games' (probably a reference to Labour's initial hovering
between the London PPS and the Lublin PPS), therefore, 'we must declare
... that the British Labour Party is a socialist party, which seeks to achieve
socialism by its methods'.[72]

What increasingly angered both the PPS and the PSIUP, however, was
that the respect they showed for the (north-)Western parliamentary road
to socialism was far from mutual. During the May 1946 International
Socialist Conference in the English resort of Clacton-on-Sea, Cyrankiewicz
set out to 'underline the difference between our methods of struggle and
those used in the West'. Yet the reception was mostly hostile. '[P]ersonal

[71] Lelio Basso, 'Socialismo europeo (i)', *Quarto Stato*, 15 September 1946. www.leliobasso.it/
documento.aspx?id=cf99e9daef3d5143ea3b0399083d2fo1 (last consulted: 27 June 2018).
[72] Rada Naczelna (31 March 1946), AAN, PPS, 235/II/6, fo.32.

attacks' had appeared 'even in the left-wing *Tribune*', whereas 'the tone of the accounts' of some sister parties bore witness to feelings of 'superiority'.[73]

On the second day of his party's April 1946 congress, PSIUP parliamentarian and Central Committee member Lucio Mario Luzzato likewise remonstrated against the notion that there were no other pathways to socialism than 'the road of the ballot paper'. To be sure, he conceded, the Italian socialists were currently committed to the maintenance of 'democratic legality' (more on the reasons for that in the Constitutions section of this chapter). But that did not mean, as 'a foreign representative' had claimed the previous day, that 'the function of a socialist party is as it is' – that it stopped at the defence of parliamentary democracy. For 'the fundamentals of democracy' were not merely 'formal' or 'negative',

> only renunciatory in the sense that we affirm that we would in no situation deviate from the democratic path. No. You know that it is not like that, because all of you who want democracy know that tomorrow, where that is necessary, we would resort to any means the reaction forces upon us to defend socialism and the rights of workers.[74]

For the ČSSD and the SFIO, on the other hand, there was an indissoluble link between socialism and parliamentary democracy. Right from the outset, then, the two parties directed their efforts towards a rapid return to parliamentary normality. They were strong supporters of the provisional parliaments, set up in both countries pending the first parliamentary elections, as counterweights to all-powerful provisional governments. According to Vincent Auriol, the French Consultative Assembly provided 'a solution' for socialist grievances about the rightward thrust of the first De Gaulle government. Warning that withdrawing support from the government in an 'anti-constitutional' regime would not make De Gaulle go, he called on socialist delegates to the Consultative Assembly to instead be 'assiduous' and use their budget-setting powers to weigh upon the government in questions like subsidies for faith schools.[75] Fierlinger too argued that the creation of the Czechoslovakian Provisional National Assembly had been 'a step in the right direction'. For even if its unelected status meant it did not yet 'give full expression to the real principle of

---

[73] 'Protokół posiedzenia CKW PPS' (14 June 1946), AAN, PPS, CKW, 235/III/2, fo. 58. Indeed, Anita Prazmowska has pointed out that, as 'European political life became polarised by the Cold War, the Polish Socialists felt both abandoned and misunderstood by their West European counterparts'. Prazmowska, 'The Polish Socialist Party', p. 352.

[74] 'XXIV Congresso del Partito Socialista Italiano di Unità Proletaria', 14 aprile 1946, seduta pomeridiana, ACS, Carteggio Nenni, Busta 88, Fasc 2193, pp. 68–9.

[75] OURS, CD SFIO, 25 January 1945.

parliamentary democracy', it had given 'the people ... a wider representation' while maintaining 'the peace necessary for the further successful
reconstruction of the State'.[76]

As the provisional chambers made way for properly elected parliaments,
the ČSSD's and the SFIO's commitment to parliamentarism only grew
stronger. The two parties were adamant that, as far as they were concerned,
parliament was now both the foremost arena for and the ultimate arbitrator of national decision-making. They placed great emphasis, therefore,
on their parliamentary factions being able to operate free from outside
constraints. This was the main reason the French socialists put forward a
proposal to quit the 'Delegation of the Left' – bringing together the PCF,
the SFIO, the Radicals, the Human Rights League, and the CGT to bolster
the Left's position within the first De Gaulle government – almost immediately after the November 1945 legislative elections. At the first post-election
meeting of the Delegation, where a CGT proposal to give the Delegation
a permanent character won the approval from all but the socialists, Mayer
made it quite clear that there was now a higher authority for the SFIO
to answer to. As 'the sovereignty of the [Constituent] Assembly has to
come to full bloom', he declared, 'we must not give the public the impression that it is outside of Parliament that decisions are being taken'. The
socialists, then, would not 'be bound upon the parliamentary level'. For it
was 'incumbent upon the elected Constituent Assembly and the government formed by the national representation', read the letter with which the
SFIO broke definitively with the Delegation, 'to take responsibility for the
conduct of public affairs'.[77]

The ČSSD similarly berated other parties for disregarding their parliamentary duties. Just like those of its provisional predecessor, lamented the
ČSSD's 1946 annual report, the proceedings of the elected Constituent
Assembly were initially dictated by the needs of the government. A whole
range of parliamentary committees was 'content to rubber stamp ... governmental bills', while deputies failed to 'fulfil one of their most important
tasks: that of controlling the state economy and public administration'.
For that reason, the ČSSD decided to 'take the initiative' and 'struggle for
the improvement of parliamentary praxis'.

A first opportunity to do that presented itself when the newly formed
Gottwald government reserved the right to draft a new constitution for

---

[76] 'The Mission of Social Democracy in the New State' (November 1947), ANM, Fonds Zdeněk
Fierlinger, Karton 40, Sjezd soc. dem. v Brne, p. 12.
[77] OURS, CD SFIO, 4 December 1945.

itself. In the parliamentary debate on the governmental programme, Oldřich John, the vice-chairman of the ČSSD's parliamentary group, immediately protested that 'we cannot agree that the new constitution will be drafted by the government, i.e. for the government by the [communist-dominated] ministry of the interior – the entire business of drawing up a new constitution should instead take place on the parliamentary floor'. At first, the ČSSD's vigour seemed to falter upon parliamentary inertia once more, as the social democrats found themselves isolated and outvoted within the parliamentary sub-committee on constitutional affairs. But when the ČSSD threatened to bring matters to a head and put forward a motion withdrawing support from the constitutional paragraph of the governmental programme, the other parties caved. Before long, the government yielded as well, agreeing that 'drawing up a new constitution' was 'a matter for parliament'. It was the ČSSD's perseverance on this particular question, insisted the party's 1946 annual report, that formed the catalyst for the subsequent 'breakthrough' in parliamentary assertiveness. For 'if we can affirm today that we were able to eliminate most of our parliament's shortcomings – it now has its own rules of procedure, [its own] economic and audit commissions, [it] energetically summons ministers to provide an account of their activities, and [it] has passed a series of private members' bills – the credit for that should go to our parliamentary group'.[78]

Much as the ČSSD and the SFIO prided themselves on having bolstered parliament's standing, however, that standing was quick to come under renewed pressure. In the face of the socio-political polarisation that accompanied the drifting apart of the post-war coalitions, after all, the two parties' rivals increasingly took contentious issues to the streets.

In France, such extra-parliamentary pressure initially emanated chiefly from the movement around General De Gaulle. The bombshells repeatedly dropped by De Gaulle, often in the form of large public rallies, sparked fierce debate within the SFIO Executive. There were leaders on the left of the party – most notably Léon Boutbien (who, ironically, ended up in the Central Committee of the Gaullist Rally for the Republic in the 1970s) – who pleaded for the extra-parliamentary challenge posed by De Gaulle to be met head-on and for the Left to start organising counter-rallies. The large majority of the SFIO leadership, however, wanted the party to steer clear of street politics. It would be 'a mistake', Philip told Boutbien after the launch of the RPF, to combat De Gaulle 'on the terrain chosen by him'.[79] Roger Priou-Valjean went further. He warned that it was dangerous for socialists to claim, as Boutbien had done, that 'we should operate on the level of the "nation"' rather than on that of 'the government'. For exactly those types of arguments had been used before the war by the counter-revolutionary opponents of the Republic, who distinguished between '*le pays réel*' and '*le pays légal*' – that is, the notion at the heart of the ideology of the far right Action Française movement that the democratic institutions of the Third Republic had somehow been imposed on the 'real' France. It was 'on the parliamentary level', Priou-Valjean concluded, that the SFIO should 'fight its battles'.[80]

The socialist commitment to parliamentarism was reaffirmed in the face of that other extra-parliamentary challenge confronting France in 1947: that of the increasingly communist-led strike movement. As the strikes lost their wildcat character and began looking more and more like a concerted attempt to destabilise the government, the socialist attitude towards strikers changed too. When Auriol called for discipline in May 1947, he was no longer referring to discipline as a productivist mantra. 'Discipline', he declared, 'is above all respect for the law; the law, having been voted in by an Assembly elected by universal suffrage, is the expression of popular sovereignty.' 'Make no mistake', he continued, 'the day that this or that professional or social group purports to defend its interests, however justified these may be, by resorting to agitations or violence, they not only neglect the national interest but they threaten to plunge the country in disorder and anarchy.' By taking the law into their own hands, after all, these groups were undercutting the authority of the democratic institutions the SFIO leadership so cherished. 'In our democratic regime', Auriol concluded, 'it is for the representatives of the nation to give voice to such claims, and it is government and parliament who, having heard all parties [and] having been presented with all arguments, are entitled to decide which measures should be taken in the national interest, and only in the national interest.'[81]

The ČSSD's dedication to due parliamentary process was no less strong. This became very clear in the conflict between communist minister of agriculture Július Ďuriš and the Czechoslovakian National Assembly in early 1947. At stake were Ďuriš's attempts to bypass parliament in the enactment

[79] OURS, CD SFIO, 23 April 1947.
[80] OURS, CD SFIO, 6 September 1947.
[81] 'Discours prononcé à Annecy' (25 May 1947), Centre d'Histoire des Sciences Po, Paris (hereafter CHSP), Fonds Daniel Mayer, 1 MA 7.7, p. 7.

of six controversial bills drawn up by his ministry. Even before the bills could be discussed in government or parliament, the ministry of agriculture had extracts of them distributed among peasants. After that, the communist party machine went into overdrive. First, mass meetings were organised across the Czechoslovakian countryside, where peasants – who, according to the social democrats, 'barely knew' what was in the bills – 'pre-approved' the proposals. This, in turn, was followed by a 'full-blown campaign' for parliament to pass the bills without amendments. 'To such manipulations of parliament', insisted the ČSSD's 1947 annual report, 'we could obviously not acquiesce.' Even though the social democrats by and large took a favourable view of Ďuriš's bills, therefore, they sided with the centre-right to pass a parliamentary resolution condemning the conduct of the minister.[82]

For both the ČSSD and the SFIO, then, the defence of parliamentarism was very much a matter of principle. The only way for socialism to retain its democratic character, insisted the two parties, was to adhere to the legal and procedural rules of parliamentary democracy. With the national and international menace to parliamentary democracy growing as 1947 progressed, therefore, the maintenance of parliamentary authority increasingly became a life-or-death issue for both parties. In a world 'heading towards conflict and mutual division' once more, Fierlinger told the November 1947 congress of the ČSSD, '[s]ocial democracy, aspiring to achieve socialism by democratic means, always had to look for … the right remedy'.[83] That remedy consisted of finding 'socialist solutions, [that are] economically and politically viable', while being 'a driving force behind the legislative activities of parliament, the significance of which we have always pointed out and emphasised'. At the height of the communist and Gaullist challenges to parliamentary democracy in France, Paul Ramadier likewise banged the drum for parliament. For all the justified criticisms that could be levelled at the government, he implored on the December 1947 National Council of the SFIO, this was not a time for parliamentary deadlock. '[A]t the present moment', he declared, 'we must … show that the parliamentary regime is capable of governing France.[84]

---

[82] *Zpráva o činnosti*, p. XLII.

[83] 'Poslání sociální demokracie v novém státě' (November 1947), Archiv ČSSD, Fond 71, Část II, Karton 112, p. 13.

[84] 'Parti Socialiste – SFIO: Conseil national des 16 et 17 décembre 1947', FJJ, p. 89. http://62.210.214.184/cg-ps/documents/pdf/cons-1947-12-16.pdf (last consulted: 27 June 2018).

Constitutions

The first task for the freshly elected parliaments in each of the four countries was to draw up a new constitution. All four parties were strong supporters of the constitutional projects that reached their (intermediate) conclusions in 1946 (France), 1947 (Poland), and 1948 (Italy and Czechoslovakia), respectively. That did not mean, however, that they took similar attitudes towards constitutions and constitutionalism. For the Italian and Polish socialists, on the one hand, the adoption of a democratic constitution was a step in the right direction but by no means the end point in the political struggle for socialism. If required, they insisted, the legal boundaries of constitutionalism could and should be overstepped in that continuing struggle. For the Czechoslovakian social democrats and the French socialists, on the other, the rights and freedoms enshrined in their constitutions (in both their pre-war and post-war versions) were sacrosanct. To violate these constitutional principles, they argued, would open the door for tyranny rather than for socialism.

Much of this went back to the debate that had divided the socialist movement ever since the late nineteenth century: whether socialism could be achieved by piecemeal reforms within the context of 'bourgeois' democracy or whether it could only be the result of a proletarian revolution outside of existing legality. The ČSSD boasted that it had been one of the first European parties to resolve this debate. Already at its 1887 congress in Brno, explained Laušman, the party had 'settled' this issue in favour of those pleading for a democratic road to socialism. This line was confirmed at the subsequent Hainfeld congress (1888–89) of the Austrian Social Democratic Party, which committed social democracy across the Austro-Hungarian Empire to electoral and parliamentary politics. 'And the result', concluded Laušman, 'was that, only shortly after that, social democracy achieved a tremendous success: that, within ten years, we made the famous breakthrough of ... introducing the so-called fifth curia [which gave suffrage to all men over the age of twenty-four], through which we immediately got five Czech social democrats elected to the Viennese Imperial Council.'[85]

Within French socialism, the polemics between revolutionaries and reformists were rather more protracted. The compromise upon which the SFIO had been founded in 1905 – between the *guesdistes* rejecting any form of cooperation with bourgeois society and the *jauresistes* embracing republicanism and reform as the road to socialism – remained fragile and

---

[85] 'Zahajovací projev předsedy XXI. sjezdu čsl. sociální demokracie Bohumila Laušmana' (14 November 1947), Archiv ČSSD, Fond 71, Část II, Karton 112, p. 9.

kept the party out of government for most of the interwar period. Yet the experiences of the 1930s and early 1940s – the February 1934 crisis, the Popular Front government, and the Vichy regime – shifted the balance in favour of working within the framework of 'bourgeois' democracy. Even if official party rhetoric remained revolutionary, the post-war SFIO was firmly committed to upholding the democratic institutions of bourgeois France. Defending his new draft of the party's declaration of principles (which included, for example, replacing the principle of 'class struggle' with the more conciliatory notion of 'class action') before the August 1945 congress of the SFIO, Léon Blum stressed just how crucial political democracy was to socialism. 'All of us know now', he insisted, 'that there is an indissoluble link between socialism and democracy; that, without socialism, democracy is imperfect, but, without democracy, socialism is powerless.' That, he declared, was 'a truth written in blood'.

It is a measure of how far the French and the Italian socialists had already drifted apart by this early stage that Nenni returned 'bewildered' from the same SFIO congress. If something as fundamental as changing the party's declaration of principles had been proposed 'in the times of [Pierre] Renaudel [one of the foremost advocates of governmental participation in the pre-war and interwar SFIO] or … [Jean] Jaurès', he told the PSIUP leadership, 'it would [have been] debated for five days and five months and every word would [have been] subjected to the most thorough scrutiny'. This time, however, it appeared 'as if nobody cared', which had 'very much impressed' Nenni 'as a sign of the party detaching itself from socialist doctrine and turning its back on the interests of the working class'.[86] For the Italian socialists, after all, reaching out to bourgeois society amounted to a vote of no confidence in the revolutionary tendencies within the working class. This is how Basso denounced both those socialists 'viewing Italian politics only in terms of party competition' and 'the heirs and followers of old reformism'. What united them, he insisted, was their 'distrust of the working class' and their lack of belief in 'the revolutionary possibility inherent in class politics'.[87]

The post-war PPS was equally dismissive of attempts to reform bourgeois society from within. Far from this 'criticism of reformism' having been imposed by the communists, argued Hochfeld, it was 'part of [the]

---

[86] 'Seduta pomeridiana' (18 October 1945), ACS, Carteggio Nenni, Busta 87, Fasc. 2189, pp. 5–6. As it turned out, though, SFIO activists did care and forced Blum into retreat at a special conference in February 1946. The declaration of principles that was adopted during that conference insisted that the SFIO had 'always been and continues to be a party of class struggle'.

[87] 'XXIV Congresso del Partito Socialista Italiano di Unità Proletaria', seduta pomeridiana (April 1946), ACS, Carteggio Nenni, Busta 88, Fasc 2193, pp. 63, 65.

good traditions' of Polish socialism. For, already before the war, such leftist party leaders as Cyrankiewicz, Oskar Lange (the world-renowned socialist economist, who became the Polish ambassador at the United Nations after the war) and Bolesław Drobner (the first Polish mayor of Wrocław and deputy to the Sejm, 1944–68) had raised much the same concerns about reformism as 'we express today ... about Blum and his tactics [as well as] about [Ernest] Bevin [Labour Britain's Foreign Secretary, 1945–51 – and a much-despised figure among left-wing socialists] and his tactics'.[88] Those leftists pleading for a more revolutionary politics do indeed seem to have been in the ascendancy within the PPS well before the communists cemented their dominant position in the aftermath of the Second World War. As the Sanacja regime grew more repressive in the 1930s, after all, the PPS leadership had increasingly taken its lead from the revolutionary socialism espoused by leading Austro-Marxist Otto Bauer.[89] Bauer's claim that the proletariat could, in the face of a reactionary threat, justifiably resort to a temporal dictatorship struck a particular chord and was co-opted in the 1937 Radom Programme of the PPS.[90]

It was this issue – the use of dictatorial methods in the struggle for socialism – that sparked some of the fiercest debates within the post-war international socialist movement and ultimately saw the PSIUP ostracised from mainstream Western European social democracy along with the browbeaten Eastern European parties. For the Italian and Polish socialists, a proletarian dictatorship, while not an end in itself, could constitute a political necessity in countries like theirs. The PPS was definitely the more extreme case in this respect, as it overtly defended the repressive and violent methods the Lublin government used against political opponents. In an open letter to the Labour Party – a response to a *Tribune* article castigating the 'pro-Communist leadership of the [Polish] Socialist Party' for, among many other things, 'making a farce of the promise of free and democratic elections'[91] – Hochfeld insisted that Poland and the United Kingdom were facing altogether different political challenges. If the Tories had won the 1945 general election, he argued, Labour would have only had to wait for five years to get another shot at power. 'Not so for us', it continued. 'We are certain that, if we were to lose power, we would have

---

[88] xxvii Kongres (December 1947), AAN, PPS, 235/1-25, fo. 218.
[89] Bäcker, *Problematyka państwa*, p. 100.
[90] Heumos (ed.), *Europäischer Sozialismus*, p. 140f.
[91] 'Retreat from Potsdam', *Tribune*, 1 March 1946.

to retake it not from conservatives, but from fascists; and not at the ballot box, but in an armed struggle.'[92]

That meant, at least in the short term, that communists and socialists had to be guaranteed a commanding position in government irrespective of their true electoral strength. The Polish socialists were well aware that this involved reverting to methods – including the falsification of election results, political persecutions, and an excessive reliance on the use of force – that, as the party leadership put it somewhat euphemistically, 'are not entirely compatible with elements of our traditions'.[93] Yet these same democratic traditions, suggested the party programme that was put before the August 1945 congress of the PPS, had let down Polish socialism in the past. 'At the current historical moment', it proclaimed, 'the Polish Socialist Party should concentrate its efforts in the first place on the problem of holding on to government.' That meant that the 'misguided principles of democracy' held by those socialists wanting to show 'far-reaching toler-ance to political opponents' were to be 'revised'. For the 'fascist centres' that had existed in pre-war Poland were not about to resign themselves to the new order and would 'not shy away from deception, sabotage, and assassinations'.[94] In these circumstances, insisted chairman of the pro-gramme commission Feliks Mantel, the PPS 'cannot forsake the use of force, which at the present moment could prove crucial for the victory of socialism'.[95]

More recent scholarship has suggested, however, that the Polish socialists were never truly at ease with the blatant violations of constitutionalism on the part of the communists and the (communist-dominated) security services. These accounts stress socialist efforts, especially after the January 1947 elections, to restore civil liberties and the rule of law through the so-called Little Constitution – adopted in February 1947 as a temporary replacement for the 'fascist' 1935 Sanacja Constitution; a full new con-stitution was only enacted in 1952.[96] While such accounts are certainly helpful in debunking the old myth that the Lublin PPS consisted exclu-sively of communist stooges, they seem to overstate the extent of 'socialist humanism'. Hochfeld, for one, was at great pains to draw a clear distinc-tion between his 'Marxist' humanism and the 'revisionist' humanism he

[92] Julian Hochfeld, 'List do towarzysza z Labour Party', *Przegląd Socjalistyczny*, 1 April 1946, pp. 3–8.
[93] XXVII Kongres (December 1947), AAN, PPS, 235/I-25, fo. 220.
[94] 'Projekt Uchwała Programowa' (August 1945), AAN, PPS, 235/I-7, fo. 12.
[95] XXVI Kongres (August 1945), AAN, PPS, 235/I-12, fo. 254.
[96] See e.g. Pięta-Szawara, 'Socialíści w Sejmie Ustawodawczym', pp. 94–102; Syzdek and Syzdek, *Zanim zostanie zapomniany*, p. 130.

attributed to Blum – insisting that 'the jump from the state of necessity [the proletarian dictatorship] to the state of freedom' was 'by no means simple'.[97] And for all of their demands that the PPS should exert more influence over the running of the security services, socialist leaders strongly supported the principle of reverting to violence against the 'reactionary' opponents of popular democracy.[98]

Perhaps Edward Osóbka-Morawski summed up the PPS attitude towards constitutionalism best when he argued that 'integral democracy is not yet possible in Poland'. 'We have some twenty years of Sanacja rule, of captivity, [and] of massive clerical involvement in a reactionary regime behind us', he declared – 'that is not a balance of power conducive to integral democracy'. The new government, therefore, needed some time to level the playing field. If it had 'offended the democratic conscience and socialist morality' in doing so, concluded Osobka, 'that is transitory … Five years should suffice to level the chances of the reactionary and democratic camps – so that we will not have to offend the democratic conscience by the time of the next election.'[99]

The post-war PSIUP leadership, conversely, was always extremely careful to operate within the margins of constitutionalism. In fact, it often used very legalistic and constitutionalist arguments to defend the governmental coalition with bourgeois parties. Nenni drew on such arguments to respond to his critics on 'the self-proclaimed left' of the PSIUP – i.e. those socialists who, yearning for their party to take a much more combative stance on such issues as the disempowerment of the liberation committees, were urging an exit from the government. 'If we allow ourselves to be removed from power today', Nenni told the PSIUP's Central Committee in October 1945, 'the perspective of a Constituent Assembly as a legalistic solution will disappear.' A new right-wing government, after all, would surely repudiate the commitments entered into by the coalition government: 'discussions about the date [for elections to] and the content

[97] Julian Hochfeld, 'Z zagadnień socjalistycznego humanizmu', *Przegląd Socjalistyczny*, 1 May 1947, pp. 13–20.
[98] Roman Bäcker notes that the post-war PPS leadership was united in viewing 'parliamentary democracy … as redundant or even harmful for Poland, which needed a strong government to achieve a similar civilisational transformation as had been achieved by Cromwell, the French Revolution, Lenin, and Stalin'. The terror that had followed the French Revolution, he goes on, served both as a model and as a justification for socialist leaders – with 'the Jacobin guillotine' becoming 'a symbol … for the absolution of the terror committed by the Ministry for Public Security'. Bäcker, *Problematyka państwa*, pp. 97–8.
[99] 'Sprawozdanie stenograficzne z obrad Rady Naczelnej PPS' (4 December 1946), AAN, Akta Stanisława Szwalbego, Box 13.

of a Constituent Assembly would be kicked into the long grass and we would be heading towards a plebiscite [on the monarchy] that would be formulated in such a way as to deliver a predetermined answer'.[100]

Three months later, Nenni painted an even more alarmist picture of what would have happened had he heeded the advice of his leftist critics. 'If we had abandoned government', he insisted, 'the country would find itself in a truly dramatic situation.' For 'in southern Italy, the communist and socialist workers' movement would already have been outlawed, we would already have seen exiles arriving here [in Rome], and we would have been mourning the victims of a civil war – which, with the Allies in the country, we would have lost before it even began'.[101]

In this respect, there were repeated allusions to 'the Greek scenario' – where the Left had walked out of a government of national unity in 1944, only to find itself facing not only the domestic Right but also the Western Allies in an unwinnable civil war. Time and again, PSIUP leaders reminded their party that 'the Greek scenario' was one to avoid at any price. Should the PSIUP embark on the same 'adventures' as the Greek Left, admonished Nenni, 'we would sacrifice the lives of our best comrades and, worse still, the possibility of making democracy succeed'.[102] Such views were echoed even by those who had been active within the revolutionary liberation committees. Nino Gaeta, who had formerly been the socialist vice-chairman of the Napoli liberation committee, warned the April 1946 PSIUP congress that 'breaking national unity' would leave Italy in an even more terrible position than Greece. For while Greece had at least been an Allied country during the war, Italy was bound by the conditions of its armistice with those same Allies. By practising 'a different politics than that of national unity' and 'adopting sectarian and factitious positions', therefore, 'we would ruin Italy forever'.[103]

When the DC finally undid the national unity government in May 1947, such fears only intensified. Speaking at one of the first meetings of the PSIUP Directorate after the communists and socialists had been removed from government, Nenni agonised over the prospect of opposition. 'The state apparatus is right-wing', he declared. Thus far, the Left had been able to 'frustrate' this apparatus 'by our presence in government. But in what

[100] 'Comitato Centrale' (17 October 1945), ACS, Carteggio Nenni, Busta 87, Fasc. 2189, p. 18.
[101] 'Relazione Nenni al Comitato Centrale' (7 January 1946), ACS, Carteggio Nenni, Busta 87, Fasc. 2190, p. 8.
[102] 'Seduta pomeridiana' (18 October 1945), ACS, Carteggio Nenni, Busta 87, Fasc. 2189, p 13.
[103] 'XXIV Congresso del Partito Socialista Italiano di Unità Proletaria', 12 aprile 1946, seduta pomeridiana, ACS, Carteggio Nenni, Busta 88, Fasc 2193, pp. 41–2.

kind of situation will we find ourselves after a couple of months of opposition?'[104] With left–right polarisation mounting across the continent over the months that followed and neighbouring France increasingly finding itself in an insurrectionary state, the situation did indeed seem to deteriorate steadily. By November, Luigi Cacciatore was expressing fears of worker agitations getting out of hand in Italy too. 'There is a danger', he argued, 'of sliding to a situation of the French type, thereafter to a situation of the Greek type.' In these circumstances, it was incumbent upon the socialists 'to rebuild the foundations, which are currently diluted, for a democratic development of political life in Italy'.[105]

Yet the PSIUP's commitment to constitutionalism always seemed to be motivated more by expediency than by principle. In view of their country's geo-political position within the Western bloc, reasoned Italian socialists, adhering to the rulebook of 'bourgeois' democracy offered far better hopes of survival than engaging in violent struggle with the bourgeoisie. That did not mean, however, that they were opposed to communist and socialist parties using force if and when they were in a more 'favourable' position to do so. As other Western European socialists and social democrats began asking more and more questions of the methods used in the 'popular' democracies in Eastern Europe, then, PSIUP leaders stubbornly kept praising 'the great efforts at renewal to which, after Russia, the countries of Eastern Europe have been subjected' – culminating in the congratulatory telegram it sent Fierlinger in the wake of the Prague Coup.[106]

For unlike its Western European and, as we will see, Czechoslovakian counterparts, the post-war PSIUP refused to draw an absolute distinction between democratic and dictatorial trajectories to socialism. Whether a country arrived at socialism by democratic and peaceful means or by dictatorship and violence, Basso explained, depended on how far into the revolutionary process the proletariat took power. If it did so at the very start of a revolution, as in the Russian Revolution, there was bound to be a transitory period of repression and violence. But if the proletariat only rose to power towards the end of a revolutionary cycle, with the disintegrating old regime practically handing over power, democratic rules could be observed. It followed that 'the differences between democracy and dictatorship are formal rather than substantial'. They were 'different methods

---

[104] 'Riunione Direzione' (16 June 1947), ISRT, Fondo Foscolo Lombardi, Partito Socialista Italiano, Direzione Nazionale, Busta 4, Fasc. 21, fo. 34.
[105] 'Riunione Direzione' (19 November 1947), ISRT, Fondo Foscolo Lombardi, Partito Socialista Italiano, Direzione Nazionale, Busta 4, Fasc. 21, fo. 110.
[106] FN, Carteggio Nenni, Busta 47, Fasc. 2033, fo. 220.

of struggle' to be sure, 'but the application of one over another does not depend on the free choice of individuals'. Instead, it was 'the historical situation in which a revolution develops, that is, the balance of power between the classes at the moment of a take-over [of political power], that determines which method of struggle the proletariat should adopt'.[107]

The ČSSD and the SFIO, on the other hand, were adamant that there was a clear-cut choice between democracy and dictatorship and that true socialists should always opt for the former. Right from the outset, the two parties made it quite clear that, as far as they were concerned, there was only one road to socialism. Speaking at his party's first post-war congress, ČSSD secretary general Blažej Vilím vowed that 'Czechoslovakian social democracy is and remains the party, which will always pursue a democratic road to realise its ideals and construct a socialist state'. The seven-year struggle against Nazi terror, he argued, 'has convinced us of the meaning of political freedom and the value of personal freedom'.[108] Vilím's French counterpart, Daniel Mayer, addressed the SFIO's first post-war congress in remarkably similar terms. 'We should be a veritable "social democracy"', he declared, 'i.e. those who create socialism without losing for a moment the sense of freedom and democracy … bringing together at the same time ardent revolutionaries, partisans of profound social and economic trans-formations, and passionate republicans, enamoured by the liberty … of which we only know the price once we have lost it'.[109]

It was not only their wartime experiences of violent repression and dictatorship, however, that accounted for the ČSSD's and the SFIO's commitment towards a democratic road to socialism. In defence of their constitutional approach, they pointed at least as much to the degenerations of the dictatorial road to socialism embarked on by the interwar Soviet Union. The French socialists were the more outspoken critics of Bolshevism.[110] According to Mayer, the Soviet experience proved that

---

[107] Lelio Basso, 'Socialismo al bivio', *Quarto Stato*, 30 April 1946. www.leliobasso.it/documento.aspx?i d=6cbd24b3168fba005bb7ae3912995Ide (last consulted: 27 June 2018).

[108] 'Protokol xx. Manifestačního Sjezdu Československé Sociální Demokracie', Archiv ČSSD, Fond 71, Část II, Karton III, p. 120.

[109] 'Parti Socialiste – SFIO: Congrès national extraordinaire des 9, 10, 11 et 12 novembre 1944', FJJ, p. 26. http://62.210.214.184/cg-ps/documents/pdf/cong-1944-11-09.pdf (last consulted: 27 June 2018).

[110] Even when the PCF was still part of the government, the perversions of Bolshevism and the Soviet system were a constant feature within anti-communist SFIO propaganda. That only intensified when the communists were no longer a coalition partner. See e.g. 'Le Parti Socialiste et la défense des libertés', Arguments et Ripostes, Bulletin Intérieur du Parti Socialiste (S.F.I.O.), 15 October 1946, OURS; 'Théorie et pratique de la conception bolcheviste du syndicalisme', Fiches Socialistes: Arguments et Ripostes, December 1947.

structural socio-economic reforms, seen as the starting point for democratic renewal by the Italian and Polish socialists, did not by themselves
suffice to liberate humanity from oppression. To be sure, such reforms
as nationalisations or the empowerment of factory councils gave freedom
'its full significance, its full meaning'. But '[w]e know now that economic
transformations are not the essential condition [for freedom] and, in any
case, do not exactly lead to freedom, because there is no freedom in Soviet
Russia'.[111] Dumas denounced the Soviet road to socialism in still stronger
terms. 'We want to create socialism in freedom', he argued, 'and we cannot
say that Soviet Russia is the traditional country of socialism.' For 'the dictatorship that was installed there more than twenty years ago is not the
necessary and temporary dictatorship described by Karl Marx, but the dictatorship of a new aristocracy'.[112]

The Czechoslovakian social democrats, possibly in view of the huge
popularity that the Soviet Union had garnered in Czechoslovakia by first
rejecting the Munich diktat and subsequently liberating the country from
Nazi rule, practised more restraint in their criticisms of the Soviet model.
They did very much insist, however, that this model was not applicable
in post-war Czechoslovakia. Even those on the pro-communist left of the
ČSSD agreed that the 'Czechoslovakian road to socialism' had to be a
democratic one. Speaking to workers in Plzeň, Fierlinger explained that
'we want to secure our revolution not by a bloody civil war, but by the
democratically expressed will of the entire nation'. In doing so, he argued,
'we will avoid superfluous bloodshed, domestic conflicts, and unnecessary economic losses'.[113] Evžen Erban similarly stressed how, in post-war
Czechoslovakia, 'a new social order' was being built 'with retention of the
traditional forms of political democracy'. In this respect, he declared, the
Czechoslovakian revolution had much more in common with the medi-
eval Hussite 'revolution' than with the Russian Revolution of 1917. The
methods used during the October Revolution, after all, were 'specifically
Russian' and could not be exported to 'a state of developed industrial capitalism and parliamentary democracy' like interwar Czechoslovakia.[114]

---

[111] 'Parti Socialiste SFIO: 38ème Congrès national, 29, 30, 31 août et 1er septembre 1946', FJJ, pp. 78–
9. http://62.210.214.184/cg-ps/documents/pdf/cong-1946-08-29.pdf (last consulted: 27 June 2018).
[112] OURS, CD SFIO, 23 April 1946.
[113] 'Naše revoluce bude uskutečněna demokratickou cestou', Nový Den, 19 July 1945.
[114] 'Projev posl. Evžena Erbana, generálního tajemníka Ústřední rady odborů, na II. krajské všeodborové
konferenci KOR v Plzni' (15 June 1947), VA, Krajské Odborové Rady 1945–1960, Karton 1, Inv.
j. 16 – KOR Plzeň 1947.

The notion of nationally specific trajectories to socialism was of course very much part of Soviet discourse during the first post-war years, and was actively propagated by communist parties eager to showcase their democratic credentials. Yet the Czechoslovakian social democrats and the French socialists were quick to question the sincerity of the communists' apparent new commitment to the rule of law. Already at the August 1945 SFIO congress, Philip pointed out that communists and socialists had an altogether different approach to practising politics. For the communists, he explained, the conquest of power justified the use of any tactical means, regardless of their 'moral value' or their 'intellectual contradictions'. The socialists, on the other hand, placed themselves within a democratic regime, 'knowing full well that the proper functioning of that regime presupposes [the observance of] a number of moral rules, a number of just rules that are accepted by all democrats'.[115] Speaking in name of the SFIO's Northern Federation at the party's August 1946 congress, Eugène Thomas – the socialist minister for the postal service in sixteen different post-war governments – was more blunt. Even though communists and socialists both used such slogans as 'democracy' and 'freedom', he declared, 'we do not have the same definitions of those concepts'. For 'we all know that the communist party is essentially an anti-democratic party ... [and w]e also know very well that, if the communists were to rise to power in our country, that would mean the end of freedom, would mean concentration camps, exile, [or] death for us'.[116]

Such assessments of communist intentions were inspired in no small part by reports about the situation in Eastern Europe. Even if early post-war Czechoslovakia was by far the most democratically governed country in Soviet-dominated Europe, its social democrats too increasingly complained about communist violations of constitutional processes. Over the course of 1947, the ČSSD became more and more anxious over the (communist-dominated) security services' ever-tightening grip on public life. The party vehemently protested when the (communist-led) ministry of the interior tried to use a law dating back to the Austro-Hungarian period to enforce police presence at all public meetings, and managed to get the police banned from meetings in all provinces where the communists were lacking a majority.[117] In spite of such local successes, however, there was no halting

---

[115] 'Parti Socialiste – SFIO: 37ème Congrès national des 11, 12, 13, 14 et 15 août 1945', FJJ, p. 296. http://62.210.214.184/cg-ps/documents/pdf/cong-1945-08-11.pdf (last consulted: 27 June 2018).

[116] 'Parti Socialiste SFIO: 38ème Congrès national, 29, 30, 31 août et 1er septembre 1946', FJJ, pp. 267–8. http://62.210.214.184/cg-ps/documents/pdf/cong-1946-08-29.pdf (last consulted: 27 June 2018).

[117] *Zpráva o činnosti*, pp. XLVIII–XLIX.

the forward march of dictatorship. When the communists began calling for a wholesale purge of the security services after the 'uncovering' of an 'anti-state conspiracy' in Slovakia in September 1947, the ČSSD once again insisted that the rule of law be observed. Although the social democrats were in favour of removing all 'reactionaries and anti-democrats' from public life, Laušman insisted, 'this purge has to take place within the legal framework of the state'. In questions like these, after all, 'only the relevant laws of the republic can decide – we will fight any ulterior motives together with all true democrats'.[118]

But such protestations were to no avail. During an October 1947 meeting of the ČSSD's parliamentary group, deputies raised alarm over recent communist activities. Ivan Frlička – the chairman of the ČSSD's Slovakian wing – noted that 'everything that is currently happening in Slovakia is being driven by the KSČ'. The communists, he warned, were trying 'to break the [Slovakian] Democratic Party after the Hungarian model' – i.e. through the use of piecemeal 'salami tactics', by which the non-communist politicians and parties were eliminated one by one. What was worse, Miroslav Sédlak – one of the many social democratic parliamentarians who would go on to support Laušman in the November 1947 party leadership election – claimed to have obtained confidential KSČ instructions outlining how the communist domination of the trade union movement could be used to erode social democracy from within.[119]

As it turned out, however, the communists never really had to apply 'salami tactics' to Czechoslovakia, as they managed to eliminate the other parties in a single stroke during the Prague Coup. It was the shock of seeing a democratic country going totalitarian in a matter of days that accounts for the huge backlash that the Prague Coup caused among those supporting a parliamentary and constitutional road to socialism. Within weeks, the parties condoning the events in Prague would find themselves out of or sidelined by the international socialist movement. By April 1948, Léon Blum, in many ways the spiritual father of the parliamentary road to socialism, launched a stark attack upon the concept of popular democracy. He still started on a conciliatory note, arguing that he understood that many 'honest men' had wanted to start from a tabula rasa in 1945

---

[118] 'Zahajovací projev předsedy XXI. sjezdu čsl. socialní demokracie Bohumila Laušmana' (14 November 1947), Archiv ČSSD, Fond 71, Část II, Karton 112, p. 12.

[119] 'Schůze klubu poslanců' (1 October 1947), NA, Fonds Bohumil Laušman, III Pisemnosti související s ústřední, veřejnou a politickou činnosti B. Laušmana, Karton 34, Souvicející činnosti v soc. dem. 1928–1948, pp. 2–3.

and rid themselves of those usual forms of democracy they considered 'outdated and inefficient – especially the parliamentary form'. But those men, he continued, who currently claimed to be building a new, popular democracy upon the ruins of representative democracy might well one day regret 'having worked for authoritarian and totalitarian regimes'. For by justifying police state methods as a necessary evil, they were rapidly approaching the point of no return. Even Rosa Luxemburg, Blum explained, had defined the dictatorship of the proletariat as a transitory phase during which interior legality, including universal suffrage, would be suspended, but the substance of democracy – personal rights and freedoms as enshrined in freedom of the press, freedom of reunion, freedom of association and freedom of thought – would be safeguarded. Without that, Blum insisted, the dictatorship of the proletariat 'would be nothing short of a full-fledged dictatorship, of a personal or collective tyranny'.[120]

Conclusion

We have seen in this chapter that the two sets of parties took completely opposite attitudes towards the three key 'bourgeois' institutions of elections, parliaments, and constitutions. Contrary to what historians of post-war (Western) European socialism have argued, therefore, there was no across-the-board socialist conversion to a parliamentary road to socialism. To be sure, in their rejection of 'bourgeois' legalism, the PPS and the PSIUP found themselves in the minority within the post-war international socialist movement (see Chapter 8). But that does not mean we should dismiss their views as peculiar to these two countries. Within most of the post-war European socialist parties, after all, there was a vociferous minority supporting the conception of a 'popular' democracy.[121]

How can we explain that anti-parliamentarianism became a majority position within the PPS and the PSIUP when, at the same time, the

---

[120] Léon Blum, 'Construire l'Europe pour aller vers le socialisme' (9 April 1948). www.lours.org/archives/defaultacae.html?pid=373 (last consulted: 27 June 2018).

[121] This became very obvious when the PPS organised an international conference for 'left-wing and revolutionary socialists' in June 1948. Only three parties sent an official delegation: the ČSSD and the Hungarian Social Democratic Party (both of which were already completely under communist control by that time) as well as the PSIUP. But the conference was also attended by a variety of left-wing dissidents that were or had until very recently been part of leading Western European socialist parties, including Pierre Stibbe (one of the leaders of the Bataille Socialiste movement, which was excluded from the SFIO in 1948) and Konni Zilliacus (the Labour MP for Gateshead, who was expelled from the Labour Party in 1949 to be readmitted in 1952).

ČSSD and the SFIO (re-)affirmed their commitment to parliamentary politics? First and foremost, we have to return here to the four parties' historical experiences with democracy and dictatorship and to the lessons they drew from their own national and Europe's interwar history. The lessons of the past had convinced the Czechoslovakian social democrats and the French socialists that democratic socialism could only be achieved through elections, parliaments, and constitutions. For not only had their own experiences with 'bourgeois' parliamentary democracy been by and large positive, but the degenerations of both fascist and communist dictatorships also taught them that there was no viable alternative to a parliamentary road to socialism. For the Italian and Polish socialists, conversely, the interwar experience with parliamentary democracy had been largely negative. Far from bringing socialism closer, they stressed that it had ushered in right-wing dictatorship in their own and a string of other European countries.

By themselves, though, historical experiences and lessons cannot account for the divergence between the two sets of parties in its totality. Italy and Poland, after all, were hardly the only countries that had succumbed to authoritarian or fascist dictatorship in interwar Europe. That had been the case in countries like Austria and Germany as well – yet the post-war socialist parties in these countries never advocated a radical departure from the parliamentary road to socialism. A further crucial factor in the four parties' attitudes towards 'bourgeois' democracy, therefore, was their perceptions of the democratic preparedness of their own societies. As we have seen in the previous chapter, the ČSSD and the SFIO were confident of the sound democratic beliefs of the overwhelming majority of their electorates. When the two parties lost elections, accordingly, they tended to blame themselves. The PPS and the PSIUP, on the other hand, felt that their underdeveloped, rural, and Catholic societies were not yet ready for the temptations of democratic politics. For that reason, the two parties felt they could justifiably disregard electoral outcomes and eliminate 'reactionary' parties even if these had majority popular support.

To these historically and socially informed perceptions, however, we still need to add a third dimension that we have not discussed thus far: the opposite views that the two sets of parties took of the merits of representative democracy itself. The 'bourgeois' institutions of elections, parliaments, and constitutions were of course part and parcel of the representative system, but, according to Basso, a new order could not be based on such existing institutions:

> [W]henever a new regime, whether political or social, has toppled the existing regime, that movement is condemned to failure if it, to legitimise and justify itself, immediately reverts to the institutions of the political, economic, or social regime it has abolished ... All of the political revolutions of the nineteenth century have failed or succeeded to the extent that they have taken the precaution of a transitory dictatorship between the destruction of the old regime and the legal installation of the new.[122]

We have analysed the socialist arguments for and against such a transitory dictatorship in this chapter. The question remained, however, of what would develop in the place of the 'old' institutions of elections, parliaments, and constitutions. It is to that question that we will turn our attention in the next chapter.

---

[122] Basso, 'Sul socialismo europeo', FLB, Fondo Lelio Basso, Serie 15, Fasc. 6, p. 25 bis. The actual quote was made by Blum in 1919, but Basso (approvingly) cited it in the above 1948 article to attack what he regarded as the hypocrisy of leading Western European socialists over the Prague Coup.

CHAPTER 7

Democracy from Below

In March 1945, Pietro Nenni received a letter from a concerned Pier Paolo Fano – the socialist trade unionist who had become the Italian representative at the International Transport Workers' Federation during his exile in London. In the letter, Fano expressed his misgivings about the PSIUP's plans for a radical overhaul of industrial relations. More specifically, he took issue with the socialist campaign to bestow wide-ranging competencies upon the revolutionary factory councils that were taking over industrial management across post-liberation Italy. For this campaign, he explained, had approached the question of worker self-management 'more from a political than from an economic point of view'.

Yet it was in the economic realm that Fano expected difficulties to arise. 'I believe that it is dangerous for the economic success of those industries and for their consolidation in the nation's hands', he warned, 'to give factory councils the direct power to decide over the technical, financial, and commercial problems of their firm.' It was far from certain, after all, that it would be possible 'to find a sufficient number of workers capable of taking on these responsibilities in the majority of factories' or that there would be 'sufficient harmony both within the factory council and between [the factory council] and the director of a company to allow for the decisions necessary for the prosperity of the firm to be taken with sufficient speed and authority'. In these circumstances, Fano went on, it would be very difficult to identify the culprit when things started to go wrong in a factory. It was for that exact reason that the interwar Soviet Union, 'after a failed experiment with worker self-management based on councils', had decided 'to entrust the running of every factory to a single person – the director, chosen, but not elected, on the basis of competency'. And even the British Labour Party, 'notwithstanding that the cultural level of the British worker is certainly higher than that of the Russian [worker] at the time of the [October]

[R]evolution', had 'a similar solution in mind' for the administration of the nationalised sector.[1]

The question of direct grassroots participation in economic as well as political decision-making certainly divided post-war socialist opinion. For some socialists, the revolutionary liberation committees and factory councils that had sprung up in the wake of the war and taken over vital functions of local and industrial administration offered unique opportunities for democratic renewal. First and foremost, the experience of direct democracy within such grassroots participatory bodies promised to (re-) animate electorates that had been left disoriented by dictatorship and war. Secondly, the introduction of worker self-management in ownerless companies extended democracy beyond the narrow confines of the political arena and into the everyday life of the working class. Other socialists, however, were less convinced about the invigorating effects of direct grassroots participation in political and economic life. For in the immediate aftermath of the liberation, local assemblies often challenged the authority of both national party leaderships and the traditional institutions of representative democracy. As the mouthpiece of an increasingly aggrieved working class, moreover, the organs of workplace democracy were quick to question some of the core tenets of the reconstruction programmes to which socialist leaders had signed up. At the root of the socialist divide on participatory democracy, therefore, were profound disagreements as to whether democratisation and socialisation should be bottom-up or top-down processes.

This chapter aims to demonstrate that the four parties found themselves on opposite ends of this divide and how this was linked closely to their conceptions of democracy. The Italian and Polish socialists, on the one side, embraced grassroots participation as a crucial stepping stone towards the democratisation of their societies. In their view, popular participation in public life was key to the democratic (re-)education of their backward populations. For that reason, they insisted on the recognition of grassroots participatory bodies as full players in political and especially economic decision-making. That meant the guidance provided by ordinary workers, through such intermediaries as factory councils or cooperatives, had to be taken seriously by those in power. The Czechoslovakian social democrats and French socialists, on the other side, increasingly viewed grassroots participation as a menace not only to the fulfilment of their economic plans but also to the resumption of parliamentary normality. In fact, they often dismissed participatory democracy as no more than a guise for the

[1] Pier Paolo Fano to Nenni, 9 March 1945, FN, Carteggio Nenni, Busta 44, Fasc. 2025, fo. 98.

political machinations of the communists. Yet their calls for the revolutionary councils to be subordinated to more readily controllable political and socio-economic structures as quickly as possible were not merely the product of their growing anti-communism. What mattered at least as much was a distinct belief that political and economic decision-making was to remain the prerogative of party and trade union elites with a more lucid view of the bigger national picture. In bringing to light these divergences between the two sets of parties, the chapter adds a fresh dimension to a scholarly debate in which socialist views have frequently been ignored, misunderstood, or taken for granted.

Confronting the Council Movement

The reconstruction effort was often set in motion by local committees. In the power vacuum left by the departed or toppled local elites of the wartime regimes, former Resistance cells transformed themselves into liberation committees or factory councils and took responsibility for such crucial tasks as food distribution, clearing rubble off the streets, and rebooting paralysed industrial production. The autonomy and discipline of these bodies has captured the imagination of many historians. In their view, the popular assemblies that took charge of local decision-making and the works councils that placed themselves at the head of factories abandoned by their collaborationist owners carried the germs of a veritable worker democracy – a decentralised system of direct democracy and worker self-management fundamentally different from both American market capitalism and Soviet state capitalism. Much of the earlier work on the theme focused on post-war Germany, where the Antifa council movement has often been taken to have offered an alternative to Americanisation and Sovietisation.[2] More recently, though, various case studies have observed how grassroots participatory bodies challenged returning elites as well as occupying armies across post-liberation Europe.[3] Almost invariably, such

---

[2] The standard work on the Antifa remains: Lutz Niethammer, Ulrich Borsdorf, and Peter Brandt (eds.), *Arbeiterinitiative 1945: Antifaschistische Ausschüsse und Reorganisation der Arbeiterbewegung in Deutschland* (Wuppertal: Hammer, 1976). See also Boehling, *A Question of Priorities*. More recently, Gareth Pritchard has challenged the idea that the Antifa did in fact offer a 'Third Way' out of Americanisation and Sovietisation. See his *Niemandsland: A History of Unoccupied Germany, 1944–1945* (Cambridge/New York: Cambridge University Press, 2012).

[3] See e.g. Peter Heumos, 'State Socialism, Egalitarianism, Collectivism: On the Social Context of Socialist Work Movements in Czechoslovak Industrial and Mining Enterprises, 1945–1965', *International Labor and Working-Class History*, 68 (2005), pp. 47–74; Pierangelo Lombardi (ed.), *L'illusione al potere. Democrazia, autogoverno regionale e decentramento amministrativo nell'esperienza*

accounts convey a sense of missed chances and lost illusions as 'the opportunity for radical democratic change' was not capitalised upon.[4]

That the radical challenge to 'politics as usual'[5] came undone within mere months of the liberation, historians in this tradition often attribute to the formidable coalition confronting the post-war council movement. First of all, both the American and Soviet occupiers, fearful of any rival authority emerging under their watch, tended to be ill-disposed to the grassroots bodies that mushroomed at the moment of liberation.[6] More important still were the hesitant and contradictory attitudes that returning communist leaders adopted towards the radicalism among their rank and file. For even if their activists often dominated liberation committees and factory councils, communist leaders arrived with clear instructions not to get embroiled in any undertakings that might disquiet the bourgeoisie or the Western Allies. Instead, they were to showcase Stalin's good faith by calling on liberation committees to surrender their weapons to the authorities and supporting the restoration of 'order' on the shop floor.[7]

This strand of historiography has, however, by and large disregarded socialist attitudes towards grassroots participatory bodies. The scarce references to socialist parties that scholarship on the post-liberation council movement does provide, moreover, point in different directions. Some historians claim that the socialists were at least as dismissive of grassroots participation as the communists, if not more so.[8] Others argue, though, that socialist leaders took a far more positive view of participatory structures,[9] only to be defeated by communists in government.[10]

---

dei CLN (1944–45) (Milan: F. Agneli, 2003); Robert Mencherini, *La Libération et les enterprises sous gestion ouvrière, Marseille, 1944–1948* (Paris: L'Harmattan, 1994).

[4] Eley, 'Legacies of Antifascism', p. 79.

[5] Eley, *Forging Democracy*, p. 271.

[6] Gareth Dale, *Popular Protest in East Germany, 1945–1989* (London/New York: Routledge, 2005), p. 43; Eley, 'Legacies of Antifascism', p. 94.

[7] See for this approach e.g. Behan, *The Long Awaited Moment.*

[8] According to Geoff Eley, for example, '[t]he [British] Labour Government's main model of reform was paternalistic and bureaucratic. A blend of Fabian progressivism (giving people what was good for them) and authoritarian trade unionism, it had little room for participatory democracy.' And Charles S. Maier claims that the French communists 'did support new schemes for a workers' voice in the tripartite management boards ... for the nationalised industries .... But they had to retreat in the face of MRP and Socialist countermeasures to ensure a more technical supervision.' See Eley, *Forging Democracy*, p. 296; Charles S. Maier, 'The Two Postwar Eras and the Conditions for Stability in Twentieth-Century Western Europe', *American Historical Review*, 86/2 (1981), pp. 327–52, 338.

[9] See, on the post-war French and Italian socialists, Andrieu, 'La France à gauche de l'Europe', *Le Mouvement Social*, 134 (1986), pp. 131–53, 134–9.

[10] In contrast to what Maier claims above (Maier, 'The Two Postwar Eras', p 338), Martin McCauley argues that, 'participating in government', the PCF 'ignored socialist plans for the nationalisation of large-scale industry, economic planning, and co-determination'. See: Martin McCauley, *The Origins of the Cold War, 1941–1949* (London/New York: Longman, 1995), p. 48.

As is so often the case with scholarly assertions about the post-war socialist parties and popular movements, such claims tend to be based on anecdotal evidence rather than a systematic study of socialist attitudes.[11] A more thorough analysis of the attitudes the two sets of parties adopted towards the question of grassroots participation reveals that the positions taken by individual socialist parties varied greatly and that these positions were, in any case, never analogous to those of the communists.

The PPS and the PSIUP, on the one hand, were considerably more anxious than their communist coalition partners about the (looming) disempowerment of the council movement.[12] For the Polish socialists, this anxiety concerned the fate of factory councils above all – in view of the ongoing struggle between the Soviet occupiers and the Polish underground, there was no scope for Resistance-led liberation committees in post-liberation Poland, after all. Yet factories abandoned by their German owners or supervisors did fall under worker control in the wake of the liberation[13] and the Lublin government initially encouraged the spontaneously formed worker committees that took over management.

Right from the outset, though, the socialists found cause to question the sincerity of the communist commitment to worker self-management. The protracted discussions about the decree empowering the revolutionary factory councils within the Lublin government had already left the socialists with the impression that the PPR was dragging its feet on the issue.[14] These suspicions were confirmed when the communist-dominated ministry of industry, within four months of the decree finally being passed in February 1945, issued new guidelines stripping factory councils of their financial and technical co-decision rights. Speaking at a September 1945 plenum of the PPS and PPR leaderships, Edward Osóbka-Morawski made it quite clear that the socialists were unimpressed. The significance of factory councils, he declared, was 'often … not appreciated'. In the face of the 'tendency to limit the competencies of factory councils', he reminded the communists

[11] Claire Andrieu (in 'La France à gauche de l'Europe'), for example, seems to base her claims regarding the French socialists in large part upon the attitudes taken by the provincial SFIO organisation in the Allier department and on a tract written by SFIO Executive member Suzanne Charpy. As we will see below, however, their views were rejected by the large majority of the SFIO leadership.

[12] On the PPS and the PSIUP and the question of participatory democracy, see Jan de Graaf, 'More than Canteen Control: Italian and Polish Socialists Confronting Their Workers, 1944–1947', *International Review of Social History*, 59/1 (2014), pp. 71–98, 89–92.

[13] Kenney, *Rebuilding Poland*, pp. 57–8.

[14] See: Jaime Reynolds, 'Communists, Socialists and Workers', pp. 519–22.

that the introduction of factory councils represented 'a major reform' and that their role could not be 'reduced to canteen control etc.'[15]

The PSIUP similarly campaigned for wide-ranging powers to be devolved to the Italian National Liberation Committees, which came in the form of both liberation committees (CLN) and factory councils (CLNA). According to Nenni, the CLN(A) reflected the 'democratic will of the people' far better and commanded far greater 'moral authority' than the average local appointee of the Allied Control Commission.[16] Pending local elections, therefore, the socialists claimed '[a]ll power' for the CLN.[17]

Yet with the partial exception of the Action Party, such claims found little resonance with the PSIUP's coalition partners and, far from being empowered, the position of the CLN(A) was steadily eroded under the first Bonomi government. This was one of the issues that contributed to the first major crack in socialist–communist unity of action during the post-war years, as the PSIUP refused to follow the PCI in joining the second Bonomi government. In the communiqué explaining this decision, the PSIUP castigated the prime minister for having failed 'to encourage the truly democratic forces in their desire to permeate [and] radically renew ... the old monarchical state organisation, still completely tainted by fascist remains'. Instead, he had 'doggedly pursued his design to humiliate the new organisms that arose in the country through the national liberation struggle – true [and] vital cells of democracy – and to restore the old bureaucratic and monarchical Italy'.[18]

The reason that the PPS and the PSIUP felt so strongly about the disempowerment of the post-war council movement was that they had envisioned these councils playing a key role in the democratic re-education of disoriented electorates. In fact, the two parties considered popular involvement in grassroots participatory bodies a crucial stepping stone towards the development of democratic and socialist beliefs in their societies. Providing ordinary people with a forum to discuss their everyday

---

[15] 'Protokół z wspólnego posiedzenia CKW PPS i KC PPR' (28 September 1945), AAN, PPS, CKW, 235/III/6, fo. 3.

[16] Pietro Nenni, 'Tutto il potere ai Comitati di Liberazione Nazionale: Il caso di Firenze', *Avanti!*, 9 November 1944.

[17] The slogan '*Tutto il potere al CLN*' ('all power to the CLN') – an obvious allusion to Lenin's 1917 dictum demanding 'all power to the Soviets' – was first coined in the clandestine *Avanti!* of 26 February 1944 and remained the PSIUP's quasi-official slogan at least until the party joined the Parri government in May 1945. See, for an explanation of the concept, Pietro Nenni, 'Tutto il potere ai Comitati di Liberazione Nazionale', *Avanti!*, 14 October 1944.

[18] 'La crisi del primo governo Bonomi: Dichiarazione del Partito Socialista al Paese' (10 December 1944), *Orientamenti: Bollettino di Commento e di Indirizzo Politico*, 18 January 1948, pp. 13–14.

problems and take action to resolve them, after all, direct participation in such bodies would be a far more effective school of democracy than voting for distant representatives in parliamentary elections had ever been. For that reason, the Italian and Polish socialists very much fostered the development of such local and workplace consultative bodies as liberation committees, factory councils, and cooperatives.

Much of this went back to the dim views, outlined in the previous chapter, that PPS and PSIUP leaders took of their own electorates. Socialist leaders in both countries argued that the political backwardness of their societies, deepened by the experiences of dictatorship and war, presented them with enormous challenges. In a country where 'the democratic consciousness has always been very scarce and where fascism had free rein for twenty years to erode it still further', explained Lelio Basso, 'our task is immense'. To be sure, worker participation in the anti-fascist Resistance and the liberation struggle had 'contributed considerably to the education and the political preparation of the masses'. '[B]ut we cannot deny', he continued, 'that, within the same working population, there are still vast groups, especially among women and youngsters, who do not partake in the political struggle [and] who do not show an interest in political problems'. And it was in 'this absenteeism, which easily generates scepticism and distrust', that 'the roots of all anti-democratic movements' were to be found.[19]

For the PPS, Adam Rapacki – the socialist minister of shipping in the first Cyrankiewicz government – described the political acumen of Polish society in similarly derogatory terms. The Polish people, he claimed, 'emerged from Polish history ... a little anarchical and hysterical, socially still immature, [and] not always understanding that a revolution is happening before their eyes'. A socialised economy, then, would not by itself 'suffice for the creation of socialism'. What was needed was '*a socialisation of popular consciousness*'.[20]

It was in this socialisation effort that the PPS and the PSIUP imputed a key function to grassroots participatory bodies. Such organisms as factory councils and cooperatives, Stanisław Szwalbe told communist leaders in September 1945, 'have a key educational function and the government

[19] Lelio Basso, 'Per una coscienza democratica', *Avanti!*, 29 August 1945. www.leliobasso.it/documento. aspx?id=1fb14f1db3eb10586206df1cbf448089 (last consulted: 27 June 2018).
[20] Adam Rapacki, 'Odcinek spółdzielczy', *Przegląd Socjalistyczny*, 1 April 1946, pp. 12–15. Emphasis in original.

should rely on them'.[21] And if governments were to draw upon grassroots participatory bodies, ordinary workers were to be drawn into them. As early as June 1944, Nenni warned workers against viewing the various workplace councils that had come into being during the liberation struggle as 'no more than an expedient' – as a means to fill the power vacuum left by managers who had fled or been expelled, to secure the successful transition from a fascist to a democratic administration, and to revise the fascist management model. Wherever workers took such views, he insisted, it was 'the duty of socialists to immediately raise awareness ... of the immense importance of councils and of their infinite possibilities for development'. For 'the function of councils' was 'not provisional, but permanent; not conservative, but revolutionary'. They constituted 'the cells of a new democratic society, which should ... lead to the amalgamation of the *homo economicus* and the *homo politicus*'.[22]

According to the Italian and Polish socialists, therefore, the true significance of grassroots participatory bodies lay in their ability to combine the economic emancipation (to which we will return in the following section) with the political (re-)education of the working class. Their accessible nature, after all, offered countless people with no experience of (democratic) politics the chance to acquaint themselves with some of the basic elements of democracy: discussion, compromise, and working together. To overcome the 'political analphabetism' afflicting large parts of Italian society, argued Basso, 'we should start from concrete problems'. That meant 'engaging workers, clerks, [and] peasants with the problems of their firm ... make them discuss ... salaries, the cost of living, [and] food, housing, [and] heating problems; gradually accustoming them to link their immediate demands to more complex questions and to move from a particularistic to a more general understanding of class relations'. To achieve that, however, it was

> necessary to get peasants [and] workers, especially women and youngsters, to attend meetings where their problems are discussed – factory meetings, trade union meetings, meetings of mass organisations – [and to get them to] participate in elections for internal commissions, for factory councils, for their local CLN ... for trade union bodies, as well as for the organs of the Youth Front and the Union of Italian Women.[23]

[21] 'Protokół z wspólnego posiedzenia CKW PPS i KC PPR' (28 September 1945), AAN, PPS, CKW, 235/III/6, fo. 16.

[22] Pietro Nenni, 'La democrazia dei consigli', *Avanti!*, 13 June 1944.

[23] Lelio Basso, 'Per una coscienza democratica', *Avanti!*, 29 August 1945. www.leliobasso.it/documento.aspx?id=1fb14f1db3eb10586206df1cbf448089 (last consulted: 27 June 2018).

Julian Hochfeld ascribed similar virtues to participation in the cooperative movement, which, after the disempowerment of the factory councils, became the chief grassroots darling of the PPS. Cooperatives, he explained, represented 'consumer self-government', with ordinary workers taking responsibility 'for the satisfaction of their own needs'. In that sense, cooperatives were 'a school of democracy in everyday life – a vibrant democracy, [being] cultivated constantly; not a ballot paper once every few years ... but [consumers taking] an immediate interest ... in their own affairs'. Cooperatives were not merely 'a branch of the democratic state', therefore, 'but its crucial component, in large part making up its democratic content'.[24]

For the Italian and Polish socialists, this educative function of popular participation always outweighed its party-political function. Socialist leaders in both countries repeatedly stressed that securing genuine mass engagement with politics was far more important than making short-term party gains. That meant the traditional focus on recruiting new members was to be abandoned. Nenni went as far as to suggest that the post-liberation surge in the PSIUP's membership, probably the result of quite a few members of Mussolini's PNF jumping ship, was unwelcome. Party membership, he argued, was of 'moral value' and should not be regarded as a necessity to find a job.[25] Basso, for his part, emphasised that it made no sense to unleash any form of propaganda, let alone socialist propaganda, upon the 'apolitical' masses.[26] The work of politicising these groups consisted of 'day-to-day contact with the life of the masses, that is with factory, company, and rural life' – meaning that the PSIUP could no longer 'simply be an electoral machine, which springs into action [only] on special occasions'.[27]

The PPS leadership even urged its party activists to treat the January 1947 elections to the Sejm as an educational opportunity. 'We desire that the elections represent not only the usual fight for power, that the election campaign is made up not only of agitations', insisted the document that the

[24] Julian Hochfeld, 'O istotną treść spółdzielczości' (November 1945), in Julian Hochfeld (ed.), *My socjalisci: Ze stanowiska socjalistycznego realizmu* (Warszawa: Spółdzielnia Wydawnicza Wiedza, 1946), pp. 259–60.

[25] Pietro Nenni, 'Che cos'è e cosa vuole il Partito Socialista', *Avanti!*, 23 July 1944.

[26] Lelio Basso, 'Per una coscienza democratica', *Avanti!*, 29 August 1945. www.leliobasso.it/documento. aspx?id=1fb14f1db3eb10586206dfcbf448089 (last consulted: 27 June 2018).

[27] Lelio Basso, 'L'aspetto politico dei nuclei aziendali', *Quarto Stato*, 30 June 1946. www.leliobasso.it/ documento.aspx?id=e23c39b2efef8f1eae37279209501c11 (last consulted: 27 June 2018).

party's manifesto commission spread among regional party representatives, '[but] that they are part of [our] educational work, which could lead a majority of the nation to an understanding of reality.' For that reason, 'our electoral action cannot be conceived as the usual agitations', with the sole goal of winning the most votes. Instead, it had to be 'another large-scale attempt to persuade society'.[28]

In order to see through the popular conversion to participation first, democracy next, and socialism ultimately, then, the PPS and the PSIUP felt they had to reinvent themselves as a different type of party – as parties taking their lead from the working masses rather than the other way around. That involved the creation of new bodies allowing party leaderships to remain in touch with the concerns at their grassroots. As the number of paid PPS functionaries rose above one thousand, explained Włodzimierz Reczek, the party was looking to avoid 'the grave ills of [interwar] German social democracy', where 'paid functionaries detached themselves from the masses, stopped understanding the masses, [and] gave up on activism among the masses'. To counter this threat, he argued, the PPS had created 'a system of councils' – economic, professional, peasant, and women's councils 'energising broad circles of socialists and effectively controlling professional party functionaries'. The fact that these councils emerged 'quickly and often as a result of the spontaneous initiative of grassroots party cells' was testimony to 'the aptness of our decision'.[29]

Basso likewise insisted on the need for new forms of socialist engagement with the party grassroots. In his view, the local party section no longer answered to the requirements of a mass proletarian party. He listed a string of practical reasons, including time constraints, inadequate transport links, and in-house duties, complicating efforts to draw workers into (mostly evening) sessions of local party sections. But even those workers who did attend would be reluctant to take the floor, he continued, 'intimidated by the presence of "notables"', the 'lawyers or professors' who often led local party sections. While such notables tended to be 'able speakers on general issues', they lacked 'direct contact with the rank and file' – leaving workers with the impression that 'their personal experience [and] their specific problems do not carry real significance'. That, in turn, led to 'erroneous party attitudes, a gulf between the opinions of [party] leaders and

[28] 'Sprawozdanie stenograficzne z obrad Rady Naczelnej PPS' (4 December 1946), AAN, Akta Stanisława Szwalbego, Box 13.
[29] Ibid.

the demands at the grassroots, [and] an insufficient interchange in party life'.[30]

It was for these reasons that Basso championed the creation of socialist factory cells. 'If the party takes its decisions in contact with the factories', he insisted, 'its decisions will never be reckless and will always have the entire working class behind them.' For the factory cell activist 'brings to party discussions not only his personal point of view, but an echo of all his colleagues' voices; and, in turn, imparts upon his colleagues the significance and conclusion of the discussions conducted within the cell'. It was only by virtue of this 'continuous exchange of sentiments, reactions, and ideas between ... the qualified minority of party activists and the entire work-force of a company', argued Basso, 'that the [factory cell] activist acquires a genuine influence over ... the non-organised masses; an influence ... that would be sacrificed and lost if the political activism of a single company's workforce was dispersed over various local sections, where members lacked direct and daily contact with non-members'.[31]

Hochfeld similarly called for the PPS to be open to the input of non-members. Responding to outrage over 'non-party' workers (in all likeli-hood communist stooges) calling on the PPS to step up its 'verification' effort (i.e. the purge of former members of the WRN Resistance organ-isation) during a factory meeting in Wrocław, he defended the principle of non-members passing judgement on the PPS. The PPS, he claimed, 'is more than a party, [it is] a movement'. If the party were to someday enter elections on its own, after all, 'it will turn out that we have far more voters than members'. And all of these people had 'the right to speak up and to scrutinise ... the PPS'. Rather than being 'so resentful', therefore, the PPS should 'approach the masses with an open mind and tell them: "we are your party; by all means control what is going on in our party, because we are connected to you and ... are part of the Polish nation"'.[32]

For the Czechoslovakian social democrats and the French socialists, on the other hand, democratic politics was to be a far more orderly process in which the initiative resided firmly with party elites. As a consequence, they were quick to demand the disbandment of the revolutionary council

---

[30] Lelio Basso, 'Per conoscersi meglio', *Avanti!* (Milanese edition), 2 November 1945. www.leliobasso. it/documento.aspx?id=8be4cc201e75fa27ebf46b80f5195499 (last consulted: 27 June 2018).

[31] Lelio Basso, 'L'aspetto politico dei nuclei aziendali', *Quarto Stato*, 30 June 1946. www.leliobasso.it/ documento.aspx?id=e23c39b2efef8f1eae37279209501c11 (last consulted: 27 June 2018).

[32] xxvii Kongres (December 1947), AAN, PPS, 235/I-25, fos 216–17.

movement. In fact, they often viewed this movement as the spearhead of the communist challenge to democratic legality.

That was certainly how most SFIO leaders viewed the French liberation committees. The first post-liberation meetings of the SFIO Executive were dominated by the question of the Departmental Liberation Committees (CDL) – which, especially in southern France, frequently rode roughshod over the authority of government-designated departmental prefects by installing themselves as the departmental administration and appointing municipal councils. The radicalism practised by these communist-dominated CDL left socialist leaders with serious misgivings about the true intentions of the communists. Gaston Defferre, then the mayor of Marseille, complained bitterly about 'communist demagogy' within the CDL.[33] Adrien Tixier, who, as the socialist minister of the interior in the first two De Gaulle governments, was responsible for dealing with the CDL, demanded that all political parties take 'an extremely firm stand' against the abuses committed by the departmental liberation committees – berating the communists in particular for failing to support the government to which they belonged.[34] Jules Moch even drew a comparison between post-liberation France and pre-revolutionary Russia, 'where the Soviets pursued a politics in opposition to that of the Kerensky government and the Duma'.[35] The SFIO Executive heeded his advice to not allow 'a third administration alongside the prefectural [and governmental] administration', instructing the party's parliamentary group to dismiss the departmental administrations the CDL had already formed and postpone any further administrative appointments until local elections had been called.[36]

The Czechoslovakian social democrats likewise wanted their liberation committees and revolutionary factory councils to be replaced by properly elected bodies as quickly as possible. First of all, this concerned the national committees (NV) – local and provincial government bodies that the exiled Czechoslovakian government had called into being in December 1944 to replace the 'alienated' pre-war administrative apparatus and rule liberated (parts of) Czechoslovakia pending the return of the government.[37] Even if the NV lacked the spontaneous character of liberation committees elsewhere in Europe, therefore, their improvised nature offered the communists ample opportunities to strengthen their

[33] OURS, CD SFIO, 13 November 1944.
[34] Ibid.
[35] Ibid.
[36] OURS, CD SFIO, 22 November 1944.
[37] Frommer, *National Cleansing*, pp. 45–6.

grip upon the state nonetheless. The KSČ readily acknowledged this, its leader Klement Gottwald crediting the NV for providing the party with 'a clean slate' as regards the state apparatus, for being 'a thorn in the side' of its coalition partners, and for constituting 'the main arena for the political struggle'.[38] The communist domination[39] of these bodies that, having been charged with the maintenance of law and order in the area under their control, often played a crucial role in sanctioning the abuses of the security services was a cause for rising concern within the ČSSD leadership. 'In many national committees', claimed the party's 1946 annual report, 'key positions are occupied by people, whose actions only create distrust towards the new bodies of popular administration.'[40] The ČSSD manifesto for the May 1946 parliamentary elections, accordingly, included the demand that the NV be 'founded on a solid basis' and 'duly elected'.[41]

If the anti-communist message was still implicit here, the ČSSD was more outspoken in the question of the revolutionary factory councils. Time and again, the social democrats insisted that elections to these councils – which had been installed in the heat of the liberation struggle but were still in place by 1947 – be held to reflect 'the current balance of forces' within factories.[42] According to the social democrats, after all, the present councils were far too one-sided and were constantly being abused for party-political purposes.[43] In terms of their make-up, they put forward much the same arguments as they had done against the NV – claiming that, in many factory councils, there were 'representatives who only diminish the significance of these organs'. What caused their 'greatest distrust', however, was that these councils were 'made up almost exclusively of communists'.[44]

The ČSSD and the SFIO insisted, accordingly, that the post-war council movement, far from democratising political and economic life, often represented the law of the jungle. Underneath their severe protests against the communist perversions of grassroots politics, however, lay

---

[38] Quoted in ibid, p. 47.
[39] Benjamin Frommer points out that the communists headed 46 per cent of the NV in the Czech lands in early 1946, with 'the Party's stranglehold on the national committees' growing 'even tighter' after the May 1946 elections. See Frommer, *National Cleansing*, p. 47f.
[40] *Zpráva o činnosti*, p. XXII.
[41] Ibid., p. XXVII.
[42] 'Dělnictvo volá po volbách do závodních rad', *Nový Den*, 11 August 1946.
[43] Zdeněk Fierlinger, for example, told the November 1947 ČSSD congress that communist–social democratic struggles had arisen primarily where 'the original revolutionary factory councils remained for a long time'. In these places, after all, the factory council had 'often used political pressure … for party purposes'. 'The Mission of Social Democracy in the New State' (November 1947), ANM, Fonds Zdeněk Fierlinger, Karton 40, Sjezd soc. dem. v Brne, p. 28.
[44] *Zpráva o činnosti*, p. XLIV.

more fundamental objections to direct popular participation in political decision-making. Democracy, the two parties proclaimed, consisted of free and fair elections, and the decisions of elected representatives were not to be challenged from below. That meant the political initiative resided with local, provincial, and national party leaders rather than with grassroots activists.

This was reflected in the arguments the ČSSD and the SFIO employed against communist conceptions of local democracy. Right from the outset, the French socialists made it quite clear that they were not about to follow the communists in creating 'a new democratic legality'.[45] At stake were communist proposals to convoke 'patriotic' or 'popular' assemblies – meetings at which the entire population of a given town or village could elect local representatives by a show of hands. When this had been tried in post-liberation Corsica, Vincent Auriol told the November 1944 congress of the SFIO, gross irregularities had come to light. Lorries had driven 'from one village to another' to transport 'voters' to places where majorities were 'shaky' and, as a consequence, up to 80 per cent of votes cast had been declared invalid in some localities.[46]

It was not only the widespread opportunities for electoral fraud, however, that pitted the French socialists against direct democracy in such assemblies. The entire process of electing representatives during public meetings, they argued, violated key principles of democratic politics. For one thing, it allowed powerful local actors to bully their way to power. '[W]e cannot accept assemblies', insisted Daniel Mayer, 'where agent provocateurs might interfere, or men who go from town to town hurling abuse, sometimes at gunpoint.'[47] Even if their pressure was less explicit, moreover, the very dynamics of a public vote enabled local employers to exert undue influence on its outcome. In this respect, argued Auriol, the assemblies corresponded 'in no way to the spirit of France, to that freedom, that secret ballot that the Republic gave all voters forty years ago to liberate them from the pressures of rural squires and city bosses'.[48] It followed, as Mayer put it, that assembly politics was 'not ... what democracy looks like'. '[F]or democracy', he explained, 'is expressed in elections with voting

---

[45] OURS, CD SFIO, 13 March 1945.

[46] 'Parti Socialiste – SFIO: Congrès national extraordinaire des 9, 10, 11 et 12 novembre 1944', FJJ, p. 122. http://62.210.214.184/cg-ps/documents/pdf/cong-1944-11-09.pdf (last consulted: 27 June 2018).

[47] Ibid., p. 32.

[48] Ibid., p. 123.

booths [and] ballots, and not in so-called popular assemblies which are no more than a caricature ... and do not reflect democracy at all'.[49]

The Czechoslovakian social democrats likewise indicated that the communist version of participatory politics was incompatible with their conception of democracy. Their protests concerned communist challenges to the decisions of properly elected local representatives. This became very clear in the controversies surrounding the elections of new NV chairmen (effectively city mayors or provincial governors) after these organs had been given a fresh distribution of seats based on the local results in the May 1946 parliamentary elections. The ČSSD leadership had instructed its municipal sections and provincial departments to vote for the candidate of the largest party locally, as long as that candidate could 'guarantee harmonious cooperation between all parties of the National Front'. In most cases, these elections went by smoothly. But in Olomouc and Plzeň, where the KSČ had become the largest party, the communists fielded candidates that were 'unacceptable' to the social democrats.[50] When these candidates were subsequently defeated, the communists launched a series of strikes and demonstrations to prevent the installation of the elected chairman. These challenges to due democratic process met with strong social democratic condemnation. The national ČSSD daily castigated the communists for trying to pick and choose from democratic outcomes. 'There is only one democracy', it insisted, 'and all attempts to subvert the implementation of a democratically taken decision by means of public speeches, work stoppages, etc. represent a diktat and an intimidation.'[51]

The polemics waged during the Plzeň episode demonstrate how, as far as the ČSSD was concerned, this one and only democracy was representative rather than participatory. Time and again, the social democrats stressed that they had followed proper channels in electing a new mayor. The stipulations issued by the ministry of the interior prescribed that the reconstituted national committees were to elect a chairman during their first session and, by a margin of thirty-one to twenty-three votes, the Plzeň national committee had done so.[52] 'For every man of democratic convictions', argued a commentary in the local ČSSD press, 'that would have been the end of the affair.' But there was 'a different [version of] democracy, communist democracy, for which the guidelines of the ministry of

[49] Ibid., p. 41.
[50] *Zpráva o činnosti*, pp. xxxiv–xxxv.
[51] 'Odpověď představenstva naší strany a Práva lidu plzeňským komunistům', *Nový Den*, 2 July 1946.
[52] 'K volbě předsedy národního výboru Plzni', *Nový Den*, 28 June 1946; 'To že má byti demokracie?' *Nový Den*, 29 June 1946.

the interior … do not count and Josef Ullrich[53] has to become mayor of Plzeň at any cost'. To that end, the communists had staged several factory walkouts and assembled a crowd outside city hall – threatening the mayor-elect with 'a defenestration, a lynching, and similar' if he were to take up his new function. The social democrats were adamant, though, that they would 'succumb neither to violence nor to demonstrations'. For 'nobody else than the rightful national committee' was entitled 'to decide over its chairman, and certainly not the mob in the street'.[54]

What outraged the ČSSD even more than the communist attempt at mob rule, however, was the blatant politicisation of (officially non-partisan) workplace organisations. The party insisted that the resolution signed by the leader of the provincial KOR as well as by the chairmen of all major Plzeň factory councils – claiming that the mayoral election had not been 'in accordance with the will of the people', calling for a fresh national committee vote on the matter, and urging the mayor-elect to hand back the committee's chair to Ullrich in the meantime – lacked 'any legal standing'. Factory councils and trade unions, after all, had no stake in political appointments such as these – that was 'a matter exclusively for political parties'.[55]

This sharp delineation between the remit of political parties and that of workplace bodies was reflected in the ČSSD's attitude towards factory cells. When the KSČ, quickly followed by the ČSNS, started (re-) building its factory cells in the summer of 1945, the social democrats immediately pointed to the dangers entailed in this operation. Now that the once fragmented trade union movement was finally united and factory councils had been empowered, explained Blažej Vilím at the October 1945 ČSSD congress, factory cells could only be a divisive force. In fact, he predicted that the creation of such bodies would 'necessarily' lead to 'turf wars' between factory cells on the one side and trade unions and factory councils on the other – as political functionaries, 'overcome by narrow

---

[53] The political career of Josef Ullrich, the leader of the KSČ in post-war Plzeň, was shrouded in controversy. Back in the summer of 1945, when the position of chairman of the revolutionary Plzeň NV first had to be filled, his main intra-party rival for the post died in suspicious circumstances. Just as he was on his way to Prague – allegedly carrying with him a file on Ullrich's inappropriate behaviour in the Buchenwald concentration camp – his car crashed. Rumours that Ullrich's supporters had staged the accident were widespread at the time. See: Jakub Šlouf, 'Rivalita komunistické strany a sociální demokracie na Plzeňsku v letech 1945–1948. Poválečné dědictví prvorepublikových tradic', in Zdeněk Kárník, Jiří Kocian, Jaroslav Pažout, and Jakub Rákosník (eds.), *Bolševismus, komunismus a radikální socialismus v Československu*, Vol. VI (Prague: Dokořán, 2009), pp. 113–37, 118.

[54] 'To že má byti demokracie?' *Nový Den*, 29 June 1946.

[55] Ibid.

party interests', would not be likely to resist the temptation to meddle in trade union affairs. Yet the other parties had been impervious to the ČSSD's arguments, Vilím declared, leaving the social democrats with no choice but to follow suit. From an organisational point of view, however, it was clear from the outset that social democratic factory cells remained very much secondary to local ČSSD sections. '[A]ll of our party's factory cell activists are first and foremost members of municipal sections', concluded Vilím, which was to remain 'the focal point of our activities'.[56]

Within the post-war SFIO, factory cells were accorded a similarly subordinate role. The statutes of the Socialist Enterprise Groups (GSE), adopted at the August 1945 SFIO congress, by and large limited their remit to spreading socialist propaganda among workers and providing the party leadership with information about worker sentiments and the economic fortunes of their companies. Neither individual GSE nor the National Commission of GSE had any say, accordingly, in setting local and national party policy, which remained the exclusive prerogative of the local SFIO section and the national SFIO Executive, respectively, while 'any incursion into the trade union domain' was likewise strictly prohibited.[57]

In the increasingly volatile political and workplace climate of the first post-war years, however, it was difficult to restrict the GSE to this narrow brief. By the summer of 1947, therefore, in the aftermath of a serious clash between the SFIO Executive and the GSE at Renault, which had supported the strike that ushered in the collapse of *tripartisme* in May, the party leadership set out to tighten its grip upon factory activists. Complaining that 'certain GSE comrades' suffered from 'misconceptions', Guy Mollet reiterated that the GSE's 'objective' consisted of 'making sure party slogans reverberate in the social environment of adherents'. Just how much of a one-way street this was supposed to be becomes apparent from the new organisational scheme put forward by the SFIO Executive,

---

[56] 'Protokol xx. Manifestačního Sjezdu Československé Socialní Demokracie', Archiv ČSSD, Fond 71, Část II, Karton III, pp. 123–5.

[57] 'Parti Socialiste SFIO: 38ème Congrès national, 29, 30, 31 août et 1er septembre 1946', FJJ, p. 110. http://flipbook.archives-socialistes.fr/index.html?docid=51052&language=fra&userid=0 (last consulted: 27 June 2018). In this respect, the GSE were to serve much the same objective as their interwar pre-cursor – the Amicales Socialistes. Donald N. Baker has argued that '(t)he *Amicales Socialistes* were not created by the wing of the party eager to evangelize the masses … On the contrary, the men who created the *Amicales Socialistes* aimed at only modest and defensive goals – chiefly to stabilize the volatile working class, to combat the rising influence of the Communists in the labour movement, and to further party recruitment. The leadership's conception of the front organization required a strict subordination to the party hierarchy.' See Donald N. Baker, 'The Socialists and the Workers of Paris: The Amicales Socialistes, 1936–1940', *International Review of Social History*, 24/1 (1979), pp. 1–33, 30.

which banned the GSE from so much as discussing party politics. What is more, the practice, dating back to the interwar precursor of the GSE, the Amicales Socialistes, of allowing non-member 'sympathisers' to partake in GSE meetings was to be discontinued. '[T]he GSE should be made up only of party members', chair of the SFIO's Reorganisation Commission André Ferrat argued, 'for it cannot be the case that the GSE can escape party discipline'.[58]

Socialising Socialism

On the face of it, the two sets of parties had rather more in common regarding the question of worker control of and participation in economic decision-making. In the immediate aftermath of the liberation, each of the four parties championed such new bodies of worker democracy as factory councils and cooperatives, calling for their creation and empowerment as well as for their autonomy vis-à-vis the state. At least in public, therefore, post-war socialist leaders insisted that the economy, even if large parts of it were to fall under the auspices of the state, would in fact be socialised.

The economic paragraph of the draft programme the PPS leadership drew up in 1945, for example, demanded that both the nationalised (i.e. all enterprises employing a workforce of more than fifty) and the private sectors be subjected to 'social control' – by 'worker delegates and factory councils' within factories and through 'the indirect representation of consumers' within branch organisations.[59] For the PPS, however, worker participation in economic life was to reach its apogee in the third sector of the Polish economy – the rural and urban cooperatives that were meant to promote the exchange of products between city and countryside. '[I]n a socialist Poland', Szwalbe declared at the August 1945 PPS congress, 'we want to socialise rather than nationalise trade'. This was to be achieved by 'cooperativisation', he argued, which was 'the highest form of socialisation'.[60]

The leadership of the PSIUP, for its part, advocated the wholesale socialisation of economic life. The draft resolution that Sandro Pertini prepared for a November 1944 convention of the (still clandestine) Northern Italian PSIUP called for worker self-management in both agriculture and industry.

---

[58] OURS, CD SFIO, 9 July 1947.
[59] 'W walce o socjalizm – Projekt Programu Polskiej Partii Socjalistyoznej' (30 June 1945), AAN, PPS, 235/1-7, fo. 48.
[60] XXVI Kongres (August 1945), AAN, PPS, 235/1-12, fo. 54.

'[M]unicipal agricultural cooperatives managed directly by workers' were to be created on expropriated estates in the countryside. In urban areas, meanwhile, 'the integral socialisation' of all state-subsidised and monopolistic industries, as well as the entire finance sector, was to find its expression in 'decentralised management by autonomous entities that implement a national plan'.[61] And such views do not seem to have been confined to the more radical socialist leaders in the occupied north. In liberated Rome, after all, Nenni was likewise calling for 'the expropriation and cooperative management of landed estates' and 'the socialisation of the trusts and monopolistic industry ... which should be managed directly by factory councils'.[62]

If not going as far as that, André Philip did feel the need 'to clarify' what the SFIO had in mind when it demanded nationalisations. Speaking at the party's November 1944 congress, he drew a sharp line between *étatisme* (a state-controlled economy) and nationalisations. The former, he explained, was 'no more than the spread of bureaucracy, with direction by experts and senior administrative cadres – not that different from capitalism itself'. Nationalisations, on the other hand, presupposed 'regional decentralisation, the rejection of every technical dictatorship, and the participation of the working class at all administrative levels'.[63] The resolution adopted by the congress reiterated these points. The 'socialisation of the commanding heights of the economy', it insisted, 'should lead neither to state capitalism nor to the bureaucracy of which the current monopoly constitutes an example'. To steer clear of that, factories were to be 'managed by workers, in association with experts [i.e. technicians and management] and representatives of the general interest [i.e. government representatives], with each of these tripartite councils ... implementing the national economic plan deliberated by the representatives of universal suffrage'.[64]

The mid-1945 programme of the ČSSD's Action Committee, finally, failed to even mention the concept of nationalisations in its description of the state take-over of the entire energy, banking, insurance, and transport sectors, of all large industrial and agricultural companies, and of all German and Hungarian property. The document made sure to warn, however, of

[61] 'Dichiarazione Politica presentata dal Segretario per l'A.I. del P.S.I.U.P. al Convegno Interregionale A.I.' (November 1944), ACS, Carteggio Nenni, Busta 87, Fasc. 2184, p. 2.
[62] Pietro Nenni, 'La repubblica ci unisce', *Avanti!*, 15 October 1944.
[63] 'Parti Socialiste – SFIO: Congrès national extraordinaire des 9, 10, 11 et 12 novembre 1944', FJJ, p. 180. http://62.210.214.184/cg-ps/documents/pdf/cong-1944-11-09.pdf (last consulted: 27 June 2018).
[64] Ibid., pp. 281–2.

the dangers entailed in this operation. The 'bureaucratisation' of economic life, insisted the programme, was to be avoided 'by any means'. For that reason, the running of 'socialised enterprises' was to be entrusted to 'local and stakeholder bodies', which were better placed to 'oversee their proper operation than the central authorities'.[65]

In their rhetoric, then, the socialists were certainly among the strongest supporters of wide-ranging powers for workplace co-decision bodies. Yet several historians have suggested there was little more to this than rhetoric, as the four parties were very much complicit in undermining such bodies. If the Eastern European socialist and social democratic parties initially tried to steal a march on the communists by their 'greater socio-political radicalism', argues Peter Heumos, they subsequently went along with communist and bourgeois efforts to 'contain, channel into trade union structures, and disempower' factory councils. The parties, after all, championed 'the hierarchic-authoritarian company model of the Soviet Union', while 'their economic and technical cadre, which carried significant weight within the party apparatus above all in Czechoslovakia and Poland, only considered worker participation a motivational tool to increase production'.[66]

The PSIUP and the SFIO come off even worse in academic accounts, which tend to position them well to the right of the communists on the question of worker participation in economic decision-making. With regard to post-war France, for example, Xavier Vigna claims that, whereas the factory councils that came into being in the aftermath of liberation could count on (limited) support from the communists, they 'upset those socialist politicians most attached to the industrial order of things, including the minister of production Robert Lacoste'.[67] For post-war Italy, meanwhile, Marialuisa-Lucia Sergio suggests that it was the PSIUP's Rodolfo Morandi who contributed most to the curbing of factory councils' competencies – first in his role as chairman of the overarching CLN for northern Italy, by stripping them of all powers in questions of (managerial) dismissals and purges, and subsequently as minister of industry in the second De Gasperi government, by drawing up an extremely restrictive legal framework for factory councils that was 'quasi-opposed' to communist perspectives. '[I]n

---

[65] 'Program akčního výboru – Československé sociální demokracie', Archiv ČSSD, Fond 71, Část II, Karton III, p. 10.

[66] Peter Heumos, 'Arbeiterschaft und Sozialdemokratie', p. 30, 33.

[67] Xavier Vigna, 'France after the Liberation: The Labour Movement, the Employers and the Political Leaders in their Struggle with the Social Movement', in Stefan Berger and Marcel Boldorf (eds.), *Social Movements and Challenges to Economic Elites after the Second World War* (Cham: Palgrave Macmillan, 2018), pp. 63–80, 70.

spite of ... all [their] rhetoric', she concludes, it was the socialists who 'closed the book on the CLN (especially in their version as organs of company self-management and social control) to return to the rules of parliamentary representation and, above all, to affirm a new democracy based on parties'.[68]

In their (near-)exclusive focus on the fate of the revolutionary factory councils and the question of worker self-management, such accounts tend to brush over the broader macro-economic role that socialists envisioned workplace co-decision bodies playing. This role lay first and foremost in framing and adapting government economic planning. Yet even if each of the four parties committed themselves to the principle of direct grassroots participation in the formulation and execution of economic plans, they quickly parted ways when it came to the practical implementation of this principle.

The Italian and Polish socialists, on the one side, insisted that economic planning always had to take its lead from grassroots bodies. In their view, plans that were imposed from above would necessarily result in the creation of a dictatorial command chain in the productive process and the proliferation of bureaucracy within the national economy. In both countries, however, the participatory structures upon which the socialists had pinned their hopes of democratising economic life found themselves under increasing political pressure.

In Poland, this pressure had its origins in communist efforts to bring all economic activity under state control. For the disempowerment of the revolutionary factory councils was but the first step in the communist campaign to create a top-down command economy after the Soviet model. The next was the establishment of state-wide conglomerates for every branch and an increasing propensity for the state to appoint industrial managers. Much like the communist attitude towards worker self-management, these measures were quick to attract socialist criticism.

As early as February 1946, Jan Topiński – together with Hochfeld probably the most important ideologue of the post-war PPS – was warning of 'centralising tendencies' in the administration of the nationalised sector. To counter these tendencies, he urged nationalised companies to take a page out of the book of the cooperative movement. In concrete terms, he advocated the creation of a 'supervisory board' for every nationalised factory, on which workforce representatives (picked by trade unions for larger companies and by factory councils for smaller companies), consumer

---

[68] Marialuisa-Lucia Sergio, *De Gasperi e la "questione socialista"*, pp. 57–8.

representatives (i.e. those other companies or cooperatives buying up the factory's produce), and state representatives would each be allocated a third of the seats. Even if these boards were to be awarded wide-ranging powers, including the right to hire and fire factory managers, there was no reason to fear that they would stray too far from government economic planning as far as Topiński was concerned. For the state could still discipline 'unruly' factories through its investment politics and would, in any case, often find the consumer representatives (who were dependent on other factories meeting their obligations to fulfil their own planning targets) on its side. What was certain, though, was that this cooperative approach to industrial administration carried less risk of 'burdening economic life with the inflexibility of a slow-moving clerical machine' and allowed for 'more freedom in social life' than using 'schematic plans that subordinate the entire economy to a bureaucratic-hierarchical template'.[69]

The chief purpose that the cooperative movement was to serve in industrial life, therefore, was to prevent the 'militarisation of dependency relations' in the planned economy. To be sure, Topiński acknowledged that a planned economy could not exist without a 'central dispositional hub that steers economic life in accordance with the directives of the plan'. The debate, though, was over 'the method of steering'. In a thinly veiled attack on the way that the communist-dominated ministry of industry was implementing economic planning, he went on to sketch the 'negative consequences' of 'directing economic life ... by command'. For by applying a highly hierarchical model to economic planning – in which planning targets were passed on 'from the ministry [of industry] to the central branch organisation, from there to the lower branch organisations, subsequently to the individual companies, and only lastly to the workplace' – it would become impossible to address unforeseen local circumstances affecting the fulfilment of plans, while the maintenance of a clerical apparatus at each sub-level would cause the costs of running the planned economy to soar. It was for these reasons, explained Topiński, that central economic plans had to be 'laconic in their formulation' and that their fine-tuning had to reflect 'impulses from below, not from above'. In this respect, he sang the praises of cooperatives, which knew 'no equal in conveying impulses from interested parties'. As cooperatives served 'the interests of the individual as consumer', he explained, the cooperative sector could grow into the 'dominant factor of coordination' in the planned economy. That meant that

---

[69] Jan Topiński, 'Struktura uspołecznionego przedsiębiorstwa', *Przegląd Socjalistyczny*, 1 February 1946, pp. 13–15.

cooperatives were to 'participate' in the local framing of government plans
even for the nationalised (heavy) industries.[70]

Far from seeing its ambit extended into the nationalised sector, however,
the cooperative movement increasingly found itself under pressure as the
Polish communists set in motion the 'battle for trade' during the spring
of 1947. As we have seen (see Chapter 2), this communist campaign to
hollow out the cooperative and private sectors of the economy triggered
the first public row between communists and socialists in post-war Poland.
Speaking at a PPS rally in Cracow in May 1947, Szwalbe insisted that
the communist attacks on the 'speculators' running cooperative and private shops had a purely political motivation – to eliminate the cooperative
movement.[71]

Of course, the cold realities of Polish political life dictated that the
communists would emerge victorious from this particular controversy
and, when the matter came before the Sejm some weeks later, the PPS parliamentary group voted in favour of granting the communist minister of
industry special powers to combat 'speculation' in the cooperative and private sectors. Even so, the passionate defence of the cooperative movement
that Szwalbe mounted during the debate tells us much about the importance that the Polish socialists attached to retaining the cooperative sector.
He explained that, as far as the PPS was concerned, cooperatives were the
'most suitable' vehicles to guarantee a 'healthy exchange between countryside and city'. If the state was now going to create its own nationalised trade
system, that could 'by no means ... come at the expense of the expansion
of cooperative trade'. That was not to argue, he went on, that the socialists
were blind to the 'shortcomings' of cooperatives or that they were looking
to establish some sort of 'cooperative republic'. But the state was already
taking many 'urgent and key economic and productive responsibilities on
its shoulders' and it 'cannot yet deal with these in an impeccable manner'.
It was clear to 'every objective observer', moreover, that 'the experiences
with nationalised trade to date' had proven 'much less successful than
[those with] cooperative [trade]'. If the PPS was all in favour of addressing
'the defects' in the cooperative sector, therefore, this could not happen
through 'a clampdown' on the cooperative movement. For the socialists
regarded cooperatives as 'an irreplaceable school of self-government and of
economic training for worker activists'. It was 'for these economic and educative reasons' concluded Szwalbe, that the PPS considered 'the broadest

[70] Jan Topiński, 'Dlaczego spółdzielczość?' *Przegląd Socjalistyczny*, 1 July 1947, pp. 22–4.
[71] Kersten, *The Establishment of Communist Rule*, p. 375.

possible development of the cooperative economy and the advance of the communal economy one of the basic and specific principles of the so-called Polish road [to socialism], of a fundamental reconstruction of the social system in Poland'.[72]

For the Italian socialists, the new economic order had to draw its inspiration from grassroots bodies too. To be sure, the broader economic context in which they had to operate was completely different, as free-market liberalism still reigned supreme in post-liberation Italy and repeated socialist calls for the introduction of state economic planning fell upon deaf ears with both the centre-right parties and the communists. Even if the attitudes that the PSIUP adopted towards economic planning were thus not rooted in practical experience, its leaders looked at the question in much the same way as did their Polish counterparts. In a discussion piece that he presented before the PSIUP Central Committee in October 1945, Angelo Saraceno – the socialist theorist, part of the group of intellectuals close to Morandi who co-founded the Institute of Socialist Studies after the liberation – was very dismissive of top-down planning. While stressing the need for economic planning as part of a larger package of industrial reform, he was alive to 'the danger of [creating] a state socialism, which is bureaucratic, centralised, and anti-democratic in substance'. For that reason, the Italian socialists did not view economic plans 'as an imposition from the centre', even if that centre found itself 'under the aegis of a socialist government'. Instead, the 'possibilities for successful planning' were linked closely to 'the functioning of a real production democracy'.[73]

Much like their Polish comrades, the Italian socialists saw workplace co-decision bodies as part and parcel of this production democracy. The focal point of their efforts to bring democracy to the shop floor were the management councils (*consigli di gestione*) that had gradually come to replace the CLNA in the wake of the liberation. These councils, upon which management and workforce representatives were each allocated half of the seats, were tasked with the day-to-day running of factories and with making decisions over investments and production programmes. For the PSIUP, however, the function of management councils transcended the individual factory. In his treatise, Saraceno explained that 'the most characteristic feature' of the socialist campaign around the management councils,

[72] 'Sprawozdanie stenograficzne z posiedzenia Sejmu Ustawodawczego' (31 May 1947). Quoted in Hanna Jędruszczak, *Wizje gospodarki socjalistycznej w Polsce, 1945–1949: Początki planowania* (Warsaw: Państwowe Wydawnictwo Naukowe, 1983), pp. 342–6.
[73] 'Relazione sulla riforma industriale – I consigli di gestione' (1945), AdL, Camera del Lavoro, Class. 5.2.2.10., Fasc. 9.

which also set it apart from communist endeavours to obtain more powers for the councils, found itself 'not so much on the company level … as on the intercompany and national level'. It was on these levels that the vertical connections between worker representatives at various factories were to usher in 'multiple processes of sectoral and regional rationalisation', which guaranteed the 'peripheral de-bureaucratisation' of the (future) planned economy. For the Italian socialists understood the management councils 'as a central element of a system that converges towards ever more organic coordination until it culminates in a true and proper planned economy'.[74]

The bottom-up and participatory planned economy that the PSIUP leadership envisioned would of course never materialise. In fact, the regrouped capitalist class would quickly come to question even the limited competencies that the management councils held on the factory level. The pushback began at Fiat, where the directors forced through an agreement that reduced the local management council to an exclusively consultative role in early 1946. What was worse, the increasingly intransigent line that the employers were adopting towards the management councils won the backing of the Christian democrats, with Alcide De Gasperi holding up the Fiat agreement as a model to be emulated by other companies in the aftermath of the June 1946 parliamentary elections.[75]

In the face of these developments, Morandi set about drawing up a legal framework that would protect the management councils against further encroachments upon their territory as he took over as minister of industry in the government that was formed after the elections. He presented his bill, which ascribed to management councils a key role in the drawing up of economic plans and awarded them deliberative powers in questions of production as well as consultative powers in questions of finance, in December 1946. Yet the bill immediately attracted the scorn of the communists, who did not believe in economic planning in the context of a capitalist economy and feared that the proposals would compromise their efforts to promote management councils 'as organs of worker control' on the factory level.[76] The liberals and Christian democrats, for their part, were up in arms about the (moderate) challenge to managerial supremacy entailed in the bill and managed to frustrate the parliamentary process for

---

[74] Ibid.

[75] Ginsborg, *A History of Contemporary Italy*, pp. 96–7.

[76] Quoted in Stefano Musso, 'Autonomia e democrazia sindacale nella *Città del lavoro*', in Alessio Gramolati and Giovanni Mari (eds.), *Il lavoro dopo il Novecento. Da produttori ad attori sociali* (Firenze: Firenze University Press, 2016), pp. 273–85, 279.

the remainder of Morandi's spell as minister of industry, before shelving the bill altogether in the changed political context of 1948.

Both within and outside of government, however, Morandi remained adamant that participatory planning offered the only way out of the economic predicament in which Italy found itself. Defending his plans before a socialist rally in Milano in March 1947, he insisted that the moderate proposals that he had put before parliament did not mean that the socialists no longer believed that more 'radical mutations in the economic order' were needed. But it was 'in the interest of the proletariat and the working masses', he went on, not to obsess over 'the confines' within which the socialists had to operate. If economic planning was going to serve the interests of the working class, though, it was imperative that central plans were open to input from ordinary workers. For the plan could not 'be a document based on simple technical criteria', argued Morandi, nor could its implementation be left to 'the normal organs of administration, working on behalf of the state'. Were economic planning to follow that path, it would certainly result only in 'a cumbersome construct of regulations and bureaucratic controls obstructing economic activity and causing a massive waste of energies'. The socialist conception of planning, therefore, involved 'a constant revision and updating of [planning] programmes'. That meant that the 'active and direct participation of the working class' in the implementation of economic plans, to be achieved 'through the recognition and limited expansion [of the competencies] of management councils', was 'indispensable'.[77] It was this participatory dimension that distinguished the socialist approach to economic planning from those of its political rivals, as Morandi could explain in more forceful terms after the Left had been removed from the Italian government in May 1947. 'The socialist plan', he told a PSIUP economic conference in November of that year, 'is implemented through a fundamental democratisation of productive life and direct worker participation in the direction and control of it.' Far from seeking to control the working class 'by administrative means', therefore, socialist planning would breathe 'fresh energies into the economy, which express and interpret the collective interest'.[78]

The very concepts – democratisation, freedom, education, etc. – that the Italian and Polish socialists used to make the case for worker participation

---

[77] 'Discorso pronunciato dal Ministro Rodolfo Morandi al Teatro Nuovo' (16 March 1947), INSMLI, Fondo Lia Bellora, Fasc. 6.
[78] 'Pianificazione e piani', *Bollettino dell'Istituto di Studii Socialisti*, November–December 1947, pp. 228–31, 231.

in economic planning reveal that the question carried acute political significance for the two parties. In liberating workers from simply having to
carry out top-down commands, irrespective of whether these came from
the state or from the capitalist, and giving them a real say over their workplace, participation in the drawing up and implementation of plans was a
cornerstone of what the PPS and PSIUP understood by economic democracy. It was for these reasons that the two parties fought so hard to preserve
the grassroots participatory structures in the face of increasing political
headwinds. Saraceno repeatedly stressed how the PSIUP campaign for the
management councils was intended to shift the question of shop floor
participation away from the purely technical realm and into the political
realm. For the management councils, he argued, were 'the foundation
and bedrock of a productive democracy, without which every desire of
[worker] control is likely to remain a gimmick of formal democracy and
get bogged down in a bureaucratic exercise'.[79] In a similar vein, Rapacki
described cooperatives as 'a political school' for the proletariat at the height
of the 'battle for trade'. Within cooperatives, after all, workers were taught
'common management … to take social responsibility and social initiative,
and to work together for the common good'.[80]

At first glance, it would seem as if the ČSSD and the SFIO shared these
views. In their publicity, after all, the two parties made sure to present
themselves as champions of grassroots participation in the implementation of economic planning. The ČSSD minority within the central trade
union leadership, for example, put forward a motion calling for 'national
committees' and 'regional and central economic stakeholder bodies' to be
involved in lower-level planning. When this proposal fell on deaf ears with
'the other parties in government', the ČSSD's parliamentary group was
quick to relaunch it as a draft law.[81] The SFIO's 1946 'Action Programme',
meanwhile, foresaw the creation of 'central councils' – made up of worker,
consumer, and state representatives – appointing managers and executing
plans within each 'socialised' sector. '[I]nside the [individual] company
and in the context of the plan', moreover, works councils were eventually
to have 'all the powers that are today possessed by a board of directors'.[82]

---

[79] 'Relazione sulla riforma industriale – I consigli di gestione' (1945), AdL, Camera del Lavoro, Class.
5.2.2.10., Fasc. 9.
[80] Quoted in Stanisław Ciesielski, 'Spory wokół koncepcji socjalistycznego humanizmu w latach
1946–1947', *Dzieje Najnowsze*, 16 (1984), pp. 21–44, 41.
[81] *Zpráva o činnosti*, pp. XLII–XLIII.
[82] 'Programme d'Action du Parti Socialiste' (1946), FJJ, pp. 25–6.

Such rhetorical bravado notwithstanding, the Czechoslovakian social democrats and the French socialists in fact took very different attitudes towards worker co-determination in economic administration to those of their Italian and Polish counterparts. The ČSSD leadership had limited confidence in workers' (or workers representatives') abilities to rise above their own narrow concerns and take decisions in their company's and/or the national interest. Already at the ČSSD's first post-war congress, Evžen Erban pointed to the many mistakes that the party had made when it had 'romantically idealised the proletariat' in the past. 'We know from political praxis and from socialist theory', he declared, 'that the working class alone, without political education, comes no further than syndicalism' – a derogatory reference to the fragmented, sector-based forms of worker representation under the First Republic. And the foremost vehicle for that political education was not workplace co-determination bodies, which, as has been claimed elsewhere, reflected these syndicalist traditions in many ways,[83] but the freshly united trade union movement. For the trade union movement, explained Erban, 'offers us great opportunities to influence the widest cadres, even their politically most backward parts, in a socialist spirit'. To achieve that, he concluded, 'we must especially endeavour for the socialist education of lower-level trade union functionaries, in order for the trade unions to be stripped of all syndicalist tendencies and for them to be infused with a profound socialist class consciousness'.[84]

While Erban called on trade unions to sort out their grassroots, Bohumil Laušman urged industrial managers to do the same. Speaking at a June 1947 conference of ČSSD managers within the nationalised sector, he expressed his surprise at the fact that, in some companies, 'every normal agenda item' was passed by the factory council. The factory council, he argued, should neither 'officiate' nor 'do business'. Its role, 'alongside its traditional social and cultural tasks', consisted of 'control' – and that did 'of course' not mean 'the control of each file', but 'the right ... to inspect company records from time to time ... to assess the quality of its management'. What was more, explained Laušman, the factory council had the duty 'to assist management in its currently very difficult tasks'. Above all, it was to make sure that 'the workforce ... realises what nationalisations mean – what they have

---

[83] Peter Heumos, 'Die Sozialdemokratie in Ostmitteleuropa 1945–1948: Zum gesellschaftlichen Potential des demokratischen Sozialismus in Polen, der Tschechoslowakei und Ungarn', in Hans Lemberg (ed.), *Sowjetisches Modell und nationale Prägung. Kontinuität und Wandel in Ostmitteleuropa nach dem Zweiten Weltkrieg* (Marburg an der Lahn: J.G. Herder Institut, 1991), pp. 51–70, 54–7.

[84] 'Protokol xx. Manifestačního Sjezdu Československé Socialní Demokracie', Archiv ČSSD, Fond 71, Část ii, Karton iii, pp. 134–5.

to offer to our people, but also which obligations they entail for all staff. In the interest of the entire workforce, therefore, the factory council was to undertake 'that there are no freeloaders within the company, that everybody is trying to work as diligently as possible, that those who in any way damage production ... are punished, that there is minimal turmoil in the production process, and that technological advances are quickly made'.[85]

The ČSSD leadership, however, increasingly felt that the majority of factory councils were not fulfilling these tasks. At the party's November 1947 congress, Václav Majer delivered a scathing attack on some of their practices, which sounded much more like an assault on the institution itself. To be sure, Majer granted that there were factory councils which functioned impeccably. There were 'others', though, which 'delay work ... and burden their companies with superfluous ideas and expenses'. If that already seemed like a negation of the consultative powers that the government had granted factory councils, Majer was not finished yet. 'Many factory councils', he continued, 'unduly interfere in company business, thereby causing conflicts between themselves and management and, as a consequence of that, unrest that harms production.'[86]

Where leaders on the left (Erban), centre (Laušman), and right (Majer) of the ČSSD were thus united in their scorn for direct worker participation in economic decision-making, the post-war SFIO saw some divisions on the issue. There was a group of leaders on the left of the SFIO Executive – most notably Suzanne Charpy, Pierre Commin, and Jean Rous – looking at grassroots participation in much the same way as the Italian and Polish socialists. Charpy hailed the two companies that had been placed under full worker self-management after the arrest or flight of their collaborationist owners – the Berliet car plant in Lyon and the Brun biscuit factory in Grenoble – as examples of socialism at work.[87] Rous, for his part, championed the 'democratic' production regime in Labour Britain, 'where the masses have been associated with the production effort and

[85] 'Projev s. ministra průmyslu B. Laušmana na konferenci soc. demokratických ředitelů a náměstků nár. podniků' (29 June 1947), NA, Fonds Bohumil Laušman, III Pisemnosti související s ústřední, veřejnou a politickou činnosti B. Laušmana, Karton 26, Projevy B. Laušmana 1940–1947, p. 3.
[86] 'Hospodářská politika Československé sociální demokracie' (November 1947), Archiv ČSSD, Fond 71, Část II, Karton 112, p. II.
[87] See the reports of the speeches that Charpy gave during her October 1946 tour of the north of France: 'Conférence du Parti Socialiste à Douai', 7 October 1946, ADN, CRR, 28 W 38454 2; 'Note de Renseignements' (Réunion organisée par le Parti Socialiste SFIO, à Anzin), 25 October 1946, ADN, CRR, 28 W 38454 2. On the experiment with worker self-management at Berliet, see also Adam Steinhouse, *Workers' Participation in Post-Liberation France* (Lanham, MD: Lexington Books, 2001).

governmental action'.[88] Commin, finally, called for 'the popular masses' to be able to participate 'in the direction and control' of economic plans.[89]

Time and again, however, these leaders stumbled upon what Rous dubbed the 'anti-participationism' of the SFIO at large.[90] Indeed, the great majority of the SFIO leadership, including all of its ministers, were distinctly less enthusiastic about worker participation of almost any kind. The divergences between the pro- and anti-participationists often came to the fore in discussions over the socialist response to strikes. During the February 1947 strike of the Parisian press operators (see Chapter 4), Rous and Charpy pressed for (members of) the SFIO Executive to meet with a delegation of socialist strikers – stating that socialist leaders should listen to what their rank and file had to say. Such party heavyweights as Mayer and Philip, however, took a far more hostile attitude towards any exchange of views with the socialist strikers, who had failed to ask the SFIO leadership for permission before joining the strike.[91] The April 1947 strike at Renault was to fray tempers once more. Charpy and, to a lesser extent, Rous came out in favour of the strike's demands.[92] What is more, Charpy backed the Renault GSE, which had defied the communist-led factory trade union command to support the strike. The actions of these factory socialists in particular met with a remarkable telling-off on the part of Mayer. In their attempts to steal a march upon the communists, he argued, the Renault GSE had 'insufficiently concerned itself about the political repercussions of their attitude'. In fact, the communists had been 'courageous' by remaining 'faithful to the commitments the government and the CGT have entered into'. 'We should not try to surpass the communists on the Left', he concluded – instead, '[t]heir language should be ours'.[93]

But even away from the charged atmosphere directly surrounding major strikes, proposals for worker's voices to be heard in economic administration met with derision among senior SFIO leaders. Time after time, then,

---

[88] OURS, CD SFIO, 3 December 1946. Rous was probably referring to the British 'Joint Production Committees' – factory bodies in which workers' representatives and management held an equal number of seats and which were entitled to 'advise' management in all production-related questions except wages. In the immediate aftermath of the war, the Joint Production Committees seem to have captured the imagination of Philip too, who ordered a number of studies into the British experience in the early stages of his tenure as minister of the national economy in 1945. Yet, by 1947, as we will now see, Philip's and most other SFIO leaders' enthusiasm for worker participation in production had cooled decisively.

[89] OURS, CD SFIO, 5 March 1947.

[90] OURS, CD SFIO, 10 December 1946.

[91] OURS, CD SFIO, 19 February 1947.

[92] OURS, CD SFIO, 30 April and 2 May 1947.

[93] OURS, CD SFIO, 30 April 1947.

Charpy's calls for a far stronger role for workplace co-determination bodies went unheeded. According to Philip, nothing much was to be expected of worker control over production. In small and medium-sized businesses, he explained, bosses could easily manipulate the workforce – as had been the case at Michelin, where workers had been 'the instruments of management in the black market for tyres'.[94] Oreste Capocci, meanwhile, claimed that workers themselves did not view participation within such bodies as factory councils or price control committees as a realistic way out of their socio-economic predicament. Communist trade unionists had been urging workers to make use of their rights within such bodies for the better part of two years, he pointed out, only for them to abandon these efforts when they realised just how ineffective they were.[95] Perhaps Moch summed up the socialist argument against worker participation best, when he told Charpy that neither the factory councils nor the GSE 'offer us effective support'. It was clear, he argued, that 'the working class has not understood its role. We are faced with a stultification of worker morality, caused by more than five years of misery as well as ... by the politics of the Communist Party.'[96]

For both the ČSSD and the SFIO, then, economic power necessarily had to reside with those at the apex of the economic pyramid: with governments and parliaments in questions of macro-economic decision-making, with trade unions in questions of worker representation, and with management in questions surrounding the production effort. The two parties, accordingly, never conceived of economic planning as a process that was to take its lead from the grassroots. As late as June 1947, an editorial in the ČSSD's theoretical weekly claimed that the recent Soviet experiences with planning 'could be of the greatest assistance to us'[97] If an SFIO propaganda document on the planned economy did denounce 'totalitarian' forms of planning, the economic model it put forward was hardly less centralised and technocratic than that of the Soviet Union. The document, after all, listed 'respect for governmental authority' – allowing the state to 'fulfil its role, which consists of arbitrating, deciding, and acting' – and a 'professional organisation' – made up of 'study, liaison, and executive organs' – as the two key requirements for a planned economy.[98]

---

[94] OURS, CD SFIO, 27 February 1947.
[95] OURS, CD SFIO, 24 June 1947.
[96] OURS, CD SFIO, 26 June 1947.
[97] 'Větší tempo', *Cíl*, 27 June 1947.
[98] 'Libéralisme ou dirigisme? Position du problème', Fiches Socialistes – Arguments et Ripostes, July–August 1947, OURS.

Conclusion

We have seen in this chapter that the two sets of parties frequently took opposite attitudes towards the question of grassroots participation in political and economic decision-making. These attitudes were linked intimately to their conceptions of democracy. For the Italian and Polish socialists, on the one side, grassroots participation was crucial to the social embedding and ultimate survival of democracy. Both in teaching their 'politically backward' electorates the fundamentals of democracy and in transforming socio-economic power relations, after all, the two parties regarded grassroots participation as the cure for the ills that had historically plagued their countries. For the Czechoslovakian social democrats and French socialists, on the other side, grassroots participation was to be limited chiefly to voting in (parliamentary) elections. In their view, any grassroots challenge to the political or economic decisions of properly elected representatives represented a dangerous affront to democracy.

Over the last two chapters, two widely divergent socialist conceptions of democracy have thus clearly come to the fore: a bottom-up participatory conception and a top-down representative conception. Yet, as we have seen, historians only tend to associate the post-war socialist parties with a representative and parliamentary politics. For that reason, they have often misconstrued the attitudes of the Italian and Polish socialists as contradictory or even, especially in the Polish case, as deceitful. In his study of the post-war PPS, for example, Jerzy Holzer has identified a fundamental paradox in the socialist struggles against the disempowerment of cooperatives in the wake of the January 1947 parliamentary elections. 'The aim of the [socialist] demands was to guarantee societal participation in the administration of the country', he explains, 'but these demands were formulated immediately after the wishes of that same society had been overridden in the coerced and falsified elections'.[99] As we have seen in the previous chapter, however, the post-war Polish socialists hardly regarded parliamentary elections as the apogee of participatory politics. From their perspective, therefore, it was perfectly consistent to acquiesce in or even lend their backing to the communist violations of constitutional legality while at the same time denouncing their attacks on such grassroots participatory bodies as the cooperatives. For it was from the institutions of economic democracy rather than from the institutions of political democracy

[99] Jerzy Holzer, *Z dziejów PPS: 1944–1948* (Warsaw: Wolność Sprawiedliwość Niepodległość, 1983), p. 26.

that the Polish socialists expected the impetus for democratic renewal to come.

In fact, for all of the filo- or even crypto-communism that historians have attributed to the post-war PPS and PSIUP, the two parties were actually highly critical of the attitudes that their communist allies took towards grassroots participation. The Italian socialists repeatedly attacked the PCI for its complete lack of internal democracy. In a September 1944 open letter to the PCI, Morandi noted that there was a fundamental difference between socialist and communist ideas about the aims and purposes of a proletarian party. For where 'the masses expressed their interests within and governed through the party' in the socialist conception, the communists saw their party as a mere 'instrument to manoeuvre the masses in accordance with the directives assigned to cadres'.[100] Even as the communists were practising a most cautious and legalistic politics during the first post-war years, socialist leaders remained sceptical of the democratic credentials of the PCI. Speaking at the April 1946 congress of the PSIUP, a characteristically rowdy affair with endless interruptions, Alberto Jacometti observed that 'the communist party is not democratic in the way that the socialist party is'. When Palmiro Togliatti had delivered his leader's address to first post-war congress of the PCI, after all, he had been able to speak 'for four hours with no one taking the floor to criticise what he had said' – that constituted 'proof that the communist party has not been sufficiently democratised'.[101]

Such misgivings about the communist approach towards the grassroots in general and towards participatory democracy more specifically stretched well beyond the party level. In fact, the kind of economic system that the Italian and Polish socialists were looking to build was in many ways the antithesis of the Soviet system. Even if they rarely mentioned the Soviet Union by name, a strong rejection of the top-down bureaucratic command economy that had been introduced there in the wake of the October Revolution was often implicit in their positions. At the height of the 'battle for trade', chief PPS economist Oskar Lange even appeared to place the pre-war capitalist economy and the communist-backed command economy on the same footing. For now that private capital had been liquidated in Poland, he pointed out, 'a danger equally harmful to

[100] 'Lettera aperta ai compagni communisti' (September 1944), in Simone Neri Serneri (ed.), *Il Partito Socialista nella Resistenza: I documenti e la stampa clandestina (1943–1945)* (Pisa: Nistri-Lischi, 1988), pp. 206–9, 207.
[101] 'XXIV Congresso del Partito Socialista Italiano di Unità Proletaria, 13 aprile 1946, seduta antemeridiana', ACS, Carteggio Nenni, Busta 88, Fasc 2193, pp. 11–12.

democracy' could emerge 'in the form of economic concentration in the hands of the state bureaucracy'.[102]

Much as the ČSSD and SFIO detested the communist abuses of participatory politics, the two parties very much shared the communist mistrust of direct grassroots participation in economic life. To be sure, especially in the immediate aftermath of the liberation, the Czechoslovakian social democrats and French socialists often spoke of shop floor co-decision bodies as building blocks of a future socialised economy. In the summer of 1945, for example, Laušman had still declared proudly that, in Czechoslovakian industry, 'not one mouse reared its head' without the permission of the factory council.[103] As it became increasingly clear that these bodies would not readily be kept to the brief that party leaders had envisioned for them and were, in any case, often dominated by communist activists, the ČSSD and SFIO were quick to embrace a top-down economic model in which the initiative resided firmly with experts at the factory and ministry level.

Once again, we can trace back the origins of these divergences between the four parties to their very different experiences during the interwar years. Over the 1920s and 1930s, the Czechoslovakian social democrats and French socialists had become increasingly embedded in the social and economic institutions of their respective states. The post-war ČSSD, of course, had a long history of working within the (economic) system, helping the social democrats to punch significantly above their reduced political weight in the politically fiercely contested struggles to provide managers for the newly nationalised industries.[104] It took the French socialists longer to come to terms with capitalist system, as the SFIO had still 'made a point of slapping down' those socialist reformers, including Moch and Philip, who had advocated the introduction of economic planning at its May 1934 congress.[105] Yet it has been observed that the experience of leading the Popular Front government caused a 'profound change of mentality' within the SFIO, as 'technicians' who had been part of or close to the government embraced Keynesianism and New Deal economics.[106]

---

[102] Quoted in Tomicki, *Polska Partia Socjalistyczna*, p. 485.
[103] Quoted in Peter Heumos, 'Betriebsräte, Einheitsgewerkschaft und staatliche Unternehmens-verwaltung. Anmerkungen zu einer Petition mährischer Arbeiter an die tschechoslowakische Regierung vom 8. Juni 1947', *Jahrbücher für Geschichte Osteuropas*, 29 (1981), pp. 215–45, 220.
[104] Lenká Kalinova, *Společenské proměny v čase socialistického experimentu: k sociálním dějinám v letech 1945–1969* (Prague: Academia, 2007), p. 97.
[105] See: Nord, *France's New Deal*, pp. 27–8.
[106] Bergounioux and Grunberg, *Le long remords du pouvoir*, pp. 154–6.

Just as the Czechoslovakian social democrats and French socialists were becoming part of the social and economic elite in their countries, however, events were moving in the opposite direction in interwar Italy and Poland. The more radical line on worker self-management and popular participation that the post-war PPS and PSIUP adopted thus reflected their interwar disillusions with reformism and with working within the (economic) system more generally. The Italian socialists had never had a significant foothold in the state economic institutions, and a good deal of the experience of working within the system was lost to the post-war PSIUP when many of its old trade union stalwarts defected to Saragat's PSLI. If the Polish socialists did initially build up a strong position in the state socio-economic institutions during the 1920s, it has been noted how the attitudes that the interwar PPS took towards grassroots participation began to radicalise as the socialists were systematically removed from the state apparatus under the Sanacja regime.[107]

[107] Bäcker, *Problematyka państwa*, p. 92.

CHAPTER 8

The International Road to Socialism

In his role as international secretary of the Labour Party, Denis Healey criss-crossed Europe during the first post-war years to attend socialist party congresses and International Socialist Conferences. Drawing on these experiences, he penned some very instructive notes on the European socialist parties in early 1948. In Scandinavia, thirteen million people lived 'under Labour rule' that was 'empirical, gradualist, quietist, [and] not doctrinaire'. There had been 'little nationalisation and [there is] great scope for private industry'. In the Benelux countries and France, the socialist parties had a 'Marxist anticlerical tradition but [an] empirical experience – [c]entrist'. They were facing 'strong competition by C.P. and Catholics', though, and the SFIO in particular was 'badly organised, disciplined and led'. In East Central Europe, the socialist parties had 'no ultimate protection against [a] determined C.P. attempt to liquidate them'. There was a 'fascist danger and no background of democracy except [in] Czechoslovakia'. Socialists in Germany and Austria had to operate in the shadow of the four occupying powers. The future of socialism in Germany still hung in the balance, but the Austrian socialists were 'tough, experienced, [and] well led' and 'would now win [elections]'. In southern Europe, by contrast, the socialist parties were 'suppressed or in opposition'. The Romanian social democrats had already been forced into a merger with the communists and the same fate awaited their Bulgarian counterparts. If the PSIUP did not find itself in that position yet, it was nonetheless 'seen as part of East Europe'.[1]

From the British perspective, the post-war European socialist movement was thus fractured along manifold lines of ideological make-up, political tradition, and socio-economic approach. As we have seen (see Introduction), however, this is not reflected in the historiography of post-war international socialism, which views the debates between the European

[1] LHASC, LPA, LP/ID, Box 13.

socialist parties almost exclusively through the prism of the emerging Cold War. In the resultant narrative, 'conflicts between the Western powers and the Soviet Union triggered conflicts between the socialist parties of East and West' right from the outset.[2] It should come as no surprise that the Eastern European socialists come off particularly badly in such accounts. Historians of post-war (Western) European socialism have frequently written them off as fellow-travellers or crypto-communists, who did the bidding of the Soviet Union first and foremost.[3] Their short-lived involvement with post-war international socialism, hence, has primarily been described as a nuisance for those Western European parties seeking to press ahead with a properly social democratic and Atlanticist agenda.[4] Even if more recent work has shown greater consideration for the arguments the Eastern European socialists put forward, these histories mostly fail to conceive of the polemics within the post-war international socialist movement in anything other than clear-cut East–West terms.[5]

This chapter aims to show that the fault lines between the post-war European socialist parties instead ran both within and across the two putative blocs. The origins of these divides, moreover, long predated the geo-political division of the continent after the Second World War. To make these arguments, the chapter revisits the divergences and debates within the post-war international socialist movement from a reconstruction rather than a Cold War perspective. In its analysis of the transnational interchanges of the post-war European socialist parties, therefore, the chapter highlights how the socio-economic and political cross-connections between the two halves of the continent made for unlikely bedfellows and unexpected adversaries within the international socialist movement. For even if historiography has mostly turned a blind eye to these alignments and altercations, the post-war socialists themselves were very much aware that the conditions on the ground in liberated Europe did not correspond to the geo-political realities of East and West. As the Cold War began taking shape, accordingly, the quest to keep open the channels of communication with like-minded parties on the other side of the Iron Curtain took on greater and greater urgency for the European socialist parties.

[2] Julius Braunthal, *Geschichte der Internationale*, Vol. 3 (Hanover: J.H.W. Dietz, 1971), p. 170.
[3] Steininger, *Deutschland und die Sozialistische Internationale*, pp. 77, 83; Guillaume Devin, *L'Internationale Socialiste: Histoire et sociologie du socialisme international (1945–1990)* (Paris: Presse de la Fondation Nationale des Sciences Politique, 1993), p. 25.
[4] Klaus Misgeld, 'As the Iron Curtain Descended', pp. 51–7.
[5] See e.g. Heumos, *Europäischer Sozialismus*, pp. 13–46; Sørensen, *Denmark's Social Democratic Government*, pp. 55–9.

By reassembling the dealings of the pan-European socialist movement from its re-inception in the wake of the liberation to its acrimonious split after the Prague Coup, the chapter does not merely place the post-war experiences of the four parties that have been at the heart of this study in a broader context. It also calls into question a central plank of the historiography of twentieth-century socialism. This particular strand of historiography has always possessed a certain Whiggish quality, observing a quasi-linear progression from the revolutionary Marxism that the socialist parties had still espoused at the turn of the century to their embrace of parliamentary democracy and socio-economic reformism during the Cold War.[6] The post-war years represent a key watershed in this narrative. For this was supposedly the period when the centrist and social democratic model provided by the British or Swedish roads to socialism became a universal template for the (Western) European socialist parties.[7] Even though some continental parties stubbornly refused to dispense with revolutionary rhetoric, for which they were duly punished by the electorate, the socialists had in practice come to terms with 'bourgeois' democracy and capitalism.[8] Recounting how the post-war international socialist movement actually drifted apart and eventually split over exactly these questions, this chapter demonstrates that the debate over the proper trajectory to socialism was as contentious as ever.

Getting Acquainted

The post-war international socialist movement represented a multi-layered patchwork of bilateral and multilateral dealings between socialist parties. Before the formal Socialist International was reconstituted in 1951, these dealings were coordinated first (1946–47) by the Socialist Information and Liaison Office (SILO) and thereafter (1947–51) by the Commission of International Socialist Conferences (COMISCO). These bodies met

---

[6] Sassoon, *One Hundred Years*. There are likewise strong overtones of this in the introductory chapter to the recent *Palgrave Handbook of Social Democracy in the European Union*. See Fabien Escalona, Matthieu Vieira, and Jean-Michel De Waele, 'The Unfinished History of the Social Democratic Family', in Fabien Escalona, Matthieu Vieira & Jean-Michel De Waele (eds.), *The Palgrave Handbook of Social Democracy in the European Union* (New York: Palgrave Macmillan, 2013), pp. 3–29.

[7] Stefan Berger, 'Communism, Social Democracy and the Democracy Gap', p. 6; paper presented at international workshop 'The International Labour Movement on the Thresholds of Two Centuries' in Flemingsberg (Sweden), October 2002. www.arbark.se/pdf_wrd/berger_int.pdf (last consulted: 27 June 2018).

[8] Sheri Berman, *The Primacy of Politics*, pp. 188–95; Orlow, *Common Destiny*, p. 4.

regularly and were responsible for organising the biannual International Socialist Conferences, in which all recognised European socialist parties (and some non-European parties too) partook. But post-war international socialism did not stop there. The socialist parties of (East) Central Europe and Scandinavia, all part of national government, held regional conferences during which they discussed the intensification of economic and political collaboration between their countries and parties. The various socialist party congresses, moreover, offered further opportunities for visiting fraternal delegates to exchange views and build relations. There were purely bilateral contacts, finally, as socialist parties frequently invited their foreign sister organisations to send over delegations to get acquainted with the conditions in and take account of the achievements of their countries.

For the diffuse character of post-war international socialism, however, one party clearly took a leading role. The British Labour Party had already replaced the German Social Democratic Party (SPD) as the dominant party of European socialism after 1933, and its role in the wartime coalition government and especially its subsequent landslide election victory cemented this status. Almost all socialist parties initially idolised Labour and wanted a piece of it. When Labour secretary general Morgan Phillips addressed the October 1945 ČSSD congress, he was greeted by 'an almost embarrassing reception'.[9] The Dutch Labour Party (PvdA), for its part, went as far as to reprint several of Labour's election posters in the run-up to the May 1946 parliamentary elections in the Netherlands – urging voters to '[d]o what Tommy did: he chose Labour. The Dutch [should] choose the [PvdA].'[10] At Labour headquarters, meanwhile, a steady flow of letters was coming in from European socialist parties practically begging Labour leaders to show more interest in their problems, to take up their cause, or to meet with their delegations.

While it was probably an overstatement to suggest, as the Polish communists did, that Labour was 'the cock of the socialist roost' and that foreign socialists went to Britain 'for instructions', the Labour Party certainly was the sine qua non of post-war international socialism.[11] At the outset, it even fell to Labour to make unilateral decisions on the very composition of the international socialist movement. As the convenor and host of the first post-war International Socialist Conference, to be held

---

[9] Quoted in Heumos, *Europäischer Sozialismus*, p. 334.
[10] See D.J. Elzinga and Gerrit Voerman, *Om de stembus: verkiezingsaffiches 1918–1998* (Amsterdam: Veen, 2002), pp. 84–91.
[11] Kirby to Healey, 28 November 1946, LHASC, LPA, LP/ID, Box 8.

at the seaside resort of Clacton in May 1946, the Labour Party had to determine which parties to invite. This was a particularly thorny decision for those Eastern European countries where the socialist movement had split into a pro-communist government party and an exiled or opposition anti-communist party. In the spring of 1946, Labour's National Executive Committee discussed the matter and decided to invite neither the government nor the opposition social democrats from Bulgaria and Romania; as it turned out, though, a delegation from the government Romanian Social Democratic Party (PSDR) showed up in Clacton anyway and was admitted to the conference. But the question simply could not be avoided with regard to Poland. As part of the wartime London government-in-exile, the London PPS had built close relations with the Labour Party. Much to the dismay of the Londoners, however, Labour worked by the 'principle … of inviting only one party from each country and that must be the "legal" or "official" one' – meaning that the invitation went to the Lublin PPS.[12]

Even if Labour had thus ruled in favour of those Eastern European socialists working closely with the communists, the Hungarian, Romanian, and Polish delegations arrived in Clacton with plenty of complaints about their portrayal in the West and especially in the Western socialist press. We have already seen how the Polish socialists repeatedly scolded the British socialist magazine *Tribune* for its alleged lack of understanding of the situation in Poland (see Chapter 6). During the Clacton conference, the Hungarian and Romanian social democrats echoed such sentiments. The Hungarian delegate rejected accusations that his party was 'betraying democratic principles' through its close alliance with the communists. In a country where 'the majority of the population is anti-democratic', he insisted, 'we cannot afford to split the working class forces'. The methods of 'our young and virile democracy' had to be pardoned, therefore, for without them 'there will be a new Fascism in Hungary'.[13]

The Romanian delegate took an even more uncompromising line. 'Our foreign comrades have often criticised the lack of democracy in Romania', he declared, 'but it is difficult to prove to the Romanian peasant that there is such a thing as democracy.' There was no point in 'talking to them about two kinds of democracy [bourgeois and popular democracy], as they have never known any kind of democracy'. The PSDR held these views on the

[12] Quoted in Heumos, *Europäischer Sozialismus*, p. 141.
[13] All of the accounts and quotes in the following section are drawn from the 'short precis of the reports' presented at the Clacton conference. LHASC, LPA, LP/ID, Box 3.

basis of not only 'our own history', but also the fateful interwar experiences of other countries: 'We have learnt to see the war was a result of the failure of the German and Italian masses to fight [the] reaction; we do not want to make the same mistakes or allow a Romanian Hitler to climb to power on universal suffrage.'

These accounts bear a strong resemblance to those the PPS consistently put forward to defend its united front with the communists. True to form, the Polish delegate in Clacton explained that 'our Polish democracy must have other weapons to protect herself than the British democracy'. These 'measures of protection', he added, 'were a necessary and unpleasant evil'. What is striking is that none of these themes found their way into the report of the ČSSD delegate. Far from approaching the upcoming parliamentary elections with ominous premonitions of a fascist take-over, he struck a combative and quietly optimistic note. The main electoral adversaries, moreover, were not some shady 'reactionaries', but the communists of the KSČ. To be sure, he acknowledged, the KSČ had been 'the strongest party' in Czechoslovakia since the liberation, and it outnumbered the ČSSD by more than two to one in terms of membership. But reports of a massive swing to the communists might well be 'exaggerated'. The 400,000 ČSSD members, after all, were 'really Socialists and had not joined the Party because of the Russian liberation. Their voting in the next elections would show.'

In their strong focus on the electoral struggle, the Czechoslovakian social democrats already had more in common with their Western European sister parties. What is more, most Western parties seemed to share their analysis that, after an initial post-liberation communist surge, the tide was now turning in their favour. The Belgian delegate pointed out that whereas the communists had expected to gain fifty seats in the wake of the liberation, they actually only gained fourteen seats in the February 1946 parliamentary elections. The communist performance in the subsequent elections to the Senate, moreover, suggested a further slump in their popular appeal. While the Danish delegate did have to report significant losses to the communists in the October 1945 parliamentary elections, he insisted this was 'only a passing stage'. For the communist vote had collapsed in the March 1946 municipal elections and the social democrats were 'now waiting for an opportunity to call fresh General Elections, when the results will be very different'.

All of this shows that, for socialist parties right across continental Europe, the first year following the liberation had been dominated by the communist challenge. Of the nineteen parties present in Clacton, noted

Healey after the conference, 'more than twelve found Communist intrigue a minor or major nuisance, while even some of the Parties which collaborate with the Communists on particular issues showed the usual psychological effects of a shotgun wedding'.[14] These symptoms were by no means limited to the Eastern European socialists. The report of the French delegate, for example, demonstrated that the SFIO was still coming to terms with its inferiority complex towards the communist PCF. 'We have a very strong Communist Party', SFIO international secretary Salomon Grumbach pointed out, 'whose influence among the working classes is stronger than ours was recently.' The huge 'enthusiasm aroused' by PCF leaders was 'of first importance for the future of France'. It was for that reason, he explained, that the SFIO had called for the two parties to merge in November 1944. After 'events' had proven that organic unity was impossible for the moment, however, the socialists had failed to challenge the communists with sufficient vigour. This had 'caused confusion and disappointment among the workers' and was also 'why the Communist Party Youth Organisations are stronger than ours'.

More generally, almost all parties that were working with the communists both in government and beyond expressed some misgivings about the true intentions and democratic credentials of their (coalition) partners. To pander to the 'real desire' for a communist–socialist merger among workers, the Belgian socialists had held joint demonstrations with the communists. But the Belgian delegate made quite clear that the two parties had 'separate organisation[s] and aims' and that communist aims remained as suspect as ever: 'The Communist Party wish[es] to be in the Government in order to know what is going on, and to control administration.' The delegate of the Finnish Social Democratic Party, meanwhile, noted that his party had been 'very hard pressed' by the communists. '[As] elsewhere', he explained, the Finnish communists had been attempting to break social democratic independence 'by infiltration'. While these attempts had been 'partly resisted', 'important posts in the government and elsewhere have had to be filled by communist sympathisers'.

Even among those socialist parties that had entered into a united front with the communists, strong doubts about communist methods and aims persisted. The Hungarian delegate pointed out that '[t]he Socialist Party, and the whole country to a certain extent, are suspicious of the Communist Party, as the 1918 experience [when the short-lived Hungarian Soviet Republic under the Bolshevik Béla Kun had unleashed a wave of terror]

---

[14] Healey to Editor of the *Daily Worker*, 29 May 1946, LHASC, LPA, LP/ID, Box 3.

is remembered still'. For the Romanian social democrats, such suspicions had their basis in the everyday practice of collaborating closely with the communists. When the PSDR had started to work with the communists in 1943, noted its delegate, 'we believed in fusion with them'. But the social democrats had 'resented [the] pressure' that the communists had put them under and had now 'abandoned' their earlier designs. Since then, it had been the communists who had 'made the concessions', as the PSDR had 'pushed the Communist Party out of many fields' and 'taken away many members' from it. In a similar vein, the Italian delegate pointed out that, in the wake of the liberation, 'considerable pressure had been brought to bear to bring about a fusion with the Communists'. But those who had left the PSIUP for the PCI were now 'showing signs of returning', as it was 'becoming obvious that the Communists in Italy are not democratic'.

What initially divided the post-war socialist parties was not so much their attitudes towards the communists as their appraisals of the broader socio-economic and political playing field. In this respect, we can divide the parties in Clacton into three rough groupings. The Labour Party and the Scandinavian socialist parties (apart from the Finnish social democrats), and increasingly the Austrian Socialist Party (SPÖ) too, felt strong enough to take on the communists and the bourgeois parties at once. In Britain, Norway, and Sweden, the socialists had an absolute parliamentary majority and firmly rejected any form of collaboration with the communists. The 'only way' for communists to collaborate with the social democrats in his country, quipped the Swedish delegate, was 'to join the [Swedish] Labour Party as individual members'. As for the bourgeois parties, it would be 'a very long time' before they 'could take over the Government'. While the SPÖ was still part of a tripartite coalition with the communists and the Catholics, the results of the November 1945 parliamentary elections had given the party much encouragement. By taking 45 per cent of the vote and dwarfing the communists in the process, boasted the Austrian delegate, the SPÖ had 'achieved one of the best results amongst the European countries' in both 'Socialist representation' and 'maximum unity inside the working class'. Even though the Catholics had won 50 per cent of the popular vote and an outright parliamentary majority, their position was already weakening as men were 'com[ing] back' from their wartime displacement. For the 'electoral majority' had been 'imposed by the women'.

The Benelux socialist parties, the SFIO, and also the ČSSD conceded that they had lost significant ground to the communists in the wake of the liberation. After weathering the initial storm, however, they were now ready to take the electoral fight to the communists. For these parties, accordingly, there could be no question of pacts or alliances with their foremost rivals for the working-class vote. If anything, they were already verging closer on the Catholic and/or bourgeois-liberal parties to their immediate right. Much like the ČSSD and the SFIO (see Chapter 5), the Dutch PvdA complained bitterly about outright communist demagoguery at election time. In a situation where paper and good transport links were still lacking, lamented the Dutch delegate, 'the most primitive forms of propaganda' prevailed. That meant the communist slogan of 'higher wages, lower prices' had 'proved most successful'. He was much milder about his Catholic coalition partners, though, whom he described as 'partly progressive and partly conservative'. The French delegate spoke of the MRP in remarkably similar terms. Even if 'the militant Catholicism' of the MRP had 'misled many people', he explained, it was still a 'partly Left and partly Right' party 'with some progressive programmes'.

According to the Eastern European socialist parties (apart from the ČSSD) and the PSIUP, exactly such a progressive and democratic party in the political centre was lacking in their countries. This was true even of their centre-right coalition partners. It was 'very easily seen', insisted the Italian delegate, that the Christian democrats of the DC were 'neither [C]hristian nor democratic'. In what was certainly a reference to the Independent Smallholders' Party, which had won 57 per cent of the vote in the November 1945 parliamentary elections, the Hungarian delegate made mention of 'strong Conservative and landed interests in the Government'. For the Romanian social democrats, the vices of the (centre-)right did not stop there. 'You will be surprised to find', their delegate told the Clacton conference, 'that the only Parties that are not anti-[S]emitic in Romania are the Socialist and Communist Parties.' The point was that, for all of their obvious flaws, the communists were still the only true allies for socialists in the struggle against 'fascist and nationalist forces' (the Polish delegate), the 'strong reactionary movement' (the Italian delegate), and the 'traces' of '25 years of ... military terror' (the Hungarian delegate).

The Clacton conference thus laid bare the divergences between the European socialist parties. In these circumstances, most parties had little appetite to re-establish the Socialist International anytime soon. Only the Belgian and French socialists, hoping to redress their domestic weaknesses through membership of a prestigious international organisation, called for the speedy reconstitution of the Second International. But the British and Scandinavian parties, bolstered by their electoral successes, were 'not prepared to consider any external interference in their own affairs'.[15] The Eastern European socialists, for their part, had no desire to be part of an organisation in which they would be outnumbered by (Western) parties that took a rather dim view of communist–socialist united fronts. The parties represented in Clacton agreed, therefore, that the international socialist movement would keep its informal and non-binding character for the time being. There were to be 'periodic conferences', at which the European socialist parties would 'exchange views without necessarily producing formal resolutions'. Any decision on political questions or the admission of new members, moreover, would have to be taken unanimously.[16]

Building a Movement

The year that followed the Clacton conference nonetheless saw a substantial intensification of international socialist collaboration. There were three more full International Socialist Conferences: one special conference hosted by the SFIO in Paris (August 1946) and two regular conferences organised by the SILO in Bournemouth (November 1946) and Zurich (June 1947). There were also two regional 'Danube Conferences' in Prague (December 1946) and Budapest (May 1947), which brought together socialist delegations from Austria, Bulgaria, Czechoslovakia, Hungary, Poland, and Romania. Unlike the Clacton conference, the chief purpose of which had been to exchange information about the political and socio-economic situation in which socialist parties found themselves, these conferences were dominated by particular questions. The Paris conference sought to flesh out a common socialist platform against the Franco regime. The Bournemouth conference was marked by long discussions over the question whether the German SPD was to be readmitted to the international socialist movement. These discussions were continued at the Zurich conference, which also addressed the schism in Italian socialism and saw a fresh Franco-Belgian push for the reconstitution of the Socialist International. As for the Danube Conferences, these were devoted to fostering economic cooperation in a region where the demise of Germany as the main trade partner had created a vacuum. Both at these conferences and in the margins of socialist party congresses, however, the broader socio-economic and political debates between the parties continued.

---

[15] Denis Healey, 'The International Socialist Conference 1946–1950', *International Affairs*, 26/3 (1950), p. 366.
[16] Ibid., p. 367.

These debates in many ways reproduced the divergences that were already on display at the Clacton conference. This was manifest in the rifts that opened up at the Paris conference on Franco Spain. There were two items on the agenda of the conference: taking diplomatic action against the Franco regime and coordinating support for the Spanish underground. On both counts, however, the conference failed to make much headway. On the diplomatic front, this was due primarily to Labour's blanket refusal to countenance any resolution that would force its government to reverse its policy of tacit backing for Franco. Quickly after taking power, the Labour government had decided that British interests were best served by Franco staying in place.[17] At the conference, accordingly, the Labour delegate took a most uncompromising line – even threatening to withdraw from the conference altogether if the final resolution were to call either for a boycott of Spain or for the United Nations to take steps against Franco. Even if Labour's attitude caused disillusionment among those who had expected more of a 'socialist foreign policy', most parties grudgingly accepted it as a fact of life within the post-war international socialist movement. Such was the sway that Labour held over its sister parties that it could basically bully its way to desirable outcomes.[18]

More contentious than the diplomatic question, therefore, was the question of actual support for anti-Franco groupings inside and out-side Spain. Here the argument revolved around the relations between communists and socialists once more. In his report of the conference, Julian Hochfeld noted how he, Lelio Basso, and the Swiss delegate had tried to 'counteract the obsessive anti-communism that reigns supreme in the West'.[19] Yet their calls for communists and socialists to work together in the anti-Franco movement were rejected by most Western European socialists. The Belgian chair immediately shot down a Romanian amendment that mentioned communist–socialist collaboration on Spain. Working with the communists on Spain, or on any other question for that matter, was anathema to the Dutch PvdA as well. The Dutch social democrats wanted nothing to do with the main anti-Franco organisation in the Netherlands, which one PvdA leader privately described as being 'infected by communists'.[20] Instead, the Dutch delegate in Paris underlined

---

[17] On the Labour government and Franco Spain see Qasim Ahmad, *Britain, Franco Spain and the Cold War, 1945–1950* (New York: Garland, 1992).

[18] Upon his return from the Franco conference, for example, the Dutch delegate informed the PvdA Executive that the resolution adopted in Paris had 'to a large extent taken into account the British position'. IISH, Archief PvdA, inventory number 1, Dagelijks Bestuur, 6 September 1946.

[19] Quoted in Heumos, *Europäischer Sozialismus*, p. 167.

[20] IISH, Archief PvdA, inventory number 22, Partijbestuur, 25 October 1946.

how Catholic politicians could be won for the campaign against the Franco regime. For when two PvdA MP's had put a resolution condemning Franco before the Dutch parliament, he explained, 'all Catholic MPs had fully agreed'.[21]

It was this none too implicit desire to work with Catholics rather than with communists that astonished and enraged more left-wing socialists. In their view, it was one thing for the Labour Party or for the Scandinavian socialist parties to reject any form of collaboration with the communists. With their overall parliamentary majorities, after all, these parties were strong enough to implement socialism on their own. But for the continental socialists to align themselves with non-Marxist parties to their right at the expense of proletarian unity with the communists amounted to class betrayal.

This was of course exactly the kind of criticism that left-wing socialists would later level at the SFIO. Before the collapse of *tripartisme* in France, however, it was two other parties that bore the brunt of their indignation: the Dutch Labour Party and the Austrian Socialist Party. Basso was particularly scornful of the new PvdA – a party that had only come into being in February 1946, after the pre-war Social Democratic Workers' Party had merged with two smaller progressive-liberal and left-Protestant parties. If the Dutch social democrats had in the past made 'a remarkable contribution to Marxist studies', he lamented, the party that had emerged from the merger stood 'completely outside of the Marxist tradition'.[22] For when Basso had asked one PvdA representative which bonds held together the diverse groups that made up the new party, the answer had been most telling: 'We are all anti-Marxists'. Their decision to force the communists into opposition and enter into a governmental coalition with the Catholics, moreover, was always going to end in disaster: 'There is no doubt that such a politics, which breaks proletarian unity, destroys any possibility of socialist action … and is therefore a reactionary politics.'[23]

In much the same terms, Hungarian social democrat and MSzDP Central Committee member Imre Vajda reported back from the December 1945 SPÖ congress. Having himself participated in the February 1934 uprising of the Republican Defence League, Vajda now found 'the spirit' of such famous Austro-Marxists as Otto Bauer and Max Adler to be absent from

[21] Van der Goes van Naters to Partijbestuur PvdA, 18 September 1946, IISH, Archief PvdA, inventory number 2680.

[22] Lelio Basso, 'L'Internazionale', *Avanti!*, 4 June 1948.

[23] Lelio Basso, 'Socialismo Europeo (1)', *Quarto Stato*, 15 September 1946.

the congress. What had been lacking, he noted, was 'a Marxist critique, with which the superficial political interpretations of many questions would have been rejected and the core problems would have been exposed'. In economic terms, its single-minded focus on the economic recovery of Austria had blinded the SPÖ to the need for structural reforms. For if the economy were to pick up without large-scale nationalisations having taken place, capitalism would emerge stronger rather than weaker. As for the political landscape, the SPÖ regarded the communists as 'irrelevant' and worked more closely with the Catholics of the new Austrian People's Party. According to Vajda, though, that party looked set 'to follow the trajectory of its interwar predecessor, the Christian Social Party'. In the wake of the First World War, after all, there had been 'truly democratic leaders' at the helm of that party as well. '[W]ithin a couple of years', however, these progressive Catholics had been:

> supplanted by the reactionary clique of [Ignaz] Seipel [the Catholic prelate, whose two terms as Chancellor of Austria during the 1920s saw a marked increase in para-military violence] and, from there on, there was a direct line through [Engelbert] Dollfuss [the Chancellor of Austria from 1932 to 1934, who established a dictatorship and ruled by decree from 1933] and [Kurt] Schuschnigg [who had succeeded the assassinated Dollfuss as Chancellor in 1934 and sustained the authoritarian regime until the 1938 *Anschluss*] to Hitler.

Vajda's prognosis for Austria and the SPÖ was bleak, therefore. 'The general impression of political life in Austria', concluded his report, 'has convinced me that we are on a better road both as a country and as a social democratic party.'[24]

The Polish socialists very much shared this analysis. In its report of the November 1946 SPÖ congress, the PPS delegation noted that the Austrian socialists stood 'under the manifest influence of the Labour Party'. The hero's welcome that the congress had given Morgan Phillips revealed as much: 'He was photographed and mobbed from all sides. Every one of his words was greeted by emphatic nodding. He gave the impression of a colonial plantation owner.' Oscar Pollak, the editor of the national SPÖ newspaper, served as the 'mouthpiece' of Phillips at the congress. In his speech, he had divided the European socialist parties into three groups. The first consisted of 'communist annexes' – parties that had 'passed the point of no return' by forming an electoral bloc with the communists. The second was made up of parties that found themselves squeezed between

---

[24] Quoted in Heumos, *Europäischer Sozialismus*, pp. 426–35.

stronger communist and right-wing blocs and were reduced to steering a middle course between these two extremes. The third – and the SPÖ self-identified as belonging to this group – were 'independent socialist parties that aspired to play a leading role in their countries'. Even though Pollack did not name names, it was clear that he counted the PPS among the 'communist annexes'.[25] If the Austrian socialists had thus more or less written off the PPS, the Polish delegation was equally scathing of the SPÖ. It was a party of the old 'social democratic tradition', observed its report, 'which has failed to revise its concepts and has absolutely no concrete programme for the current problems of Austria.'[26]

In this respect, the Czechoslovakian social democrats once again struck a different tone from their Eastern European counterparts. The ČSSD report of the same November 1946 SPÖ congress was altogether milder with regard to the Austrian socialists. It painted an overall picture of a strong and united party, which looked likely to prevail in the next elections. What needed work, however, were the relations between the SPÖ and the ČSSD. The report noted how the Austrian socialist press paid little attention to Czechoslovakia. It had printed no articles whatsoever on the nationalisation of industry or the introduction of economic planning, while the communist press had loudly banged the drum for the socio-economic reforms in post-war Czechoslovakia. This had given many SPÖ activists 'the impression that political life in Czechoslovakia is completely dominated by the communist party'. One SPÖ parliamentarian had even asked the Czechoslovakian delegate whether the ČSSD press criticised the communists at all.[27] It was perhaps to dispel such ideas that the ČSSD insisted on inviting the SPÖ to Prague to partake in the first Danube Conference.[28]

For those Western European socialists more familiar with the situation in Czechoslovakia often took a more positive view of the country and its social democrats. Indeed, in transnational contact with its Western sister parties, the ČSSD took great pains to present Czechoslovakia as a country where socialism had been introduced by democratic means. In its message to the August 1946 SFIO congress, the ČSSD boasted that Czechoslovakia

[25] This was also the impression with which the ČSSD delegate left the congress. In his report, he observed that whereas the Czechoslovakian social democrats 'apparently' found themselves in group two, group one 'alluded … above all to Poland'. Quoted in Heumos, *Europäischer Sozialismus*, pp. 365–6.

[26] AAN, PPS, Wydz. Zagraniczy, 235/XIX-15, fos 7–14.

[27] Quoted in Heumos, *Europäischer Sozialismus*, pp. 360–7.

[28] Heumos, *Die Konferenzen*, p. 22.

had 'surmounted' the dictatorship of the proletariat. The lessons of the Soviet Union, it explained, could not be applied to 'states … of a great and ancient tradition and of a democratic culture'. In Czechoslovakia, after all, it had been possible to 'place economic power in the hands of the people' without having recourse to dictatorial methods.[29] These efforts to place Czechoslovakia and the ČSSD in a better light quickly paid off. Already at the Clacton conference, several delegates had 'expressed a keen interest in our nationalisation of industry and of the banks'. Even the Labour ministers Emanuel Shinwell and Aneurin Bevan had asked for specific information about the nationalisation programme.[30]

When PvdA chairman Koos Vorrink visited Czechoslovakia in August and September 1946, he was similarly impressed by the nationalisation 'experiment' that the country was undertaking. So 'educational and interesting' was this experiment that he urged the PvdA leadership 'to send three or four expert party members to Czechoslovakia' to examine the nationalisation programme locally. Vorrink was also much heartened by the political attitude of the ČSSD, both towards the communists and on the broader question of democracy. In a personal conversation, Blažej Vilím had assured him that, while 'contact' with the communists was unavoidable, 'unity' was out of the question. 'As soon as the communists turn to non-democratic methods', he had added, 'they will find us on their path.' This 'combative spirit', noted Vorrink, had also been on display at the large ČSSD rally in Liberec that his hosts had invited him to attend. To the 'rapturous applause' of the 'many thousands present', Bohumil Laušman had declared that 'we have not fought one form of dictatorship to bow down for another'. In the conclusion of his report, Vorrink acknowledged that he could have written a more pessimistic analysis of the communist hold over political life in Czechoslovakia. But he had been encouraged by 'the steadfast democratic beliefs and combativeness' of the non-communist parties. In their declarations, there had been 'no sign of defeatism or of a cowardly fear of communism'. The fact that their 'unconditional loyalty to the Western democratic spirit' went hand in hand with a 'radical progressiveness', Vorrink insisted, 'makes it a moral duty for us have confidence in their grand programme for Czechoslovakia – which one of our comrades described as the peaceful introduction of a socialist system on the principles of Western civilisation'.[31]

[29] Quoted in Heumos, *Europäischer Sozialismus*, p. 352.
[30] Quoted in Heumos, *Europäischer Sozialismus*, p. 338.
[31] 'Enkele aantekeningen naar aanleiding van mijn reis naar Tsjecho-Slovakije (27 augustus tot 5 september 1946)', IISH, Archief PvdA, inventory number 2286.

Such statements bear testimony to the strong resonance that the Western democratic tradition had for the Czechoslovakian social democrats. They felt increasingly ill at ease, accordingly, in communist-dominated Eastern Europe. While the Czechoslovakian social democrats 'continue their struggle against the communists', wrote the Prague correspondent of the PvdA newspaper Richard Jokel in May 1947, 'they regret that the socialist parties in other Central and Eastern European countries succumb as soon as they are exposed to communist pressure'. Or, as one ČSSD secretary had put it: 'We were a democratic island in fascist surroundings between 1933 and 1939 and we are a democratic island in communist surroundings today – it is as unpleasant.'[32]

If the ČSSD was thus verging ever closer on its Western European sister parties, the PSIUP was moving in the opposite direction. This became very clear when the Zurich conference discussed the Italian question. After a conference sub-commission had heard representatives of the secessionists, several Western delegates called upon the PSIUP to bury the hatchet with Giuseppe Saragat's PSLI. Healey insisted that, if reunification was not yet possible, the PSIUP and PSLI should at least present a common list at the next elections. To that end, he suggested the two parties hold a joint conference, chaired by a respected foreign socialist, in the next six weeks. There was not much time, he warned, as 'polarisation in Italy is mounting and, if we fail to check that polarisation, socialism in Italy will be finished for a long time'. He had a clear message for those in the PSIUP claiming that an electoral deal with Saragat would make many of its members leave for the PCI: '[T]hat will happen in any case if you have communists in your ranks'. It was 'better', he explained, 'to let them go'. For 'you cannot call yourself a socialist if you would rather draw up an electoral programme with the Communist Party than with a Socialist Party which contains many old comrades'.[33]

While the Swedish delegate backed these proposals, the French delegate wanted to go further still. He called for an international socialist commission, led by the veteran Belgian socialist Louis De Brouckère, to be sent to Italy 'to create the climate' in which a reunification could take place. In the meantime, moreover, the PSLI was to be admitted to International Socialist Conferences as an observer without voting rights. But Basso, who

---

[32] IISH, Archief PvdA, inventory number 1314.
[33] All of the accounts and quotes in the following section are drawn from two documents: a 'short summary of the proceedings' of the Italian Commission in English and a longer protocol of its deliberations in French. See IISH, Socialist International Archives (hereafter SIA), inventory number 235.

represented the PSIUP in the sub-commission, was having none of it. He rejected any foreign intervention, as 'the Italian question does not exist'. As for a common list, the PSLI was welcome to join a larger electoral bloc with the PCI and the PSIUP. An exclusive alliance between the PSIUP and the PSLI, however, was not going to 'increase the socialist vote'. And to allow the PSLI as an observer would only encourage dissidents in other parties to create further schisms. In Basso's view, therefore, the only thing the Zurich conference could do was 'to address itself to the secessionists and ask them to re-enter the [PSIUP]. We are waiting for them.'

The Hungarian and Polish delegates gave Basso their backing. In doing so, Hochfeld even drew a direct comparison between Italy and Poland. The Polish socialists, he explained, had set themselves the task of making sure that the economic reconstruction of Poland followed 'the principles of democratic socialism'. This was no easy task in 'a country where the Communists are revolutionaries, but [are] not very democratic'. In these circumstances, it was of first importance for socialist parties to be 'strong and united'. As the Italian socialists had to work with 'a strong and revolutionary Communist Party' too, the secessionists had made a 'grave error' by breaking away. The conference, he insisted, should call on them to re-enter the PSIUP 'without conditions'.

Of course, this was a minority viewpoint. Once the sub-commission reached the voting stage, Hochfeld's proposals were comprehensively defeated. Instead, the sub-commission recommended the two socialist parties to examine common action in the next elections, and looked set to admit the PSLI as an observer. As it turned out, though, the PSIUP managed to get its way on both counts. First, Basso stopped the sub-commission from taking a vote on observer membership for the PSLI by threatening that the PSIUP would walk out of the conference if the PSLI was admitted. Subsequently, during the plenary session, Nenni succeeded in persuading some of his 'personal friends' among the delegates to withdraw the recommendation 'on the grounds that it would in some way seem to condone the action of the secessionists', – thereby, as Healey lamented after the conference, 'giving carte blanche to Nenni and the extremists in the old party'.[34]

The failure to make any headway on the Italian question was symbolic of a broader malaise in post-war international socialism. In fact, the Zurich conference deferred all the major questions that were before it. Even though the voting rules had been altered prior to the conference to

[34] 'Notes on the Minutes of the Zurich Conference', LHASC, LPA, LP/ID, Box 13.

allow decisions to be made by a two-thirds majority, the conference had to establish no fewer than three study and fact-finding commissions. The first had to decide which of the two Bulgarian socialist parties was to be admitted to the international socialist movement. The second was a liaison committee 'appointed to keep in touch with' the German SPD after that party saw its bid to be readmitted to international socialism defeated by a single vote. The third was to formulate 'useful proposals as to the ideological bases, organisation, and methods of action' of a future Socialist International.[35] Even if the work of these commissions allowed the next conference to make progress on these three issues, the rift within the post-war international socialist movement was to grow only wider over the months to follow.

Drifting Apart

For the Zurich conference met in an increasingly fraught international atmosphere. Just days before its start, United States secretary of state George Marshall had announced the European Recovery Plan that came to be known by his name. Even if the Marshall Plan originally had a pan-European scope, and as such elicited some hopes for united socialist action, it quickly became a very divisive issue between the European socialist parties. The establishment of the Cominform in September 1947 saw them drift apart still further. For the founding manifesto of that organisation not only divided the world in a Soviet-led 'democratic camp' and an American-led 'imperialist camp', but also launched a blistering attack on several leading Western socialists. Such 'right-wing socialists as Blum in France, Attlee and Bevin in England, Schumacher in Germany, Renner and Schärf in Austria, Saragat in Italy etc.', it read, had a special role to play in the imperialist designs of the United States. It was their task to 'try and hide the true predatory nature of imperialism under the mask of democracy and socialist phraseology'. In doing so, these 'imperialist lackeys' contributed to the 'disintegration of the working class', while 'poisoning its class consciousness'.[36] Long gone, then, were the days of the popular fronts or of the post-liberation coalitions of the Resistance. As the communists reverted to their 1920s sectarianism, the time had come for socialists to show their hand.

---

[35] 'Conférence socialiste internationale – Zurich, 6/8 juin 1947', IISH, SIA, inventory number 235, fo. 286.
[36] Quoted in Braunthal, *Geschichte*, p. 635.

This pressure to take sides was building not only as a consequence of the emerging Cold War, though. Even within the various socialist parties, there was a distinct feeling that the status quo in the international socialist movement was becoming untenable. At the August 1947 SFIO congress in Lyon, the party leadership came under fire for its overly indulgent attitude towards the Eastern European and Italian socialists. Marceau Pivert, on the anti-Stalinist left of French socialism, claimed that international secretary Grumbach had allowed himself to be 'blackmailed' by Nenni over the PSLI. For it was the PSLI, he insisted, that 'is the most close [to us], that is the party of the Third Force in Italy'. He also had a strong message for the fraternal delegation of the PPS. 'Do not mistake our welcome, our courtesy, for our approval of the massive arrests that you are trying to cover up', he declared to applause. To be sure, the party leadership fought back, with Léon Boutbien and Grumbach scolding Pivert for his ignorance both of the fault lines within the international socialist movement and of the situation in which the Eastern European socialists found themselves.[37] But the mood among the party faithful was very clear. Whereas the congress propelled Pivert onto the SFIO Executive, Grumbach was voted off the Executive for the first time since the war.[38]

The first meeting of the study commission on the Socialist International, which followed the Lyon congress, gave the PSIUP and the Eastern European socialist parties a chance to respond to the allegations that had been levelled at them. The Czechoslovakian, Italian, and Polish delegates complained about the shocking levels of ignorance that had been on display in Lyon. But whereas the ČSSD delegate limited herself to calling for 'a better information service', Basso for the PSIUP and Stanisław Dobrowolski for the PPS went much further. 'Much has been spoken in Lyon', noted Dobrowolski, 'about the Bulgarian Social Democratic Party and its collaboration with the Communist Party. But are there not [socialist] parties which collaborate in their countries with elements that we consider to be fascists?' In Poland, he explained, such 'fascist elements are still very strong'. The PPS, therefore, had to 'cooperate with anyone who rejects fascism'.

Basso echoed these sentiments. There were countries, he insisted, 'where the outcome can only be socialism or fascism'. In this respect, he drew a

---

[37] The protocols of the congress are available at http://62.210.214.184/cg-ps/documents/pdf/cong-1947-08-16.pdf (last consulted: 27 June 2018).
[38] In a letter to Denis Healey, Charles Dumas pointed out that Grumbach's dismissal had everything to do with his attitudes vis-à-vis the PSLI and the Eastern European socialist parties. Dumas to Healey, 21 September 1946, LHASC, LPA, LP/ID, Box 2.

distinction once more between the conditions in Britain on the one side and those in continental Europe on the other. With its absolute majority, he explained, the Labour Party could afford to keep the communists at arm's length. In countries where communist parties were stronger, however, 'the question of working-class unity' was paramount. It was in this context that Basso publicly singled out the SFIO for the first time. The situation in France, he warned, 'raises the concern that that country is sliding towards fascism'. In his view, this had everything to do with narrow-minded socialist ideas about democracy. 'We need to reformulate', argued Basso, 'what we mean by democracy.' So far, the socialist conception of democracy had been 'very petit-bourgeois, as was manifest in the Lyon resolution' – which had pitted 'democratic socialism' against 'totalitarian Stalinism' first and foremost.[39] '[W]hen talking about democratic methods', instead, 'there should be only one concept for socialists: the victory of the working class'. For that reason, the PSIUP was 'in accordance with the politics of both Britain and Poland'.[40]

While the Italian socialists respected and to an extent admired the British road to socialism (see Chapter 6), it was the Polish road to socialism to which they could really relate. In fact, relations between the PPS and the PSIUP had grown much closer during the summer of 1947. In late August, Basso and Nenni had visited Poland as official guests of the PPS. Over the months that followed, they invoked the Polish road to socialism with increasing frequency. For in Poland too, a communist-socialist bloc was facing strong Catholic and nationalist opposition.[41] The main difference, as Nenni noted during his stay in Warsaw, was that communists and socialists in Poland had 'power ... firmly in their hands'.[42] Much more than the unavailable British road, therefore, it was the Polish road to socialism that came to serve as a model for the Italian socialists.

The increasing closeness of the PPS and the PSIUP unnerved many Western socialists. Especially after the PPS published a resolution that basically endorsed the Cominform worldview and called for 'the creation of a united front of Communists and Socialists on the international scale', there were intense rumours about the pending formation of a 'Socinform'

---

[39] The full text of the resolution is available at www.archives-socialistes.fr/app/photopro.sk/archives/detail?docid=12216 (last visited: 27 June 2018).
[40] Archiv ČSSD, Fond 71, Karton 182, fos 309–312; IISH, Archief PvdA, inventory number 2680; AAN, PPS, Wydz. Zagraniczy, fos 1–9.
[41] Emanuele Rossi, *Democrazia come partecipazione: Lelio Basso e il PSI alle origini della Repubblica, 1943–1947* (Rome: Viella, 2011), pp. 270–1.
[42] Pietro Nenni, *Tempo di Guerra Fredda. Diari 1943–1956* (Milan: Sugarco, 1981), 26 August 1947.

of left-wing socialist parties.[43] Even if these reports were denied by Basso[44] and dismissed by Healey,[45] something of the kind does initially seem to have been on the agenda of the PPS. Immediately after the establishment of the Cominform, PPS secretary general Józef Cyrankiewicz privately approached ČSSD chairman Zdeněk Fierlinger with a proposal to form a close-knit bloc of Central European socialist parties. The plan was apparently for these parties to form a separate information bureau, along the lines of the Cominform, within the international socialist movement. It was only after the broader ČSSD leadership had rejected this proposal that the PPS went public with its campaign for an international communist-socialist front. First, a manifesto calling for a 'Workers' International' of communists and socialists was published in the national PPS newspaper *Robotnik*.[46] Subsequently, the party leadership sent its sister parties translated versions of the resolution, which caused much consternation among Western socialists. Not only did it fully associate the PPS with the Cominform's two-camp theory, after all, it also echoed its attacks on 'right-wing socialists' in the West. For '[i]n many countries', the resolution noted, 'rightist-socialist politicians are capitulating before the dollar offensive', and were thus 'defending the interests of American imperialism'.[47]

It was this sort of rhetoric that won the PPS its reputation as no more than a Soviet agency within the international socialist movement, as one of these Eastern European socialist parties that found itself under 'remote control' from Moscow.[48] This was certainly not how contemporary observers saw it, however. For even leading Western socialists considered the international agenda of these parties to be genuine and perfectly consistent with their historical experience. As far as the Hungarian and Polish parties were concerned, explained Healey in late 1947, ' "Eastern democracy" is at least an advance on the pre-war regimes, and they believe that an American victory in a hot or cold war would subject them to a new white terror'.[49] In their view, accordingly, their countries' close alliance with the Soviet Union represented the best guarantee against the return of the reaction.

These views had in large part been shaped, especially among the Hungarian social democrats, by the questionable role that the Western

[43] Healey to Kirby, 3 November 1947, LPA, LP/ID, Box 8.
[44] 'Accantonata la ricostruzione dell'Internazionale Socialista: Il secessionismo è considerato liquidato', *Avanti!*, 4 November 1947.
[45] Healey to Matteotti, 3 November 1947, LHASC, LPA, LP/ID, Box 8.
[46] LHASC, LPA, LP/ID, Box 9.
[47] IISH, Archief PvdA, inventory number 2702.
[48] Steininger, *Deutschland*, p. 83.
[49] 'The Antwerp Conference', LHASC, LPA. LP/ID, Box 13.

powers had played in interwar central Europe. Even Anna Kéthly – the leader of the MSzDP parliamentary group, who was seen in the West as one of the most reliable anti-communist Hungarian social democrats[50] – had precious few illusions about the Western democracies. She had not forgotten how, in the aftermath of the First World War, the American and British control authorities present in defeated Hungary had not lifted a finger when a counter-revolutionary dictatorship was installed. 'Thousands of Hungarian workers were murdered', she lamented, 'while one British diplomat reported back: "A Christian government, a Christian country".'[51] If these were the sentiments on the anti-communist right of Hungarian social democracy, the verdict on the pro-communist left was harsher still. Speaking at the January 1947 MSzDP congress, justice minister István Ries declared that there were 'some social democrats who want to work with the Soviet Union and the communists with one hand and no heart – I want to do so with both hands and all my heart'. As for those 'social democrats who keep pointing to the example of the Western democracies', he insisted that he 'would not even want to live in a so-called Western democracy'.[52]

We have already seen how the Czechoslovakian social democrats took an altogether more positive attitude to the West in general and the concept of Western democracy in particular. As it became increasingly clear that Czechoslovakia was set to become part of the Eastern bloc, therefore, upholding the fraternal relations with the Western socialist parties took on a still greater significance for the ČSSD. When the party leadership discussed the Cyrankiewicz proposals for a 'Socinform', several speakers pointed to the community of interest between Czechoslovakian social democracy and mainstream Western socialism. Those socialist parties pursuing an 'independent politics' vis-à-vis the communists, observed Václav Majer, would have to 'reckon with a [communist] offensive sooner or later; for the moment, that offensive is being conducted against the French and English parties'. Vilím, for his part, expressed his dismay that the Cominform manifesto targeted democratic socialism rather than 'the actual reaction'. The fact that the manifesto had 'not singled out, for example, Churchill but Attlee' demonstrated as much. In these circumstances, socialists from

[50] Janos Jemnitz, 'Soziale und politische Probleme nach dem Zweiten Weltkrieg. Die Erfahrungen und internationalen Verbindungen der ungarischen sozialdemokratischen Partei (1945–1947)', in Dieter Staritz and Hermann Weber (eds.), *Einheitsfront Einheitspartei. Kommunisten und Sozialdemokraten in Ost- und Westeuropa 1944–1948* (Cologne: Verlag Wissenschaft und Politik, 1989), pp. 230–65, 247.

[51] IISH, Archief PvdA, inventory number 1315.

[52] Nationaal Archief, The Hague, Archief Ministerie van Buitenlandse Zaken: Code Archief 1945–1954, nummer toegang 2.05.117, inv. nr. 14183.

East and West had to close ranks. For '[t]he communists follow the same tactics at the international level as they do at home, i.e. they try to undermine the social democratic movement. Just like we do at home, we must also reject these tactics on the international level.'[53]

The months that followed saw the Czechoslovakian social democrats step up their efforts to reach out to the Western socialist parties. At the November 1947 ČSSD congress in Brno, international secretary Vilém Bernard explicitly sang the praises of the Labour Party. 'In our region', he explained, there was a widespread belief 'that the socialist world stops at the Stettin–Trieste line'. But 'the British example shows us that this is not true'. If anything, he argued, the nationalisations of Labour Britain were more impressive 'that those of any Eastern European country'. For not only had the Labour government implemented its nationalisation programme 'without any foreign assistance', it had also come up against 'American capital' in doing so.[54] In an interview with the SFIO newspaper *Le Populaire* later that month, Laušman similarly disowned the idea that there was no socialism beyond the Stettin–Trieste perimeter. What is more, he took great pains to underline that Czechoslovakia was a modern constitutional democracy. 'Our nation is sufficiently developed and cultured', he insisted, 'not to accept or endure any form of government other than substantive democracy.'[55]

These efforts to disassociate Czechoslovakia and the ČSSD from the Eastern bloc had the desired effect. In his report of the Brno congress, Healey noted how Western delegates had been struck by 'the immediate response' to every mention of democracy and independence. He explained that '[t]he word "democracy"' had 'a great political significance' in Czechoslovakia, 'for example in relation to the factory elections where the Communists have been using terrorism as a weapon'. What was also 'noticeable' was that even the pro-communist wing of the ČSSD 'tried to justify its policy purely on grounds of expediency or necessity while accepting the same principle as the anti-Communist wing'. For '[i]n Poland, Hungary, Italy, indeed even in England', he pointed out, 'the pro-Communist wing tries to justify its attitude in principle and on theoretical grounds'. From the Western perspective, therefore, the Brno congress had been most encouraging. One delegate, marvelled Healey, had even been

---

[53] Quoted in Heumos, *Die Konferenzen*, pp. 155–7.
[54] AAN, PPS, Wydz. Zagraniczny, 235/XIX-43, fos 4–5.
[55] *Le Populaire*, 25 November 1947.

'warmly applauded' for a speech 'in the course of which he went so far as to offer a defence of American foreign policy'.[56]

It was against this backdrop that the socialist parties from East and West came together in late November 1947 for the International Socialist Conference in Antwerp. There were two major items on the agenda of the conference: world peace and international economic reconstruction. Right from the outset, however, the discussions between the parties were overshadowed by the tense international situation.

This became especially clear in the debate about world peace. Opening the deliberations, former Labour Party chair Harold Laski set out the British position. The Labour Party, he declared, understood that the Eastern European socialists had little choice but to work with the communists. What they did ask was for them 'to uphold the principles of democratic socialism' in doing so. As for the international situation, the Labour Party was opposed to the division of Europe and of Germany into rival blocs. But the Marshall Plan, provided that it did not come with political preconditions, represented 'a step towards European independence'. Far from sealing off West from East, after all, it would contribute to the recovery of Europe and the rebalancing of the world economy, from which Eastern Europe would also benefit indirectly. Towards the end of his declaration, Laski turned directly to the Eastern delegations. 'Say what you want about American imperialism', he told them, 'but you cannot say the Labour government is imperialist.' Quite the contrary: 'the achievements of the Labour government represent the best that socialism has produced in any country'.[57]

In the ensuing discussion, the Italian and Polish delegations once more rallied to the defence of the communist-socialist united front. For the PSIUP, Nenni insisted that the resolution would explicitly state 'that we are facing a counter-revolutionary threat'. Apart from Greece and Spain, 'where the counter-revolution is already victorious', that threat was 'strongest in Italy and France'. In these circumstances, he declared, socialists had work towards the 'realisation of [communist–socialist] unity of action on both the national and international levels'. On the international level, that meant siding with the Soviet Union against American intervention in Western Europe. It was impossible, claimed Nenni, 'to see

---

[56] Quoted in Heumos, *Europäischer Sozialismus*, p. 389.
[57] All of the accounts and quotes in the following section (i.e. on the socialist debate on world peace) are drawn from two slightly different protocols (one in German and one in French) of the International Socialist Conference in Antwerp. See IISH, SIA, inventory number 236.

the Marshall Plan in isolation from the Truman Doctrine'. The Truman Doctrine, he went on, 'gives the United States the right to intervene, for political and strategic reasons, in a certain number of countries'. This had 'created an abominable situation in Greece'. To be sure, Nenni conceded that the Soviet Union had also intervened the internal politics of countries in its sphere of influence. From a socialist perspective, however, American and Soviet intervention could not be placed on the same footing. For '[i]n Poland, the Soviet Union has put arms in the hands of the proletariat; in Italy, the United States and Britain have disarmed us'.

This intervention, as Nenni put it himself, 'scandalised' many Western delegations.[58] Max Buset, the leader of the Belgian delegation, accused Nenni of peddling 'half-truths' about the United States. On the Soviet Union, moreover, Buset found himself 'unable to agree with more than a quarter of what Nenni has said'.

But the most severe clash was yet to come. After PPS delegate Kazimierz Rusinek had weighed in with further warnings about American intervention and about the situation in Greece and Spain, Vorrink had heard just about enough. 'Up to this point', he complained, 'I have heard much criticism of the United States and Great Britain, whereas the Soviet Union is apparently beyond reproach.' Vorrink went on to give an account of the 'political repression' he had 'witnessed and heard about' during his recent travels to Eastern Europe. While he understood the 'difficulties' facing the Eastern parties, surely they had to draw a line somewhere. How was it possible, he asked, for them 'to go on like this'?

This elicited an angry response from Hochfeld. The Polish socialists, he admonished, did not wish to be treated like 'poor relations'. Nobody had forced them to work with the communists, after all – they had done so of their own free will. Quoting Engels, Hochfeld went on to argue that 'freedom is the recognition of necessity. For the PPS believed that 'the working class should take power by whatever means [necessary] to implement its reforms'. In doing so, the Polish socialists had been 'good humanists' for having 'taken power with a minimum of bloodshed'.

If the debate on world economic reconstruction was somewhat less contentious, it saw similar rifts open up between the parties. These rifts revolved around two questions: the actual socio-economic approach that the conference resolution would endorse and the broader problem of the Marshall Plan. On the first point, the ČSSD delegation recommended that the resolution call for widespread nationalisations and for a struggle

[58] Nenni, *Diari*, 29 November 1947.

against 'international cartels'. But the Western delegations raised strong objections on both counts. According to the Dutch delegate, 'struggle against the cartels' was no more than a slogan. The British and Belgian delegates, for their part, claimed that there were no cartels that operated outside of governmental control in their countries.[59] As for the question of nationalisations, the Swedish delegate pointed out that his party did 'not consider the nationalisation of industry as a step towards socialism' and demanded that the resolution limit itself to calling for the nationalisation of 'certain key industries'.[60]

Where it was thus the mainstream Western parties seeking to water down the more radical dimensions of the resolution, things were the other way around as far as the Marshall Plan was concerned. The British and Norwegian delegates insisted that the conference come out strongly in favour of the Marshall Plan. The conference served 'a single purpose', argued the Norwegian delegate: '[for us] to get behind this plan and declare that socialist workers welcome it'. The British delegate agreed wholeheartedly, arguing that 'a warm welcome' for the Marshall Plan should be 'at the heart of the resolution'. But the Eastern and Italian delegations took an altogether different view. The Italian delegate warned that the Marshall Plan did not contribute to 'the socialist reconstruction of Europe'. The PSIUP would only be able to support the Marshall Plan, he explained, if it was 'underpinned and accompanied by socialist measures, above all nationalisations'. The Czechoslovakian delegate, who spoke also on behalf of the Hungarian and Polish delegations, was similarly sceptical. Given that the United States Congress would have the final say in the matter, he pointed out, it was far from clear that the Marshall Plan would not come with anti-socialist provisions.[61] For that reason, he called for the Marshall Plan to be placed 'under United Nations auspices so as to assure the neutrality of American aid'.[62]

Even if the ČSSD made common cause with the other Eastern parties in the economic debate, the reference to the United Nations was most telling of its broader approach. In fact, in the second half of 1947, the Czechoslovakian social democrats had increasingly pinned their hopes on economic and political collaboration through the United Nations as a means of counteracting bloc-building.[63] At the Antwerp conference too,

[59] Archiv ČSSD, Fond 71, Karton 117, fo. 94.
[60] AAN, PPS, Wydz. Zagraniczy, 235/XIX-119, fo. 16.
[61] Archiv ČSSD, Fond 71, Karton 117, fos 93–4.
[62] IISH, SIA, inventory number 236.
[63] Cf. 'Socialistické strany a OSN', Archiv ČSSD, Karton 182, fos. 457–67.

avoiding confrontation between the socialists of East and West was the
chief aim of the ČSSD. Its delegate had largely sat silent as the Italian
and Polish delegates outraged the mainstream Western parties during the
debate on world peace, limiting himself to a short statement in which he
distanced the ČSSD from the Cominform manifesto.[64] In the economic
debate, moreover, the ČSSD quickly accepted defeat on the question of
international cartels. As for the Marshall Plan, the Czechoslovakian delegation went along with a Franco-Swedish compromise proposal that stopped
short of mentioning the Marshall Plan by name and called for economic
collaboration between the two halves of the continent.

The PPS and PSIUP delegations, by contrast, were in no such conciliatory mood. Even though the Czechoslovakian delegate had formally
already spoken in his name, the PPS representative in the economic
debate could not resist having another go at the Western socialists over
the Marshall Plan. Far from being a welcome 'step towards the [eco-
nomic] collaboration between the nations of Europe', as the Franco-
Swedish proposal had suggested, he insisted that 'the Paris conference [at
which the sixteen countries that had signed up to the Marshall Plan had
met in July 1947] was the first step towards the capitalist reconstruction
of Europe'. This triggered a further clash with the Belgian and Dutch
delegations. While the Belgian delegate branded the Polish position
'absurd', the Dutch delegate concluded that this constituted further proof
that 'a common language' between socialists from East and West could no
longer be found.[65]

The atmosphere got no better when the full conference reassembled to
discuss and vote on the resolutions on world peace and international economic reconstruction. On behalf of the PPS and the PSIUP, Basso tabled
an amendment to the resolution that had been prepared by the world
peace sub-commission. Introducing the amendment, Basso explained that
the Italian and Polish socialists were 'opposed to the Third Force spirit
among the majority of the parties at this conference'. The 'division of the
world into two camps', he insisted, 'is a fact that we have to acknowledge;
[and] in the current struggle, the communists are the natural allies for
socialists'. The amendment itself, which echoed many of the views that
Nenni had expressed in the debate on world peace, was met by a strong
rebuke from Laski. When the conference proceeded to take a vote on the

[64] 'Protokoll der Internationalen Sozialistischen Konferenz Antwerpen 28. November – 2. December
1947', p. 7. IISH, SIA, inventory number 236.
[65] AAN, PPS, Wydz. Zagraniczy, 235/XIX-119, fo. 15.

amendment, it was defeated by fourteen votes to three – with only the Hungarian, Italian, and Polish delegations voting for it.[66]

With the amendment out of the way, the conference went on to adopt the draft resolution on world peace. It committed the socialist parties to opposing 'any policy directed towards' the creation of 'opposite "blocs"', expressed confidence in the United Nations as 'the only international institution capable of assuring peace', and condemned the situation in Greece and Spain.[67] None of the parties voted against the resolution, but the Dutch, Hungarian, Italian, and Polish delegations did abstain. While the three left-wing parties could no longer bring themselves to support the resolution after their amendment had been voted down, the Dutch delegate denounced the resolution as 'completely one-sided' for failing to criticise the repression in Eastern Europe alongside that in Greece and Spain.[68] Even if the resolution on international economic reconstruction was adopted unanimously in the end,[69] it was thus clear that the post-war international socialist movement was approaching breaking point.

Towards the Split

After the Antwerp conference, the loveless marriage between the left-wing and mainstream socialists lasted for another three months. Although there were no more full International Socialist Conferences during that period, the first meeting of the freshly created COMISCO in January 1948 saw further portents of a pending split. The Prague Coup cemented that process. As the PSIUP and the Eastern European parties were either removed from COMISCO or left the organisation of their own accord, there were two rival international socialist movements for a brief while. But the forced communist–socialist mergers in the East quickly ended that situation, ensuring that what remained of the European socialist movement entered the Cold War more united than it had been for years.

---

[66] 'Protokoll der Internationalen Sozialistischen Konferenz Antwerpen 28. November – 2. December 1947', pp. 20–1. IISH, SIA, inventory number 236.

[67] 'Notes on the Antwerp Conference of Socialist Parties, November 28 – December 1, 1947', LHASC, LPA, LP/ID, Box 13.

[68] 'Protokoll der Internationalen Sozialistischen Konferenz Antwerpen 28. November – 2. December 1947', p. 9. IISH, SIA, inventory number 236.

[69] The Polish delegate had put forward two leftist amendments upon the economic resolution. But '[f]or formal and tactical reasons', i.e. the fact that they would almost certainly be defeated, the PPS delegation decided not to put these amendments to a vote. AAN, PPS, Wydz. Zagraniczy, 235/XIX-19, fo 17.

The drift towards the split had already set in at the Antwerp confer-ence. For the outcome of that conference left socialists from both halves of the continent disillusioned about the prospects of further collabor-ation. The mainstream Western parties were particularly frustrated about the failure to make much progress on the question of the Marshall Plan. These parties now began overtly contemplating a schism. In Antwerp, the Dutch delegation had already 'canvassed the possibility of holding a regional conference restricted to parties which approve the Marshall Plan'.[70] It was the Norwegian Social Democratic Party (DNA) that took these designs to the next level. At a meeting of the Scandinavian social democratic leaderships in December 1947, DNA secretary general Haakon Lie described the Antwerp conference as a 'fiasco'. As long as the Eastern European parties remained part of COMISCO, he concluded, there was little hope of any 'improvement in the conditions for inter-national socialist collaboration'. For that reason, the DNA suggested that the Danish, Norwegian, and Swedish social democrats seize the first meeting of COMISCO the following month to call for a regional con-ference of the Western European socialist parties. In the absence of the meddlesome Eastern European socialists, after all, this conference would finally allow the mainstream Western parties to take an unequivocal stand on such 'current international questions' as the Cominform and the Marshall Plan.[71]

The left-wing socialists had likewise left Antwerp much disillusioned. They were particularly disheartened by the unwillingness, on the part of the mainstream Western parties, to countenance any criticism of the Marshall Plan. Given their uncompromising attitude in Antwerp, it is perhaps not surprising that that the Dutch social democrats bore the brunt of the left-wing condemnation. Vorrink had spoken 'the language of Truman', complained Nenni after the debate on world peace.[72] For the PPS delegation too, the demeanour of the Dutch social democrats demonstrated 'how little they care about socialism' and 'how badly they want the United States to regard the Netherlands as its best debtor'. But if the Dutch certainly took the most strident position, 'the shadow of the dollar' had hung over the entire conference. 'We must fear', warned the report that the PPS delegation drew up, 'that American aid will serve as an

---

[70] 'The Antwerp Conference', LHASC, LPA, LP/ID, Box 13.
[71] Klaus Misgeld, *Sozialdemokratie und Außenpolitik in Schweden. Sozialistische Internationale, Europapolitik und die Deutschlandfrage 1945–1955* (Frankfurt/New York: Campus, 1984), pp. 123–4.
[72] Nenni, *Diari*, 29 November 1947.

economic "Maginot line" for Western Europe ... subduing vigilance and distracting from unpleasant realities'.[73]

What was even more disturbing for the left-wing socialists, though, was what Nenni described as 'the defection of the Czechoslovaks'.[74] At previous International Socialist Conferences, the Eastern European parties had always voted as a bloc on such contentious issues as the readmission of the SPD or the re-establishment of the Socialist International. But in Antwerp, the ČSSD voted first against the Italo-Polish amendment and subsequently in favour the resolution backed by the mainstream Western parties.

For the left-wing socialists, this sudden change of tack had everything to do with the defeat of Fierlinger at the Brno ČSSD congress. As ČSSD chairman, Fierlinger had always maintained excellent relations with the other Eastern European socialist parties. These parties were furious about his dismissal in Brno. Hochfeld, who had represented the PPS at the Brno congress, immediately denounced the election of Laušman and the broader course embarked upon by the ČSSD in a *Robotnik* article. Over the next couple of months, the PPS and the MSzDP would largely cold-shoulder the new centrist ČSSD leadership, while trying to keep in touch with Fierlinger through back channels. This became very clear when a ČSSD delegation, led by new party chairman Laušman, visited the December 1947 PPS congress in Wrocław. On the first day of the congress, the PPS leadership taunted the delegation by having a personal message from Fierlinger read out to the congress. Later that day, just as Laušman finished his fraternal address, a heckler shouted out 'long live Fierlinger!' That night, the official ČSSD delegation quit the congress, leaving but an observer.[75]

In its disavowal of Laušman and the new ČSSD leadership, the PPS had the full support of the Hungarian social democrats. In a letter to his Polish counterpart, MSzDP secretary general Árpád Szakasits assured Cyrankiewicz that he was 'in complete agreement' with the tough line that the PPS had taken vis-à-vis the ČSSD. 'We continue to be in contact with comrade Fierlinger', he pointed out, 'whose work we need to support in the strongest possible terms.' In this respect, he was dismissive of the ČSSD's overtures, probably in an attempt to patch up its relations with the MSzDP and the PPS after Antwerp and Wrocław, for the three parties

---

[73] AAN, PPS, Wydz. Zagraniczy, 235/XIX-116, fos 15, 17.
[74] Nenni, *Diari*, 30 November 1947.
[75] Archief PvdA, Map 2703.

to have a joint meeting in January 1948. Even though left-wing socialists would find themselves in the majority at such a meeting, he argued, it could also 'give way to misunderstandings'. For it might leave 'the mistaken impression' that the MSzDP and the PPS still considered the ČSSD 'a party of the Left'.[76]

Of course, as we have seen, there was nothing sudden about the ČSSD's abandonment of the explicitly left-wing course that it had steered in the wake of the liberation. The replacement of Fierlinger by Laušman, therefore, was the result rather than the cause of a longer process which saw the ČSSD return to its pre-war social democratic roots. The new ČSSD leadership was well aware that this involved a rupture with its erstwhile Eastern allies in the international socialist movement. But that was a price worth paying to strengthen its bonds with the mainstream Western parties. Explaining its decision to go against the PPS at the Antwerp conference, the ČSSD delegation pointed out that it had found Basso's amendment 'unconvincing'. The resolution backed by the mainstream Western parties, on the contrary, corresponded 'fully with the programme and politics of our party'. What had particularly delighted the delegation was its 'rejection of a politics of bloc-building'. The implicit[77] repudiation of the Cominform manifesto also chimed with 'the position taken by our Central Executive Committee'. To be sure, the Czechoslovakian delegation had objected to the resolution explicitly defending Blum from the Cominform attacks, pointing out that his name was still associated with the Munich diktat in Czechoslovakia and that this passage could be used against the ČSSD back home. But even if the ČSSD had found itself 'isolated' in calling for a resolution that did not name names, the delegation had not viewed this as sufficient ground for rejecting the resolution as a whole. For 'the political significance of the resolution' lay very much in the fact that almost 'all Western socialist parties voted for it'.[78]

It was against this backdrop that the pan-European socialist movement met for one last time at the inaugural meeting of COMISCO in January 1948. The meeting was dominated by the question of the Marshall Plan

---

[76] Szakasits to Cyrankiewicz, 23 December 1947, AAN, PPS, 235/xix-144.
[77] The resolution on world peace did not mention the Cominform by name. It did, however, express regret at 'the aggravation of the divisions within the international working class, provoked by the attacks of which democratic socialism has recently been the object. The Conference rejects the attacks on Socialist Parties, particularly those directed against the Socialist Parties of Great Britain and France and against men like Blum and Attlee.' 'Notes on the Antwerp Conference of Socialist Parties, November 28 – December 1, 1947', LHASC, LPA, LP/ID, Box 13.
[78] Archiv ČSSD, Fond 71, Karton 117, fo. 92.

once more. On behalf of the Norwegian social democrats,[79] Lie suggested that there would be a regional conference exclusively for socialist parties supporting the Marshall Plan in March 1948. Thereupon, the Polish delegate retorted that what Lie had proposed did not qualify as a regional conference. The issue at hand was political rather than regional, after all, and the statutes of COMISCO did not allow for separate political conferences. But Lie had come prepared for exactly this, and posited that the Labour Party would call the conference instead.[80] Phillips immediately answered that his party was more than happy to do this, thus presenting the Polish delegation with a fait accompli. Furious at being outmanoeuvred like this, the PPS released a statement that it would call a conference for socialist parties opposed to the Marshall Plan as the meeting broke up.

The international socialist movement had thus all but split in two by early 1948. There was still a third group of parties in continental Europe, however, that refused to accept that the fissure was irreversible. During the COMISCO meeting itself, the Belgian, French, and Swiss delegations had insisted that there was to be an all-party conference devoted to 'Economic Reconstruction in Europe in relation to the Marshall Plan'. At such a conference, explained Grumbach, the Eastern parties 'might be able to agree to a large number of measures, even if they could not carry all of them out'. But none of the socialist parties in the Soviet sphere of influence had any desire to go anywhere near the Marshall Plan. Even the Finnish social democrats, who did not find themselves in nearly as precarious a position vis-à-vis the communists as the Eastern European socialists, were adamant in this respect. In the grand scheme of things, declared the Finnish delegate, it was 'preferable to have economic rather than political difficulties'. Faced with the opposition of both the Eastern and most of the mainstream (north-)Western parties, then, an all-party conference on the Marshall Plan was a non-starter from the beginning.[81]

But even if the Czechoslovakian social democrats had thus little choice but to vote against this particular proposal, they very much shared the broader sentiment of keeping socialists from East and West together. Unlike the Hungarian social democrats, noted Jokel in January 1948, they

[79] Seeking to remain neutral in the emerging struggle between East and West, the Swedish social democrats had been very much opposed to the Norwegian proposals. Much to their dismay, however, the DNA decided to push ahead with the scheme regardless. See Misgeld, *Sozialdemokratie und Außenpolitik*, p. 124.

[80] Lie later explained that he had coordinated this approach with Denis Healey beforehand. See ibid., p. 124.

[81] Steininger, *Deutschland*, p. 92.

wanted nothing to do with the 'politics of splits' pursued by the PPS. The ČSSD had no plans, accordingly, 'to partake in the Warsaw conference [the international conference for socialist parties opposing the Marshall Plan] if that conference represents an attempt to create a left-wing bloc within the international socialist movement'.[82] In these efforts to prevent COMISCO from falling apart, the Czechoslovakian social democrats increasingly seem to have viewed the SFIO as a key partner. Already at the Antwerp conference, the ČSSD delegation had found the French socialists far more willing to engage in ideological discussions about such issues as nationalisations and international cartels than the other mainstream Western parties.[83] As the rift with their Eastern sister parties grew deeper over the months that followed, therefore, the Czechoslovakian social democrats more and more looked towards the SFIO for guidance and support. In early 1948, the ČSSD invited Guy Mollet to their country for top-level talks with the new leadership team.

So it happened that Mollet found himself in Czechoslovakia just as the governmental crisis that led to the Prague Coup got underway. His discussions were understandably dominated by these events and Mollet later declared that he had been 'dumbfounded' by the 'optimism' that the Czechoslovakian social democrats had still exuded.[84] His visit, and the broader course that the ČSSD had steered ever since the Brno congress, nonetheless raised considerable alarm among the Polish socialists. The PPS leadership much feared that the 'rightist elements' at the helm of the ČSSD 'might easily be led astray during the present crisis ... and be tempted to play the role of a "third force"'. For that reason, the PPS decided to send its own (uninvited) delegation to Prague, a week after Mollet's visit, to 'influence the ČSSD Central Committee in the spirit of a leftist-socialist and revolutionary politics'.

The PPS delegation, consisting of four Central Executive Committee members, arrived in Prague in the wake of the resignation of the centre-right ministers from the Czechoslovakian government. Its chief aim, accordingly, was to persuade the ČSSD to take up the communist offer of a new, exclusively communist-socialist government. The delegation first got in touch with Fierlinger and several leading communists. On the second day of its stay, it officially approached the ČSSD leadership and requested a meeting 'with the decision-making people in the party'. Laušman agreed

---

[82] Jokel to Thomassen, 19-01-1948, IISH, Archief PvdA, inventory number 551.
[83] Archiv ČSSD, Fond 71, Karton 117, fo. 95.
[84] CD SFIO, 5 March 1948.

and a joint conference was scheduled for the afternoon of February 22nd. During this conference, the Polish speakers pointed to 'the influence of the Czech crisis on the struggle of Western European workers, particularly in Italy', stressed the need for strong bonds between left-wing socialists in East and West, and warned of the dangers of 'sitting on the fence' and 'playing the Third Force'. The report drawn up by the PPS delegation does not explicate how individual ČSSD leaders responded, but points out that the conference saw several leading social democrats move leftwards and left the right wing around Bernard and Vilím 'clearly isolated'. The delegation even went so far as to claim that the conference exerted 'a decisive influence' upon the subsequent developments within the ČSSD, boasting that its intervention had 'neutralised the influence of Guy Mollet', 'undermined the mood of the ČSSD's extreme right wing, and 'made it easier for the left wing to put the Party onto the right path'.[85] That was very much an overstatement of the visit's impact, as it was communist force rather than socialist persuasion driving events by that stage. But the Prague Coup certainly did see the ČSSD return to the fold of left-wing Eastern socialism.

The Prague Coup also represented a key turning point in the relations between the PSIUP and the mainstream Western socialist parties. These relations had already cooled substantially after the Antwerp conference. The Labour Party, for example, chose not to send a fraternal delegate to the January 1948 PSIUP congress. There were 'various reasons' for this, explained Healey in a confidential letter to the Labour attaché at the British Embassy in Rome, but the first was that 'Morgan Phillips was rather shocked by the line which Nenni and Basso took at Antwerp, which seemed to him more Cominformist than Stalin'. It was not just the Labour Party that had grown increasingly disillusioned with the PSIUP. The 'bulk of the French and Belgian [socialist] Parties', noted Healey, 'would much prefer to treat the PSLI as a fraternal body ... if they could be convinced that the PSLI was in fact a mass party of the Italian working class'.[86]

The Prague Coup was the final straw. Within days, the National Executive of the Labour Party issued a statement noting that the Prague Coup closed 'a period in post-war history'. For 'a nation conceived in the principles of liberty, outstanding in its devotion to parliamentary democracy, has for the second time in ten years fallen victim to aggression from without aided by treachery from within'. The events in Czechoslovakia carried 'a warning

[85] 'Report of the Special Action of the Polish Socialist Party in Prague, 21–25 February 1948', *Cold War International History Project Bulletin*, 11 (1998), pp. 143–8.
[86] Healey to Braine, 23 December 1947, LHASC, LPA, LP/ID, Box 3.

and a lesson', the statement went on, for those 'Democratic Socialists still free to choose their future'. The people of Czechoslovakia, after all, had been 'united alike in their will for friendship with the Soviet Union and in their determination to carry through great social and economic transformations, without sacrificing [the country's] democratic heritage'. But that national unity had been 'shattered in a week' by a 'Communist minority … afraid of defeat in free elections'. What had happened in Prague offered clear evidence that there was no possibility of honest collaboration with the communists: 'slave or enemy – there is no third way'. There could 'no longer' be 'any prevarication' on the question of democracy and socialism, accordingly: 'Socialism is meaningless without democracy … Any attempt to achieve Socialism by means which deny democracy and human rights, particularly by the operation of an all-powerful secret police, must lead inevitably to a dictatorship, indistinguishable in its impact on the common man from Fascism.' For socialist parties, therefore, 'Czechoslovakia is an acid test of sincerity. Those who seek to condone this crime show that they are false to the principles of Democratic Socialism for which the Labour Party stands.'[87]

Condoning the events in Czechoslovakia was of course exactly what the PSIUP leadership did. Upon learning that Basso and Nenni had sent Fierlinger a congratulatory telegram, Healey and Phillips immediately flew to Rome for a last-ditch attempt to talk the Italian socialists out of their alliance with the communists. As these efforts proved hopeless, the Labour Party and the SFIO decided to invite representatives from the PSLI to the International Socialist Conference on the Marshall Plan.[88] A PSIUP delegation, consisting of Rodolfo Morandi and PSIUP international secretary Tullio Vecchietti, did still turn up for the COMISCO meeting that preceded the conference. Morandi launched another 'vicious' attack upon the SFIO, and upon Blum and Mollet in particular. But when the other parties wanted to discuss the Fierlinger telegram, the PSIUP delegation refused and left the meeting.[89]

Thus freed from left-wing interference, the mainstream Western parties passed a resolution that by and large confirmed the split. COMISCO had 'tried consistently to maintain cordial relations between Socialist Parties of all countries', claimed the resolution, 'but it notes that many

[87] *Report of the 47th Annual Conference of the Labour Party held in the Spa Grand Hall, Scarborough, May 17-May 21, 1948* (hereafter: Labour Party Conference Report, 1948) (London: The Labour Party, 1948), p. 23.
[88] 'The Labour Party and Italy', LHASC, LPA, LP/ID, Box 13.
[89] CD SFIO, 24 March 1948.

of them have been forced to submit to communist control or disappear altogether'. The responsibility for the split, therefore, rested squarely 'with the Cominform and with the policies through which the Cominform has tried exclusively to serve the interests of the Soviet Union'. As for the individual socialist parties, the Bulgarian, Hungarian, and Romanian parties had 'excluded themselves' from COMISCO by agreeing to a merger with the communists. The Czechoslovakian social democrats, for their part, had 'clearly shown their desire for independence at their Brno Congress'. But they had been 'betrayed to the Communists by a few of their leaders'. For that reason, COMISCO could no longer accept the ČSSD leadership 'as representative of socialism'. To the PPS and the PSIUP, 'which are at present following the same path to absorption', COMISCO launched 'a final appeal'. It called upon the two parties 'to remain faithful to socialism and democracy, to regain their freedom of action while there is still time'. It was for them 'to prove by their deeds that, faced with the choice between subjection to the Cominform and free socialist cooperation in European reconstruction, they have chosen the socialist way'.[90]

What the Italian and Polish socialists understood by socialism, however, was no longer compatible with the mainstream Western conception. Within days of the COMISCO meeting, the PPS severed its ties with the organisation.[91] In what was probably an attempt to delay the official admission of the PSLI, the Italian socialists preferred to leave their relations with COMISCO in limbo for the time being – waiting for the mainstream Western parties to take disciplinary action against the PSIUP at the June 1948 International Socialist Conference in Vienna.[92] But the fissure was real all the same, and for the next couple of months the PSIUP would be a full member of the PPS-led counter-movement for left-wing socialists. It was the only major Western party to attend the Warsaw conference in May 1948, as relations between the Italian and Polish socialists grew ever closer. During another sojourn in Poland in the summer, Nenni noted how 'the Polish road to socialism is materialising'. He spent some days in the 'recovered territories' in Western Poland, where he visited an exposition on the reconstruction of the region. It was, he explained, 'a remarkable display of what Poland has managed to achieve in this land of the

[90] Labour Party Conference Report, 1948, pp. 24–5.
[91] For the letter with which the PPS withdrew from COMISCO see Heumos, *Europäischer Sozialismus*, pp. 249–51.
[92] On the expulsion of the PSIUP from COMISCO and its arduous way back into the Socialist International see Simona Colarizi, 'I socialisti italiani e l'internazionale socialista: 1947–1958', *Mondo Contemporaneo*, 2 (2005), pp. 1–62.

Oder'. For the exposition had been 'inspired by four grand themes: power to the people, land to the peasants, industry to the nation, [and] culture for the masses'. It had thus exhibited what Nenni described as 'the exploits of the revolution'. In this respect, he concluded, 'the Poles can be particularly proud of themselves'.[93]

Conclusion

By 1948, there were thus two rival visions of socialism in Europe. The first was centrist and reformist, in which socialist parties sought to implement a 'capitalism with a human face' in (coalition) governments.[94] The second was leftist and revolutionary, in which socialist parties worked exclusively with the communists to overturn capitalism altogether.

If the Cold War made sure that these rival visions could no longer co-exist peacefully in one and the same international movement, the divisions between the post-war European socialists were themselves not a consequence of the Cold War. In fact, there was mutual misunderstanding and mistrust right from the outset. The mainstream Western parties had always struggled to reconcile what was happening in Eastern Europe with their ideas of democratic socialism. The notion that the Eastern European socialists were no more than puppets in communist-controlled governments, so prominent in the Western (socialist) press in the wake of the liberation, proved very persistent. As late as December 1945, Pollak had told the Hungarian social democrats in no uncertain terms that they were 'repeating the failures of 1919', having 'surrendered the[ir] party to the communists'.[95] Even about the political situation in Czechoslovakia, widely regarded as 'a bastion of democracy' in the wider region,[96] there was some concern among the Western socialists. A country where the political landscape was to be constitutionally limited to five parties and where there was no parliamentary opposition, noted Vorrink after his August 1946 visit to Czechoslovakia, was 'certainly not a full-fledged democracy'.[97]

The left-wing socialists, for their part, had all along accused the mainstream Western parties of timidity in the face of a resurgent bourgeois and

---

[93] Nenni, *Diari*, 31 July and 2 August 1948.
[94] This was the proclaimed objective of the Swedish Social Democratic Party. Berger, 'Communism, Social Democracy', p. 6.
[95] Heumos, *Europäischer Sozialismus*, p. 431.
[96] Misgeld, *Sozialdemokratie und Außenpolitik*, p. 124.
[97] 'Enkele aantekeningen naar aanleiding van mijn reis naar Tsjecho-Slovakije (27 augustus tot 5 september 1946)', IISH, Archief PvdA, inventory number 2286.

capitalist class. They were often left bewildered by the seeming Western indifference towards such structural economic reforms as nationalisations and land reform. It was with this impression that Vajda had left the December 1945 SPÖ congress. Even if its programme committed the party to nationalisations, he explained, SPÖ secretary general Adolf Schärf had shelved any plans for a state take-over of heavy industry by pointing out that the economic agenda of the SPÖ was rejected by 'the majority of the electorate'. Instead, the SPÖ would focus its efforts as part of the coalition government on the introduction of 'a welfare and administrative state'.[98] For the left-wing socialists, however, the introduction of welfare provisions and other forms of state intervention within the framework of a capitalist economy hardly amounted to the establishment of socialism. In fact, the PSIUP leadership increasingly came to define the interventionist policies pursued by the Labour government as ' "progressive policies", oriented towards a moderate redistribution of income, rather than "socialist policies", directed towards structural changes of class relations'.[99] The PPS was still more scathing about what the mainstream Western socialist parties had achieved in the social and economic realms. In many countries, concluded the report that the PPS delegation drew up after the Antwerp conference, 'socialism is, or aspires to be, no more than a correction upon the capitalist system'. While Labour Britain was 'rigorous in its principles', it was 'flexible in practice'. As for the parties in the continental West, these frequently had 'lovely slogans', but were 'in effect cultivating conservatism'.[100]

The social democratic and reformist template provided by the British and Scandinavian parties, the most successful members of the post-war international socialist movement in electoral terms, thus certainly did not win universal socialist approval. Speaking shortly after the rupture within COMISCO, Basso drew a sharp distinction between his 'democratic socialism' and the 'social democracy' of the mainstream Western socialist parties. Whereas the former aspired to 'open the road to power to the oppressed classes', the latter accepted 'the mastery of the capitalist class and only puts up a fight on the question of the division of income'.[101] To be sure, this was a minority viewpoint within the post-war international socialist movement all along. But to measure the socialist parties

[98]	Heumos, *Europäischer Sozialismus*, p. 427.
[99]	Michele Mioni, 'The Attlee Government and Welfare State Reforms in Post-War Italian Socialism (1945–1951): Between Universalism and Class Policies', *Labor History*, 57/2 (2016), pp. 277–97, 287.
[100]	AAN, PPS, 235/XIX-116, fo. 17.
[101]	'L'ampio discorso polemico del compagno Lelio Basso', *Avanti!*, 29 June 1948. www.leliobasso.it/documento.aspx?id=c8814a5089f7412215291650b35cd957 (last consulted: 27 June 2018).

in post-war continental Europe only by the extent to which they succeeded in emulating the British or Scandinavian model is to distort the debates within and between them. It is very telling that studies employing such a social democratic teleology often mention the French and Italian socialist parties in the same breath.[102] By and large disregarding the very significant divides between these parties during the first decade and a half following the Second World War, such accounts tend to write off both the SFIO and the PSIUP as parties that 'still didn't hear the music and continued to proclaim their dedication to classic, prewar ideological goals such as transcending capitalism entirely'.[103] It is only by extending our thus far exclusively northwards perspective eastwards that we can understand post-war continental socialism in its full complexity.

[102] See e.g. Berman, *The Primacy of Politics*, pp. 192–5; John T. Callaghan, *The Retreat of Social Democracy* (Manchester/New York: Manchester University Press, 2000), p. 18.
[103] Berman, *The Primacy of Politics*, p. 188.

Conclusion

To contemporary socialists, it was perfectly obvious that the eventual dividing lines between 'East' and 'West' did not correspond to the reality on the ground in post-war Europe. In their view, the continent was above all divided between modern and backward countries. This was why the Prague Coup had such enormous reverberations among the mainstream Western socialist parties. Speaking on May Day 1948, Labour prime minister Clement Attlee made clear that Czechoslovakia was nothing like its Eastern bloc neighbours. For when the communists had had recourse to 'force or fraud' in Bulgaria, Hungary, Poland, and Romania, he explained, '[e]xcuses were offered which had a certain plausibility or even validity. It was said that Russia had to ensure that her neighbours were reliable friends. It was said that these countries never had any real democracy.' But the recent events in Czechoslovakia had 'opened the eyes' of many observers. 'Here was no backward State. Here was a country with a fine democratic tradition. Yet because there was a strong possibility that the forthcoming elections would give a majority against the Communists, action was taken and a dictatorship established.'[1]

There were thus certainly two Europes in the wake of the liberation. It was just that these two Europes did not take the shape that we know from more traditional Cold War-centric accounts. Away from the Cold War divide, the two Europes actually faced very similar challenges: fighting off rampant inflation, coming to terms with substantial industrial unrest, and making a success of broad-based governmental coalitions. By analysing the processes of socio-economic and political reconstruction in meticulous detail, more recent studies of individual countries have much enriched our understanding of how politicians in East and West grappled with these challenges.[2] The aims of this book were different. In taking a

---

[1] LPA, LP/ID, Box 13.
[2] Conway, *The Sorrows*; Lewis, *Workers and Politics*; Pittaway, *The Workers' State*; Kenney, *Rebuilding Poland*. See also the essays in Stefan-Ludwig Hoffmann, Sandrine Kott, Peter Romijn, and Olivier

pan-European perspective, which explores the reconstruction effort both from the bottom up and from the top down, it sought to make broader generalisations about the fortunes of the socialist parties in post-war (continental) Europe. In doing so, the book has shed fresh light on the history of post-war European socialism in at least three ways.

In the first place, it has offered an explanation of the political weakness of socialism in post-war continental Europe that is rooted in longer-term socio-economic and political trends. As we have seen, historians have tended to look at the post-war tribulations of the continental socialist parties only through a narrow political prism: either portraying the socialists and their political programmes as victims of the Cold War or faulting the socialists for refusing to abandon their outmoded Marxism. Both of these approaches suffer from serious shortcomings, to which we will return below. What is striking, though, is that such accounts often neglect the more structural changes that the interwar and war years had wrought on the broader social, economic, and political climate in which the continental socialists had to operate. For these changes had certainly not worked to the benefit of socialist parties.

In political terms, the manifold legacies of right-wing dictatorship put socialist parties at a disadvantage vis-à-vis their direct political rivals. Having been at the sharp end of the repression meted out by fascist regimes and their authoritarian predecessors, socialists and communists were already starting from well behind their (centre-)right coalition partners in organisational and personnel terms. And socialist parties, which were less accustomed to underground survival than their communist counterparts and whose tight-knit sub-cultures never really recovered from the blows delivered to them during the interwar years, found it all the harder to make up the lost ground. It was for these reasons, explained Pietro Nenni, that the DC found itself in a 'privileged position' compared with the PSIUP. For when 'we were in prison, in exile, or wound up' under fascism, the Christian democrats still had their 'natural centre of activity in parishes, so that [their organisation] never vanished [completely]'.[3]

In economic terms, the austerity programmes required to rebuild war-ravaged countries put further pressure on socialist parties. To be sure, these programmes had the backing of communists and centre-right parties as well, but socialist parties saw their vote squeezed from two sides as the post-war economic hardships heightened class tensions. This was what Yves Dechezelles was alluding to when he argued that the 'principal reason' for the losses that the SFIO had suffered in the November 1946 parliamentary elections was 'of an economic order'. For the 'worsening of the [economic] situation', he explained, 'renders the antagonisms between the various classes more acute still'.[4] In such circumstances, socialist parties bled support to the main rivals to their left and right. On the one side, the communists often thrived on worker misery, which they could exploit with their penchant for populist campaigns. On the other, the spectre of inflation rallied the (lower) middle classes behind the centre-right. In the final analysis, therefore, the post-war continental socialist parties could not placate one key segment of their electoral coalition without alienating the other. It was only in the transformed economic context of the 1960s that the continental socialists could begin to reassemble this coalition.

If the problems that the socialist parties were facing in the political and economic realms had been caused by forces that were beyond their control, this was certainly not the case for the difficulties they experienced in coming to terms with their war-torn societies. In fact, the socialist elites that returned from exile or emerged from the underground were frequently their own worst enemies in their interactions with the newcomers that had entered public and industrial life before and during the war. These newcomers had brought along a set of demands and interests, often framed around the local community, that socialist leaders neither understood nor respected very much. As a consequence, the post-war socialist parties struggled to find a common language even with a significant part of the working class in their historic heartlands. For there was often a profound disconnect between the worldview of unskilled rural migrants or those employed in the public sector and the ideas espoused by socialist leaders still identifying primarily with the aristocracy of labour of skilled workers in large factories.

Nowhere was this disconnect as marked, or as damaging from an electoral perspective, as in the relations between socialist parties and women. The frail position from which socialist parties, and the post-war Left more generally, suffered among female voters was probably the single-most significant factor contributing to their political weakness.[5] This was linked to

---

[4] CD SFIO, 13 November 1946.
[5] For even if there were significantly more women than men in post-war France, female voters still only made up 47 per cent of the total SFIO electorate during the Fourth Republic. The respective number for the MRP is estimated at between 58 and 62 per cent. See Duchen, *Women's Rights*, p. 39;

the dismissive attitudes that male elites up and down the post-war labour movement took towards women in general and towards female concerns more specifically. For much as socialist leaders publicly professed their support for efforts to get more women involved in politics, party cultures proved most resistant in this regard. Despite repeated calls to give female candidates a decent shot at winning (parliamentary) seats, the percentage of women in the SFIO parliamentary group actually more than halved between 1945 and 1956. Worse, women made up less than 1 per cent of all departmental councillors that the SFIO provided during the Fourth Republic.[6] In a broader sense, female socialist activists were often left with the feeling that their efforts were not being taken seriously within the party. In an open letter to her male comrades, one female PPS activist complained about 'the nearly epidemic habit of patronising and ridiculing us'. 'You can ridicule us as individuals', it went on, 'but ridiculing our contribution to party work is detrimental to all of us.'[7]

The belittling attitudes that male socialist elites adopted towards the female activists within their own ranks were reflected in the attitudes they took towards the bread-and-butter grievances that were formulated by ordinary women in their industrial strongholds. We have seen how socialist leaders tended to dismiss such grievances as pettiness that had its roots in the political backwardness of women. What they did not seem to realise was that their boasts about such political achievements as the nationalisation programme, the introduction of economic planning, or even democracy itself often failed to resonate or backfired among the working-class women who could not get enough food on the table to feed their families. To be sure, socialist leaders had rare moments of lucidity about the unattractiveness of their offer to female voters, usually in the wake of election defeats. When the SFIO National Council met to discuss the disappointing socialist showing in the June 1946 parliamentary elections, Daniel Mayer concluded that '[o]ur propaganda is too abstract. In the future, we will have to talk a bit less about grand principles and a bit more about *ravitaillement*, about small business, and about the everyday affairs of women.'[8] Yet irrespective of whether this outreach to female voters was

---

Richard Vinen, *Bourgeois Politics in France, 1945–1951* (Cambridge/New York: Cambridge University Press, 1995), pp. 46–55.

[6] Noëlline Castagnez, 'La notabilisation du PS-SFIO sous la Quatrième République', *Vingtième Siècle. Revue d'histoire*, 96 (2007), pp. 35–46, 37.

[7] Quoted in Malgorzata Fidelis, *Women, Communism, and Industrialization in Postwar Poland* (Cambridge: Cambridge University Press, 2010), p. 54.

[8] 'Parti Socialiste SFIO. Conseil national du Palais de la Mutualité, 9 juin 1946', FJJ, p. 10.

packaged as socialist propaganda aimed more purposely at women or as efforts to draw women into grassroots discussion bodies, the point was often still to remake women in the image of the 'politically conscious' male proletarian. The ČSSD's campaign to enrol more women into productive work must be seen in this light. For if the struggle for women's rights consisted primarily of 'relieving women of domestic chores so that they could become workers like men' for the Czechoslovakian social democrats (and communists), the programme of the centrist-nationalist ČSNS spoke more directly to the social environment of women by calling for the legal recognition of housekeeping as valuable work.[9]

What this book has demonstrated is that their failure to reconcile themselves to the political, economic, and social consequences of the interwar and war years hurt the prospects of the socialist parties in post-war continental Europe far more than any of the political difficulties they were confronted with after the liberation. Its second contribution to the historiography of post-war European socialism thus lies in its challenge to the Cold War conceptual constructs of 'East' and 'West' that still predominate in this field. Of course, the budding East–West conflict cannot be discounted completely in the post-war histories of the four countries and parties. This is especially true for Poland, where Soviet security forces were a constant presence that intervened decisively in the civil war between the government and the remnants of the wartime underground. If the influence that the superpowers wielded in Czechoslovakia, France, and Italy was not nearly as pervasive, such geo-political turning points as the announcement of the Marshall Plan or the establishment of the Cominform nonetheless had a significant impact on domestic politics in each of the three countries.

As far as post-war socialist leaders were concerned, however, any pressure exerted by the two superpowers paled in comparison with the pressure exerted by forces closer to home. We have seen how the Polish socialists often considered Stalin to be on their side when they went to Moscow to settle their domestic disputes with the communists. The Czechoslovakian social democrats likewise had significantly more confidence in Soviet leaders than in their communist coalition partners. During his mid-1946 visit to Czechoslovakia, Koos Vorrink was told time and again that Stalin had given his personal blessing to a democratic 'Czechoslovakian road to socialism' – with one journalist of the national ČSSD newspaper even claiming that 'Stalin and Molotov are better Czechs than the Czech communists'.[10] If the

---

[9] Feinberg, *Elusive Equality*, p. 197.
[10] 'Enkele aantekeningen naar aanleiding van mijn reis naar Tsjecho-Slovakije (27 augustus tot 5 september 1946)', IISH, Archief PvdA, inventory number 2286.

Italian socialists certainly did not view the United States as a benevolent force, they by no means regarded American meddling as the gravest danger facing Italian democracy. When, on the eve of the Left's removal from the Italian government, the PSIUP Directorate discussed the deterioration of relations within the coalition, Luigi Cacciatore warned his colleagues not 'to lend excessive weight to American pressure'. Insofar as the Americans were pushing for the communists to be removed from the government, he explained, that was because they wanted to see an end to the economic deadlock paralysing the coalition. 'Far more serious' than any American pressure was 'the pressure from the Vatican'.[11]

For each of the four parties, therefore, the foremost threat to socialism and democracy came from within. In fact, the coming of the Cold War did little to change longer-held views about the popular constituencies and political allies upon which socialism could draw and rely. For these views, as we have seen, had deep roots in the national histories and social structures of the four countries. Strengthened by the lived experience of the interwar and war years, it was these views that provided post-war socialist leaders with their main frame of reference in questions of socio-economic and political reconstruction.

The PPS and PSIUP, even if they found themselves in national government for the first time in their existence, essentially remained anti-system parties. Ever since its 'maximalist' wing had defeated its reformist wing in 1912, the PSIUP had by and large rejected a parliamentary road to socialism. When the PSI became the largest force in parliament following the 1919 elections, many elected socialist deputies barely turned up – so confident were they of an imminent proletarian revolution. The subsequent rise of fascism, with the active or tacit support of the right-wing parties and the bourgeoisie, only deepened socialist beliefs that nothing was to be gained from working through the 'bourgeois' institutions. To be sure, the exiled PSI committed to the restoration of parliamentary democracy as a short-term goal upon its reunification with the PSU in 1930, but notions of class struggle were never quite abandoned. In fact, the leaders of the socialist underground within Italy, including Rodolfo Morandi and Lelio Basso, were already infusing more radical ideas around worker self-management and direct democracy into socialist thinking.[12]

---

[11] 'Riunione Direzione' (3 May 1947), ISRT, Fondo Foscolo Lombardi, Partito Socialista Italiano, Direzione Nazionale, Busta 4, Fasc. 21, fo. 16.

[12] Alexander De Grand, *The Italian Left in the Twentieth Century: A History of the Socialist and Communist Parties* (Bloomington: Indiana University Press, 1989), pp. 31–73.

Within the PPS, the move away from a parliamentary and reformist road to socialism came rather later. It was only once the Sanacja regime turned increasingly authoritarian in the late 1920s, and socialists were driven out of the state apparatus, that the party embraced a more radical conception of socialism. Still, much as historians have disputed that the post-war PPS reflected the traditions of Polish socialism,[13] many of the party's attitudes can be traced back to the 1930s. Whether it was by making the first overtures regarding cooperation with the communists, by adopting a new party programme no longer excluding a transitory dictatorship, or by championing grassroots democracy and worker self-management, the interwar PPS was very much on the road towards becoming the post-war PPS.

The ČSSD and the SFIO, conversely, considered themselves part of a system that was worth defending. For both parties, these beliefs had their origins all the way back in the nineteenth century. In its insistence on a robust defence of 'republican' rights and freedoms, the post-war SFIO in many ways reproduced the discourse that the French Left had employed ever since the formation of the Third Republic in 1870. What is meant here is the notion that there were 'two Frances': a Catholic, monarchical, and authoritarian France on the one side and a secular, republican, and democratic France on the other.[14] It was this notion that had prompted the French socialists to seek alliances with non-proletarian parties in the Republican camp following such political calamities as the Dreyfus Affair and the February 1934 Crisis.[15] Of course, the context was fundamentally different during the post-war years, when we might well speak of 'three Frances'. Yet, in the face of the fresh pressure under which the Fourth Republic found itself from 1947 onwards, the SFIO quickly reverted to what it knew best: uniting with moderate and democratic allies against the 'Caesarism'[16] of General De Gaulle and the new foe of Stalinism.

---

[13] See e.g. Norman Davies, *Heart of Europe: The Past in Poland's Present* (Oxford: Oxford University Press, 2001), pp. 75–81.

[14] On the 'two Frances', see Robert Tombs, *France 1814–1914* (London/New York: Longman, 1996), pp. 145–6.

[15] On how the socialists and Radicals pulled together in the face of such crises, see e.g. Daniela Neri-Ultsch, *Sozialisten und Radicaux – eine schwierige Allianz: Linksbündnisse in der Dritten Französischen Republik, 1919–1938* (Munich: Oldenbourg, 2005).

[16] This was how Léon Blum put it when, in October 1947, he claimed that Republican freedoms were under attack from both the Left and the Right: 'There exists a communist danger against personal and civil liberties. But against the same liberties there exists a Caesarist danger of which we must be aware, before which we do not have the right to close our eyes.' Quoted in William I. Hitchcock, *France Restored: Cold War Diplomacy and the Quest for Leadership in Europe, 1944-1954* (Chapel Hill/London: University of North Carolina Press, 1998), p. 85.

If the Czechoslovakian social democrats often drew on a nineteenth-century discourse too, theirs was one of national unity rather than division. In their view, history had pitted an overwhelmingly democratic Czech nation against those forces and movements wanting to impose 'foreign' dictatorial models on it. There were stark echoes of this discourse in a speech that Bohumil Laušman delivered in the wake of the communist victory in the May 1946 parliamentary elections. 'When we talk about socialism', he explained, 'we do not mean a socialism that copies foreign models, but … we have in mind a socialism that springs from our own history … from the spirit of our people and our nation'.[17] As it became increasingly clear that the Czechoslovakian communists were seeking to implement a foreign model of their own, therefore, the post-war ČSSD drew ever closer to the centrist and centre-right parties with which it had historically held up 'Czech' values.

As this book has shown, however, the divergences between the two sets of parties must not be viewed in an exclusively (party-)political context. These divergences also had their origins in the way that socialist leaders looked at their respective societies. The attitudes taken by the ČSSD and the SFIO still revolved around the traditional industrial heartlands of the two parties. Within the SFIO leadership, a distinctly northern perspective, which took a negative view of socio-political radicalism, often prevailed. Already at the November 1944 SFIO congress, Mayer was at pains to put some distance between the SFIO and the factory occupations which had raised the spectre of 'bolshevisation' in central and southern France. If he still paid lip service to the local and provincial socialists who had placed ownerless factories under worker self-management, he immediately added that 'the measures taken … are insufficient [by themselves] and … should be followed by large-scale nationalisations'. What is more, he was quick to point to the 'danger' entailed in the operation. For the experiment of worker self-management was taking place 'in the most unfavourable conditions: raw materials do not arrive on time or at all, there is a lack of fuel, orders cannot be fulfilled, etc.'. It was to be feared, therefore, that the enemies of socialism would try 'to take advantage of these circumstances to make life very difficult for you – in order to show that socialism cannot be implemented [anywhere] because it did not succeed in Allier, in Toulouse,

---

[17] 'Volby a čs. sociální demokracie' (1946), NA, Fonds Bohumil Laušman, III Pisemnosti související s ústřední, veřejnou a politickou činnosti B. Laušmana, Karton 34, Souvicejíci činnosti v soc. dem. 1928–1948, p. 11.

or in Saint-Raphaël'.[18] Over the years to follow, the SFIO leadership would take an increasingly uncompromising line towards those party members or branches challenging its top-down conception of socialism. We have seen how the SFIO Executive clamped down on those local and factory activists who refused to toe the party line during strikes. And in June 1947, the national office of the Young Socialists, which had supported the landmark strike at Renault the previous month, was even dissolved by the SFIO leadership.[19]

A similar process by which the old stalwarts of reformism gradually reasserted control over the party apparatus was clearly underway, until it was cut short by the Prague Coup, within the post-war ČSSD. Here too, the fightback against the brand of radical politics practised by the communists often had its roots in the interwar bastions of 'right-wing social democracy'. It was no coincidence that the first real showdown between communists and social democrats over this politics came in Plzeň, where a moderate and anti-communist branch of the ČSDSD had built up a dominant position during the interwar years. Over time, such branches were to regain the upper hand within the post-war ČSSD. This was to become very clear during the inner-party crisis that was unleashed by the publication of the communist–social democratic Unity Pact in September 1947. For in the power struggle that followed the signing of the pact, the successful movement to replace Zdeněk Fierlinger as ČSSD chairman drew its strength primarily from the traditional working-class bulwarks of Plzeň and Ostrava.

The focal point of the politics of the post-war PPS and PSIUP, by contrast, shifted away from their traditional industrial strongholds and to the rural communities where elections were won and lost. Much of what was distinctive about their agenda was aimed specifically at educating the peasantry. The struggles that the Polish socialists fought for the survival of the cooperative movement were part and parcel of their 1944 promise to deliver a 'socialism for the working and peasant class'.[20] For not only did they envision cooperatives playing a vital role in the exchange of products between city and countryside, they also attributed great virtues

---

[18] 'Parti Socialiste – SFIO: Congrès national extraordinaire des 9, 10, 11 et 12 novembre 1944', FJJ, p. 213. http://62.210.214.184/cg-ps/documents/pdf/cong-1944-11-09.pdf (last consulted: 27 June 2018).

[19] See, on the post-war Young Socialists, Jean-Jacques Aymé, *Jeunesses Socialistes, 1944–1948* (Nantes: Amalthée, 2008).

[20] Michał Śliwa, 'Tendencje w socjalistycznej myśli agrarnej w Polsce', in Andrzej Jaeschke, Michał Śliwa, and Barbara Stoczewska, *Z dziejów polskiej myśli socjalistycznej* (Warsaw: Państwowe Wydawn. Nauk., 1985), pp. 21–38, 38.

to cooperative practices in winning over backward peasants to democracy and socialism. The attitudes taken by the Italian socialists were likewise formulated with an express view to politicising the rural masses in the backward south. In fact, it was with reference to this effort that Basso defended the policy of forming electoral blocs with the communists. 'In the south', he explained, 'we have a rural population that is politically uneducated, which identifies not with political parties but with the general interests of its class'. In these circumstances, a socialist-communist bloc had 'proved efficient'.[21]

The social rootedness of the divides between the continental parties has, however, largely been lost on the (comparative) history of post-war European socialism. This strand of historiography is still dominated by an idealist and teleological approach, which weighs the continental socialist parties first and foremost by the extent to which they co-opted key elements of a social democratic programme around anti-communism, reformism, and the embrace of parliamentary democracy. In accounts adopting this approach, the continental parties always come up short on one or more of these counts. This book, conversely, has ventured to address the socialist parties on the post-war continent in their own right, without preconceived ideas about the overall direction in which socialism should be heading. Its third contribution to scholarship on the post-war continental socialist parties therefore lies in its critical interrogation of the dominant paradigm that sees the history of European socialism as progressing in an essentially straight line from Bebel to Blair.[22]

As we have seen, the post-war era occupies a special place in this particular narrative. For this was supposedly the period when the continental socialist parties definitely abandoned their reservations about 'bourgeois' parliamentary democracy and started working towards piecemeal reforms within the context of the capitalist system. In academic work on the theme, this sea change is often traced back to the lessons that socialists had drawn from recent history.[23] With the fateful socio-political upheavals of the interwar years fresh in mind, the post-war socialist parties were desperate to form alliances across class boundaries. In many countries, this involved close collaboration with Catholic and/or Christian democratic parties in a system of corporatist decision-making. Their 'post-war consensus' around

---

[21] IISH, SIA, inventory number 235.
[22] I am indebted to one of the two anonymous reviewers for this formulation.
[23] Escalona, Vieira, and De Waele, 'Unfinished History', pp. 14–17; Berger, 'Democracy', pp. 26–7.

'the values of capitalism and democracy' has thus frequently been described as a natural consequence of the experience of totalitarianism and war.[24]

This book has demonstrated that the socialist conversion to a reformist and parliamentarist politics was anything but a self-evident or uncontested affair. In fact, it has pointed out that the lessons that the European socialists drew from the interwar and war years were far from uniform. That is not to argue that the concept of the 'post-war consensus' has no explanatory value. It certainly captures the post-war political landscape in several European countries quite well. Yet it is important to remember that the post-war consensus only had limited reach. Consensus politics worked wonders in countries like Austria,[25] where Left and Right were roughly equally strong and where socialist–Catholic collaboration seemed to offer the only way forward after the violent struggles of the 1930s. But in countries like Italy and Hungary, where communists and socialists barely scraped together one-third of the popular vote, there was really no electoral basis for the Right to meet the Left halfway. Small wonder that socialists in such countries had few illusions about a parliamentary road to socialism.

These political outcomes were, in turn, closely linked to prevailing societal relations. For in countries with large, and frequently illiterate, peasant majorities, the domination of church and clergy in the countryside put Catholic and conservative forces at a huge advantage vis-à-vis the parties of the working class. In such circumstances, there was little potential for consensus politics to take hold. But in countries where the industrial proletariat, if certainly not finding itself in the majority, could at least join forces with the lower middle classes to form a credible counterweight to the agrarian and bourgeois classes, the Left tended to be strong enough to demand a place at the negotiating table. The post-war consensus, therefore, was only available to that part of the continent that was at least relatively modern, industrial, and urbanised.

All of this goes to show that the European socialist parties could hardly start from a blank slate in 1945. This is what makes the repeated historiographic attempts, especially in English-language literature, to apply universal models to the history of post-war continental socialism so problematic. Such accounts frequently suggest that there were clear templates for the post-war continental socialists to follow. The British Labour Party

[24] See e.g. Tony Judt, *Postwar: A History of Europe since 1945* (London: Penguin Press, 2005), pp. 256–65; Vinen, *A History*, pp. 358–404.
[25] In history textbooks, post-war Austria is often held up as the poster boy of the post-war consensus. For a more detailed analysis, see Günter Bischof and Anton Pelinka (eds.), *Austro-Corporatism: Past, Present, Future* (New Brunswick, NJ: Transaction Publishers, 1996).

had just shown the way, after all, by winning an overall majority on a manifesto that reached out to non-proletarian sections of the population. In Scandinavia, meanwhile, the social democrats dominated governments for decades on end by making their peace with capitalism and focusing their energies on building a welfare state. That the continental socialist parties did not manage to emulate these successes and never quite made it past the 30 per cent mark in electoral terms, these historians attribute to their struggles with 'the vestiges of Marxist teleology'.[26] If only the continental socialists had abandoned their revolutionary fantasies earlier, conservatives and Catholics could not have 'gotten a jump on them'[27] to become the dominant force in post-war European politics.

In its fixation on universal models, however, the (English-language) historiography of post-war European socialism has underestimated the tenacity of national political cultures.[28] To be sure, its landslide election victory had won the Labour Party enormous international prestige, with even some centrist and Catholic parties looking to emulate its success in becoming a catch-all party for working people.[29] But to take up the teachings of the British or Scandinavian roads to socialism was by no means a guarantee for success. The Dutch PvdA went to great lengths to model itself after the Labour Party, but the longed-for electoral breakthrough failed to materialise.[30] When Mayer was replaced by Guy Mollet as secretary general of the SFIO, moreover, his *travaillisme à la française*[31] had already failed to deliver success at two parliamentary elections. Much as historians have derided Mollet's decision to take the SFIO back to its traditional Marxist comfort zones, it is worth remembering that when the

---

[26] Orlow, *Common Destiny*, p. 4.

[27] Berman, *The Primacy of Politics*, p. 188.

[28] I have dealt with the non-applicability of the British and Scandinavian models to the continental socialist parties in far greater detail in Jan De Graaf, 'The Golden Age and Its Malcontents: Continental Socialists facing the British and Scandinavian Models', *Austrian Journal of Historical Studies/Österreichische Zeitschrift für Geschichtswissenschaften*, 29/1 (2018), pp. 111–124.

[29] Dieter A. Binder, for example, has argued that the Labour Party, along with the Hungarian Smallholders' Party, was the most important template for the post-war (Catholic) Austrian People's Party – with the party going so far as to present itself as 'Austria's Labour Party' during the campaign for the 1945 parliamentary elections. See Dieter A. Binder, ' "Rescuing the Christian Occident" and "Europe in US": The People's Party in Austria', in Michael Gehler and Wolfram Kaiser (eds.), *Christian Democracy in Europe Since 1945*, Vol. 2 (London/New York: Routledge, 2004), pp. 139–54, 139.

[30] On the post-war PvdA and the idea of an electoral breakthrough: Bram Mellink, 'Tweedracht maakt macht. De PvdA, de doorbraak en de ontluikende polarisatiestrategie (1946–1966)', *Bijdragen en Mededelingen betreffende de Geschiedenis der Nederlanden*, 126/2 (2011), pp. 30–53.

[31] Pascal Delwit, 'Partis et système de partis en France de 1945 à nos jours', in Pascal Delwit (ed.), *Les partis politiques en France* (Brussels: Éditions de l'Université de Bruxelles, 2014), pp. 7–33, 10–12.

French socialists finally did win an overall majority in 1981, they did so on an explicitly left-wing programme.

Much as they would come to loathe Mollet and the SFIO, the Italian and Polish socialists completely agreed that the road to socialism had to tap into national traditions and histories. When they cited the British or Scandinavian experiences, accordingly, it was often to point out that that model was simply not applicable to their countries. Speaking at the International Socialist Conference in Antwerp, Julian Hochfeld made quite clear that British prescriptions would never lead to socialism in countries like Poland. For whereas it was 'possible to take a democratic road to socialism' in Britain, this was 'not the case in countries where the fascist threat is still strong'.[32] Most PSIUP leaders were equally dismissive of claims that the British or Scandinavian models carried any lessons for their party and country. Giuseppe Saragat and his followers certainly liked to raise these models as evidence that socialism thrived there where it was not associated with communism.[33] Yet Sandro Pertini spoke for the majority when he argued that 'an educated man' like Saragat would do better to base his views on 'the objective Italian situation' rather than on that 'in Britain and [some] other countries'. For, contrary to Saragat's claims that Labour's landslide showed that there was 'no longer a danger of a violent return of the reaction', the reality was that 'we are emerging from a dictatorship imposed by violence, Germany is emerging from a dictatorship imposed by violence, and a dictatorship imposed by violence still exists in Spain'.[34]

It was thus primarily from the experiences of countries that had also suffered through (or were still suffering through) prolonged periods of right-wing authoritarian or fascist dictatorship – Austria, Germany, Hungary, Spain, and increasingly also Greece – that the post-war PPS and PSIUP drew their inspiration. By placing the Italian and Polish socialists in this broader European context, we can arrive at a far better understanding of what drove the two parties. For there is little point in only weighing the PSIUP against its (north-)Western European counterparts, often countries with completely different socio-economic and political backgrounds, and then dismissing it as an anomaly. By the same token, we cannot fully explain the politics of the Czechoslovakian social democrats without

---

[32] Quoted in Steininger, *Deutschland*, p. 293.
[33] Ennio Di Nolfo, *La Repubblica delle speranze e degli inganni: l'Italia dalla caduta del fascismo al crollo della Democrazia cristiana* (Florence: Ponte alle grazie, 1996), p. 232.
[34] Quoted in Stefano Caretti (ed.), *Sandro Pertini. Dal delitto Matteotti alla Costituente. Scritti e discorsi: 1924–1946* (Manduria: Lacaita, 2008), p. 149.

reference to the Western democratic tradition they so cherished. If we really want to make sense of post-war European socialism and, by extension, post-war Europe as a whole, we have to transcend the Iron Curtain that still exists in historiography.

In doing so, as this book has demonstrated, we always have to start from the social realities that underlie politics. Just how strong an imprint social structures left on political life became painfully obvious after the PSIUP finally broke with the PCI in the late 1950s. As the PSIUP tentatively started to make its way back into the international socialist movement, it hosted a delegation of the Norwegian DNA in Rome. But even ten years into the Cold War, with all of its homogenising effects, the two parties still seemed to be living in completely different worlds. 'They talk about class struggle and Marxism like we used to do thirty years ago', noted Haakon Lie, who led the Norwegian delegation; 'perhaps that is because their socio-economic situation resembles that of us back then'.[35]

---

[35] Quoted in Giovanni Scirocco, *Politique d'Abord: Il PSI, la Guerra Fredda e la Politica Internazionale, 1948–1957* (Milan: Edizione UNICOPLI, 2010), p. 264.

Bibliography

A UNPUBLISHED DOCUMENTS

The Czech Republic

Archiv České Strany Sociálně Demokratické, Prague (Archiv ČSSD)
  Fond č. 71
Archiv Města Plzně, Plzeň (AMP)
  Zápisy o schůzich Národního Výboru a rady Okresního Národního Výboru
    a Místního Národního Výboru statutárního města Plzeň 1945
  Zápisy o schůzich rady Místního Národního Výboru statutárního města
    Plzeň 1946/1
Archiv Narodního Muzea, Prague (ANM)
  Fonds Zdeněk Fierlinger
Narodní Archiv, Prague (NA)
  Fonds Bohumil Laušman
Státní Oblastní Archiv v Plzni, Plzeň (SOA Plzeň)
  Fonds Krajský Výbor KSČ Plzeň
Všeodborový Archiv – ČMKOS, Prague (VA)
  Krajské Odborové Rady 1945–1960
  Organizační oddělení ÚRO

France

Archives Departmentales du Nord, Lille (ADN)
  Commissariat Régional de la République
Archives Nationales du Monde du Travail, Roubaix
  Fonds CGT Lever à l'usine de Haubourdin
Centre d'Histoire des Sciences Po, Paris (CHSP)
  Fonds Daniel Mayer
Centre d'Histoire Social, Paris (CHS)
  Fonds Marceau Pivert

Fondation Jean Jaurès, Paris (FJJ)
'Parti Socialiste – SFIO: 37ème Congrès national des 11, 12, 13, 14 et 15 août 1945'
'Parti Socialiste SFIO: 38ème Congrès national, 29, 30, 31 août et 1er septembre 1946'
'Parti Socialiste – SFIO: 39ème Congrès national des 14 au 17 août 1947 (partie 2)'
'Parti Socialiste – SFIO: Congrès national extraordinaire des 9, 10, 11 et 12 novembre 1944'
'Partit Socialiste SFIO: Conseil national 3 et 4 décembre 1946'
'Parti Socialiste – SFIO: Conseil national des 16 et 17 décembre 1947'
'Parti Socialiste – SFIO: Conseil National du mardi 6 mai 1947'
'Parti Socialiste – SFIO. Conseil national du Palais de la Mutualité, 9 juin 1946'
'Programme d'Action du Parti Socialiste'
Office Universitaire de Recherche Socialiste, Paris (OURS)
Compte rendu des débats du Comité Directeur, 1944–1969, 26 February 1945
'Procès-verbaux des réunions du Comité Directeur du congrès de Paris, 9–12 novembre 1944 au 37e congrès national, 11–15 août 1945'

Italy

Archivio Centrale dello Stato, Rome (ACS)
Carteggio Nenni
Archivio del Lavoro, Milano (AdL)
Camera del Lavoro
Fondazione di Studi Storici Filippo Turati, Firenze (FFT)
Partito socialista italiano (Psi) – Direzione nazionale
Fondazione Lelio e Lisli Basso Isocco, Rome (FLB)
Fondo Lelio Basso
Fondazione Nenni, Rome (FN)
Carteggio Nenni
Istituto Nazionale per la Storia del Movimento di Liberazione in Italia, Milano (INSMLI)
Fondo CLN Regionale Lombardia
Fondo Lia Bellora
Istituto Storico della Resistenza in Toscana, Florence (ISRT)
Fondo Foscolo Lombardi

The Netherlands

International Institute of Social History, Amsterdam (IISH)
Archief Partij van de Arbeid
Socialist International Archives
Nationaal Archief, The Hague
Archief Ministerie van Buitenlandse Zaken

Poland

Archiwum Akt Nowych, Warsaw (AAN)
Akta Stanislawa Szwalbego
Fonds Henryk Wachowicz
Polska Partia Socjalistyczna
Archiwum Panstwowe w Łodzi, Łódź (APŁ)
DK PPS Czerwona
DK PPS Fabryczna
DK PPS Górna
DK PPS Ruda Pabianicka
DK PPS Śródmieście Lewa
DK PPS Śródmieście Prawa
DK PPS Tramwaje
Wojewódzki Komitet PPS w Łodzi

United Kingdom

Labour History Archive and Study Centre, Manchester (LHASC)
Labour Party Archives

B PUBLISHED DOCUMENTS

Blum, Léon, *Les devoirs et les tâches du socialisme: Discours prononcé à la Conférence des Secrétaires de Fédérations Socialistes Paris, le 20 Mai 1945* (Paris: Éditions de la Liberté, 1945).

Caretti, Stefano (ed.), *Sandro Pertini. Dal delitto Matteotti alla Costituente. Scritti e discorsi: 1924–1946* (Manduria: Lacaita, 2008).

Heumos, Peter (ed.), *Europäischer Sozialismus im Kalten Krieg: Briefe und Berichte, 1944–1948* (Frankfurt am Main: Campus Verlag, 2004).

(ed.), *Die Konferenzen der sozialistischen Parteien Zentral- und Osteuropas in Prag und Budapest 1946 und 1947* (Stuttgart: Franz Steiner, 1985).

Hochfeld, Julian, *My socjalisci: Ze stanowiska socjalistycznego realizmu* (Warsaw: Spółdzielnia Wydawnicza Wiedza, 1946).

Jędruszczak, Hanna, *Wizje gospodarki socjalistycznej w Polsce, 1945–1949: Początki planowania* (Warsaw: Państwowe Wydawnictwo Naukowe, 1983).

Nenni, Pietro, *Tempo di Guerra Fredda. Diari 1943–1956* (Milan: Sugarco, 1981).

Neri Serneri, Simone (ed.), *Il Partito Socialista nella Resistenza: I documenti e la stampa clandestina (1943–1945)* (Pisa: Nistri-Lischi, 1988).

Neri Serneri, Simone, Casali, Antonio, and Errera, Giovanni (eds.), *Scritti e discorsi di Sandro Pertini: Volume I, 1926–1978* (Rome: Presidenza del Consiglio dei Ministri, Dipartimento per l'Informazione e l'Editoria, 1992).

Report of the 47th Annual Conference of the Labour Party held in the Spa Grand Hall, Scarborough, May 17–May 21, 1948 (London: The Labour Party, 1948).

'Report of the Special Action of the Polish Socialist Party in Prague, 21–25 February 1948', *Cold War International History Project Bulletin*, 11 (1998), pp. 143–8.

Zpráva o činnosti Československé sociální demokracie k XXI řádnému sjezdu v Brně 14.–16. XI. 1947 (Prague: Československá Sociální Demokracie, 1947).

C NEWSPAPERS AND PERIODICALS

Avanti!
Avanti! (Milanese edition)
Bollettino dell'Istituto di Studii Socialisti
Cíl
Ill Giornale dell'Emilia
La Revue Socialiste
Le Marteau Piqueur: Feuille de propagande du Groupe socialiste des Mines de Ledoux
Le Populaire
Nový Den
Orientamenti: Bollettino di Commento e di Indirizzo Politico
Právo Lidu
Przegląd Socjalistyczny
Quaderni di Giustizia e Libertà
Quarto Stato
Sesto Proletaria
Socialismo
Tribune

D ONLINE RESOURCES

Léon Blum, 'Construire l'Europe pour aller vers le socialisme', 9 April 1948. www.lours.org/archives/defaultacae.html?pid=373.

E LITERATURE

Abrams, Bradley F., *The Struggle for the Soul of the Nation: Czech Culture and the Rise of Communism* (Lanham, MD: Rowman & Littlefield, 2004).
'The Second World War and the East European Revolution', *East European Politics and Societies*, 16/3 (2002), pp. 623–64.
'Who Lost Czechoslovakia? Reconsidering the Communist Takeover 50 Years Later', *Intermarium Online Journal*, 3/3 (1999), pp. 1–13. www.columbia.edu/cu/ece/research/intermarium/vol3no3/abrams.pdf.
Agnew, Hugh, *The Czechs and the Lands of the Bohemian Crown* (Stanford, CA: Hoover Institution Press, 2004).
Agosti, Aldo, *Palmiro Togliatti: A Biography* (Oxford/New York: I.B. Tauris, 2008).
Rodolfo Morandi: Il pensiero e l'azione politica (Bari: Laterza, 1971).
Ahmad, Qasim, *Britain, Franco Spain and the Cold War, 1945–1950* (New York: Garland, 1992).
Andrieu, Claire, 'La France à gauche de l'Europe', *Le Mouvement Social*, 134 (1986), pp. 131–53.

Le programme commun de la Résistance: Des idées dans la guerre (Paris: Éditions de l'Érudit, 1984).

Aymé, Jean-Jacques, *Jeunesses Socialistes, 1944–1948* (Nantes: Amalthée, 2008).

Bailey, Christian, 'The European Discourse in Germany, 1939–1950: Three Case Studies', *German History*, 28/4 (2010), pp. 453–78.

Baker, Donald N., 'The Socialists and the Workers of Paris: The Amicales Socialistes, 1936–1940', *International Review of Social History*, 24/1 (1979), pp. 1–33.

Bäcker, Roman, *Problematyka państwa w polskiej myśli socjalistycznej lat 1918–1948* (Toruń: Wydawnictwo Uniwersytet Mikołaja Kopernika, 1994).

Histoire politique de la France depuis 1945 (Paris: A. Colin, 1996).

Behan, Tom, *The Long Awaited Moment: The Working Class and the Italian Communist Party in Milan, 1943–1948* (New York: P. Lang, 1997).

'"Riding the Tiger": The Italian Communist Party and the Working Class of the Porta Romana Area of Milan, 1943–1948', *The Italianist*, 10 (1990), pp. 111–50.

Berger, Stefan, 'Communism, Social Democracy and the Democracy Gap', paper presented at international workshop 'The International Labour Movements on the Thresholds of Two Centuries' in Flemingsberg (Sweden), October 2002. www.arbark.se/pdf_wrd/berger_int.pdf.

'Democracy and Social Democracy', *European History Quarterly*, 32/1 (2002), pp. 13–37.

Bergounioux, Alain, 'Socialisme français et social-démocratie européenne', *Vingtième siècle, revue d'histoire*, 65 (2000), pp. 97–108.

Bergounioux, Alain, and Grunberg, Gérard, *L'ambition et les remords: Les socialistes français et le pouvoir (1905–2005)* (Paris: Fayard, 2005).

Le long remords du pouvoir: Le Parti socialiste français 1905–1922 (Paris: Fayard, 1992).

Berman, Sheri, *The Primacy of Politics: Social Democracy and the Making of Europe's Twentieth Century* (Cambridge/New York: Cambridge University Press, 1995).

Berstein, Serge, 'French Power as Seen by the Political Parties after World War II', in Josef Becker and Franz Knipping (eds.), *Power in Europe: Great Britain, France, Italy, and Germany in a Postwar World, 1945–1950* (Berlin/New York: De Gruyter, 1986), pp. 163–84.

Bessel, Richard, 'Establishing Order in Post-War Eastern Germany', *Past and Present*, Supplement 6 (2011), pp. 139–57.

Béthouart, Bruno, 'Le MRP, un nouveau partenaire', in Serge Berstein, Frédéric Cépède, Gilles Morin and Antoine Prost (eds.), *Le Parti socialiste entre Résistance et République* (Paris: Publications de Sorbonne, 2000), pp. 257–68.

Binder, Dieter A., '"Rescuing the Christian Occident" and "Europe in US": The People's Party in Austria', in Michael Gehler and Wolfram Kaiser (eds.), *Christian Democracy in Europe Since 1945*, Vol. 2 (London/New York: Routledge, 2004), pp. 139–54.

Bischof, Günter, and Pelinka, Anton (eds.), *Austro-Corporatism: Past, Present, Future* (New Brunswick, NJ: Transaction Publishers, 1996).

Boehling, Rebecca, *A Question of Priorities: Democratic Reforms and Economic Recovery in Postwar Germany: Frankfurt, Munich, and Stuttgart under U.S. Occupation, 1945–1949* (Providence, RI: Berghahn Books, 1996).

Bösch, Frank, *Die Adenauer-CDU: Gründung, Aufstieg und Krise einer Erfolgspartei 1945–1969* (Stuttgart: Deutsche Verlags-Anstalt, 2001).

Braunthal, Julius, *Geschichte der Internationale*, Vol. 3 (Hanover: J.H.W. Dietz, 1971).

Buton, Philippe, 'L'éviction des ministres communistes', in Serge Berstein and Pierre Milza (eds.), *L'Année 1947* (Paris: Presses de Sciences Po, 2000), pp. 339–55.

Cabada, Ladislav, 'Vztahy sociálních demokratů a komunistů v období první a druhé Československé republiky', in Hynek Fajmon, Stanislav Balík, and Kateřina Hloušková (eds.), *Dusivé objetí: historické a politologické pohledy na spolupráci sociálních demokratů a komunistů* (Brno: Centrum pro Studium Demokracie a Kultury, 2006), pp. 14–24.

Cafagna, Luciano, *Una strana disfatta: La parabola dell'autonomismo socialista* (Venice: Marsilio, 1996).

Callaghan, John T., *The Retreat of Social Democracy* (Manchester/New York: Manchester University Press, 2000).

Caridi, Paola, and Di Nolfo, Ennio, *La scissione di palazzo Barberini: la crisi del socialismo italiano, 1946–1947* (Napoli: Edizioni Scientifiche Italiani, 1990).

Cartier, Emmanuel, 'The Liberation and the Institutional Question in France', in Andrew Knapp (ed.), *The Uncertain Foundation: France at the Liberation, 1944–1947* (Basingstoke/New York: Palgrave Macmillan, 2007), pp. 23–40.

Castagnez, Noëlline, 'La notabilisation du PS-SFIO sous la Quatrième République', *Vingtième Siècle. Revue d'histoire*, 96 (2007), pp. 35–46.

Churaň, Milan, *Kdo byl kdo v našich dějinách ve 20. století* (Prague: Libri, 1994).

Ciesielski, Stanisław, 'Spory wokół koncepcji socjalistycznego humanizmu w latach 1946–1947', *Dzieje Najnowsze*, 16 (1984), pp. 21–44.

Clark, Martin, *Modern Italy 1871–1995* (London/New York: Longman, 1996).

Colarizi, Simona, 'I socialisti italiani e l'Internazionale Socialista: 1947–1958', *Mondo Contemporaeno*, 1/2 (2005), pp. 1–62.

Conway, Martin, 'The Age of Christian Democracy. The Frontiers of Success and Failure', in Thomas Kselman and Joseph Buttigieg (eds.), *European Christian Democracy: Historical Legacies and Comparative Perspectives* (Notre Dame, IN: University of Notre Dame Press, 2003), pp. 43–67.

'The Rise and Fall of Western Europe's Democratic Age, 1945–1973', *Contemporary European History*, 13/1 (2004), pp. 67–88.

The Sorrows of Belgium: Liberation and Political Reconstruction, 1944–1947 (Oxford/New York: Oxford University Press, 2012).

Courtois, Stéphane, and Lazar, Marc, *Histoire du Parti communiste français* (Paris: Aubier, 1992).

Coutouvidis, John, and Reynolds, Jaime, *Poland 1939–1947* (New York: Holmes & Meier, 1986).

Dale, Gareth, *Popular Protest in East Germany, 1945–1989* (London/New York: Routledge, 2005).

Davies, Norman, *Heart of Europe: The Past in Poland's Present* (Oxford: Oxford University Press, 2001).

De Felice, Renzo, *Rosso e nero* (Milan: Baldini & Castoldi, 1995)

Degl'Innocenti, Maurizio, *Storia del PSI. III, Dal dopoguerra ad oggi* (Rome/ Bari: Laterza, 1993).

De Graaf, Jan, 'European Socialism between Militant and Parliamentary Democracy: A Pan-European Debate, 1945–9', *European Review of History/ Revue européenne d'histoire*, 26 (forthcoming). www,tandfonline.com/doi/ful l/10.1080/13507486.2018.1491530.

'The Golden Age and Its Malcontents: Continental Socialists facing the British and Scandinavian Models', *Austrian Journal of Historical Studies/ Österreichische Zeitschrift für Geschichtswissenschaften*, 29/1 (2018), pp. 111–24.

'More than Canteen Control: Italian and Polish Socialists Confronting Their Workers, 1944–1947', *International Review of Social History*, 59/1 (2014), pp. 71–98.

'Old and New Democracy: Placing the Italian Anomaly in a European Context', in Jens Späth (ed.), *Does Generation Matter? Progressive Democratic Cultures in Western Europe, 1945–1960* (Cham: Palgrave Macmillan, 2018), pp. 151–70.

'Outgrowing the Cold War: Cross-Continental Perspectives on Early Post-War European Social Democracy', *Contemporary European History*, 22/2 (2013), pp. 331–342.

' "The Usual Psychological Effects of a Shotgun Wedding". British Labour and the Socialist Parties in Eastern Europe, 1945–1948', *Bohemia*, 50/1 (2010), pp. 138–62.

De Grand, Alexander, *The Italian Left in the Twentieth Century: A History of the Socialist and Communist Parties* (Bloomington: Indiana University Press, 1989).

' "To Learn Nothing and to Forget Nothing": Italian Socialism and the Experience of Exile Politics', *Contemporary European History*, 14/4 (2005), pp. 539–58.

Delwit, Pascal, 'Partis et système de partis en France de 1945 à nos jours', in Pascal Delwit (ed.), *Les partis politiques en France* (Brussels: Éditions de l'Université de Bruxelles, 2014), pp. 7–33.

Devin, Guillaume, *L'Internationale Socialiste. Histoire et sociologie du socialisme international (1945–1990)* (Paris: Fondation Nationale des Sciences Politiques, 1993).

Diamond, Hannah, 'Miners, Masculinity and the "Bataille du Charbon" in France 1944–1948', *Modern & Contemporary France*, 19/1 (2011), pp. 69–84.

Di Nolfo, Ennio, *La Repubblica delle speranze e degli inganni: l'Italia dalla caduta del fascismo al crollo della Democrazia cristiana* (Florence: Ponte alle grazie, 1996).

Di Scala, Spencer, *Renewing Italian Socialism: Nenni to Craxi* (Oxford: Oxford University Press: 1988).

Duchen, Claire, *Women's Rights and Women's Lives in France, 1944–1968* (London: Routledge, 1994).

Eley, Geoff, *Forging Democracy: The History of the Left in Europe, 1850–2000* (Oxford/New York: Oxford University Press, 2002).

'Legacies of Antifascism: Constructing Democracy in Postwar Europe', *New German Critique*, 67 (1996), pp. 73–100.

Elgey, Georgette, *Histoire de la IVe République: La République des illusions 1945–1951* (Paris: Fayard, 1965).

Ellwood, David, *Rebuilding Europe: Western Europe, America and Postwar Reconstruction* (London/New York: Longman, 1992).

Elzinga, D.J., and Voerman, Gerrit, *Om de stembus: verkiezingsaffiches 1918–1998* (Amsterdam: Veen; 2002), pp. 84–91.

Escalona, Fabien, Vieira, Matthieu, and De Waele, Jean-Michel, 'The Unfinished History of the Social Democratic Family', in Fabien Escalona, Matthieu Vieira, and Jean-Michel De Waele (eds.), *The Palgrave Handbook of Social Democracy in the European Union* (New York: Palgrave Macmillan, 2013), pp. 3–29.

Feinberg, Melissa, *Elusive Equality: Gender, Citizenship and the Limits of Democracy in Czechoslovakia, 1918–1950* (Pittsburgh, PA: University of Pittsburgh Press, 2006).

Fidelis, Malgorzata, *Women, Communism, and Industrialization in Postwar Poland* (Cambridge: Cambridge University Press, 2010).

Fogg, Shannon Lee, *The Politics of Everyday Life in Vichy France: Foreigners, Undesirables, and Strangers* (Cambridge: Cambridge University Press, 2009).

Forlenza, Rosario, 'A Party for the Mezzogiorno: The Christian Democratic Party, Agrarian Reform, and the Government of Italy', *Contemporary European History*, 19/4 (2010), pp. 331–49.

Frommer, Benjamin, *National Cleansing: Retribution Against Nazi Collaborators in Postwar Czechoslovakia* (Cambridge: Cambridge University Press, 2005).

Ganapini, Luigi, *Una città, la guerra: Lotte di classe ideologie e forze politiche a Milano, 1939–1951* (Milan: F. Agneli, 1988).

Ginsborg, Paul, 'The Communist Party and the Agrarian Question in Southern Italy, 1943–1948', *History Workshop Journal*, 17/1 (1984), pp. 81–101.

A History of Contemporary Italy: Society and Politics 1943–1988 (London/New York: Penguin Books, 1990).

Giovagnoli, Agostino, *L'Italia nel nuovo ordine mondiale: politica ed economia dal 1945 al 1947* (Milano: Vita e Pensiero, 2000).

Górecki, Wojciech, 'Strajki robotnicze w Łodzi w latach 1945–1947', in Jerzy Eisler and Krystyna Kersten (eds.), *Polska 1944/45–1989: studia i materiały II* (Warsaw: Instytut Historii Polska Akademia Nauk, 1997), pp. 93–121.

Graham, Bruce Desmond, *Choice and Democratic Order: The French Socialist Party, 1937–1950* (Cambridge: Cambridge University Press, 1994).

The French Socialists and Tripartisme 1944–1947 (London: George Weidenfeld and Nicholson, 1965).

Grenard, Fabrice, *Les scandales du ravitaillement: détournements, corruption, affaires éttouffées en France, de l'Occupation à la Guerre Froide* (Paris: Payot, 2012).

Gross, Jan T., 'Social Consequences of War: Preliminaries to the Study of Imposition of Communist Regimes in East Central Europe', *East European Politics and Societies*, 3/2 (1989), pp. 198–214.

'Themes for a Social History of War Experience and Collaboration', in István Deák, Jan T. Gross, and Tony Judt (eds.), *The Politics of Retribution in Europe: World War II and Its Aftermath* (Princeton, NJ: Princeton University Press, 2000), pp. 15–36.

'War as Revolution', in Norman Naimark and Leonid Gibianskii (eds.), *The Establishment of Communist Regimes in Eastern Europe, 1944–1949* (Boulder, CO: Westview Press, 1997), pp. 17–40.

Gruber, Helmut, and Graves, Pamela M. (eds.), *Women and Socialism, Socialism and Women: Europe between the Two World Wars* (New York: Berghahn Books, 1998).

Harsch, Donna, 'Public Continuity and Private Change? Women's Consciousness and Activity in Frankfurt, 1945–1955', *Journal of Social History*, 27/1 (1993), pp. 29–58.

Healey, Denis, 'The International Socialist Conference 1946–1950', *International Affairs*, 26/3 (1950), pp. 363–73.

Heumos, Peter, 'Arbeiterschaft und Sozialdemokratie in Osteuropa 1944–1948', *Geschichte und Gesellschaft*, 13 (1987), pp. 22–38.

'Betriebsräte, Einheitsgewerkschaft und staatliche Unternehmensverwaltung. Anmerkungen zu einer Petition mährischer Arbeiter an die tschechoslowakische Regierung vom 8. Juni 1947', *Jahrbücher für Geschichte Osteuropas*, 29 (1981), pp. 215–45.

'Die Sozialdemokratie in Ostmitteleuropa 1945–1948: Zum gesellschaftlichen Potential des demokratischen Sozialismus in Polen, der Tschechoslowakei und Ungarn', in Hans Lemberg (ed.), *Sowjetisches Modell und nationale Prägung. Kontinuität und Wandel in Ostmitteleuropa nach dem Zweiten Weltkrieg* (Marburg an der Lahn: J.G. Herder Institut, 1991), pp. 51–70.

'State Socialism, Egalitarianism, Collectivism: On the Social Context of Socialist Work Movements in Czechoslovak Industrial and Mining Enterprises, 1945 1965', *International Labor and Working-Class History*, 68 (2005), pp. 47–74.

'Zum industriellen Konflikt in der Tschechoslowakei 1945–1968', in Peter Hübner, Christoph Kleßmann, and Klaus Tenfelde (eds.), *Arbeiter im Staatss ozialismus: Ideologischer Anspruch und soziale Wirklichkeit* (Cologne: Böhlau, 2005), pp. 473–98.

(ed.), *Europäischer Sozialismus im Kalten Krieg: Briefe und Berichte, 1944–1948* (Frankfurt am Main: Campus Verlag, 2004).

Hitchcock, William I., *France Restored: Cold War Diplomacy and the Quest for Leadership in Europe, 1944–1954* (Chapel Hill/London: University of North Carolina Press, 1998).

Hoffmann, Stefan-Ludwig, Kott, Sandrine, Romijn, Peter, and Wieviorka, Olivier (eds.), *Seeking Peace in the Wake of War: Europe 1943–1947* (Amsterdam: Amsterdam University Press, 2015).

Holzer, Jerzy, *Z dziejów PPS: 1944–1948* (Warsaw: Wolność Sprawiedliwość Niepodległość, 1983).

Horn, Gerd-Rainer, *European Socialists Respond to Fascism: Ideology, Activism, and Contingency in the 1930s* (Oxford/New York: Oxford University Press, 1996).

Horn, Gerd-Rainer, and Gerard, Emmanuel (eds.), *Left Catholicism, 1943–1955: Catholics and Society in Western Europe at the Point of Liberation* (Leuven: Leuven University Press, 2001).

Iazhborovskaia, Inessa, 'The Gomułka Alternative: The Untravelled Road', in Norman Naimark and Leonid Gibianskii (eds.), *The Establishment of Communist Regimes in Eastern Europe, 1944–1949* (Boulder, CO: Westview Press, 1997), pp. 123–38.

Jemnitz, Janos, 'Soziale und politische Probleme nach dem Zweiten Weltkrieg. Die Erfahrungen und internationalen Verbindungen der ungarischen sozialdemokratischen Partei (1945–1947)', in Dieter Staritz and Hermann Weber (eds.), *Einheitsfront Einheitspartei. Kommunisten und Sozialdemokraten in Ost- und Westeuropa 1944–1948* (Cologne: Verlag Wissenschaft und Politik, 1989), pp. 230–65.

Judt, Tony, *Marxism and the French Left: Studies on Labour and Politics in France, 1830–1981* (New York: New York University Press, 2011).

Postwar: A History of Europe since 1945 (London: Penguin Press, 2005).

Kalinova, Lenká, *Společenské proměny v čase socialistického experimentu: k sociálním dějinám v letech 1945–1969* (Prague: Academia, 2007).

Kamiński, Łukasz, *Polacy wobec nowej rzeczywistości, 1944–1948: formy pozainstytucjonalnego, żywiołowiego oporu społecznego* (Toruń: A. Marszałek, 2000).

Kaplan, Karel, *The Short March: The Communist Takeover in Czechoslovakia 1945–1948* (London: C. Hurst & Company, 1987).

'Tschechoslowakische Sozialdemokratie und tschechoslowakische Kommunisten 1944–1948', in Dieter Staritz and Herman Weber (eds.), *Einheitsfront Einheitspartei. Kommunisten und Sozialdemokraten in Ost- und Westeuropa 1944–1948* (Cologne: Verlag Wissenschaft und Politik, 1989), pp. 280–304.

Das verhängnisvolle Bündnis: Unterwanderung, Gleichschaltung und Vernichtung der tschechoslowakischen Sozialdemokratie 1944–1954 (Wuppertal: Pol-Verlag, 1984).

Kenney, Padraic, *Rebuilding Poland: Workers and Communists, 1945–1950* (Ithaca, NY: Cornell University Press, 1997).

Kersten, Krystyna, *The Establishment of Communist Rule in Poland, 1943–1948* (Berkeley/Los Angeles/Oxford: University of California Press, 1991).

Kleßmann, Christoph, 'Betriebsräte, Gewerkschaften und Arbeiterselbstverwaltung in Polen (1944–1958)', *Jahrbücher für Geschichte Osteuropas*, 29 (1981), pp. 185–214.

Kochanowicz, Jacek, 'Początki planowania w Polsce po II wojnie światowej w perspektywie porównawczej', in Alexsander Łukaszewicz, Elżbieta Mączyńska, and Jerzy Wilkin (eds.), *Ekonomia i ekonomiści w czasach przełomu* (Warsaw: Polskie Towarzystwo Ekonomiczne, 2010), pp. 203–22.

Kokošková, Zdeňka, Jiří Kocian, and Stanislav Kokoška (eds.), *Československo na rozhraní dvou epoch nesvobody* (Prague: Ústav pro soudobé dějiny, 2005).

Kořalka, Jiří, 'Českoslovanská Sociálně Demokratická Strana Dělnická', in Jiří Malíř and Pavel Marek (eds.), *Politické strany: vývoj politických stran a hnutí v českých zemích a Československu 1861–2004* (Brno: Doplněk, 2005), pp. 213–39.

Kuklík, Jan, 'Československá Sociálně Demokratická Strana Dělnická', in Jiří Malíř and Pavel Marek (eds.), *Politické strany: vývoj politických stran a hnutí v českých zemích a Československu 1861–2004* (Brno: Doplněk, 2005), pp. 683–709.

Lachaise, Bernard, 'La creation du Rassemblement du Peuple Français', in Serge Berstein and Pierre Milza (eds.), *L'Année 1947* (Paris: Presses de Sciences Po, 2000), pp. 328–37.

Lagrou, Pieter, *Legacy of Nazi Occupation: Patriotic Memory and National Recovery in Western Europe* (Cambridge: Cambridge University Press, 2000).

Lewis, Jill, *Workers and Politics in Occupied Austria, 1945–55* (Manchester/ New York: Manchester University Press, 2007).

Lombardi, Pierangelo (ed.), *L'illusione al potere. Democrazia, autogoverno regionale e decentramento amministrativo nell'esperienza dei CLN (1944–45)* (Milan: F. Agneli, 2003).

Loth, Wilfried, 'Die französische Linke und die "Einheit der Arbeiterklasse" 1943–1947', *Vierteljahrshefte für Zeitgeschichte*, 35/2 (1987), pp. 273–88.

Lukes, Igor, 'The 1948 Coup d'État in Prague Through the Eyes of the American Embassy', *Diplomacy & Statecraft*, 22/3 (2011), pp. 431–49.

Macartney, C.A., *The Habsburg Empire, 1790–1918* (New York: Macmillan, 1969).

Maier, Charles S., 'The Two Postwar Eras and the Conditions for Stability in Twentieth-Century Western Europe', *American Historical Review*, 86/2 (1981), pp. 327–52.

Malgeri, Francesco, *La stagione del centrismo: politica e società nell'Italia del secondo dopoguerra (1945–1960)* (Soveria Manelli: Rubbettino, 2002).

Marcucci, Gabriella Fanello, *Il primo governo De Gasperi (Dicembre 1945 – Giugno 1946): Sei mesi decisivi per la democrazia in Italia* (Soveria Mannelli: Rubbettino, 2004).

Marks, Gary N., 'Communist Party Membership in Five Former Soviet Bloc Countries, 1945–1989', *Communist and Post-Communist Studies*, 37/2 (2004), pp. 241–63.

Mattera, Paolo, *Storia del PSI: 1892–1994* (Rome: Carocci, 2010).

Mazower, Mark, 'Reconstruction: The Historiographical Issues', *Past and Present*, 210, Supplement 6 (2011), pp. 17–28.

Mazower, Mark, Feldman, David and Reinisch, Jessica (eds.), *Post-War Reconstruction in Europe: International Perspectives, 1945–1949* (Oxford/New York: Oxford University Press, 2011).

McCauley, Martin, *The Origins of the Cold War, 1941–1949* (London/New York: Longman, 1995).

McMillan, James, *France and Women, 1789–1914: Gender, Society and Politics* (London/New York: Routledge, 2002).

Mechoulan, Eric, 'Le SFIO et les grèves', in Frédéric Cépede Berstein, Gilles Morin and Antoine Prost (eds.), *Le Parti socialiste entre Résistance et République* (Paris: Publications de Sorbonne, 2000), pp. 205–22.

Mellink, Bram, 'Tweedracht maakt macht. De PvdA, de doorbraak en de ontluikende polarisatiestrategie (1946–1966)', *Bijdragen en Mededelingen betreffende de Geschiedenis der Nederlanden*, 126/2 (2011), pp. 30–53.

Mencherini, Robert, *Guerre froide, grèves rouges: Parti communiste, stalinisme et luttes sociales en France: Les grèves 'insurrectionnelles' de 1947–1948* (Paris: Syllepse, 1998).

La Libération et les enterprises sous gestion ouvrière, Marseille, 1944–1948 (Paris: L'Harmattan, 1994).

Milward, Alan, *The Reconstruction of Western Europe* (London: Routledge, 1992).

Mioni, Michele, 'The Attlee Government and Welfare State Reforms in Post-War Italian Socialism (1945–1951): Between Universalism and Class Policies', *Labor History*, 57/2 (2016), pp. 277–97.

Misgeld, Klaus, 'As the Iron Curtain Descended: the Co-ordinating Committee of the Nordic Labour Movement and the Socialist International between Potsdam and Geneva (1945–1955)', *Scandinavian Journal of Social History*, 13/1 (1988), pp. 51–7.

Sozialdemokratie und Außenpolitik in Schweden. Sozialistische Internationale, Europapolitik und die Deutschlandfrage 1945–1955 (Frankfurt/New York: Campus, 1984).

Mistry, Kaeten, 'The Case for Political Warfare: Strategy, Organization, and US Involvement in the 1948 Italian Election', *Cold War History*, 6/3 (2006), pp. 301–29.

Moldenhauer, Harald, ' "Ihr werdet Euch dem Sozialismus ohne blutigen Kampf annähern." Kommunistische Blockpolitik und "Gleichschaltung" der Parteien in Polen, 1944–1948', in Stefan Creuzberger and Manfred Görtemaker (eds.), *Gleichschaltung unter Stalin: Die Entwicklung der Parteien im östlichen Europa 1944–1948* (Paderborn: F. Schöningh, 2002), pp. 85–122.

Morgan, Philip, *Fascism in Europe, 1919–1945* (London/New York: Routledge, 2002).

Musso, Stefano, 'Autonomia e democrazia sindacale nella *Città del lavoro*', in Alessio Gramolati and Giovanni Mari (eds.), *Il lavoro dopo il Novecento. Da produttori ad attori sociali* (Firenze: Firenze University Press, 2016), pp. 273–85.

Nehring, Holger, 'What was the Cold War?' *The English Historical Review*, 127 (2012), pp. 920–49.

Neri Serneri, Simone, *Resistenza e democrazia dei partiti: I socialisti nell'Italia del 1943–1945* (Manduria/Bari/Rome: Piero Lacaita, 1995).

Neri-Ultsch, Daniela, *Sozialisten und Radicaux – eine schwierige Allianz: Linksbündnisse in der Dritten Französischen Republik, 1919–1938* (Munich: Oldenbourg, 2005).

Niethammer, Lutz, Borsdorf, Ulrich, and Brandt, Peter (eds.), *Arbeiterinitiative 1945: Antifaschistische Ausschüsse und Reorganisation der Arbeiterbewegung in Deutschland* (Wuppertal: Hammer, 1976).

Nord, Philip, *France's New Deal: From the Thirties to the Post-War Era* (Princeton, NJ: Princeton University Press, 2010).

Orlow, Dietrich, *Common Destiny: A Comparative History of the Dutch, French and German Social Democratic Parties, 1945–1969* (New York/Oxford: Berghahn Books, 2000).

Pavone, Claudio, *Una guerra civile: saggio storico sulla moralità nella Resistenza* (Turin: Bollati Boringhieri, 1991).

Pernes, Jiří, *Takoví nám vládli: komunističtí prezidenti Československa a doba, v níž žili* (Prague: Brana, 2003).

'Vztahy ČSSD a KSČ v době třetí republiky', in Hynek Fajmon, Stanislav Balík, and Kateřina Hloušková (eds.), *Dusivé objetí: historické a politologické pohledy na spolupráci sociálních demokratů a komunistů* (Brno: Centrum pro Studium Demokracie a Kultury, 2006), pp. 25–33.

Pięta-Szawara, Anna, 'Socialíści w Sejmie Ustawodawczym wobec zmian ustrojowych w Polsce w 1947 roku', *Polityka i Społeczeństwo*, 6 (2009), pp. 94–102.

Pittaway, Mark, *The Workers' State: Industrial Labor and the Making of Socialist Hungary, 1944–1958* (Pittsburgh, PA: University of Pittsburgh Press, 2012).

Pons, Silvio, 'Stalin and the European Communists after World War Two (1943–1948)', *Past and Present*, 210, Supplement 6 (2011), pp. 121–38.

'Stalin and the Italian Communists', in Melvyn P. Leffler and David S. Painter (eds.), *Origins of the Cold War: An International History* (New York/London: Routledge, 2005), pp. 205–20.

'Stalin, Togliatti, and the Origins of the Cold War in Europe', *Journal of Cold War Studies*, 3/2 (2001), pp. 3–27.

Pottrain, Martine, *Le Nord au cœur: historique de la Fédération du Nord du Parti Socialiste, 1880–1993* (Lille: SARL de Presse Nord-Demain, 1993).

Pradoux, Martine, and Gilles Morin, 'Daniel Mayer et la SFIO, 1944–1958', *Matériaux pour l'histoire de notre temps*, 51/52 (1998), pp. 24–32.

Prazmowska, Anita, *Civil War in Poland 1942–1948* (Basingstoke: Palgrave Macmillan, 2004).

Poland: A Modern History (London/New York: I.B. Tauris, 2010).

'The Polish Socialist Party, 1945–1948', *East European Quarterly*, 34/3 (2000), pp. 337–59.

Pritchard, Gareth, *The Making of the GDR: From Antifascism to Stalinism* (Manchester: Manchester University Press, 2000).

Niemandsland: A History of Unoccupied Germany, 1944–1945 (Cambridge/ New York: Cambridge University Press, 2012).

Pynsent, Robert B., 'Misoteutonic Myths: Lopping Noses in Hussite Nationalism and Love's Sweet Cure', in Alexander Wöll and Harald Wydra (eds.), *Democracy and Myth in Russia and Eastern Europe* (New York: Routledge, 2008), pp. 98–121.

Reinisch, Jessica, 'Comparing Europe's Post-War Reconstructions: First Balzan Workshop, Birkbeck College, London, 28 October 2005', *History Workshop Journal*, 61/1 (2006), pp. 299–304.

Reynolds, Jaime, 'Communists, Socialists and Workers: Poland, 1944–1948', *Soviet Studies*, 30/4 (1978), pp. 516–39.

Révész, László, *Die Liquidierung der Sozialdemokratie in Osteuropa* (Berne: Schweizerisches Ost-Institut, 1971).

Rioux, Jean-Pierre, *The Fourth Republic 1944–1958* (Cambridge: Cambridge University Press, 1987).

Rossi, Emanuele, *Democrazia come partecipazione: Lelio Basso e il PSI alle origini della Repubblica, 1943–1947* (Rome: Viella, 2011).

Rossi-Doria, Anna, 'Italian Women Enter Politics', in Claire Duchen and Irene Bandhauer-Schöffmann (eds.), *When the War Was Over: Women, War and Peace in Europe, 1940–1956* (London/New York: Leicester University Press, 2000), pp. 89–102.

Sabbatucci, Giovanni, *Il riformismo impossibile: Storia del socialismo italiano* (Rome: Laterza, 1991).

Sadoun, Marc, *Les socialistes sous l'occupation: résistance et collaboration* (Paris: Presse de la Fondation Nationale des Sciences Politiques, 1982).

Sassoon, Donald, *One Hundred Years of Socialism: The West European Left in the Twentieth Century* (London/New York: I.B. Tauris, 1996).

Schneer, Jonathan, 'Hopes Deferred or Shattered: The British Labour Left and the Third Force Movement, 1945–49', *The Journal of Modern History*, 56/2 (1984), pp. 197–226.

Scirocco, Giovanni, *Politique d'Abord: Il PSI, la Guerra Fredda e la Politica Internazionale, 1948–1957* (Milan: Edizione UNICOPLI, 2010).

Scot, Jean-Paul, 'Contradictions d'une tentative de "voie française"', *Nouvelles FondationS*, 3/3–4 (2006), pp. 104–9.

Sergio, Marialuisa-Lucia, *De Gasperi e la 'questione socialista': l'anti-communismo democratico e l'alternativa riformista* (Rome: Istituto Luigi Sturzo, 2004).

Shennan, Andrew, *Rethinking France: Plans for Renewal 1940–1946* (Oxford: Oxford University Press, 1989).

Sláma, Jiří, and Kaplan, Karel, *Die Parlamentswahlen in der Tschechoslowakei 1935– 1946–1948* (Munich: Oldenbourg Verlag, 1986).

Sørensen, Vibeke, *Denmark's Social Democratic Government and the Marshall Plan, 1947–1950* (Copenhagen: Museum Tusculanum Press, 2001).

Spałek, Robert, 'Między pragmatyzmem a zdradą. Zawłaszczenie PPS w Kraju (1944–1948)', in Robert Spałek (ed.), *Polska Partia Socjalistyczna. Dlaczego się nie udało? Szkice. Wspomnienia. Polemiki* (Warsaw: Instytut Pamięci Narodowej, 2010), pp. 145–242.

Steege, Paul, *Black Market, Cold War: Everyday Life in Berlin, 1946–1949* (Cambridge: Cambridge University Press, 2009).

Steinhouse, Adam, *Workers' Participation in Post-Liberation France* (Lanham, MD: Lexington Books, 2001).

Steininger, Rolf, *Deutschland und die Sozialistische Internationale nach dem Zweiten Weltkrieg* (Bonn: Verlag Neue Gesellschaft, 1979).

Strachura, Peter D., *Poland, 1918–1945: An Interpretive and Documentary History of the Second Republic* (London/New York: Routledge, 2004).

Strobach, Vít, and Mareš, Jan, 'Třída dělníků i žen? Proměny chápání genderových vztahů v českém dělnickém hnutí (1870–1914)', *Střed: Časopis pro mezioborová studia Střední Evropy 19. a 20. století*, 2 (2012), pp. 34–68.

Syzdek, Eleonora, and Syzdek, Bronisław, *Zanim zostanie zapomniany* (Warsaw: Wydawnictwo Projekt, 1996).

Śliwa, Michał, *Demokracja polska: idee, ludzie, dzieje* (Warsaw: Wydawnictwo Sejmowe, 2010).

'Tendencje w socjalistycznej myśli agrarnej w Polsce', in Andrzej Jaeschke, Michał Śliwa, and Barbara Stoczewska, *Z dziejów polskiej myśli socjalistycznej* (Warsaw: Państwowe Wydawn. Nauk., 1985), pp. 21–38.

Šlouf, Jakub, 'Rivalita komunistické strany a sociální demokracie na Plzeňsku v letech 1945–1948. Poválečné dědictví prvorepublikových tradic', in Zdeněk Kárník, Jiří Kocian, Jaroslav Pažout, and Jakub Rákosník (eds.), *Bolševismus, komunismus a radikální socialismus v Československu*, Volume VI (Prague: Dokořán, 2009), pp. 113–37.

Taddei, Francesca, *Il socialismo italiano nel dopoguerra: Correnti ideologiche e scelte politiche, 1943–1947* (Milano: Franco Agneli, 1984).

Tombs, Robert, *France 1814–1914* (London/New York: Longman, 1996).

Tomicki, Jan, *Polska Partia Socjalistyczna,1892–1948* (Warsaw: Książka i Wiedza, 1983).

Tumblety, Joan, 'Responses to Women's Enfranchisment in France, 1944–1945', *Women's Studies International Forum*, 26/5 (2003), pp. 483–97.

Ventresca, Robert, *From Fascism to Democracy: Culture and Politics in the Italian Election of 1948* (Toronto/Buffalo: University of Toronto Press, 2004).

Vigna, Xavier, 'France after the Liberation: The Labour Movement, the Employers and the Political Leaders in their Struggle with the Social Movement', in Stefan Berger and Marcel Boldorf (eds.), *Social Movements and Challenges to Economic Elites after the Second World War* (Cham: Palgrave Macmillan, 2018), pp. 63–80.

Vinen, Richard, *Bourgeois Politics in France, 1945–1951* (Cambridge/New York: Cambridge University Press, 1995).

A History in Fragments: Europe in the Twentieth Century (London: Abacaus, 2002).

Walker, Ignacio, 'Democratic Socialism in Comparative Perspective', *Comparative Politics*, 23/1 (1991), pp. 439–58.

Weber, Fritz, *Der kalte Krieg in der SPÖ: Koalitionswachter, Pragmatiker und revolutionäre Sozialisten* (Vienna: Verlag für Gesellschaftskritik, 1986).

Wrona, Janusz, *System partyjny w Polsce, 1944–1950: miejsce-funkcje-relacje partii politycznych w warunkach budowy i utrwalania systemu totalitarnego* (Lublin: Wydawn. Uniwersytetu Marii Curie-Skłodowskiej, 1995).

Zaremba, Marcin, *Die grosse Angst. Polen 1944–1947: Leben in Ausnahmezustand* (Paderborn: Ferdinand Schöning, 2016).

Index